C AND DEFENSE

CONFLICT AND DEFENSE

A General Theory

Kenneth E. Boulding

Professor of Economics
Institute of Behavioral Sciences
University of Colorado

Lanham • New York • London

Copyright © 1962, 1988 by

Kenneth E. Boulding

University Press of America,® Inc.

4720 Boston Way
Lanham, MD 20706

3 Henrietta Street
London WC2E 8LU England

All rights reserved

Printed in the United States of America

British Cataloging in Publication Information Available

Library of Congress Cataloging-in-Publication Data

Boulding, Kenneth Ewart, 1910–
 Conflict and Defense.
 Includes index.
 1. Peace. 2. Social conflict. 3. International
   relations. I. Title.
JX1963.B6954   1988   327.1'6   88–27677
ISBN 0–8191–7112–3 (pbk. : alk. paper)

All University Press of America books are produced on acid-free paper.
The paper used in this publication meets the minimum requirements of
American National Standard for Information Sciences—Permanence of Paper
for Printed Library Materials, ANSI Z39.48–1984.

CONTENTS

PREFACE TO THE UNIVERSITY PRESS OF AMERICA EDITION	vii
PREFACE	xv
1. STATIC MODELS OF CONFLICT	1
2. THE DYNAMICS OF CONFLICT: RICHARDSON PROCESS MODELS	19
3. THE CONTRIBUTION OF GAME THEORY	41
4. THE THEORY OF VIABILITY	58
5. THE INDIVIDUAL AS A PARTY TO CONFLICT	80
6. THE GROUP AS A PARTY TO CONFLICT: THE ECOLOGICAL MODEL	105
7. THE GROUP AS A PARTY TO CONFLICT: THE EPIDEMIOLOGICAL MODEL	123
8. THE ORGANIZATION AS A PARTY TO CONFLICT	145
9. CONFLICT BETWEEN THE INDIVIDUAL, THE GROUP, AND THE ORGANIZATION	166
10. ECONOMIC CONFLICT	189
11. INDUSTRIAL CONFLICT	208
12. INTERNATIONAL CONFLICT: THE BASIC MODEL	227
13. INTERNATIONAL CONFLICT: MODIFICATIONS AND APPLICATIONS OF THE BASIC THEORY	248
14. IDEOLOGICAL AND ETHICAL CONFLICT	277
15. CONFLICT RESOLUTION AND CONTROL	305
16. EPILOGUE: THE PRESENT CRISIS OF CONFLICT AND DEFENSE	329
INDEX	345

PREFACE
To the University Press of America Edition

The babies who were born when *Conflict and Defense* was written are now about 28 and presumably actively participating in the world around them. What does this book have to say to this generation, or more importantly perhaps, what does it not say that might be said if it were written now? *Conflict and Defense* was a very early product of what has come to be known as the peace research movement, embodied in journals, books, institutes around the world, programs in universities, and professional societies, especially the International Peace Research Association, which attracts over 300 people from all around the world at its biennial meetings. *Conflict and Defense* has reached the status of a "Citation Classic" and has been cited in over 360 publications.[1] Somebody must have read the book! I have used it myself recently as a textbook in a course on The Theory of Conflict. Much, of course, has happened in these 28 years, and if I were writing it today it would certainly not be quite the same book. I am particularly grateful, however, to the University Press of America for reprinting it in its original form, so that it can perhaps have some impact on the next generation.

[1] *Conflict and Defense: A General Theory,* featured as the "Citation Classic," *Current Contents* (Social & Behavioral Sciences), 18, 43 (Oct. 27, 1986): 20; and *Current Contents* (Arts & Humanities), 8, 43 (Oct. 27, 1986): 20.

A whole book could be written—and one day perhaps will be—on the history of conflict thought in the last generation. The patterns of thought have not changed very much. This has been a period of what might be called "normal science" rather than a period of revolutionary change. The static models of conflict (Chapter 1) have not changed very much. There has been a little more "economics imperialism," the attempt on the part of economics to take over the other social sciences. There have been some contributions from psychology on decision-making pathologies. What still remains to be done here is a much more careful study of who are the parties to conflict, particularly in the case of groups and organizations. Even in the case of the individual, studies of multiple personalities suggest that a single person, and especially a powerful person, is a "group." Bismarck is supposed to have said "I am a committee." The single unified person of "economic man" oversimplifies the complexity of actual human behavior.

There has been some development of Richardson process analysis (Chapter 2), introducing a few more variables, without, I think, changing the fundamental model. I have even made some contribution to this myself in "The Parameters of Politics."[2] In this article I extend the Richardson process to three parties and show that if an equilibrium is to be reached, that is, a balance of power, the reaction coefficient, that is, how much each party will raise armament expenditures in response to a perceived one percent increase in the other party's, cannot be more than about 0.7, whereas in a two-party system this is 1.0 or less. I have not seen anything on the n-party case as n gets larger. Oddly enough, the economist's concept of perfect equilibrium may be relevant here.

Game theory (Chapter 3) has continued to stimulate a good deal

---

[2]Kenneth E. Boulding, "The Parameters of Politics," *University of Illinois Bulletin* (Urbana), 63, 139 (July 15, 1966): 1-21. Reprinted in Kenneth E. Boulding, *Collected Papers* (Boulder: Colorado Associated University Press), Vol. V, pp. 195-215.

of work in the last generation, mainly in terms of the two-party game.³ The subject is still very lively today, as witness the remarkable work of Robert Axelrod⁴, which suggests that if the parties are given a tit-for-tat strategy, that is, no more than one eye for an eye or one tooth for a tooth, this is likely to be most successful. This theory has been criticized since by Jack Hirshleifer and Juan Carlos Martinez Coll,⁵ but it still continues to arouse a great deal of interest.

From the point of view of its practical applications to conflict, however, game theory has a fundamental weakness: it assumes that the parties to conflict are known and given. In fact, both the origins and the effects of organized conflict are remarkably obscure. What might be called "unconscious conflict," that is, the real dynamics of the distribution of welfare around the human population, often bears very little relation to conscious conflict. Thus, a union wins a strike, but who loses? Either the people who might have been employed if wages had not risen or the customers who have to pay higher prices. The employer against whom the conflict was ostensibly waged may even benefit. Military defeat often results in both an economic and a cultural expansion of the defeated party at the expense of the victor. Empire often impoverishes the imperial power. Game theory is merely a very abstract theory of conscious conflict. It has very little to say about unconscious conflict, which may be much more important.

Chapters 4 to 9 really represent the beginning of an evolutionary theory of conflict, seeing conflict as merely one element in the vast process of evolutionary and ecological interaction which moves us

---

³See especially Anatol Rapoport and Albert Chammah, *The Prisoner's Dilemma, A Study in Conflict and Cooperation* (Ann Arbor: University of Michigan Press, 1965), for a fairly popular exposition.
⁴Robert Axelrod, *The Evolution of Cooperation* (New York: Basic Books, 1984).
⁵Jack Hirshleifer and J.C.M. Coll, "What Strategies Can Support the Evolutionary Emergence of Cooperation?" Working Paper No. 58. (Los Angeles: University of California Center for International and Strategic Affairs, February 1987).

as a total system through time. A good deal of my work (and publications) since writing *Conflict and Defense* has been devoted to the study of this larger system.[6] The role of conflict in this larger process is a matter of great conflict itself between the "dialecticians," who see conflict as the most important part of the process, and "evolutionists" like myself, who see conflict as occasionally significant, but on the whole a minor part of the process of overall interaction of species in the immense complexity of mutational and selective processes.

Since writing *Conflict and Defense* my main interest in the international field has been in the development of a theory which might be called the "evolution of peace," as reflected in my book *Stable Peace*[7]. It is interesting to note that the biologists are beginning to see that evolution is not a continuous process, but is marked by some quite sharp discontinuities. This is what is called "punctuational evolution."[8] The evolutionary process seems to consist of periods of relative stability, with rather small and gradual changes, which are divided by short periods of very rapid and dramatic change, leading into a new periods of stability. These transition periods may be induced by some catastrophe which opens up all sorts of new niches for new mutations that would not have survived before. A transition may also happen through simply passing over some kind of systems boundary in which positive feedback processes—the more A, the more B; the more B, the more A—become more prominent rather than the negative-feedback processes which lead towards equilibrium (if A gets too big, it will get smaller; if it gets too small, it will get bigger). Punctuated

---

[6]See Kenneth E. Boulding, *A Primer on Social Dynamics: History as Dialectics and Development* (New York: Free Press, 1970), *Ecodynamics: A New Theory of Societal Evolution* (Beverly Hills, Calif.: Sage Publications, 1978), *Evolutionary Economics* (Sage, 1981).

[7]Kenneth E. Boulding, *Stable Peace* (Austin: University of Texas Press, 1978).

[8]See Steven Peterson and Albert Somit, eds., "Punctuated Equilibria Theory," special issue of *The Journal of Biological and Social Structures* (forthcoming).

evolution leads to the perception of stages. Thus, the age of big reptiles and dinosaurs was succeeded by the age of big mammals, as dinosaurs became extinct, perhaps because of some catastrophe about which there is still a good deal of disagreement.

It is very tempting to divide human history into stages—the paleolithic, the mesolithic (which seems to have been something of a catastrophe), the neolithic, leading into agriculture, which releases resources for increased human learning—pottery, weaving, metallurgy—which leads into weaponry, which leads into civilization. Now we seem to be in a transition period of very rapid change, between civilization and something that can be called "post-civilization." This transition is very far from being complete and indeed it may not be accomplished, but it is certainly within the realm of the possible. And there is at least some probability that it will lead to a world without war and without poverty.

One must always be careful about "stages" because there is continuous change as well as discontinuous change and it is not always easy to say where one stage ends and the next stage begins. Nevertheless, it seems not unreasonable to postulate four stages in the development of international systems, which may also be found in other conflicts. Each of these stages, it should be emphasized, may be found in different places at the same time, and it is quite possible to retrogress, that is, to go from what normally would be a later stage to an earlier one. The four stages are: (1) *stable war,* in which war goes on all the time, perhaps with some ups and downs of intensity. Southeast Asia seems to have been in this condition for over 50 years. Stable war, however, is very expensive and destructive. It is not surprising that it tends to pass over into the second stage, (2) *unstable war,* where war is interrupted by periods of peace, although war is still regarded as the norm and peace as just a time of wound licking and preparing for the next year. The Middle East has a good deal of this kind of quality. We see the beginnings of it even in the early civilizations, with the development of royal marriages, diplomacy, trade, and so on.

(3) Unstable war tends to pass over, perhaps rather imperceptibly, into something that might be called *unstable peace,* in which peace is regarded as the norm and war as the interruption. This has been very common in human societies. It certainly characterizes the European world and its expansions, from the end of the Thirty Years' War (1688). It is especially characterized by deterrence, that is, peace maintained by the fear of mutual threats. But this has a profound tendency to be unstable. Indeed, unless there is some probability of it breaking down, it will not deter in the short run. Historically it always has broken down, usually within one generation. We have had nuclear deterrence now for over 40 years, and the enormous cost of it probably makes it more stable than what might be called "conventional deterrence." But it too will break down if we wait long enough. Just how soon it is hard to say, but almost certainly within 100 years. The proof here is that if the probability of nuclear weapons going off were zero, they would not deter anybody. But since that probability is not zero, if we wait long enough they will go off.

(4) The fourth stage is *stable peace,* something which has only been achieved in the last 150 years or so, perhaps as a result of the continuing increase in the cost and the danger of war. This is the situation in which two independent countries have no plans whatever to go to war with each other, though they might sometimes go to war with other people. It seems to have been achieved first in Scandinavia, when the Swedes and the Danes, who had fought each other for centuries, suddenly stopped fighting each other, sometime after 1815. Stable peace spread to North America about 1870; to Western Europe, Australasia, and Japan after the Second World War. We still, of course, do not have it between the United States and the Soviet Union. What we have is unstable peace. The great problem of the present age is how to expand this area of stable peace, first to include the relations between the United States and the Soviet Union, then to the Third World. We cannot rule out the possibility that stable peace itself might break

down, but the longer it lasts, the more stable it gets, that is, the more it becomes a habit. The probability of war between the United States and Canada, or between Britain and France, has been reduced now to virtually zero. The greatest obstacle to stable peace is the organizations of the military themselves, what might be called "unilateral national defense organizations." These are organizations indeed which have to have an enemy in order to justify their budgets, so they are skilled at conflict creation rather than at conflict management. It is hardly an exaggeration to say that the greatest conflict in the world today is between the united military forces of the world that form a single system, each dependent on the other, and the human race as a whole. This is, again, one of these real conflicts that is not visible or organized, except to a very small degree in peace movements.

Looking back now on 1960, when this book was written, from 1988, what can we say about the world? Certainly over large parts of the world stable peace now seems closer, but the area of stable peace has not expanded perceptibly. The conflict between the military and the civilian population has taken a severe toll, for instance, in Argentina internally; in the war between Iran and Iraq, which seems like an utterly meaningless sacrifice of young life; in the nuclear arms race, which has continued, at least until 1987, with the Reagan-Gorbachev Agreement, which is very minor, but at least a sign of hope. A larger intellectual effort is going into the study of peace at the present than it was in 1960, but this is infinitesimal compared with the intellectual resources that still go into war and the means of destruction. Nevertheless, there are signs of hope. The Strategic Defense Initiative ("Star Wars") of Mr. Reagan is itself implicitly a recognition that national defense has broken down and that it can no more defend a country than the castle walls could defend a baron after the invention of gunpowder. A large proportion of the scientific community believes that SDI is humbug, that it cannot be successful, that it is not a defensive structure but an increase in offensive destructive power, and that it is more likely to bring on a nuclear war than to prevent it. As a symbol of the breakdown of national defense, however, it offers hope that genuine security, in terms of stable peace, may be sought. The motto for the next century should really be "National Security, Not National Defense." The lesson of history is that change is possible and indeed inevitable, and good change is possible though not inevitable, but is made more probable by the process of human learning, towards which I hope this little volume will be a small contribution.

Kenneth E. Boulding
Institute of Behavioral Science
University of Colorado-Boulder
February 1988

PREFACE

The origin of this book in my own mind can be traced back to a passionate conviction of my youth that war was the major moral and intellectual problem of our age. If the years have made this conviction less passionate, they have made it no less intense. The book, therefore, is not a work of that idle curiosity which, according to Veblen, is the motivator of pure science. It is driven rather by that practical curiosity which inspires applied science. Nevertheless, it is a work of pure theory, that is, of the abstract imagination. It gives no easy recipe for the abolition of war or for the general control of conflict, though it does, I hope, demonstrate exactly why in our own age these tasks have become a necessity. It does not deal, except by way of occasional illustration, with the current historical situation in detail, for it has been inspired not only by a practical end but by the belief that applied science cannot succeed unless it guides its empirical study by reins, however loose, of pure abstract theory. In particular, this work is the result of a conviction that the intellectual chassis of the broad movement for the abolition of war has not been adequate to support the powerful moral engine which drives it and that the frequent breakdowns which interrupt the progress of the movement are due essentially to a deficiency in its social theory.

Although a theory of war and peace and of international relations is perhaps the most important part of this work, it is by no means the whole of it, because of another conviction which grew in my mind largely as the result of a year of fruitful discussion at the Center for Advanced Study in the Behavioral Sciences in Palo Alto, California, in 1954 and 1955. This was the conviction that, in order to develop a theoretical system adequate to deal with the problem of war and peace, it is necessary to cast the net wider and to study conflict as a general social process of which war was a special case. Out of a small group of scholars who shared this conviction grew first the *Journal of Conflict Resolution*, beginning in 1957, and then the Center for Research in Conflict Resolution at the University of Michigan in 1959. Although I must claim sole responsibility for all the mistakes in this book, whatever value it contains owes a great deal to the work of the Conflict Resolution group. I am particularly grateful to a group of colleagues who participated in a seminar in the theory of conflict in 1956. It is entirely appropriate, therefore, that this book appear as a publication from the Center for Research in Conflict Resolution.

Whatever originality this book may possess is a matter of building rather than of brickmaking; most of the bricks were made by others and my main task has been to fit them together into a reasonably coherent structure. My own training and background are revealed both in the method, which is largely that of theoretical economics, and in the central theoretical structure, which is largely based on the theory of oligopoly, that is, of competition among few firms. The substance of the book, however, is not "economics" in the usual sense of the word: it is, I hope, a new theoretical abstraction from the general phenomenon of conflict; it draws for its models on many of the other social sciences and its principal application is to the theory of international relations. The book is divided roughly into two parts. In the first nine chapters I attempt to develop a general theory of conflict which will be applicable to most, if not all, cases. In the remaining chapters I concentrate on the application of this theory to special cases, with more emphasis on the differences among the various kinds of conflict rather than on their similarity.

I owe so much to so many that personal acknowledgments would be either invidious or unduly voluminous. Bread-and-butter courtesy, however, requires thanks to the Ford Foundation for a summer grant which enabled me to write the first draft, to the University College of the West Indies and the Rockefeller Foundation for a golden year in Jamaica that produced the final version, and to the University of Michigan, my home base, which puts up with some eccentric activity from one of its professors of economics.

KENNETH E. BOULDING

Ann Arbor, Michigan
October, 1960

1

STATIC MODELS OF CONFLICT

Conflict is an activity that is found almost everywhere. It is found throughout the biological world, where the conflict both of individuals and of species is an important part of the picture. It is found everywhere in the world of man, and all the social sciences study it. Economics studies conflict among economic organizations—firms, unions, and so on. Political science studies conflict among states and among subdivisions and departments within larger organizations. Sociology studies conflict within and between families, racial and religious conflict, and conflict within and between groups. Anthropology studies conflict of cultures. Psychology studies conflict within the person. History is largely the record of conflict. Even geography studies the endless war of the sea against the land and of one land form or one land use against another. Conflict is an important part of the specialized study of industrial relations, international relations, or any other relations.

The question, therefore, arises, "Is there a general phenomenon of conflict, and, therefore, a general theory of conflict, that applies in all these areas, or is the type of conflict that is studied in one area quite different from that studied in another?" It seems reasonable to suppose that conflict does exhibit many general patterns, that the patterns of conflict in industrial relations, international relations, interpersonal relations, and even animal life are not wholly different from one another, and that it is, therefore, worth looking for the common element. On the other hand, we should be surprised if there were no differences; the pattern of conflict in international relations, for instance, is not the same as in industrial or interpersonal relations. Just as it is important to perceive the similarities in different situations, so it is important to perceive the differences. These differences cannot be perceived, however, without a general theory to serve as a standard of comparison. It is my contention that there is a general theory of conflict that can be derived from many different sources and disciplines. In developing this theory, I shall first show the essential similarities in all conflict situations in a series of models of broad application. Then, in applying these to various special conflict situations, the differences among these situations will be more clearly revealed in terms of divergences from the general models.

There are two broad types of general model of any system—the static (including comparative statics) and the dynamic, or process, which takes sequences of events specifically into account. For both these types of model of conflict, however, there is the following general framework of concepts:

1. *The Party.* A conflict is a situation that involves at least two parties, so that the first concept must be that of a party. A party is a *behavior unit*, that is, some aggregate or organization that is capable of assuming a number of different positions while retaining a common identity or boundary. A behavior unit may be a person, a family, a species of animals or artifacts, a class of ideas, a theory, or a social organization such as a firm, a nation, a trade union, or a church. The mere aggregate of people called Smith, however, is not a behavior unit, simply because this aggregate does not behave as a unit. It makes sense to say that John Smith does something; it makes no sense to say that Smiths do something, simply because Smiths have no sufficiently common or organized characteristic. Under some circumstances, a crowd may be a behavior unit, because crowds sometimes do things as crowds. It might even make sense to say

that all titmice or all Philadelphia Biddles are a behavior unit, if certain circumstances make all titmice or all Biddles react in much the same way. The test that decides whether an aggregate is a behavior unit, then, is whether it can be the subject in a sentence with a verb of action. Not all behavior units are parties to conflict, though most of them probably are. A behavior unit becomes a party when it becomes involved in conflict with another behavior unit. A party is something that cannot actually exist in the singular—they must come at least in pairs.

2. *Behavior Space.* Before we can proceed to a formal definition of conflict we must examine another concept, that of behavior space. The *position* of a behavior unit at a moment of time is defined by a set of values (subset, to be technical) of a set of variables that defines the behavior unit. These variables need not be continuous or quantitatively measurable. The different values of a variable must, however, be capable of simple ordering; that is, of any two values it must be possible to say that one is "after" (higher, lefter, brighter than) the other. Thus, for a person we might have the variable "angry." We might specify five grades of anger, say, speechless with anger, very angry, moderately angry, a little peeved, not angry at all. At any one time, a person must occupy one of these positions. We can, of course, specify as many grades as we wish. In the case of a quantity like height or weight, there may be in theory an infinite number of grades. In practice, even here we have only a finite number: if we measure weight only in pounds, for instance, an adult person will have one or two hundred possible positions of this variable; even if we measure it in ounces, there are only two or three thousand possible positions. We see that there is no essential difference, therefore, between a quantity, which we think to measure exactly, and a quality. A quantity merely has a larger number of grades.

The *history* of a behavior unit is the record of the positions it has occupied at successive moments of time. We can think of a position as a single frame of a movie reel. The history, then, is the successive frames of the reel. History, however, stops at the present; all possible future positions of the behavior unit are what we mean by its behavior space. Back from the present, the history of the behavior unit unfurls as a single reel; forward from the present, there is not a single reel but a great many different possible future reels. It is this set of future positions that comprises the behavior space. There is not an infinite number of such reels because the set of potential positions is limited by the existence of *laws*. A law is a stable relationship between positions at different dates. Thus, if we have a body falling in a vacuum under a constant acceleration of 32 feet per second, the law of its movement tells us that there is only one possible place for it to be at each moment. It will have fallen 16 feet by the end of the first second, 64 feet by the end of the second second, and so on. This is an extreme case in which there is only a single set of future positions. In the case of complex systems like human and social systems, we cannot define the future positions uniquely. Nevertheless there are limits. I am sure I shall not be on the moon tomorrow, I am pretty sure I shall not be in New York, and, in fact, I am pretty sure I shall be right here where I am today, which is where I plan to be. There is a possibility, however, that my plans might change—the death of a relative, an urgent matter of business, and so on. I might be able to range these possible futures in order of their present likelihood, starting with the highly probable and going down to the impossible. This is the usual form of laws in social science.

3. *Competition.* Competition in its broadest sense exists when any potential positions of two behavior units are mutually incompatible. This is a broader concept than conflict, as we shall see, in the sense that, whereas all cases of conflict involve competition, in the above sense, not all cases of competition involve conflict. Two positions are mutually incompatible if each excludes the other, that is, if the realization of either one makes impossible the realization of the other. Thus, suppose we have two populations of different biological species, A and B. If an expansion of A makes an expansion of B impossible, and vice versa, we have a case of simple mutual

competition. The intensity of competition depends on the likelihood of each behavior unit moving into the incompatible area. Thus we might have a situation in which an expansion of A would preclude an expansion of B, but, for some reason, an expansion of A is very unlikely. In that case, the competition will be weak. In an extreme case, we may have potential competition, where if A expanded, B would diminish but where there is no actual competition because A does not, in fact, expand.

4. *Conflict.* Conflict may be defined as a situation of competition in which the parties are *aware* of the incompatibility of potential future positions and in which each party *wishes* to occupy a position that is incompatible with the wishes of the other. Our definition of conflict includes two little words, "aware" and "wishes," each of which is laden with philosophical dynamite. The nature of awareness is very obscure. Nevertheless, there is a clear difference between, say, the competition of land forms and the competition of animals, men, and societies. One can even postulate a condition of competition among animals or men that would not involve conflict, because there would be no awareness of the competitors. Thus, suppose we had two species of insects, one of which fed by day and the other by night on the same food supply. They might be in intense competition, in the sense that an increase in the number of one would force a diminution in the number of the other, but they might be totally unaware of each other's existence. Similarly, the world of man is so complex that many individuals and groups may be in competition and yet be quite unaware of the fact. Even where people are aware of potential conflict, there may be no actual conflict if there is no desire on the part of one party to occupy a region of its behavior space from which it is excluded by the other. Thus it is impossible for two people to sit on top of a flagpole at the same time. In this area, there is competition between them, and if they are aware of this, there is potential conflict. If, however, neither party has any desire to sit on the flagpole or even if only one party has this desire, the conflict will not become actual.

In an actual conflict situation, then, there must be awareness, and there must also be incompatible wishes or desires. If the concept of awareness raises philosophical difficulties, the concept of desire is haunted by the ghosts of agelong disputes about free will and determinism. We can escape them only by a heroic process of abstraction by which we hope to achieve a workable theory of behavior. The particular abstraction that we use is the idea of a *value ordering*. We suppose that the relevant parts of a party's image of its potential positions can be ordered on a scale of better and worse; that is, of any two positions, we can say either that one is better than the other or that they are equally good. This is what is called a *weak* ordering. A *strong* ordering is one in which we can always say of any two positions which is better and in which there are no two positions to which the party is indifferent. Weak orderings are probably less likely to lead to conflict than strong orderings. A pliable, good-natured person has many positions that are of about equal value to him; if he is excluded from one he simply goes to another without any sense of loss. An inflexible, opinionated person whose orderings tend to be strong, and who always knows quite positively which of two positions he prefers, is likely to run into conflict if his best position happens to be occupied by someone else.

We suppose, then, that there is an *ordered set* of positions of a behavior unit. This need not cover all conceivable positions; we do not bother to order very remote possibilities. In a conscious or unconscious form, however, the ordering is likely to extend over a range of positions in the vicinity of the present position. Thus I could say with some certainty that I would prefer a raise in salary to no raise at all or that I prefer a vacation and no new car to a new car and no vacation. This ordered set is pretty certain to extend beyond the set of possible positions, which is defined by the *boundary of possibility*.

The boundary of possibility is the next important concept. It defines certain limitations on the positions I could occupy, say, tomorrow, imposed by various physical, psychological, legal, and financial restrictions. I could not, for instance, be in Australia, simply because planes do not travel that fast. This is a physical limitation. I could not be in London, even though this might be physically possible, because my passport has expired, or even if I had a valid passport, because I cannot afford the trip. It would not be too difficult to draw on a map of the world my possibility boundary—a line that divides the world into two regions, one containing all the places to which I can go and the other containing all the places to which I cannot go. The same concept can be applied to my general behavior space. Thus I cannot, at any rate, tomorrow, be a very different person from what I am, but I can be a little different; there is a rough boundary here between possible and impossible changes in my personality or general conduct.

The *behavior* of a behavior unit consists in its moving to the best position possible, i.e., the point within its possibility boundary that is higher than any other on the value ordering. This principle is illustrated, in terms that will be familiar to economists, in Fig. 1.1. Here we suppose the plane of the paper represents the behavior space of an individual located at *A*. Each point on the paper, or *field*, represents a certain state of the universe that is within the purview of the individual at *A*. We neglect here the problem of the various ways in which these can be ordered: if there are only two variables in the behavior system, the plane can then express any combination of these by a set of Cartesian coordinates. We do not limit ourselves to this condition, however; since there is an infinite number of points on the plane, there is no reason why each one should not represent a state of a multidimensional universe. We order the field only to the extent that we suppose a line (the heavy line in the figure) represents the boundary

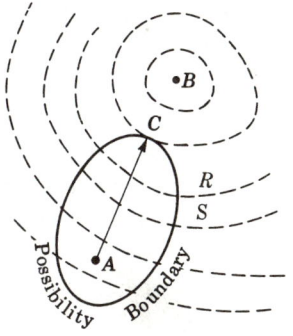

Fig. 1.1

of possibility, so that all points inside the line represent states of the universe that are possible or available to the behavior unit at A and that all points outside the line represent states that are not. We then suppose that the value ordering of the field can be represented by a surface (a *welfare function* or *utility function*) in the third dimension, such that any point R that is a higher point on this surface than another point S is better than S. On the plane, this surface can be represented by a series of contours, or indifference curves (dotted in the figure), that join all points of equal value in the value ordering, that is, to which the behavior unit is indifferent. This can only be done if the ordering is a weak ordering. In the figure, the best point that A can reach is the point C, where the possibility boundary touches its highest indifference curve. In Fig. 1.1, we suppose that B is the point of *bliss*, the best conceivable state of the universe. This, however, is outside the possibility boundary, so that the behavior unit can only get to C. This is essentially a static analysis; that is, we are not considering the time position of these various states of the universe, though of course each point on the field can represent a future time path of instantaneous states.

The tangency condition at C is significant only if certain mathematical conditions in regard to the ordering of the field are fulfilled. Thus it may not be possible to represent both the possibility boundary and the indifference curves by smooth and well-behaved curves. The utility surface, for instance, might be a mass of little pock-marked hills and valleys. The principle of selecting the point with the highest value ordering within the possibility field survives any degree of irregularity in the ordering; we simply give a *value number* to each point within the possibility set and pick out the point with the highest number. This is the most general form of the principle of *maximizing under constraint*. For some of the ensuing propositions to hold, however, the field must be well ordered at least in the sense that the behavior unit can always go from one point to the next in the vicinity.

This is a view of behavior that is derived fundamentally from the economist's theory of *rational behavior*. In the economist's vision, a man looks over the field of possible choices much as he might look over a tray of hors d'oeuvres or French pastries, orders the field according to his first, second, and third choices, and so on, and then picks out the first choice. This is a very formal theory of behavior, and if we are not careful, it can easily collapse to the empty proposition that people do what they do, for what they do is by definition the best choice. It is, however, a place to begin, and, as we shall see, it can be expanded to take account of such phenomena as the dilemma or quandary, or even what seems like irrational behavior. The rationality of behavior does not consist in the principle of selection of the first choice, which is a formal principle independent of the nature of the perceptions either of the field or of the value ordering. If a man chooses to stand on his head in the middle of the street, this is presumably because he selects this alternative as best out of all those acts which seem open to him at the moment. The distinction between rational and irrational behavior must be found in the content of the image either of the field or of the value ordering. Thus, behavior is irrational if it is based on a false image of the world or on a bad system of value ordering. The exact meaning of "false" and "bad" we leave to a fairly distant future. But it is clear that schizophrenic behavior is based on an image of the world that is at least false enough to occasion sanctions (ranging from adverse comment to incarceration) imposed by those who have power to do so and that criminal behavior is based on a value ordering that is false in much the same sense.

We shall not, at this point, go into the determinants of the value ordering, or even of the image of the field. This would carry us far into the theory of motivation and into the dynamics of personality change. For the moment, we must be content to observe that, whereas, for purposes of developing an elementary static theory, we can assume the image of the field and the value ordering of each party to be given, in dynamic theory, this is no longer true, and we shall have to consider the processes by which images are formed and changed.

Now let us consider a joint field (behavior space) with two behavior units, A_1 and A_2 (Fig. 1.2). Each point on this field represents a state of the universe that is relevant to either one or both behavior units. Possibility boundaries, as before, are drawn round the present positions of the parties at A_1 and A_2, and we suppose the possibility sets intersect in the shaded area ps_aqr_b. Each point within the shaded area, then, represents a state that is open to both parties. Suppose now there is, within the dotted line, a set of mutually exclusive states that has the property that, if one party is within this area, the other party is excluded from it; that is, if A_2 is anywhere within the dotted line, A_1's boundary of possibility drops to the area $r_a s_a t_a$, and if A_1 is anywhere within the dotted area, B's boundary of possibility shrinks to $r_b s_b t_b$. Then, the area $r_b s_a p$ is a field of potential conflict. All states within this area are open to each only if the other is not within the area. It is a field of actual conflict only if both parties wish to be within it, that is, if their highest value state lies within it. If A_1's best point is C_1 (within his original possibility boundary) and A_2's best point is C_2, neither can reach his best point if the other reaches his. If A_1 reaches C_1, then A_2's possibility area is reduced to $ps_b t_b r_b s_a p$. He will have to be content with something like the point r_b, which is somewhat less advantageous than C_2. Similar considerations obtain for A_1 if A_2 reaches C_2.

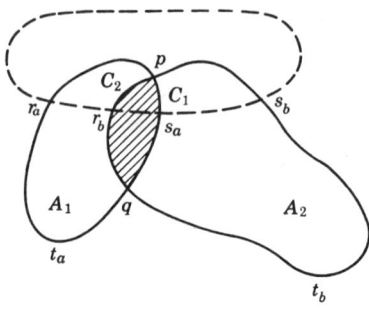

Fig. 1.2

We can now define another very important division of the field into what may be called the *conflict set* (or area) and the *trading set* (or area). We have supposed the field to be ordered for each party according to a value ordering; that is, each point in the field (each state of the joint universe) can be associated with two numbers, one representing the value ordering of party A_1 and the other of party A_2. Thus, by the combination (12,7), we mean that the point associated with this pair of numbers stands twelfth on A_1's value ordering of all points within the field and seventh on A_2's ordering. These are ordinal, not cardinal, numbers. Now suppose we pick out all the points in the field that are twelfth in A_1's ordering; they will be, say, (12,10), (12,9), (12,8), and (12,7). This is an *indifference set* for A_1; all the points have equal value for him. There will be at least one point in this set that will be the highest valued in the set for A_2. In the above example, this is (12,7), as we suppose a point that is seventh on A_2's class list is better than points that are eighth, ninth, tenth, etc. Let us call this a *superior point* of the indifference set. A superior point has the property that any other point on the indifference set is clearly a worse position, as it is worse for one party and no better for the other. Suppose now that the superior point of an indifference set for A_1 is also a superior point for the indifference set of A_2. In the above example, this would mean that, if we picked out all the points that are seventh in A_2's list, the point (12,7) will be the best for A_1; other points will be (13,7) (14,7), etc., but there will be no point (11,7). When the field has this property, the superior points form the conflict set and all other points the trading set. The meaning of these terms will again be made clear as the argument proceeds.

Let us first examine the matrix of all possible value-ordering points. It will look like Fig. 1.3. If there are points in the joint field of the two parties corresponding to every cell of this table, the parties will simply move to the point correspond-

A_1	1	2	3	4	5	–
1	(1,1)	(2,1)	(3,1)	(4,1)	(5,1)	–
2	(1,2)	(2,2)	(3,2)	(4,2)	(5,2)	–
A_2 3	(1,3)	(2,3)	(3,3)	(4,3)	(5,3)	–
4	(1,4)	(2,4)	(3,4)	(4,4)	(5,4)	–
5	(1,5)	(2,5)	(3,5)	(4,5)	(5,5)	–
–	–	–	–	–	–	

Fig. 1.3

ing to (1,1), where both are at bliss and there is no conflict. Usually, however, some points in the top left-hand corner of Fig. 1.3 will be missing from the field; that is, there may be no points in the field that have the value orderings (1,1), (1,2), (2,1), etc. Suppose that the dotted line in Fig. 1.3 cuts off all those points in the top left-hand corner that do not exist in the field. We can call this line the *upper-value boundary*.

Now let us take any cell in the matrix, say, (4,4). If we go north from this cell, A_1 is no worse off, and A_2 is better off; if we go south, A_1 is no worse off, and A_2 is worse off; if we go east, A_2 is no worse off, and A_1 is worse off; if we go west, A_2 is no worse off, and A_1 is better off. If, therefore, we go northwest (any direction between west and north), both parties are better off; if we go southeast, both parties are worse off; if we go northeast, A_1 is worse off, and A_2 is better off; if we go southwest, A_1 is better off, and A_2 is worse off. Any point in the matrix, therefore, from which it is possible to go northwest may be called a *trading point*, because from it a movement can be made that makes each party better off in his own estimation. It will be seen from Fig. 1.3 that all points that are not immediately adjacent to the upper-value boundary are trading points. These points constitute the trading set. Those points, however, that are adjacent to the upper-value boundary [in the figure, (1,5), (2,4), (3,3), (4,2), and (5,1)] are *conflict points*. From these points, no move is possible that makes both parties better off; all moves make at least one party worse off. These points constitute the conflict set. Moves northeast or southwest may be called *conflict moves*, as they make one party worse off and one party better off. Moves northwest, which make both parties better off, may be called *trading moves*. The southeast moves, which make both parties worse off, are stupid moves.

A field that has the properties of Fig. 1.3 is shown in Fig. 1.4. The solid circles are the indifferences curves of A_1, the dotted circles those of A_2. B_1 is the bliss point of A_1, B_2 of B_2. Each point of intersection of a dotted with a solid indifference curve corresponds to one cell of Fig. 1.3. Thus, the point K is the joint value ordering (4,4). The line B_1CDEB_2, which goes through all the points of tangency of the

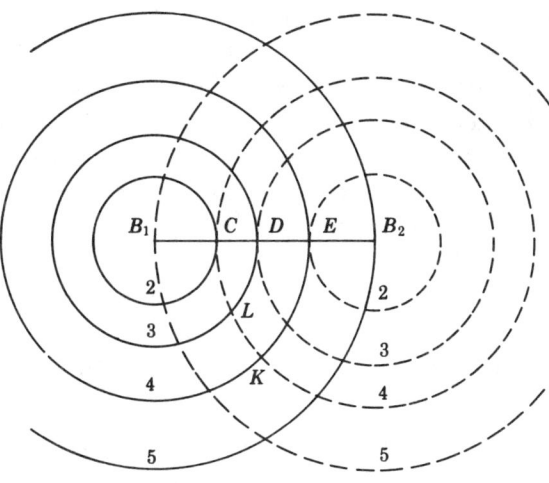

Fig. 1.4

indifference curves between the two bliss points, is the *conflict line*. All points in the conflict set [B_1 is (1,5), C is (2,4), D is (3,3), E is (4,2), and B_2 is (5,1)] are on the conflict line. Any point not on the conflict line is in the trading set. Thus, from the point K, any move within the triangular area KCE makes both parties better off and is a trading move. Trading moves are always possible as long as we are not on the conflict line; a succession of trading moves, however, eventually ends up on the conflict line. Trading always reduces the area of further trading. If we go from K to L, this reduces the trading area from KCE to LCD.

We may notice that the field in Fig. 1.4 has a *lower-value boundary* in Fig. 1.3 as well as an upper-value boundary. The value points (1,6), (1,7), (2,7), etc., and also the points (6,1), (6,1), (6,2), etc., are not represented in the field. These points occupy southwest and northeast triangles in Fig. 1.3. There is also a lower-value boundary in a southeasterly direction, when the field reaches the limit of mutual possibility; that is, there are some prospects that are the worst that could happen. In the absence of uncertainty, these lower-value

14 CONFLICT AND DEFENSE

boundaries may not be important. In considering behavior under uncertainty, as we shall see later, they may be very important. They are important, also, in delimiting the area of conflict. Thus, if the boundaries of possibility are so restricted that there is only one point in the value matrix, say, (3,3), and no other points are represented in the possible behavior field, then there is no conflict, because there is no freedom.

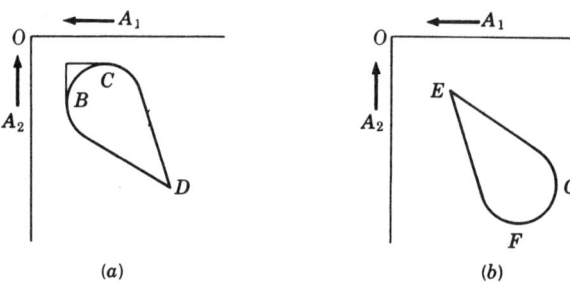

Fig. 1.5

The relation between freedom and conflict is illustrated in Fig. 1.5. Here we replace the value matrix of Fig. 1.3 by a continuous field, every point of which now represents a value-ordering point. A_1 gets better off as we move to the left, A_2 as we move upward. 0 is the bliss point for both parties. Now we suppose that those value ordering points that are contained in the joint possibility field are all found within a closed area such as BCD in Fig. 1.5a. The conflict set is, then, the line BC, where the curve BC is vertical at A_2 and horizontal at C. From any point on this line, it is impossible to make a trading move northeast; from every point within BCD not on the line, it is possible to make a trading move. Now, the *amount of freedom* in the situation is measured by the area within the possibility boundary BCD. The *range of conflict* is measured by the length of the conflict curve BC. In Fig. 1.5b, we see a situation in which the amount of freedom is about the same as in Fig. 1.5a, but the range of conflict is reduced to zero, simply because of the shape of the possibility boundary EFG; trading moves, which constitute the exercise of freedom, all lead to a single point E, and, from any point inside the boundary EFG except E, it is possible to make a trading move. Suppose now that we shrink the boundary EFG down to the single point E; again there is no conflict, but also no freedom. One of the problems of social organization is how to have possibility boundaries like Fig. 1.5b rather than like Fig. 1.5a, for this is the only way to have freedom without conflict. These measures must be taken as rough topological illustrations rather than as exact measures. It is the extent of the area of freedom, i.e., the area within the boundary of possibility, in the behavior field that is the significant measure of the freedom of choice of action of the individual. There is not a one-to-one correspondence between the area of the boundary of possibility in the behavior field of Fig. 1.4 and the corresponding area in the value-ordering field of Fig. 1.5. Thus, suppose, in Fig. 1.4, the two sets of indifference curves exactly coincided. The only value points on the behavior field would be (1,1), (2,2), (3,3), etc. The area of freedom in Fig. 1.5 would collapse to a single line from 0 at a 45° angle to both axes. The conflict set would also collapse to the point of mutual bliss, 0.

The economist will readily recognize the Edgeworth contract curve and the familiar analysis of exchange as a special case of the above system. In the theory of exchange, the behavior field consists of the possible distributions of fixed amounts of two commodities between two parties. This can be represented in the usual box diagram, as in Fig. 1.6, where O_1T is the total amount of commodity T and O_1S is the total amount of commodity S. Any point K within the rectangle O_1TO_2S represents a possible distribution of the two commodities between the exchangers A_1 and A_2. The amounts owned by A_1 are measured by the coordinates of K measured from O_1, KT_1 of T, and KS_1 of S. The amounts owned by A_2 are the coordinates of K measured from O_2, KT_2 of T, and KS_2 of S. As we move toward O_2, A_1 gets more of both commodities, and A_2 gets less. *Exchange* consists of moving in a northwest or southeast direction, for instance, from K, within the quadrants bounded by T_1KS_2 or S_1KT_2. This involves each party giving up one commodity and getting another. If the exchange is at a constant price or ratio of exchange, the exchange path is a straight line. The slope of the exchange path at any point is the ratio of exchange. On this field, we impose A's indifference curves (solid)

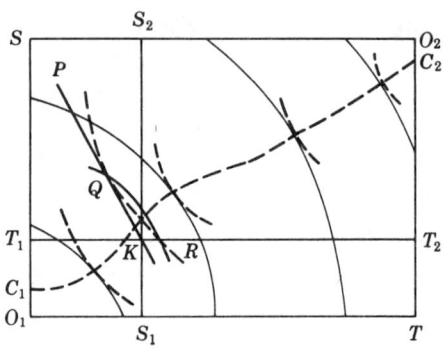

Fig. 1.6

and B's (dotted). The line through the points of tangency of these two sets of indifference curves, C_1C_2, is Edgeworth's contract curve. We see that it is identical with the concept of the conflict line developed earlier. From any position not on the contract curve, a trading path can be followed that makes both parties better off. Any trading path will be followed until it touches an indifference curve of one trader; it will not, then, pay this trader to pursue the trading path farther. If this point, however, is not on the contract curve, the terms of trade can be shifted so that trading is again possible. Thus, suppose we start at the point P and follow the trading path PK. Trade will stop at Q, where PK touches an A_2 indifference curve, because A_2 will get worse off if he trades more than this at a price equal to the slope of PK. It is possible, however, to find a new ratio of exchange, represented by the slope of a line such as QR lying between the two indifference curves that cross at Q, at which exchange will continue. It is always possible to do this as long as Q is not on the contract curve. If revision of the ratio of exchange is possible, then, there will always be a path that leads to the contract curve. Once on the contract curve, however, any move off it can be followed by a trading move back to it, so that we can regard the movement as now confined to the contract curve. As we move up the contract curve toward C_2, however, A_1 gets better off and A_2 worse off; as we move in the opposite direction, A_1 gets better off and A_2 worse off. This is why the contract curve is a *conflict curve*.

The analysis of exchange is applicable to any situation in which something is given up in return for something else. It applies, for instance, to a bargaining situation, where the exchangeables are not physical commodities but clauses in a union contract, or to an international treaty, or even to quite imponderable understandings and agreements. In any bargaining situation, we have a bargaining field, any point of which represents a state of the joint universe of the bargainers. A value ordering for each bargainer can be placed over the field as before, and, from the two value orderings, a conflict set and a trading set of positions can be developed. Within the trading set, it is possible for one side to offer to give up something and get something else—a wage increase, for instance, for union security—that will be accepted because both parties benefit. As before, however, trading leads to the conflict set, and we can consider the real problem as beginning when the conflict set is reached. At this point, a new and very important concept enters the picture—*acceptability*. A position in the field is acceptable to one of the parties if the party is willing to conclude a bargain or enter into some continuing relationship with the other party. The field can, therefore, be divided into an acceptable set and a nonacceptable set by a boundary of acceptability for each party. If the acceptable sets of the two parties do not overlap, that is, if there are no points common to both sets, no bargain can be struck. This is illustrated in Fig. 1.7a, where C_1C_2 is a contract curve (stretched out for convenience into a straight line), C_1W_1 is the acceptability set for A_1 and C_2W_2 for A_2. There are no points common to both

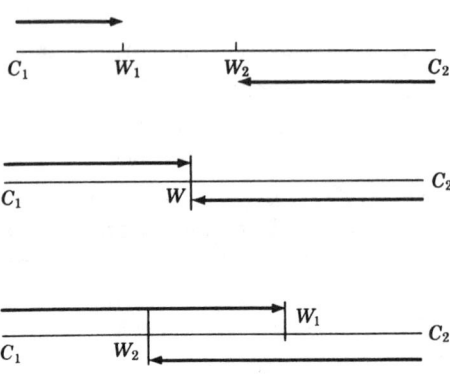

Fig. 1.7c. The bargaining area.

sets, and a bargain cannot be struck. Figure 1.7b shows the "bare bargain" case. C_1W is the acceptability set for A_1 and C_2W for A_2, and a bargain can be struck at W but nowhere else. Figure 1.7c shows a field of acceptability, W_1W_2, that is the mutually acceptable set. In the dynamics of bargaining, changes in the acceptability set are of first importance.

2

THE DYNAMICS OF CONFLICT:

RICHARDSON PROCESS MODELS

The static-equilibrium models of the previous chapter take us only a little way toward the understanding of conflict processes, though they are useful in indicating the framework within which the dynamic processes take place and perhaps in indicating the end result of these processes. All real conflicts take place in time and consist of a succession of states of a situation or field. If this succession is governed by fairly simple laws, so that there is a stable relationship between the state of today and the state of tomorrow or, say, between yesterday, today, and tomorrow, then there is a *dynamic system* that can, in general, be solved to predict the state of the system at any future date. One of the great problems in social dynamics is that the dynamic systems are not stable and are frequently subject to unpredictable change. Nevertheless, the succession of states of a social system is not random; some regularities can usually be detected, and even if the system is not stable enough to permit unconditional prediction of its future states, at least enough can usually be known about it to set limits on the probability of various future positions.

Where the dynamics of the system results in a succession of

identically similar states, the system is said to be in *equilibrium*. Many dynamic systems move toward an equilibrium; some, however, do not, and move either indefinitely onward or else toward *system breakdown*, some point at which the laws of the system change. An interesting special case is that of *cyclical equilibrium*, in which the system repeats indefinitely a certain sequence of states. Equilibrium is thus seen to be a special case of a dynamic process; indeed, the stability of an equilibrium cannot be known with certainty unless the dynamic process of which it is a special case is also known. In a stable equilibrium, the dynamic paths all converge on the equilibrium point; in an unstable equilibrium, the dynamic paths diverge away from the equilibrium point. In a circular equilibrium, the dynamic paths converge on a ring of successive states.

By way of further illustration of the properties of dynamic systems, let us consider the dynamics of a very simple behavior-field system in which a single behavior unit is moving toward the highest-valued position of its field. The history of a dynamic movement can be recorded by a path in the field, each successive point of which shows the position of the system on successive *days*, or equal time intervals. It can be represented graphically by what in *A Reconstruction of Economics* I have called a *vector line*, where the successive positions of the system on successive days are represented by the points of arrows on the path, the direction of movement being shown by the direction of the arrows.[1] Thus, in Fig. 2.1, the solid lines are indifference contours of a value surface with P_b as the maximum value. Starting from a position P_0, the behavior unit then traces out a path, climbing the value hill, and occupying positions P_1, P_2, etc., on successive days. The problem of dynamic theory, then, is to try to say something about the nature of the possible paths from all points in the field. This is relatively easy if at each point there is a unique direction of movement. Thus, suppose, in Fig. 2.1, that we assume the vector lines all cross the indifference

[1] Kenneth E. Boulding, *A Reconstruction of Economics*, New York, Wiley, 1950, Chap. 1.

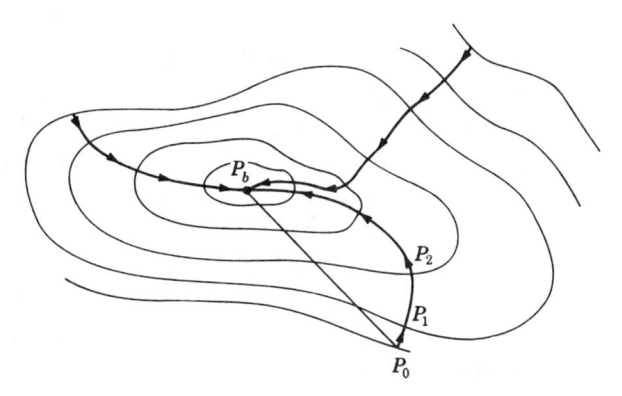

THE DYNAMICS OF CONFLICT: RICHARDSON PROCESS MODELS   21

Fig. 2.1

curves at right angles. This means that, from any point, we always climb the hill in the steepest direction, that is, in the direction in which the value is increasing most rapidly. Then, given a system of indifference curves of sufficient density, we can immediately draw a single corresponding system of vector lines that traces out the dynamic paths from roughly any position in the field. Some of these are shown in Fig. 2.1. The stability of the equilibrium is given immediately by whether the vector lines move into the equilibrium position or out from it. P_b in Fig. 2.1 is clearly a position of stable equilibrium. Thus, if Fig. 2.1 were the contours of a basin, the vector lines would show how perfectly round balls would roll down to the equilibrium at the bottom of the basin, neglecting momentum.

If momentum is taken into consideration, another element is added to the dynamic equations. This is illustrated graphically in Fig. 2.2. P_0, P_1, and P_2 are successive points in an *orthogonal path*, that is, a path that crosses all indifference curves at right angles. We suppose that, in going from P_0 to P_1, however, the body gathers momentum, which in the absence of other forces would carry it to R_2, where P_1R_2 is tangent to the curve P_0P_1 at P_1. The actual

Fig. 2.2

movement is the resolution of these two vectors, P_1Q_2. Because of momentum, a body approaching a maximum position on a curved path will rotate around it, just as a ball rotates around the bottom of a bowl when it is set rolling in an oblique path. Similarly, it is because of momentum that a pendulum swings about its point of equilibrium instead of proceeding to it and stopping there. The *cobweb theorem* in economics is an example of a rather similar phenomenon, where prices and quantities oscillate around the equilibrium point because the behavior always overshoots the mark. Momentum has to be taken into account in most social behavior systems; this is the element of habit, custom, and resistance to change.

The dynamic system that I have described is an example—and only one out of a very large number of possible examples—of a dynamic system in the small. It is described essentially by means of differential or difference equations, which tell us exactly how we get from one point to the next. A difference equation is simply a stable relationship between today and yesterday, and perhaps the day before yesterday or the day before that, depending on the degree of the equation. If we know how to get from yesterday to today and the same law applies, then we know how to get from today to tomorrow, from tomorrow to the next day, and so ad infinitum. What might be called *mechanical prediction* depends on the discovery of *stable* difference (or differential) equations.[2] This is the secret of the remarkable predictive success of the astronomers; the move-

[2] A differential equation is simply the limiting case of a difference equation in which the time interval between successive positions of the system reduces to a limiting value of zero and the differences are expressed as continuous rates of change. Thus, take what is about the simplest difference equation system—growth at a constant rate, for example, at compound interest. If x_{t-1} and x_t are the values of the sum yesterday and today and if we have growth at a constant rate, we know that $(x_t - x_{t-1})/x_{t-1} = k$, where k is the constant rate of growth. We can solve this difference equation, that is, find the explicit equation for x_{t+n}, which is, in this case, the familiar compound interest formula $x_{t+n} = x_t(1 + k)^n$. The corresponding differential equation is $dx/x\, dt = k$; that is, the proportionate rate of change of x is constant. Its solution is the continuous compounding law $x_{t+n} = x_t e^{kn}$.

ments of the planets are described by very stable, though complex, differential equations, and so their positions can be predicted indefinitely from the past into the future.

Systems in social dynamics, however, are not usually mechanical systems, nor are they capable of mechanical prediction except within very wide limits of uncertainty. A dramatic example of the failure of mechanical prediction in social systems was the debacle of the population predictions of the 1940s. Here was a system, we thought, where mechanical predictions really worked; the one thing we knew for certain about the future was that anybody who was x years old today would be either dead or $x + 1$ years old at this time next year. Hence, given certain assumptions about continuance in trends of age-specific birth and death rates, we should have been able to predict population with great accuracy. Unfortunately, these assumptions let us down, and we found in the 1950s a totally unexpected population increase in most of the Western world.

One answer to the failure of mechanical dynamics in social systems is to look for bigger and better differential equations. In a sense, this was what happened in astronomy; the circular assumed motions of the planets of Ptolemy and even Copernicus gave unsatisfactory predictions, and it was not until the more complex elliptical equations of Kepler and the great generalizations of Newton came along that astronomical predictions were placed on a firm basis. It can be argued, therefore, that, if predictions go wrong in social systems, if population movements or business cycles do not turn out as we predict, then the answer is to look for new variables, or more complex equations, in hope of finding stable relationships.

The difficulty is more fundamental than this, however. Our failure to find stable difference equations in social systems is not merely because we have not looked hard enough or because our techniques of analysis are not refined enough. Our failure is due to the fact that the equations do not exist; that is, social systems are not stable dynamically in the small, as most physical systems are. This does not mean that they are purely random or haphazard; it means, however, that the classical apparatus of physical mechanical systems, the system of simultaneous differential equations, has only a very limited applicability to social systems, because the dynamics of systems composed of intelligent beings inevitably has an epistemological or, as I have called it, an *eiconic*[3] aspect and has, therefore, a dynamics in the large. Human beings are moved not only by immediate pressures but by distant goals that are contemplated in the imagination. These goals are susceptible of change, often of dramatic change, as a result of apparently slight changes in current information. On the other hand, they also have a good deal of stability, and this gives a stability to the system in the large that it may not have in the small. Thus, to revert to Fig. 2.1, we may not be able to trace the path from P_0 with any degree of certainty, because it is not the immediate environment but the distant goal that may drive men forward, and the easy path in the present may be rejected because of the dominating pull of the distant future. Thus, in Fig. 2.1, we may reject the path $P_0P_1P_2$, even though this may be the easiest in the present, in favor of the straight line to the distant goal P_0P_b. It is this possibility of being moved in the large which perhaps differentiates man from the lower animals more than any other feature of his nature. It is this capacity which enables him to endure war, marriage, religion, and education—institutions which are also peculiar to man and which carry him to adventure and to martyrdom. This is why all equilibriums of human and social systems in the small are to be suspected. Man has the capacity of going down into innumerable valleys of humiliation because of the vision he catches of the heights on the other side.

Without further preliminaries, however, we must now get down to the consideration of the nature of conflict processes. Perhaps the most important class of these processes is what may be called

[3] Kenneth E. Boulding, *The Image*, Ann Arbor, University of Michigan Press, 1956.

reaction processes. These are processes in which a movement on the part of one party so changes the field of the other that it forces a movement of this party, which in turn changes the field of the first, forcing another move of the second, and so on. The economist is familiar with the reaction process in the theory of oligopoly, especially the theory of the price war. The political scientist meets the reaction process in the concept of the arms race, which is theoretically very similar to the price war. We find the same processes going on, however, at all levels of relationship—between union and management, between husband and wife, between king and parliament, between president and congress, between administration and faculty, between teacher and student, and even in the animal kingdom, between predator and prey, parasite and host, eater and eaten. By far the most extensive theoretical treatment of these processes has been made by Richardson, whose remarkable pioneering work is only now receiving recognition.[4] It would only be just to name these processes *Richardson processes* in his honor.

Richardson developed his system along the lines of classical physics, using differential equations. Here I propose to use a simpler graphic technique similar to that outlined in the opening paragraphs of this chapter; this does not have quite the elegance and power of Richardson's method, but it illustrates the principles involved without requiring so much mathematical skill. We shall suppose a field, then, on which a quantity or quality descriptive of each party can be measured. Suppose this quantity is the continuum "hostility-friendliness" toward the other party. Thus, in Fig. 2.3, the origin O is the neutral point for both parties. Then, along OH_a, we measure A's hostility to B, and, along OH_b, B's hostility to A. Along OF_a,

---

[4] Richardson's two great works have just been published—*Arms and Insecurity*, Pittsburgh, Boxwood, 1960; and *Statistics of Deadly Quarrels*, Chicago, Quadrangle, 1960. See also his "Generalized Foreign Policies," *British Journal of Psychology*, 1939, monograph supplement; and two articles reprinted in James R. Newman, ed., *The World of Mathematics*, New York, Simon and Schuster, 1956, pp. 1240, 1254. For a summary of his work, see Anatole Rapoport, "Lewis Richardson's Mathematical Theory of War," *The Journal of Conflict Resolution*, I (1957) 249–299.

we measure A's friendliness to B, and, along OF_b, B's friendliness to A. We assume here that hostility is simple negative friendliness, and we do not stop at this point to inquire how these quantities are measured or observed; we use these terms simply as a very general measure of attitude. We then postulate two partial equilibrium curves, an A curve, M_aA, which shows what will be A's level of friendliness or hostility for each level of B's friendliness or hostility, and a B curve, M_bB, which shows the same thing for B. For convenience, we draw these curves as straight lines, but there is no reason why they should not be curvilinear. Indeed, they probably will exhibit something like diminishing returns, so that they are likely to be S-shaped, that is, there may be some maximum degree of hostility or friendliness after which there is no reaction and the curves are parallel to their respective axes. As we have drawn the curves, we suppose that, for each party, there is a level of initial hostility, ON_a for A and ON_b for B, that shows the level of hostility of one toward the other even when the other is neutral. Both the parties of Fig. 2.3 are xenophobes. Then we suppose a positive reaction coefficient, so that both lines have positive slopes. The reaction coefficient is the amount by which the equilibrium level of hostility of the one increases per unit increase in the hostility of the other. The reaction coefficient, therefore, measures the touchiness of the parties. A touchy party has a high reaction coefficient; he reacts to an increase in the perceived hostility of the other by a sharp rise in his own hostility

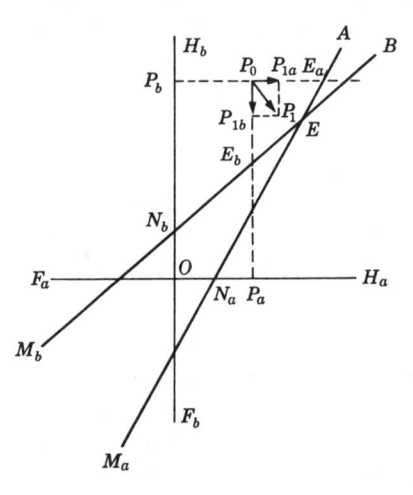

Fig. 2.3

—and similarly for friendliness. A placid party, on the other hand, has a low reaction coefficient.

In the figure, there is a point of equilibrium at the intersection of the two partial-equilibrium lines at E. In order to find out whether this is stable or unstable, however, we must examine the dynamics of the system as reflected in the vector lines. Consider a point P_0 corresponding to an A hostility of OP_a and a B hostility of OP_b. For the level of A's hostility, OP_a, B's hostility is too high; it will move, therefore, toward the B equilibrium corresponding to OP_a at E_b, as shown by the arrow P_0P_{1b}. Similarly, A's hostility is too low to correspond to B's hostility OP_b; A, therefore, moves toward E_a, following the arrow P_0P_{1a}. The effect of both these movements is shown by completing the rectangle $P_0P_{1b}P_1P_{1a}$ and drawing the arrow P_0P_1, which is a segment of a vector line. Some vector lines of this system are shown by the arrow lines in Fig. 2.4. It is clear that E is a stable equilibrium, as all the vector lines move toward it. It will be observed that, where the vector lines cross line M_bB, they are horizontal, for, on this line, there is no B component; the movement is entirely by A, as the meaning of the partial-equilibrium line is that B is satisfied. Similarly, the vector lines are vertical where they cross the partial-equilibrium line M_aA. It should be observed that this analysis is formally identical with the analysis of the ecological equilibrium of two complementary populations;

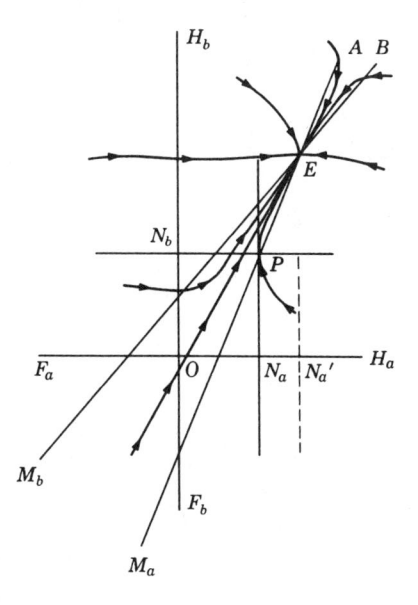

Fig. 2.4

the hostility of each is complementary with the hostility of the other.[5]

In Figs. 2.3 and 2.4, there is a stable equilibrium at E. This is the *balance of power*. Cases can easily exist in which no such equilibrium exists. Thus, suppose, in Fig. 2.3, the reaction coefficients increase, so that the lines of partial equilibrium, M_aA and M_bB, grow flatter and steeper respectively. The position of equilibrium moves farther and farther away from the origin, equilibrium being found at higher and higher levels of hostility, until when the two partial-equilibrium curves are parallel, the equilibrium point shoots off to infinity, and when they diverge, there is no stable equilibrium at all. This is shown in Fig. 2.5. There is an unstable position of equilibrium at E, which happens to be in the friendly-friendly quadrant. From any point upward and to the right of the line of unstable equilibrium, E_1EE_2, the dynamics of the system carries it to an increasingly hostile area until some boundary of the system is reached and it breaks

---

[5] See Boulding, *A Reconstruction of Economics, op. cit.*, chap. 1; and Chapter 6 of this book.

It is not difficult to show that the above system is equivalent to Richardson's system, on one simple assumption. Let a and b be the hostilities of the two parties. Then, at P_0, we write

$$\frac{da}{dt} = k(P_0E_a) \tag{2.1}$$

That is, the rate of change of A's hostility per unit time, measured by the length of the line P_0P_{1a}, is proportional to the distance of P_0 from A's partial-equilibrium point E_a.

We have, however, $P_0E_a = a_0 + r_ab - a$, where r_a is the reaction coefficient of A and a_0 ($= ON_a$) is A's initial hostility.

That is,
$$\frac{da}{dt} = ka_0 + kr_ab - ka \tag{2.2a}$$

and, similarly, we can show that

$$\frac{db}{dt} = hb_0 - hb + hr_ba \tag{2.2b}$$

Equations (2.2a) and (2.2b) are essentially Richardson's equations. They state that the rate of change of hostility of each party is a constant, less a certain proportion of the level of hostility of that party, plus a certain proportion of the level of hostility of the other party.

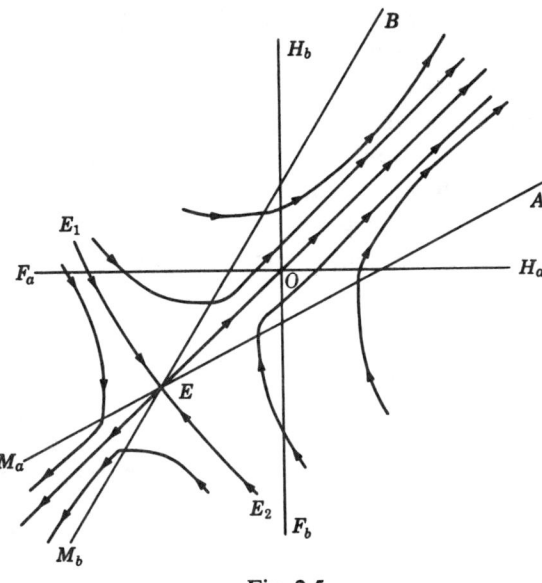

Fig. 2.5

down. There is no balance of power, or balance of hostility, or balance of arms: the arms race or the price war will go on until the system breaks down in war, or in capitulation of one side or the other, or in a mutual reorganization of the whole system. In the simpler linear system, the condition that informs us whether there is a point of stable equilibrium is that, if the product of the reaction coefficients, $r_a r_b$, is less than 1, there is a position of equilibrium and that, if it is equal to or greater than 1, there is no stable equilibrium. This condition holds no matter what the initial hostilities. Provided that there is a point of stable equilibrium, however, we can say that the larger the initial hostilities and the greater the reaction coefficients, the more hostile will be the position of equilibrium. It is interesting to notice that, in the case of Fig. 2.5, southwest of the line of unstable equilibrium, $E_1 E E_2$, there is a region of constantly increasing friendliness. Richardson himself pointed out that this is not an unknown phenomenon and that it is, in fact, the familiar phenomenon of falling in love, which is strictly analogous to the phenomenon of an arms race. A phrase from a popular song, "Lay down your arms and surrender to mine," is a succinct expression of the mathematics of this model.

It is interesting to investigate some special cases of this model for various possible forms of the particular equilibrium functions. Thus, in Fig. 2.6, we show the extreme case of the yogi who, having achieved complete detachment from the world, exhibits friendliness

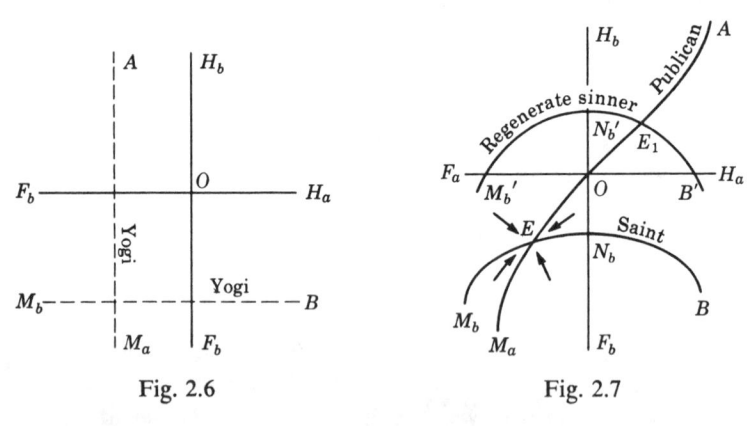

Fig. 2.6

Fig. 2.7

to the other no matter what the attitude of the other. His partial-equilibrium curve will be, say, AM_a. If there are two yogis, they have a stable but not very interesting equilibrium of friendliness at E, where the lines AM_a and BM_b intersect. A more exciting case is that of the saint. The saint has a high level of initial friendliness and, furthermore, returns good for evil as well as good for good. His partial-equilibrium curve is thus at least of the second degree, as the curve $M_b N_b B$ (Fig. 2.7). In Fig. 2.7, we show the saint combined with an ordinary person who returns good for good and evil for evil, whom, following Matthew 5:46, we might call the publican. In Fig. 2.7, we suppose him to be very ordinary indeed, so that his partial-equilibrium curve goes through the origin; he is neutral toward people who are neutral to him, hostile to those who are hostile, and friendly to those who are friendly. In Fig. 2.7, we show an equilibrium at the intersection at E:—the vector arrows show that this is stable—that is, the saint imposes friendliness on the publican. Indeed, by being sufficiently saintly, that is, by moving his partial-equilibrium curve downward, the saint can impose any degree of friendliness on the situation. In the figure, we suppose that, beyond a certain point, the publican's partial-equilibrium curve exhibits diminishing returns; that is, there are certain maximum degrees of both hatred and friendliness of which the publican is capable, and his partial-equilibrium curve will be asymptotic to these maxima. The saint, obviously, cannot impose more friendliness on the publican than he is capable of; however, by being sufficiently saintly, the saint can push the publican to the limit.

We may notice that, in order to impose friendliness on the publican, the saint must have a positive level of initial friendliness, ON_b; he must be well disposed even toward the neutral. The mere regenerate sinner, who, like the saint, returns good for both good and evil but who starts with the handicap of a positive level of initial hostility (original sin), can never force the publican into friendliness. His partial equilibrium curve is like $M'_b N'_b B'$ in Fig. 2.7; the equilibrium at E' is always in the first (hostile-hostile) quadrant.

Another case is that of the devil, who returns evil for both evil and good. In Fig. 2.8, $M_b N_b B$ is the devil's partial-equilibrium curve. If the devil is faced with the publican, the case is not much different from that of two publicans: there may be an equilibrium, as at E_1, in the hostile-hostile quadrant, or there may be no equilibrium and continually increasing hostility. If the devil is faced with the saint, however, we end up in the hostile-friendly quadrant; the saint cannot force the devil into friendliness, as he can the publican. There may be an equilibrium, as at E_2, or if the two curves do not intersect, there may be an unstable dynamic process in the hostile-friendly quadrant, with the saint getting continually more saintly and the devil continually more devilish.

A very interesting case, which was studied in some detail by

Richardson, is that of the submission of one party to another. We may suppose, to return to our first example of xenophobic publicans or nations, that a party will exhibit a positive reaction coefficient

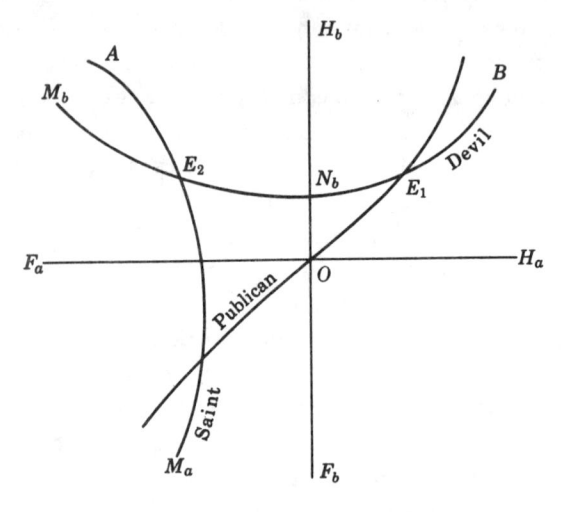

Fig. 2.8

for low levels of hostility but that, as the hostility of the other party increases beyond a certain point, the first party will become cowed and its hostility will diminish; that is, its reaction coefficient will become negative. The partial-equilibrium curve of the submissive party, therefore, exhibits a maximum hostility, as at M_b in Fig. 2.9, after which it declines. In Fig. 2.9, there is an equilibrium at E. The nature of this equilibrium, however, is very peculiar. If we trace a vector line such as $P_0 P_1 P_2 \cdots P_n$, we find that it circles around the equilibrium point in a spiral. The equilibrium has a circular solution in dynamic terms. Economists will recognize this as a case similar to that of the cobweb theorem. In extreme cases, the circle may be closed, or the spiral may explode outward toward a closed circle. The rationale of this circular movement is easy to explain. Thus, suppose we start with the point P_0, where A is very hostile and B is cowed into friendliness. Because of B's friendliness, A's hostility diminishes; A can afford to let his defenses down. As he does so, however, B becomes less cowed, and his hostility increases as we move from P_0 to P_1. Between P_1 and P_2, both hostilities increase—B's because A's level is low enough so that B is not completely cowed and A's because of fear of the rising hostility of B. From P_2 to P_3, A's hostility increases rapidly in response to B's high level of hostility, but B's declines because he is cowed by A's high hostility. From P_3 to P_4, both hostilities decline—A's because B is now adequately cowed and B's because A's hostility is now so high. From P_4, the cycle repeats itself on a diminished scale. We may note that there is a possible equivalent of this system in the friendly-friendly quadrant, where the equivalent of submission is revulsion, a diminution in the friendliness of one as a result of too much friendliness of the other. The notable cyclical movement of young people in love may be an expression of this system.

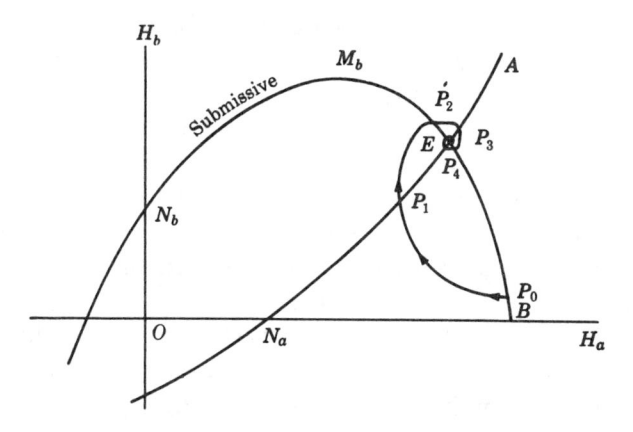

Fig. 2.9

An interesting case is that of mutual submissiveness, that is, where each party exhibits partial-equilibrium curves of the type of $N_b M_b B$ of Fig. 2.9. This is shown in the curves $N_b M_b B$ and $N_a M_a A$ of

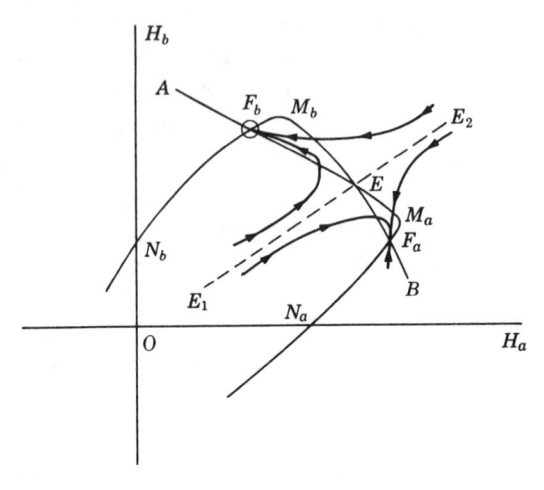

Fig. 2.10

Fig. 2.10. The field is divided into two parts by a line of unstable equilibrium E_1EE_2. There are two positions of stable equilibrium, F_a, where A is dominant and B is submissive, and F_b, where B is dominant and A is submissive. These equilibriums may be circular. As shown by the sample vector lines, from all points upward and to the left of E_1EE_2, movement takes place eventually to F_b, from all points downward and to the right, movement carries the system eventually to F_a. Which party becomes dominant, then, is a matter of where the parties start from; whoever has an initial advantage will maintain it and will eventually become dominant.

I have used the rather vague words "hostility" and "friendliness" to describe the fundamental variables of these models deliberately in order to point up the great generality of the system. We should now apply the system to special cases. Richardson[6] attempted to verify the system by applying it to the two arms races of 1908–1914 and 1929–1939. The application to the earlier period is fairly successful and indicates that the reaction coefficients and positions

[6] Richardson, *Arms and Insecurity, op. cit.*, chaps. 4, 19.

of the two opposing European systems in 1908 were such that an equilibrium might have been found at a somewhat smaller level of armaments than then existed. As it was, the system got into an explosive phase, like that of Fig. 2.5, that led to the First World War. His analysis of the arms race preceding the Second World War is much more elaborate, using a matrix of 10 nations, and is less successful. His quantitative work is seriously hampered by the lack of data and by some untenable assumptions, for instance, that the volume of trade between two countries measures the degree of friendliness between them. It is, however, pioneering work of the first magnitude, and it needs to be taken up again with the better data and means of measurement that we now have at our disposal. The problem of the measurement of hostility and friendliness is a difficult one. The problem is complicated by the fact that the significant variables here are the hostility or friendliness of each party as perceived by the other. We have, therefore, for each party, three significant reaction concepts. There is the *objective situation* as it might be perceived by an omniscient outsider. There is the situation of the first party as perceived by the second, and of the second as perceived by the first. We have here a fertile field for a theory of *misunderstanding processes*, which, however, we cannot go into at this point. The reaction of a party depends not on the objective situation but on its image of itself and the other. The reaction coefficients are likely to be high if a party feels itself to be misunderstood, that is, if it senses a gap between its own image of its behavior and its image of the other party's image of its behavior. This is particularly common in international relations, where it is customary for each nation to put the best interpretation on its own actions and the worst interpretation on the actions of its enemies.

We can now summarize some of the conclusions of the analysis of Richardson processes. The basic parameters of the particular equilibrium curves are (1) the initial hostility, (2) the initial reaction coefficient, and (3) the rate of change of the reaction coefficient with increase in hostility. This implies, of course, what is not in general strictly true, that the particular equilibrium curve can be described by a quadratic equation such as $h_1 = H_1 + (r_1 - m_1 h_2)h_2$. Here, h_1 and h_2 are the hostility levels of parties 1 and 2. Then, for party 1, H_1 is the initial hostility, r_1 the initial reaction coefficient, and m_1 the decline in reaction coefficient per unit increase in h_2, or the rate of diminishing returns in the reaction coefficient. If there are no diminishing returns ($m_1 = 0$), the reaction functions are linear ($h_1 = H_1 + r_1 h_2$ and $h_2 = H_2 + r_2 h_1$). Solving these two equations, we get

$$h_1 = \frac{H_1 + k_1 H_2}{1 - r_1 r_2} \qquad h_2 = \frac{H_2 + k_2 H_1}{1 - r_1 r_2}$$

It is clear that, the greater the initial hostilities and the greater the reaction coefficients, the greater the equilibrium level of hostility. Xenophobia and touchiness both lead to high levels of hostility. As long as $r_1 r_2 < 1$, there will be some position of equilibrium, no matter how great the initial hostilities. If the parties are sufficiently touchy, so that $r_1 r_2 > 1$, there will be no position of equilibrium (except at negative levels of hostility, and this will not be stable). If there are diminishing returns to touchiness (m_1 is positive), the equilibrium level of hostility is likely to be less than the initial touchiness would indicate. In this case, there may be an equilibrium even if levels of touchiness are high. The effect on the equilibrium of a pure change in initial hostility of one party depends on the sign and slope of the reaction function of the other. Thus, if, in Fig. 2.3, we simply increase ON_b, keeping the slope of $M_b N_b B$ the same, the equilibrium point E moves up the other reaction curve $M_a A$; in this case, both levels of hostility increase. In Fig. 2.10, if we suppose that the curve $N_b M_b B$ simply moves upward with unchanged shape, the equilibrium point F_b moves toward A along $AF_b E M_a$, and the equilibrium point F_a moves toward M_a. In the first instance, the equilibrium hostility level of A actually declines because of the increased initial hostility of B; this is, of course, because of A's submissiveness.

Up to this point, we have assumed the reaction functions to be given. We can now remove this limitation and suppose that each party may have some control over his reaction function; that is, the reaction function itself is chosen out of a certain range of possibility. This implies a certain distinction between shortsighted and longsighted equilibria. The equilibrium of a simple Richardson process is shortsighted in the sense that it assumes for each party a simple reaction to its perception of the current position of the other. If, however, we take into account the possibility of longsightedness, that is, of the possible deliberate shift of reaction functions themselves, the results of the analysis may be very different. Thus, party A can force an equilibrium on B at any point on B's reaction function (assuming this to be stable) if A can shift his own reaction function. In Fig. 2.3, for instance, A, by sliding his reaction curve M_aA right or left, could force an equilibrium on B at any point on B's reaction curve M_bB, assuming this remains unchanged.

The problem of mutual shift of reaction functions is rather complex, but, for the reader who does not mind a complicated diagram, Fig. 2.11 illustrates some of the problems involved. Here, to fix ideas, we use the illustration of a price war under conditions of imperfect oligopoly, where we have two firms producing similar though not identical commodities. This is strictly analogous to the hostility-friendliness analysis of Fig. 2.3 if we suppose that a rise in the price that one seller charges benefits the other seller by chasing customers toward him; Fig. 2.11, then, is analogous to the third quadrant of Fig. 2.3, a rise in price corresponding to an increase in friendliness. Here, then, we measure A's price P_a horizontally and B's price P_b vertically. The thin solid lines are contours of A's profit surface if profit is measured vertical to the plane of the paper. For any given price of B, A's profit first rises as he increases P_a, reaches a maximum, and then falls. The higher the price of B, the less B will sell of his product, and the less competition he will offer A, and the higher A's profit curve will be, up to the price T_b, where B sells nothing; after that, a further rise in B's price makes no difference to A's profit curve, and the contours become vertical. The thick line M_aA goes through the points where A's profit contours are horizontal. This means that, for each price of B, the line M_aA shows the price of A at which A's profits are a maximum. Assuming shortsighted reaction of A to his observation of a price of B, this is his reaction curve in the Richardson process sense. Similarly, the

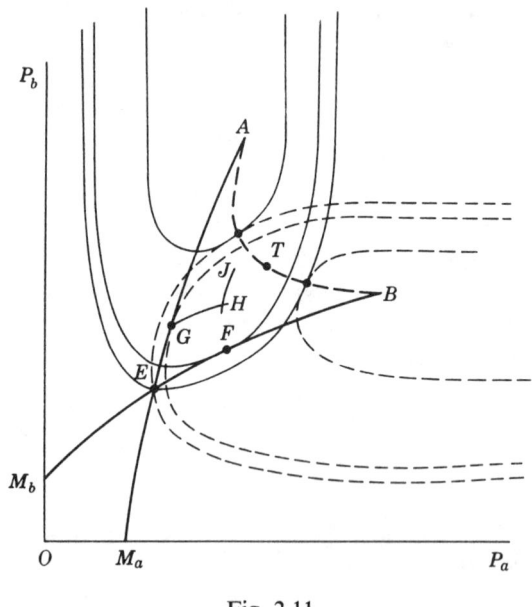

Fig. 2.11

dotted contours are profit contours of B, and M_bB is B's shortsighted reaction curve. There is a reaction equilibrium at E, where the reaction curves intersect, which is, incidentally, the Cournot solution.

If A can now control his own reaction function by longsightedness, he can do better for himself than the equilibrium at E, which is the shortsighted equilibrium. By shifting his reaction function M_aA to the right, that is, by charging a price greater than the one that would maximize his profit on the assumption that B maintains a constant price, he can push the equilibrium of the system to any point on EB, assuming that B does not change his reaction function. He will not push it beyond F, where the line M_bB is touched by one of A's profit contours, as this is the highest profit that A can attain on the line M_bB. If B now moves his reaction function first, with A's remaining constant, he can push the equilibrium to G, where B's profit contour touches M_aA, by making his reaction function GH. Now, however, A can push the equilibrium to H by shifting his reaction function to HJ, and so on. As long as one party can improve his position without worsening the position of the other by shifting his reaction function, he will do so; this process clearly ends on the conflict curve ATB, which is the locus of all points of tangency of the two sets of profit contours. The maximum joint profit (the sum of the profits of the two firms) must lie on ATB, say, at T. Here is a process almost identical with the process of recontract in exchange, which we examined in Fig. 1.6. As in that case, the solution is not determinate, in the sense that the exact location of the final point of equilibrium on the conflict curve depends on the dynamic path that is taken toward it. In Fig. 2.11, it may well be, for instance, that, if A moves first, the equilibrium may move right to the point B and stay there.

Finally, it should be noted that Richardson processes may reach some kind of a system boundary before they reach equilibrium. This is a very important phenomenon in the conflict processes of the real world, where arms races frequently lead to war, industrial disputes to strikes, marital discord to divorce, verbal quarrels to fisticuffs, theological disagreements to separations, and party strife to dictatorship. The simplest form of such a boundary is illustrated in Fig. 2.4, where we suppose that there is some level of hostility for each party, ON_a for A and ON_b for B, beyond which they will not go without system breakdown. The system cannot operate, then, above N_bP or to the right of N_aP. Which party reaches the boundary first depends on the dynamic path that is followed, for the system will change when its dynamic path hits its first boundary.

Generally speaking, the less system-tolerant the party, the more likely is it to be the system-changer. Thus, if we move N_a to the right to N_a', the system can only be changed by B; that is, B will declare war, break off relations, institute divorce proceedings, or hit A on the nose. Sometimes the system never recovers after a breakdown; one country is destroyed by the other in war, the firm is bankrupted or the union is destroyed by a strike, one party is killed in a fight or duel, or a divorced couple never see each other again. On the other hand, it not infrequently happens that, after a breakdown and an interlude of open conflict, the old system re-forms, perhaps in a slightly different pattern. Nations renew relationships after a war, a firm and a union continue after a strike, friendship survives a quarrel, and divorced people remarry each other. This alternation of systems is one way in which systems that have no true point of equilibrium or an equilibrium beyond the limits of tolerability can persist. Thus, even in the condition of Fig. 2.5, with explosive dynamics, we might suppose that the system would explode toward some boundary and be succeeded by another system that would reduce the hostilities to the point where the first system could re-form and start over again. The phenomenon of system alternation is a remarkably common one: we find it in the manic-depressive psychosis and in the alternation of war and peace, prosperity and depression, Republicans and Democrats, romanticism and classicism, and so on. The inference seems to be that, the more complex a system is, the more difficult it becomes to make it truly stable, and that the price of complexity, up to a point, seems to be alternation.

3

THE CONTRIBUTION OF GAME THEORY

In the past twenty-five years or so there has developed a set of mathematical models known as the *theory of games*. These models throw light on many aspects of conflict situations, both static and dynamic, and it is the purpose of this chapter not so much to give a general exposition of game theory as to select from it those elements and techniques which seem most useful in developing a general theory of conflict.

The basic concept of game theory is that of the payoff matrix. A *game* is a situation in which we have a certain number of parties each of which is capable of assuming one out of a given number of positions or choices (a finite number in the case of a finite game and an infinite number in the case of an infinite game). The *outcome* or the *payoff* of the game is the set of rewards or penalties accruing to each party at each combination of positions of all the parties. This outcome is expressed in the payoff matrix, illustrated in Fig. 3.1 for the simplest possible case of two parties, A and B, with two choices or positions each: A can choose either A_1 or A_2, and B can choose either B_1 or B_2. We can think of these positions either as simple choices or as complex *strategies*; a strategy is simply a rule of choice that is complex enough to take care of all possible eventualities. It makes no difference to the analysis how a position is defined: all that is necessary is that there be more than one position and the

	(Head) a_1	(Tail) a_2
(Head) b_1	$(1,-1)$	$(-1,1)$
(Tail) b_2	$(-1,1)$	$(1,-1)$

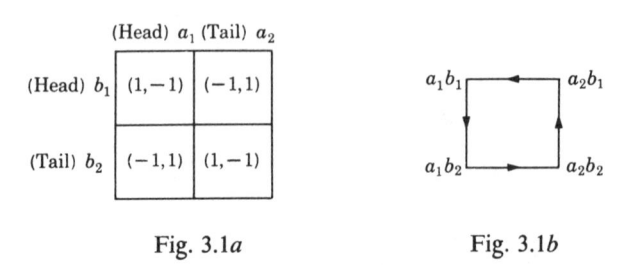

Fig. 3.1a

Fig. 3.1b

ability to choose one position among those available. In the boxes of the matrix, we write the outcomes; we adopt the convention that the first symbol represents the outcome to A, the second the outcome to B. To fix ideas, we may suppose that the matrix in Fig. 3.1a shows the outcomes of a game of matching pennies, with position 1 as head and position 2 as tail. Then we draw up the rules of the game, which is the payoff matrix: if both choices are heads (a_1b_1) or both tails (a_2b_2) B pays a penny to A, so that A's outcome is $+1$ and B's is -1; if a head and a tail come up (a_1b_2 or a_2b_1), A pays a penny to B, so that A's outcome is -1 and B's is $+1$. In Fig. 3.1b, we show a simplified pattern of the matrix expressed as what is called a *directed graph*. The dots (*nodes*) at the corners of the square represent the boxes of the matrix, and the dynamics of the system is expressed by arrows between the nodes. The dynamics of the system depends, of course, on the assumptions that are made. Suppose we assume that, if one party knows what the other is going to do, that party will move to the higher payoff for itself. Thus, suppose that A knows that B is going to adopt position b_1. Then, A will adopt position a_1; if A were already at a_2, he would move to a_1. This is the meaning of the arrow between a_2b_1 and a_1b_1 in Fig. 3.1b; the direction of the arrow shows that, for A, a_1b_1 dominates a_2b_1. Likewise, for A, a_2b_2 dominates a_1b_2. Similarly, for B, a_1b_2 dominates a_1b_1, as B will prefer a payoff of 1 to one of -1, and a_2b_1 dominates a_2b_2. It will be observed that the horizontal arrows represent A's potential shifts of choice, or dominances, whereas the vertical arrows refer to B.

It will be observed that, in Fig. 3.1b, the arrows chase each other endlessly around the square; there is no position of equilibrium. If A chooses a_1 and sticks to it, B will move to b_2; whereupon it will pay A to move to a_2, and then it will pay B to move to b_1, and then it will pay A to move to a_1, whence we repeat the circle indefinitely. We shall return to this case later. Meanwhile, consider the slightly different pattern of Fig. 3.2a. Here we suppose different rules: if two heads or two tails turn up, nobody gets anything; if B plays head and A tail, B pays A a penny; if A plays head and B tail, A pays B a penny. In Fig. 3.2b, we draw the corresponding directed graph, and we see that there is now an equilibrium position at a_2b_2. If A starts at a_1, B will go to b_2, and then A will go to a_2; if B starts at b_1, A will go to a_2, and then B will go to b_2. Once the parties have arrived at a_2b_2, it pays neither party to change his position even if he knows that the other party will continue in his present position. This type of equilibrium position, for reasons suggested in Chapter 2, may be called the shortsighted equilibrium. It is the result of a dynamics that assumes that each party simply supposes that the other party's behaviour will continue indefinitely, and reacts accordingly, and does

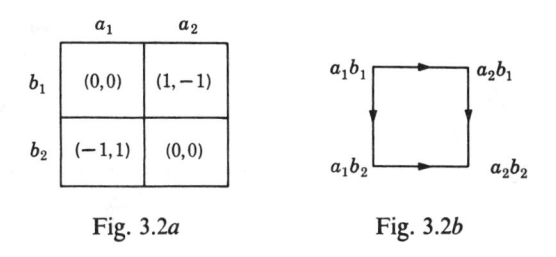

	a_1	a_2
b_1	(0,0)	(1,−1)
b_2	(−1,1)	(0,0)

Fig. 3.2a

Fig. 3.2b

not, therefore, consider the effect of the other party's reaction. The analogy with the Richardson process is no accident; these are indeed two different ways of analyzing much the same type of reaction process.

The payoff matrices of Figs. 3.1 and 3.2 have one thing in common; the sum of the payoffs in each box of the matrix is zero. They belong, therefore, to an important category of games known as *zero-sum* games, in which what any one party gains the other loses (or the others taken collectively lose if there is more than one party). Such a game neither requires any subsidy from nor pays any tax to the outside: its payoffs are internal to the game and involve a simple redistribution of some initial good among the players. Adding (or subtracting) a fixed amount to each payoff of a zero-sum game produces a *constant-sum* game, in which the sum of the payoffs in each box of the matrix is constant. The dynamics of a constant-sum game is identical with that of the zero-sum game from which it is derived. By contrast, the *variable-sum* game is one in which the sum of the payoffs in each box is not constant. This, as we shall see, has many properties different from the constant-sum game. The constant-sum game may be regarded as an interaction process of pure conflict, for any increase in the gain to one party must result in an equal decrease in the gain to the other. Variable-sum games may involve both conflict and cooperation. In a *positive-sum* game, there is at least one position in which both parties can be better off than if the game were not played. In a *negative-sum* game, there is no such position.

In constant-sum games, the payoff matrix for one party can be derived immediately from that of the other by subtracting each figure from the constant sum. Thus, in Figs. 3.1 and 3.2, B's payoff is always minus A's payoff. Frequently, only the payoffs of one party are shown in the boxes, as those of the other can immediately be derived. In a constant-sum game, it can be shown that the short-sighted-equilibrium point always occurs at a point in the matrix that has the properties of a *minimax*, or *saddle point*, that is, which is both a maximum of a row and a minimum of a column. This is illustrated in Fig. 3.3. Here we suppose a three-by-three matrix, with each party having three choices, 1, 2, and 3. (It should be noticed that a payoff matrix does not have to be symmetrical; it would be quite possible, for instance, for one party to have three choices and the other two, in which case we would have a three-by-two matrix.) In Fig. 3.3*a*, we show the directed graphs of the

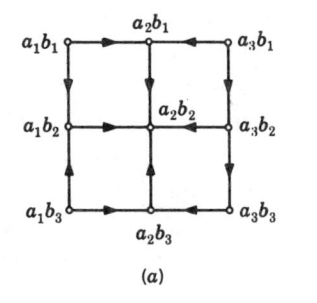

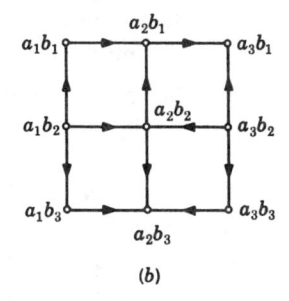

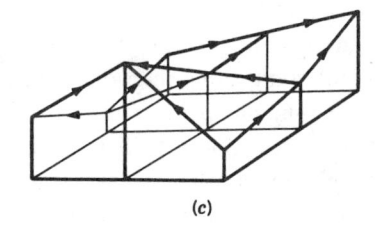

Fig. 3.3

shortsighted equilibrium, the equilibrium position being at a_2b_2, in the center of the figure. We place it in the center merely to illustrate the principle; it could just as well, of course, be at an edge or corner. Here, the vertical arrows indicate B's movements and the horizontal arrows A's movements. Thus, in the figure, we know that B's payoff at a_1b_2 is greater than B's payoff at a_1b_1. If this is a constant-sum game, however, this means that A's payoff at a_1b_1 is greater than A's payoff at a_1b_2, as A's payoff is the constant sum less B's payoff. Thus, suppose B's payoffs at a_1b_1 and a_1b_2 were 7 and 4 respectively and the constant sum were 10; A's payoffs would be $10 - 7 = 3$ and $10 - 4 = 6$. In Fig. 3.3b, then, we reverse the direction of the vertical arrows, leaving the horizontal arrows unchanged; this gives us the directed graph of A's payoff matrix, where, in each case, the arrow points from the smaller to the larger payoff. These arrows, it should be observed, have the opposite sense to the usual "greater than" or "less than" signs; it seems best, however, to preserve the arrowhead convention as indicating the potential dynamics of the system: we always go toward the larger payoff. An arrow, that is, always points uphill. We now see that, because the equilibrium point a_2b_2 in Fig. 3.3a has four arrows pointing in toward it, the same point in Fig. 3.3b has two horizontal arrows pointing in toward it, indicating that the point is a maximum along the horizontal line a_1b_2, a_2b_2, a_3b_2, but it has two vertical arrows pointing away from it, indicating that it is a minimum on the line a_2b_1, a_2b_2, a_2b_3. This, then, is a minimax. If we plot the payoffs vertically, as in Fig. 3.3c, we see that the point a_2b_2 is a saddle point; it is like the top of a mountain pass, which is the highest point going over the pass from a_1b_2 to a_3b_2 and the lowest point going along the ridge from a_2b_3 to a_2b_1.

If there is only a single minimax point in the payoff matrix, it can be shown that, if both parties choose their positions according to the principle of choosing the best of the worst, or the *maximin*, they will settle down right away at the minimax. This again is illustrated in Fig. 3.3. We suppose here that the payoff matrix is known to each party (not usually a very realistic assumption) but that neither knows which position the other will choose. We suppose, then, that A looks over the matrix. If he chooses a_1, the worst thing that can happen to him (looking down the column) is that B chooses b_2; if he chooses a_2, the worst thing that can happen to him is a_2b_2; if he chooses a_3, the worst is a_3b_3. The best of these worsts is a_2b_2, which is the minimax. A's worst from any choice can be worse than the payoffs along the mountain pass, but they cannot be better, or else the mountain-pass values become the worst. Hence, the value at the top of the mountain pass must be the maximin, or the best of the worst. Similarly, remembering that B's payoffs are minus A's payoffs, we show that B's maximin must be at the trough of the ridge, a_2b_1 to a_2b_3, which is also at the minimax a_2b_2.

The minimax equilibrium has been criticized on the grounds that the maximin is an unrealistic rule of choice, that, in particular, it is too conservative and pessimistic, and that people are more likely to choose the position that gives them the chance of the highest gain (the maximax) or, if the probabilities of the other parties' choices are known, will choose the position that gives them the highest expected value of gain, or something of this kind. These criticisms of the rule of behavior may be entirely valid, and yet they do not necessarily upset the concept of the minimax as the shortsighted equilibrium. The minimax is, in general, the only position in which knowledge of the intentions of the other party will not change the policy of either. Its claim to be an equilibrium position, therefore, rests on the assumption that, if one party adopts a position that is not at the minimax and sticks to it, the other party will find this out by observation and will move its position and a succession of such moves must eventually bring us to the minimax. In the case of the constant-sum game, the minimax, therefore, has strong claims to be a true equilibrium position, even though inertia or ignorance may act like friction to prevent the system from attaining it. As we shall see, this does not apply to the variable-sum game, where the payoff matrices of the two parties are not reciprocal to the other, and where, therefore, the very concept of a mutual minimax ceases to have meaning.

Let us now return to the circular equilibrium of Fig. 3.1 and ask whether there is any way out of this impasse. There is a fundamental theorem in the theory of games due to Von Neumann, that states that a minimax equilibrium can always be found in a finite, constant-sum, two-person game if a *mixed strategy* can be employed. By a mixed strategy, we mean making each choice at random with a given probability every time a choice is made. The sum of the probabilities of all the choices must, of course, add up to 1. Thus, in the game of Fig. 3.1, we may suppose that A has a bag with n tickets marked A_1 and $100 - n$ tickets marked A_2 and draws a ticket at random out of the bag and takes the position indicated on the ticket. A_1 is then played with a probability of $n/100$ and A_2 with a probability of $(100 - n)/100$. Suppose now, in this case, A adopted a mixed strategy, playing a_1 25 percent of the time and a_2 75 percent. By careful observation, B could deduce this strategy, and then it would pay

B to adopt a strategy of always playing b_1. As soon as A spots B's strategy, however, it will pay A to change his strategy to a pure strategy of always playing a_1, whereupon B will shift to b_2, and we are off round the circle again. If, however, A plays a mixed strategy of 50 percent A_1 and 50 percent A_2, B cannot beat this by playing any pure strategy, or even by playing any mixed strategy that differs from 50:50. When each party plays a 50:50 strategy, then, there is no incentive to change even if each party knows what the other plays. A good deal of the arithmetic of the theory of games involves the calculation of the appropriate mixed strategies for various matrices; the problem becomes very complicated as the matrix becomes larger and must be solve generally by the techniques of linear programing. These computations do not seem very relevant to the theory of conflict, however, and the reader can be referred to the standard works on the subject.[1]

An interesting question that has been somewhat neglected in the literature is that of the stability of the minimax equilibrium of a mixed strategy. In the above example, it would certainly seem that the equilibrium is unstable: if one of the parties diverges perceptibly from the 50:50 ratio, it will pay the other party to switch to a pure strategy, and we seem to be back once again in the circular movement. We should notice, incidentally, that a pure strategy is merely a special case of a mixed strategy where the probability of one position is 100 percent and of all others is zero.

We may ask with some justification why anyone would ever play a truly zero-sum game. In Fig. 3.1, as in Fig. 3.2, the long-run gains for each party are clearly zero, which will be true in any game of absolutely fair gambling. Unless, therefore, there are payoffs in terms of excitement or the pleasure of playing the game for its own sake, there would be no incentive to play the game. It is easy to devise a game, as in Fig. 3.4, where, at the equilibrium minimax (in this case, $a_2 b_2$), one party (A) has a positive gain but the other

---

[1] See especially R. Duncan Luce and Howard Raiffa, *Games and Decisions'* New York, Wiley, 1957.

party must have an equal loss and hence will refuse to play the game. If *A* tries to bribe the other party to play the game, he will have to pay him at least a penny, in which case *A*'s gain is reduced to zero and *B*'s is raised to zero. But, then again, why play the game? This illustrates a fundamental principle that, in the zero-sum game (and, in general, in the constant-sum game), there can be no bribery, for the bribe would always have to be so great as to make it not worthwhile for the briber. Bribery always suggests some kind of positive-sum game or subgame.

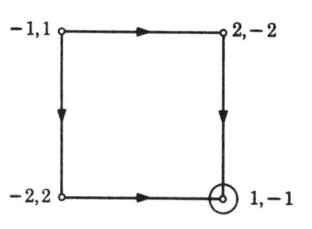

Fig. 3.4. Pure conflict.

The payoff at the equilibrium position is called the *value* of the game to the player. It represents, presumably, the greatest amount that he can be taxed (if positive) or be bribed (if negative) in order to persuade him not to play. The sum of the values of any zero-sum game to the two players together must be zero, which suggests that zero-sum games have a strong tendency not to exist. Constant-sum–positive-sum games could exist easily as far as the players are concerned except that the question arises, "Where does the positive-sum payoff come from?" as it must come from outside the game. It may, of course, come from nature, and most economic activity can be regarded in this light. There are limits imposed by some kind of conservation principle on the indefinite extension of a positive-sum game. We must note, furthermore, that, whereas a zero-sum game must be also constant-sum, a positive-sum game need not be constant-sum, and, in general, there is no reason to expect it to be so. Because most games in the real world are, in fact, both positive-sum and variable-sum, this means that the very elaborate theory of the constant-sum game has only limited applicability to most problems of conflict.

An interesting application of the variable-sum game can be made to the problem of *perverse dynamics* in social life, which we have noted in the previous chapter, that is, to situations in which the dynamics of interaction lead to positions that are worse for both parties than some alternative position. Consider, for instance, the payoff matrix in Fig. 3.5. This is a variable-sum game. Suppose it represents the decision of two competing nations whether to arm or disarm. The payoffs here are intended merely as ordinal numbers to illustrate dominance. If both nations disarm, they can devote these resources to useful objects, and both will be better off, expressed by payoffs of 1 to each. If both arm, both will be worse off, expressed by payoffs of -1 to each. If A arms and B does not, however, even though the total payoff at $a_2 b_1$ is less than at $a_1 b_1$, A is able to force a distribution of the reduced payoff, which is so favorable to him that he is better off than at $a_1 b_1$. Similarly, B is better off at $a_1 b_2$ than at $a_1 b_1$. The shortsighted dynamics of the system, then, move it inevitably to $a_2 b_2$, where the total payoff is the least of all. We may, however, suppose a long-sighted dynamics, represented by the dotted diagonal, in which each party moves to $a_1 b_1$ because each knows that, if he moves away from this unilaterally, he will soon end up at $a_2 b_2$. This could happen without any agreement or organization if both parties behave long-sightedly. If one party behaves shortsightedly, however, he can force shortsightedness on the other. Then the question arises whether there can be any organizational defenses against shortsightedness. These consist essentially in organizing to manipulate the payoff matrix. Thus, each party might bribe the other not to arm: in the matrix of Fig. 3.5, for instance, if, at the position $a_1 b_1$, B were to bribe A not to arm by an amount of $1+$, A would no longer have even a shortsighted incentive to arm; B, unfortunately, would have his shortsighted incentive to arm increased.

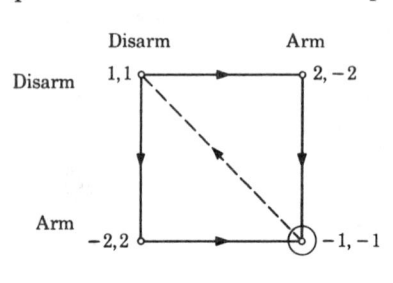

Fig. 3.5. Mixed conflict, symmetrical.

If, however, only A is shortsighted, this might lead to stability at a_1b_1. If neither party trusts the other, they might both contribute to a third party who would exact penalties on A at a_2b_1 and on B at a_1b_2. This is the police solution and is of very general applicability. Suppose, for instance, we replace "arm" by "theft" and "disarm" by "honesty"; the diagram then illustrates a dilemma of social life that, if both parties are honest, both are better off than if both are thieves, but that, if one is a thief, this forces the other to be a thief too unless the matrix can be changed by the introduction of police to penalize the rewards of one-sided theft.

A distinction can be made between those games of mixed conflict (variable-sum), in which the payoffs are such as to permit the establishment of defenses against shortsightedness, and those in which the differential payoffs are not sufficient to establish these defenses and in which, therefore, optimum solutions can only be defended by love or a sense of community between the parties. Thus, in Fig. 3.5, A can bribe B (or B, A) at position a_1b_1 not to arm by paying him $1+$, which still leaves A better off $(0-)$ than he would be at a_2b_2. If, however, the payoff at a_2b_2 were $(0, 0)$ instead of $(-1, -1)$, this would no longer be true: neither party now has enough differential between the optimum and the shortsighted equilibrium positions to make it worth their while bribing the other to stay at the optimum. Under these circumstances only mutual long-sightedness or outside police can prevent the equilibrium from moving to a_2b_2.

In Fig. 3.5, we assume the parties are symmetrical; where the parties are asymmetrical, with one large and strong and the other small and weak, it is not difficult to set up matrices such as Fig. 3.6, where there is a perpetual cycle with no equilibrium position. Here we start off at the optimum (a_1b_1), with

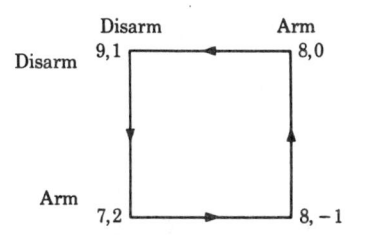

Fig. 3.6. Mixed conflict, asymmetrical.

A having 9 and B having 1. Unilateral arming, we suppose, enables B to gain 2 units from A because of his nuisance value; arming, however, costs B 1 unit. Similarly, unilateral arming enables A to squeeze 1 unit out of B, but at a cost of 2 units. Hence, if we start from mutual disarmament, it will pay (shortsightedly) B to arm and then A to arm; then, however, it pays B to be submissive and disarm, whereupon it pays A to disarm, and the cycle starts again. The similarity with the submission cycles in the Richardson process in Fig. 2.9 is striking, though not surprising, as we have here two different methods of analyzing much the same phenomenon.

In Fig. 3.7, we see a type of matrix that might be described as pure cooperation, where the optimum position for both parties is also the shortsighted equilibrium. Here it pays either party to move toward the optimum position for both at a_1b_1. This can only happen,

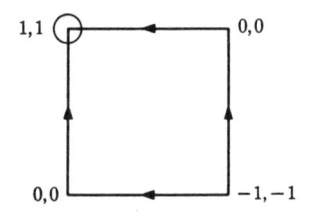

Fig. 3.7. Pure cooperation. 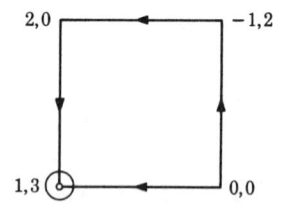 Fig. 3.8. Mixed cooperation.

of course, in a variable-sum game. In this case, the cooperation does not have to be organized, as it must be in the game of mixed conflict, for the self-interest of both parties produces the best position for either or for all. This is the type of unconscious and uncoordinated cooperation for the good of all that is postulated in Adam Smith's doctrine of the hidden hand.

We can distinguish between the pure cooperation of Fig. 3.7, in which each move benefits both parties, so that there is never a conflict of interest in a move, and the mixed cooperation of Fig. 3.8. Here, each move increases the total payoff to both parties together but does not necessarily benefit each party. Thus, from a_2b_2 (0, 0),

B will move to a_2b_1 (−1, 2), but A will be injured by the move; the total payoff is greater however at a_2b_1 (1) than at a_2b_2 (0). The rule here is that, if one party benefits, the injury to the other party, if any, must not exceed the benefit to the first. The cooperation here is mixed because there may be moves that benefit one party and injure the other. The system is cooperation, however, because the equilibrium position will always be the maximum total payoff. A system of mixed cooperation can always be reduced to one of pure cooperation with the same dynamics by a suitable system of side-payments, bribes, or, as the welfare economists say, compensating payments. Thus, in Fig. 3.8, B could pay A 1+ in position a_1b_1, and it would still pay B to move from a_2b_2 to a_2b_1, and similarly for the other moves.

The introduction of a third party into a game situation increases the complexity of the analysis enormously. It is a fairly general rule in science that the interaction of a few individuals presents extremely difficult theoretical problems; the three-body problem in physics and oligopoly in economics are good examples, and the theory of conflict is no exception. Between the two-person game and the n-person game (where n is large) lies a thorny wilderness of complexity. In the three-party situation where the over-all game is zero-sum, two parties, by forming a coalition, may create a positive-sum subgame for themselves at the expense of negative payments to the third party. The general solution of these problems is difficult. The following extension of the directed-graph technique shows how solutions might be obtained in any particular case and illustrates also the complexity of the general problem.

We suppose three individuals, A, B, and C, with two choices each, 1 and 2. a_1, then, is A's first choice, b_2 is B's second choice, and so on. There are eight combinations, shown in Fig. 3.9. The four corners of the outer rectangle correspond to the A-B combinations when C is at c_1; the four corners of the inner rectangle correspond to the same combinations when C is at c_2. The diagram may be visualized as a cube in perspective, looking head on, with the c_2 combinations behind the c_1. The horizontal connecting lines, then, indicate possible shifts in choice by A, the vertical lines by B (as in Fig. 3.1b), and the diagonal lines by C. Then, in the eight boxes, we write the payoffs—the first for A, the second for B, and the third for C. In Fig. 3.9, we suppose a zero-sum game in which the arrows then indicate the

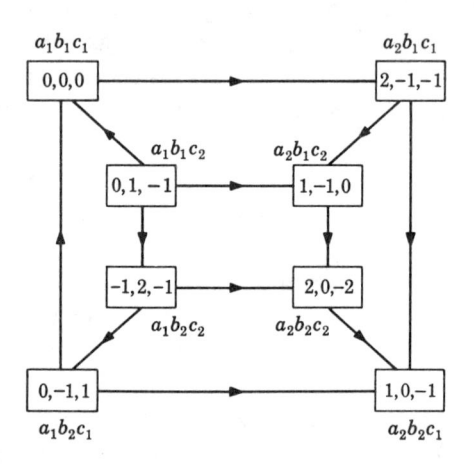

```
   a₁b₁c₁                          a₂b₁c₁
   0,0,0 ──────────────────────→  2,-1,-1
              a₁b₁c₂   a₂b₁c₂
              0,1,-1 → 1,-1,0

              -1,2,-1 → 2,0,-2
              a₁b₂c₂   a₂b₂c₂
   a₁b₂c₁                          a₂b₂c₁
   0,-1,1 ─────────────────────→  1,0,-1
```

Fig. 3.9

direction of potential shift of choice. It will be seen that there is an equilibrium position to which all the arrows converge in the bottom right-hand corner at $a_2b_2c_1$. An interesting problem arises here because of the possibility of two (or even three) shifts away from a particular position. Thus, consider the position $a_2b_1c_1$ at the top right-hand corner. It is a stable position for A. If A moves to A_2, however, and stays there, it will pay either B or C to move. If B moves, we go to $a_2b_2c_1$ at the bottom right-hand corner; If C moves, we go to $a_2b_1c_2$ at the top right-hand corner of the inner square. The actual dynamic path, therefore, depends on the order of the moves. If there is a rigid order of moves—if, for instance, B always moves before C—this will even affect the position of the equilibrium. This is not the case in Fig. 3.9, where all roads lead to $a_2b_2c_1$, but the possibility of different paths leading to different positions at equilibrium is greater, the greater the complexity of the system.

We can now trace the effects of various coalitions on the dynamics and equilibrium positions of this model. In Fig. 3.10a, we suppose that A and B unite against C. What this means is that, if a move of either A or B increases the total payoff to A and B taken together, the appropriate party will make the move. Thus, in the move from $a_1 b_1 c_2$ to $a_2 b_1 c_2$, if the parties are operating independently, it will pay A to move from the payoff 0 at $a_1 b_1 c_2$ to 1 at $a_2 b_1 c_2$ (see Fig. 3.9; the payoffs are omitted from Fig. 3.10 for the sake of simplicity). If, however, A and B are married, so that only the total gain to both matters to them, A will move from $a_2 b_1 c_2$, where the combined payoff is $1 - 1 (= 0)$, to $a_1 b_1 c_2$, where the combined payoff is $0 + 1 (=1)$. In this case, the combination reverses the movement. In two other cases, we shift from a movement to indifference (no movement), indicated by the double-arrow symbol in Fig. 3.10; in all other cases, there is no change. Change in direction of movement is indicated by ringing the symbol in Fig. 3.10. In

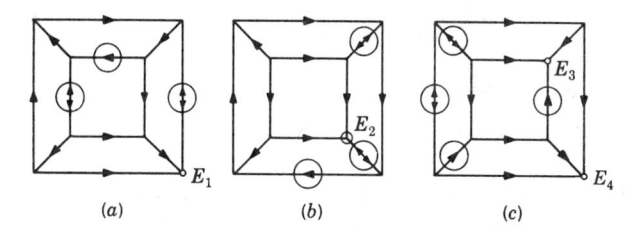

Fig. 3.10. (a) A and B against C; (b) A and C against B; (c) B and C against A.

Fig. 3.10a, there is no change in the position of equilibrium at E_1, as arrows still lead out from any other node. There is some danger of a circular solution between $a_1 b_1 c_1$, $a_2 b_1 c_1$, $a_2 b_1 c_2$, and $a_1 b_1 c_2$ if the convention is that A always moves before B. If B can move before A with some positive probability, then, at some time in the circle at

$a_2b_1c_2$, B will move instead of A, and the system goes to $a_2b_2c_2$ and then to equilibrium at $a_2b_2c_1$.

In Fig. 3.10b, we suppose a combination of A and C against B. Here, the position of equilibrium shifts in a very interesting way. On the outer square, there is a circular equilibrium: C never has any positive incentive to shift from choice 1 to choice 2, though, at two points, he is indifferent and could easily be bribed to shift. On the inner square, with C at c_2, there is an equilibrium at E_2 ($a_2b_2c_2$). In Fig. 3.10c, we suppose B and C combining against A. Here there are two points of equilibrium, depending on the path taken, one at E_3 ($a_2b_1c_2$) and the other at E_4 ($a_2b_2c_1$). If B goes first at $a_2b_2c_2$, we get to E_3; if C goes first, we get to E_4. If C goes first at $a_2b_1c_1$, we get to E_3; if B goes first, we get to E_4.

An analysis of this type can throw light on what combinations, if any, are likely to be formed. Thus it is clear that the A-B combination lacks incentive as it results in the same equilibrium position as the independent pattern. Presumably, A could afford to pay B something to join with him, but A has no incentive to do this as an individual. The only incentive for an A-B combination then would be love, that is, if B regarded A's gains as his own. In this case, the love does not even have to be mutual. The A-C combination, if it moves the equilibrium to E_2, is better for A than for C, as A moves from 1 to 2 and C from -1 to -2. A's payoff at E_2 is not big enough to compensate C, as A would have to pay 1 unit to C to compensate him for moving, and this would destroy A's incentive. Similarly, in Fig. 3.10c, there is no incentive to form the B-C combination.

This example serves mainly to illustrate the complexity of even the three-person game—and we have not even introduced mixed strategies into it. It gives a method of analysis that is applicable to any particular case but does not enable us to derive many general propositions.

The reader may wonder about the relevance of game theory, especially in its more recondite branches, to the flesh and blood conflicts that we find in the world of man. It is perhaps true at the moment that game theory operates at a level of abstraction that is a little too high to be immediately fruitful in practical conclusions. Its main weakness in application is that it abstracts from the problem of knowledge of alternatives and of the payoffs associated with them. In the general situation of decision making under uncertainty, we not only face uncertainty as to the strategies of the opponent, whether that opponent be another person or organization or merely nature, but we face great uncertainty as to the payoffs themselves. Any decision, of course, involves some image of alternative payoffs; how our image of the payoffs is affected by our previous experience is a crucial factor on which the theory of games throws but little light. The payoff matrix is a useful analytical device and, frequently, can be used to clarify a conflict situation; the notion of the minimax as an equilibrium of mutual choice is important, especially as this does not involve any assumptions about behavior beyond a certain shortsightedness in maximization. The real world, however, is much more complicated (or may be even in some respects simpler) than the Hobbesian universe of the game theorist. For a true understanding of conflict, we also have to examine love, affection, empathy, and community of feeling. These are concepts alien to the theory of games.

4

THE THEORY OF VIABILITY

Up to this point, we have taken the parties to conflict as given and have studied merely the abstract relationships between them. Now we must carry the analysis to an investigation of the parties themselves and to the factors that determine their existence and their behavior. The first problem to be considered is that of *viability*. By this, we mean the ability and the willingness of one party to destroy or eliminate another. A party that cannot be absorbed or destroyed as an independent source of decisions is said to be *unconditionally viable*. A party that can be absorbed or destroyed by another is *conditionally viable* if the party that has the power to destroy it refrains from exercising this power. The party that can absorb or destroy another is said to be the *dominant* party. Thus, a party that is conditionally viable survives only at the will of the dominant party. Perhaps two kinds of conditional viability should be distinguished. There are some situations in which it does not pay the dominant party to extinguish the other; this might be called *secure* conditional viability. There are other situations in which it would pay the dominant party to extinguish the other but in which the dominant party refrains through goodwill toward the dominated. This might be called *insecure* conditional viability.

Where we have a situation in which both parties are unconditionally viable or in which there is secure conditional viability, we have what Strausz-Hupé has called *protracted conflict*,[1] where the problem is how to control the conflict process rather than to resolve it; the resolution may come eventually through change in the character of the parties or through the growth of a sense of community between them, but it cannot come through the absorption or destruction of one party. Where we have insecure conditional viability, there is a strong tendency for the weaker party to be absorbed or destroyed by the stronger. This may be bad—making a desert and calling it peace—or it may be good—the integration of organizations that are too small to be useful or serviceable into larger and more inclusive organizations. The value judgments here are not easy; it is not always true, for instance, that absorption is good and extinction is bad, though we may reasonably have a certain prejudice in this direction. It should be observed also that, when a party is absorbed into another, it frequently retains some identity within the larger organization and that absorption may in fact mean the setting up of a larger organizational framework that actually increases in some sense the viability of the component parts. Thus, the several states within the United States are much more viable as states than they would be as independent countries. Whatever value judgments we apply to these processes, it is clear that they form an important element of the field of study of conflict.

Much light is thrown on the problem of viability by a model of spatial competition derived originally from the theory of competition of firms. Let us suppose two firms, A and B, located at A and B in Fig. 4.1a. We will suppose them to produce a single, homogeneous product. Dollars per unit of product are then measured vertically, and we suppose AH to be the price charged at the mill or point of origin, by A and BK the price charged by B. We suppose further that there is a uniform cost of transport over the field and that, at each point, a firm charges its mill price plus the cost of transport. The price charged by firm A at any point, then, is shown by line SHT. In the figure, B is a lower-price firm with a mill price BK and prices

[1] R. Strausz-Hupé, *Protracted Conflict*, New York, Harper, 1959.

at other points shown by the line *UKV*. The point *D* is where the customer prices of the two firms are equal, both being equal to *DC*. If the customers are activated by price only, so that they always

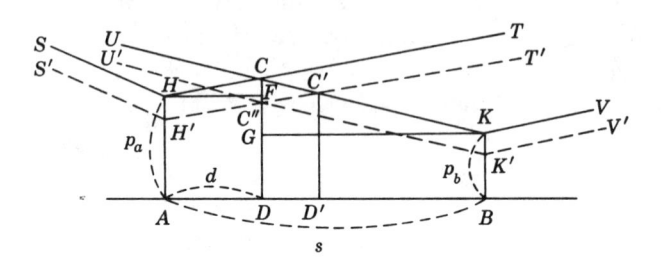

Fig. 4.1a

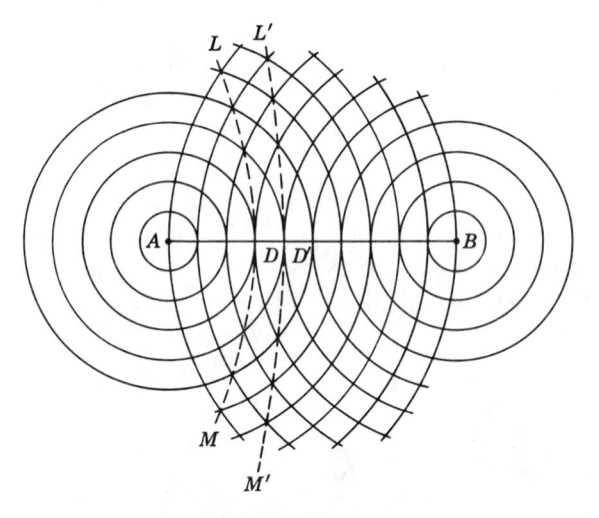

Fig. 4.1b

purchase from the firm offering the lowest price, all customers to the left of *D* will buy from firm *A*, and all to the right of *D* will buy from firm *B*.

The same pattern on a two-dimensional field is shown in Fig. 4.1b. *AB* is the same line as in the upper part. The circles round the points

THE THEORY OF VIABILITY

A and B are customer-price contours—contours of the surface generated by the lines SHT and UKV as they revolve. LDM is the line on which the customer prices of the two firms are equal. It may be called the *boundary of indifference*. Its general form is that of a hyperbola; in the special case where D is halfway between A and B, it is a straight line at right angles to AB. All customers on the left side of the boundary go to A, and all on the right side go to B.

Now consider what happens when A cuts its mill price, say, to AH'. A's customer prices are now given by $S'H'T'$. The new boundary of indifference is at D' ($L'D'M'$ in Fig. 4.1b). A has captured from B all the customers that lie in the space DD' (or between LDM and $L'D'M'$.) B can recapture them only by cutting its mill price to BK', thus pushing their boundary of indifference back to D, where DC'' is the new customer price. This is the machinery of the

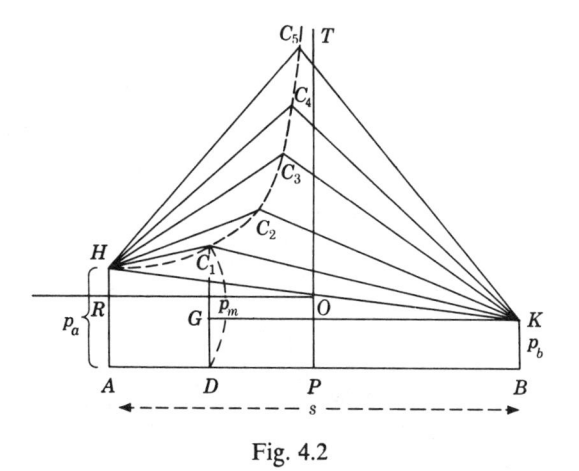

Fig. 4.2

price war. As we shall see, it has many counterparts—in advertising wars, in arms races, and so on—in fact, in all Richardson processes.

In Fig. 4.2, we show what happens with change in the unit cost of transport. A rise in the cost of transport steepens the lines HC and KC of Fig. 4.1a. As cost of transport rises, therefore, we move to positions C_1, C_2, C_3, etc. As it falls, we follow the same curve back until the cost of transport is equal to the slope of KH, at which point the boundary of indifference coincides with A. At this point, A has no customers left at all, as B can outsell him not only between A and B but also to the left of A. This is the *market-extinction point for A*; A may or may not be viable up to this point but is clearly not viable beyond it. There is a similar market extinction point for B.

Simple formulas relate these various quantities (capital letters refer to Fig. 4.1). Let p_a ($= AH$) and p_b ($= BK$) be the mill prices of A and B respectively. Let P_m ($= DC$) be the customer price at the boundary of indifference. Let d ($= AD$) be the distance of the boundary of indifference from A. s ($= AB$) is the distance between the parties. Let c be the cost of transport per unit of commodity per mile. Then,

$$c = \frac{FC}{HF} = \frac{p_m - p_a}{d} \tag{4.1a}$$

$$c = \frac{GC}{GK} = \frac{p_m - p_b}{s - d} \tag{4.1b}$$

whence $p_m = cd + p_a = cs - cd + p_b$

that is,
$$d = \frac{cs - p_a + p_b}{2c} \tag{4.2}$$

From Eq. (4.2) we notice that, when $d = 0$, that is, at A's market-extinction point,

$$p_a - p_b = cs \tag{4.3a}$$

and when $d = s$, that is, at B's market-extinction point,

$$p_b - p_a = cs \tag{4.3b}$$

It is not hard to show that the curve HC_5 in Fig. 4.2 is a rectangular hyperbola with asymptotes OT and OR.[1]

---

[1] The equation of HC_5 is obtained by eliminating c between Eqs. (4.1a) and (4.1b). This gives $p_m s - 2 p_m d + (p_a + p_b)d = p_a s$, which is a rectangular hyperbola in p_m and d. When p_m is infinite, $d = s/2$, which is the asymptote OT. When d is infinite, $p_m = (p_a + p_b)/2$, which is the asymptote OR.

In the present example, let us suppose first that the distances between the parties is fixed and is not under their control. The cost of transport we likewise suppose is not under the control of the parties. Then, the only strategies available to each consist in variations of the mill price. These can be expressed in a diagram in which p_a is measured, say, horizontally and p_b vertically, as in Fig. 3.11. Contours of equal net return can then be drawn for each party. These, it should be noticed, are the payoffs of an infinite-game matrix in which each party can choose one of an infinite number of possible values of its mill price. This is a variable-sum game, the sum, of course, being the total-profits contours of Fig. 2.11. Some problems can be illustrated, as we shall see, by reducing the infinite matrix to a simple finite set of choices.

Now let us assume that there is some bare-survival level of its net return below which the firm cannot survive and must die and above which the firm can survive indefinitely. If we define cost to include all those payments which are necessary for survival, as is customary in economic theory, then the bare-survival level of net return will be where the net return is zero. It does not matter, however, how we define net return as long as we can identify some value as bare survival. Thus, in Fig. 4.3, suppose $C_a M_a C_a'$ is that one of A's equal-net-return contours for which the net return is bare survival. A, we suppose, is the maximum net return for A at that level of p_b where B no longer influences A's net return. Then, in the area within $C_a M_a C_a'$, A can survive; we may call this A's *survival area*. Outside this area, A cannot survive and is not viable. A's survival area is shaded horizontally to reflect that fact that A can only change p_a and not p_b; that is, A's movements are

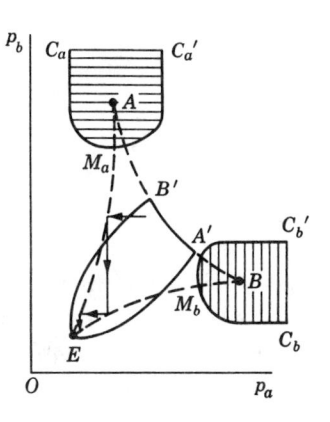

Fig. 4.3

always horizontal, unless by mutual agreement. Similarly, the vertically shaded area $C_b M_b C_b'$ is B's survival area, suggesting that B can only move vertically. In the unshaded area, neither A nor B can survive; this is the area of mutual nonsurvival.

The shortsighted dynamics of the system at Fig. 4.3, as we saw in Chap. 2, leads to mutual annihilation at E, like the two cats of Kilkenny.[2] From any point in the field, A will move horizontally to EA, then B will move vertically to BE, A will move horizontally again to EA, and so on, until the point E is reached. This is a typical Richardson process. We may note here that the same type of process can be represented in a simple finite-game matrix. Suppose that, instead of having an infinite number of prices open to them, the parties are allowed to choose only one of two prices, a high price and a low price. This is shown in Fig. 4.4. OH_b, OL_b are the high and low prices for B and OH_a and OL_a the high and low prices for A. The four cells of the matrix are at A $(H_b L_a)$, H $(H_b H_a)$, B $(L_b H_a)$, and L $(L_b L_a)$. Payoffs are suggested by the numbers, which show the net return to each party at each point. The dynamics of the system, as indicated by the arrows, leads to a shortsighted equilibrium at L (the minimax), which corresponds roughly to E in Fig. 4.3. The finite matrix is clearly not capable of very refined analysis, but it is sometimes useful in simplifying the problem and illustrating its basic dynamics.

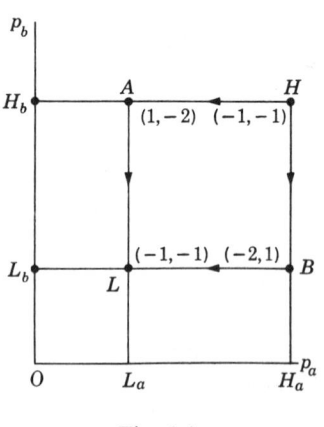

Fig. 4.4

[2] There once were two cats of Kilkenny;
 Each thought there was one cat too many,
  So they fought and they fit
  And they scratched and they bit
 'Til instead of two cats, there weren't any!

By long-sighted dynamics or by collaboration, the parties can do better than at E, as we saw in Chap. 2. By deliberate manipulation of his short-run adjustment curve and refraining from trying to maximize short-run advantage, A can push up the line EB (if B continues to maximize short-run advantage), and B can push up the line EA. By successive manipulations of the individual reaction curves, the parties may eventually land on the conflict curve AB, as we saw in Chap. 2. If, however, EA' is A's net-return contour through E, it will not pay A to go downward or to the right of it; similarly, it will not pay B to go upward or to the left of his net-return contour EB'. What might be called the *equilibrium field*, then, is the triangular area $EB'A'$. Mutual shortsightedness will land the parties at E; long-sightedness or collaboration, at its most successful, will land them on the line $A'B'$ and, if less successful, will land them somewhere within the equilibrium triangle.

In Fig. 4.3, it is clear that there is no position of mutual survival within the equilibrium field. As soon as one party disappears, however, the other party then becomes viable. If A disappears, B can move to the point B, where, for all practical purposes, p_a is infinite, and if B disappears, A can similarly move to point A. The situation, therefore, degenerates into a *game of survival*, as Shubik[3] has called it. This game of survival requires a new concept of *staying power*. We can suppose that, at every point of the p_a–p_b field, each party can survive for so many weeks. Within the survival area, of course, the staying power is infinite, as the party can survive indefinitely. We can then draw contours of equal staying power for each party; these will be roughly the same shape as the net-return contours, as we may reasonably suppose that, the less the net return, the less the staying power. The heavy line SS' is drawn through the points where the staying power of the two parties is equal. On this line, we may suppose that the Kilkenny-cats principle will operate and both parties will disappear. Above and to the left of SS', A will

[3] M. Shubik, *Strategy and Market Structure*, New York, Wiley, 1959. Chap. 10.

survive by outlasting B; below and to the right of SS', B will survive by outlasting A.

The dynamics of a game of survival or extermination is very different from that of the game of maximizing profit or minimizing loss. From a position such as R_1 in Fig. 4.5, B will lower his price and move down to something like R_2 on his side of the line of equal

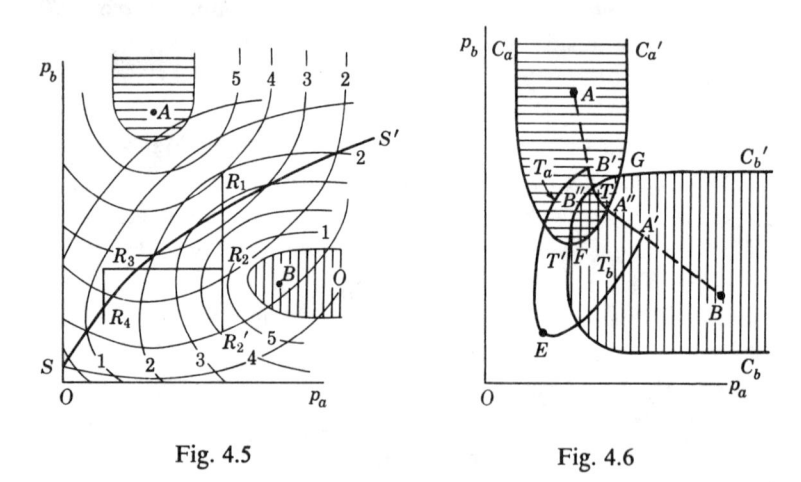

Fig. 4.5

Fig. 4.6

staying power; A will then move to something like R_3, B to R_4, and so on. This process may not even end at S, where one price is zero. It is quite possible for prices to be negative—for a firm to pay people to take their product away. Where the dynamic process ends depends on how long it takes. If, say, the parties cannot change their price oftener than once a week, then, from R_1, B may be able to drop to R_2', and A will give up immediately. It is clear that we have here a process where a great deal depends on the exact timing of changes and where, therefore, prediction is nearly impossible.

Let us now go back to the somewhat less strenuous games of maximizing net return and consider the situation of Fig. 4.6. Here, A's viability area $C_a FGC_a'$ and B's viability area $C_b FGC_b'$ intersect in the crosshatched area of mutual viability. As before, in the horizontally shaded area, only A is viable, in the vertically shaded area, only B is viable, and, in the unshaded area neither is viable. In Fig. 4.6, we see that there is a triangular area within the equilibrium field $FB''A''$ in which mutual survival is possible. Collaboration to maximize joint net return must land the parties in this area, as the point of maximum joint return must lie on the line $A''B''$. Mutual shortsightedness, of course, will lead to mutual extermination or to a game of ruin at E; independent long-sightedness may take the system within $FA''B''$ or it may not. This is a case, therefore, of possible but insecure mutual conditional viability. From any point within the area of mutual survival, either party can move to a position where the first party can survive and the second cannot. Thus, from T, party A can reduce his price to T_a, from which point B cannot move to any place where he is viable, though he can move to, say, T', where A is also no longer viable, and a game of ruin may ensue. Similarly, from T, B might move to T_b, where A is not viable at any p_a, and A can retaliate only by moving, say, to T' and again starting a game of ruin.

An interesting boundary case is shown in Fig. 4.7, where the two bare-survival contours intersect at E, where curve $C_a E C_a'$ is horizontal and $C_b E C_b'$ is vertical. E is the point of short-sighted equilibrium, and the equilibrium field $EA'B'$ is now wholly within the area of mutual survival. As long as the game is one of maximizing immediate profit, then, there is mutual viability. This is not strictly unconditional, because it is possible even for a situation like this to turn into a game of ruin, for either party can, by

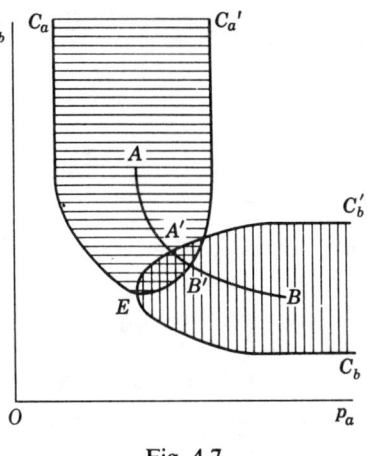

Fig. 4.7

reducing their price below that at E, force a position of mutual non-survival in which one party may expire first and the other then move to its maximum profit position at A (for A) or B (for B). The probability of a game of ruin here depends very much on the difference between the level of net return within the area of mutual survival and level A or B; the gains for the survivor of a game of ruin will have to be substantially above what he can get in the area of mutual survival if he is to risk starting the game of ruin. We might call this situation *conditionally secure* conditional viability, the condition of the security being the absence of incentive to start a game of ruin.

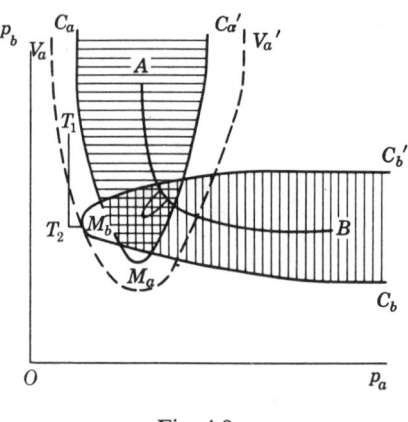

Fig. 4.8

As the areas of overlap increase and the two areas of viability expand, the viability of the parties becomes more and more secure until finally we reach a condition such as Fig. 4.8, in which one of the parties reaches unconditional viability. Let us suppose that there is some level of net return below which A will never go even in the short run. This is likely to be less than the long-run bare-survival level; that is, any firm can endure losses in the short run, but there will be some limit even to this. In Fig. 4.8, the net-return contour $V_a M_b V_a'$ corresponds to A's absolute minimum of net return. If now B's bare-survival net-return contour touches (still more if it cuts) A's absolute-minimum contour, say, at M_b, B is unconditionally viable, for A cannot move to any position which is tolerable to A and from which B cannot move to a B survival position. Thus, if we start from T_1, B can move to T_2, which forces A to move to M_b.

THE THEORY OF VIABILITY

If now A's bare-survival contour touches B's minimum-of-toleration contour at M_a, both parties are unconditionally viable, and a game of ruin cannot ever begin. The equilibrium field of the game of profit maximization is safely within the area of mutual survival. If each party identifies his bare-survival net return with his minimum of toleration, as would be the case under some conditions, even the condition of Fig. 4.7 is one of mutual unconditional viability.

We must now introduce into the analysis an element that we have hitherto neglected—the possibility of market extinction. Consider the 45° lines $U_b V_b$ and $U_a V_a$ in Fig. 4.9a. These are the lines corresponding to $p_b - p_a = cs$ and $p_a - p_b = cs$, where $cs = OU_b = OU_a$. Referring now to Eqs. (4.3a) and (4.3b) on page 62, we see that these are the *market-extinction lines*. At any point in the field below and to the right of $U_a V_a$, A's market-extinction line, A is no longer viable because p_a is so much larger than p_b that B can outsell A at and beyond A's own location. Similarly, $U_b V_b$ is B's market-extinction line and B is not viable anywhere above and to the left of this line. These market-extinction lines introduce an interesting discontinuity into the survival fields. Thus, if $C_a D_a D^a{}' C_a'$ is A's contour of bare-survival net return, it is clear that the net return

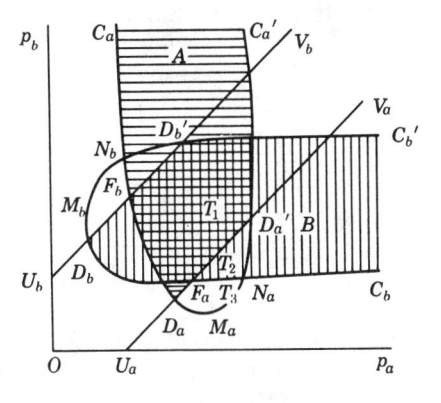

Fig. 4.9a

drops suddenly to zero, or to a negative number if there are fixed costs, as soon as we pass below the market-extinction line $D_a D_a'$, even though there may have been a positive net return immediately before reaching the market-extinction point. The lune-shaped segment $D_a M_a D_a'$ then, clearly must be excluded from A's survival field. The significance of this discontinuity can be seen clearly if we go back to Fig. 4.1a and visualize what happens as B lowers his price. The boundary of indifference D moves toward A, and A's net return will shrink in consequence. If, however, the return from the customers to the left of A is sufficient, A may still be viable and have a positive net return right up to the point where D reaches A. At this point, however, or just immediately beyond it, B captures not only all A's market between A and B but all A's market to the left of A; that is, A's market is completely extinguished, and A's net return falls to zero or below. The process corresponds to moving vertically downward, say, along the line $T_1 T_2 T_3$ in Fig. 4.9a. Up to T_2, A may continue to enjoy a positive net return; as soon as we pass T_2 on our way to T_3, however, A's net return disappears completely and suddenly as B captures the whole market. Similarly, we can show that B's survival area must exclude the lune $D_b M_b D_b'$. The effect of the introduction of the market-extinction principle is to take away from the area of mutual survival the triangular areas $F_b N_b D_b'$ and $F_a N_a D_a'$. It also has the effect of changing the area $D_b F_b N_b M_b$ from one of survival to B and nonsurvival to A to an area of mutual nonsurvival; similarly, the area $D_a F_a N_a M_a$ is changed from A survival only to no survival. If the market-extinction lines lie outside N_b and N_a, it is clear that they have no effect of viability. Where cs, that is, the cost of transport or the distance between the parties, is large, as we might expect, the parties never reach the point of market extinction, and this phenomenon is irrelevant. As c and s get smaller, however, the market-extinction phenomenon becomes of greater and greater importance as the lines $U_b V_b$ and $U_a V_a$ approach each other. Thus, in Fig. 4.9b, we

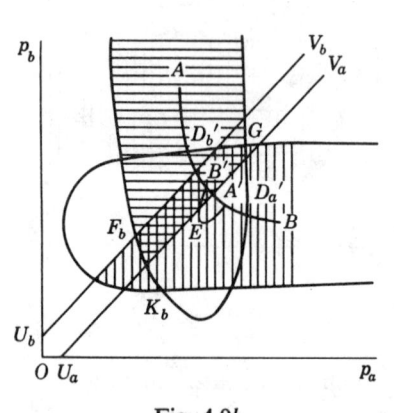

Fig. 4.9b

reproduce the condition of Fig. 4.9b except that we suppose the parties to be much nearer to each other, so that $cs\,(=OU_b = OU_a)$ is smaller. We see how drastically the area of mutual survival is reduced, so that if $cs = O$ there is no area of mutual survival at all. We see also, in Fig. 4.9b, that, assuming that the area of long-run survival is also the area of short-run toleration, A is no longer unconditionally viable in spite of the favorable profit situation because the market-viability line $U_a V_a$ has passed above the point K_b, where the two bare-minimum net-return curves intersect. In Fig. 4.9b, B can select prices at which he can survive and A cannot; consequently, the temptation to start a game of ruin is strong.

The analysis of a change in the cost of transport is more complicated, as this will change not only the market-extinction lines but also the profit contours themselves. A fall in the cost of transport, for instance, will, presumably, make each firm more profitable at each point in the p_a–p_b field unless there are very peculiar conditions of very sharply increasing internal production costs with output. A fall in the cost of transport, then, has a peculiar effect on the area of mutual survival: it not only narrows it but lengthens it as the survival areas of each party get broader. The narrowing effect, however, is likely to outweigh the broadening effect, as the narrower the area of mutual survival, the harder it is either to find a profit-maximizing equilibrium within it, and the more likely are we to run into a game of ruin. Thus we might easily find in Fig. 4.9b, for instance, that the area of profit-maximizing equilibrium $EB'A'$ lay wholly or in part outside the area of mutual survival and that a game of ruin could easily ensue. We can say with a good deal of confidence that there is some critical value of c, or of s, or of cs, below which mutual survival becomes increasingly unlikely and a game of ruin more and more likely.

Up to now, we have assumed that neither c nor s were in the control of the parties and have merely investigated what would happen if c or s changed. Now let us consider what will happen if the power to change s, let us say, is in the hands of one or the other of the parties. Suppose, for instance, that one party is already established in its location and that a second party is considering where to locate itself. This is a famous problem in economics associated especially with the name of Hotelling.[4]

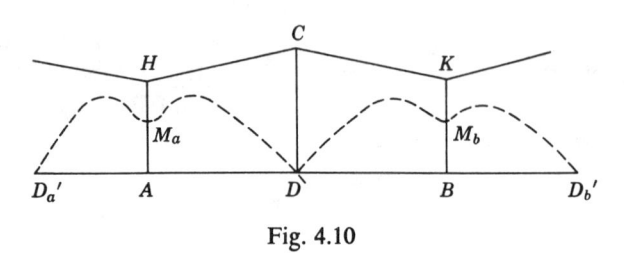

Fig. 4.10

Let us suppose first that, in Fig. 4.10, as in Fig. 4.1, we have a uniform line of customers of indefinite length with one firm already established at point A, with price AH. Let us suppose that the amount purchased by each consumer falls with a rise in the price, so that there is a price DC at which the amount bought by the consumers at this location is so small that any further geographic extension of the market brings in only as much revenue as it costs and beyond this point brings in less revenue than it costs. We can suppose at each point in the market area that there is a certain marginal net return, that is, the addition to net return that results from a 1-mile expansion of the market field. The marginal-net-return curve may have a shape like the dotted line $D'M_aD$ in Fig. 4.10. The total net return from any given market field is the sum of all the marginal net returns, that is, the area under the marginal-net-return curve in the market field. The maximum net return is given in the case of the single monopolist firm when the market field includes all those places where the marginal net return is positive, in this case, between D'_a and D,

[4] See Harold Hotelling, "Stability in Competition," *Economic Journal*, XXXIX (1929), 41–57, and Arthur Smithies, "Optimum Location in Spatial Competition," *Journal of Political Economy*, XLIX (1941), 423–439. Both these articles are reprinted in George J. Stigler and Kenneth E. Boulding, eds., *Readings in Price Theory*, Homewood, Ill., Irwin, 1952. The constructions of this chapter owe a great deal to these writers.

and the amount of this net return is given by the area between the dotted line and $D'_a A D$. This maximum net return is also a function of the price; a rise in the mill price may raise one marginal net return and lower another, depending on the slopes of the demand curve and the cost curve. There will be some price at which the maximum maximorum is attained, that is, at which the maximum net return in the market field is greater than at any other price. This will be the best mill price from the point of view of the firm. We suppose, then, that $D_a D'$ shows the effective range of A's market when A's net return is maximum. A has, then, no incentive to lower his mill price or to try to sell anything beyond his market range. We may note that A might have potential customers beyond the effective market range who would be willing to buy at his mill price plus cost of transport but that it simply does not pay him to sell to them because the additional gross return is not worth the additional cost.

Now suppose that another firm, B, enters the picture and has to decide where to locate. If he locates at, or to the right of, B, he does not interfere in any way with A's market, for D is the limit of B's effective range as well as of A's. If B moves to the right of this, as in Fig. 4.11, we see that not only is A's total net return reduced to the area under $D'_a M_a E D$ but B's is likewise reduced to $D'_b M_b E D$.

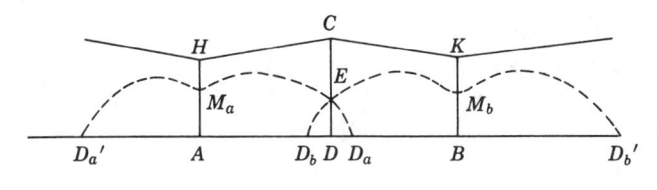

Fig. 4.11

A loses net return equal to the area $E D D_a$, but B also loses net return equal to $E D D_b$. It is clear that there is here no incentive for B to encroach on A's market. If we have unlimited space, firms will expand indefinitely into it without limiting each other, and there will be no conflict. A slight theoretical complication should be noted. The effect of encroachment is complicated by the fact that, once a firm's market has been encroached on, it may no longer pay it best to operate at the old mill price, and there will be mutual and possible competitive price adjustments; this does not affect the proposition, however, that, if there is unlimited space, there is no incentive to encroachment.

The unlimited character of the space implies that there are no nonmarket disadvantages to locating farther out rather than nearer in. In fact, of course, we may find that a firm's costs are higher as it locates farther away from some center; under these circumstances, the unlimited character of the economic space is destroyed, and there may be a case for encroachment.

The situation is entirely changed if we suppose that the market space is limited. Suppose, for instance, that, in Fig. 4.12, we have an

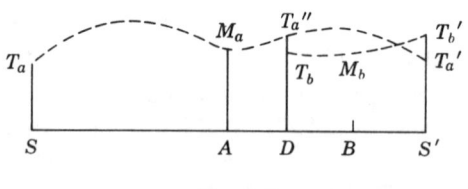

Fig. 4.12

island represented by the line SS', where S and S' are the coasts. As before, we assume a uniform distribution of customers along the line SS^1. A single firm located at A has a marginal-net-return line $T_a M_a T_a'$, where the marginal net return is still positive at the coasts, so that the effective market area of the firm covers the whole island. Again we have the problem of the optimum mill price, but we assume this has been solved. Again let us suppose a new firm B coming in. In this case, he must encroach on A's market, as there is no place where he can go without encroaching on A. Suppose he settles at B. Then, D will be the boundary of market indifference between A and B; if B's mill price is the same as A's, D will be halfway between

A and B. If $T_b M_b T_b'$ is B's marginal-net-return curve and DT_a'' is A's marginal net return at D, A's total net return is reduced to the area $ST_a T_a'' D$, and B's total net return is the area $DT_b T_b' S'$. Under these circumstances, it clearly pays B to move as close to A as he can, for as he moves closer and closer to A, the point D also moves closer and closer to A, and B's area of total net return increases. We may notice a curious indeterminacy here: if B starts out by sitting at B and A is capable of moving, it will pay A to move toward B; if there are lags in movement, therefore, or mistakes in policy, we may end up with the parties not located at the center of the island and the net return unequally distributed between them. If, however, B is wise, he will jump right next door to A, and A has then no power to get closer to him.

This is the classical Hotelling case, from which Hotelling explained the observed facts that five-and-ten's cluster on Main Street, churches on Church Row, and steel mills in Pittsburgh and even that, in a wider field, Methodists get to be indistinguishable from Baptists and all ciders are too much alike. We should notice, however, an important principle that works against the disappearance of distance between competitors. The closer B gets to A in Fig. 4.12, the closer together draw the market-extinction lines of the p_a–p_b field, as in Fig. 4.9, and the greater the probability, therefore, that the situation will turn into a game of survival or ruin in which the newcomer may easily be at a disadvantage. As B, in contemplating his optimum position, therefore, moves closer and closer to A, he is acted upon by two opposite forces: the expectation of increased net return *if* a game of ruin is avoided but the fear of an increasing chance of A forcing a game of ruin upon him from which he might not emerge victorious. If B locates right at A, then the area of mutual survival in Fig. 4.9 shrinks to a hairbreadth; the slightest divergence of one price from the other will result in the market extinction of the weaker party. We can postulate, therefore, an equilibrium distance AB, at which B reckons that the gain in net return in a game of maximization obtained by moving closer to A is not worth the danger of extinction in a game of ruin. An interesting corollary of this proposition is that the well-established old firm is always at a certain advantage relative to a newcomer, for if A is originally at the center of the island, B must be off-center, and B's net return, unless B has a much better organization than A, is bound to be less than A's.

This analysis throws some light on the difficult question of how many parties will establish themselves in a given space. It is clear, for instance, that, if we have a line of length h and if the distance between, say, D_a' and D in Fig. 4.10 is k, then we can have h/k parties without any encroachment of one on another. There may be more parties than this, in which case each party is encroached on by two others, if the line h is circular; if all parties are alike and if a length m gives a bare-minimum net return, the number of parties can be h/m.[5]

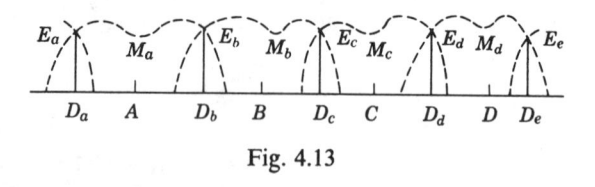

Fig. 4.13

Thus, in Fig. 4.13, we suppose that firms A, B, C, and D are squeezed into the field, where there is encroachment but not enough to carry any firm below the bare-survival net return. Thus, for firm A, the area $D_a E_a M_a E_b D_b$ is the bare-survival net return, and similarly for the others. If any more firms squeeze into the field, all firms, if they are all alike, will be carried below the level of bare survival, and a game of ruin must ensue until enough firms withdraw to bring the number of firms back to the bare-survival number. Similarly, if there are fewer than the bare-survival number, the firms will make more than bare-survival profits, and these may attract other firms in. This

---

[5] The problem is more complex in two dimensions, where the market areas dominated by each party are polygons; it is still more complicated on the surface of a sphere, where the polygons, except in the very special cases of the inscribed five regular solids, have to be irregular.

is closely analogous to the economist's concept of an industry in perfect competition with free entry.

A firm that is hemmed in by others, like B in Fig. 4.13, is much less tempted to move toward one or the other than a firm which is limited on one side by the edge of the field, like B in Fig. 4.12. If, in Fig. 4.13, B were to move toward A, it is true that it would gain something from the customers captured from A but it would also lose something to C, as the boundary of indifference between C and B moves toward B. If $D_b E_b$ is equal to $D_c E_c$, B clearly gains nothing from moving slightly toward A, for what it gains at D_b is counterbalanced by what it loses at D_c. The symmetry of the problem likewise suggests that, if all the firms are alike and the field is circular, so that there are no end firms, the market area taken by all firms will be equal.

In a two-dimensional field, the problem of "betweeness" becomes more complicated, though much the same fundamental principles apply. Thus, if we have one party, A, already established in a significantly limited field, say, a circular island, another party, B, will settle as close to the first as it can without making the danger of the game of ruin too great. A third party, C, coming in can divide the field three ways by the lines bisecting AB, BC, and AC, depending on the shape of the island. As more parties come in, the island gets divided up like a pie until finally this configuration becomes unstable; firms have to get farther and farther from the center of the island in order to get a sufficient distance away from each other until eventually there is room for someone in the middle.

We have seen that, the less the cost of transport, the greater the chance of a game of ruin for any two firms a given distance apart and the farther apart, therefore, two firms must be if games of ruin are to be avoided. A diminution in the cost of transport, therefore, inevitably diminishes the number of parties in a given field and increases their average size. If the cost of transport were zero, then a game of ruin would be probable at any distance, and the system would not find a secure equilibrium short of the absorption of the whole field by one party (monopoly). There is presumably some cost of transport somewhat above zero at which monopoly is still the only secure solution.

In this chapter, I have used the competition of firms as the most vivid example of the problem of viability, mainly because the issues stand out more sharply in this context and economists have given a good deal of thought to the problem. A little reflection, however, shows the great generality of the principles that we have developed here, and we shall use this type of analysis later, especially in the theory of international relations. The theory of the present chapter applies wherever we have a situation of two or more parties separated by some kind of space, whether this is physical, social, or organizational, and where the parties are competing for occupancy of the space in the sense that, if one party occupies it, the other cannot. Thus, nations compete for territory and for spheres of influence: this is the basic concept of international relations. Even with an organization as small as the family, there may be relations of dominance and submission as one party seeks to reach out and occupy the field of behavior of the other, or there may be relations of mutual independence and viability; furthermore, between two individuals there can be a game of ruin in which one seeks to destroy the independence or even the life of the other. In industrial relations, there is a constant source of conflict in the encroachment of one side (usually labor) on fields of decision making that have previously been the prerogative of the other (management). A frequent source of racial or group conflict is the encroachment of one group on jobs, housing, or privileges that were previously reserved for another. In all these cases, we have some concept of a space or field within which the conflict takes place, we have a concept of the location of the parties within this space, some place within the conflict space where the party is at home, and we also have a concept of a cost of transport of competitive power through the conflict space. The general principle applies that each party can be supposed to be at his maximum power at home (this may be an area rather than a point) but that his competitive power, in the sense of his ability to dominate another, declines the farther from home he operates. This is the great principle of *the further the weaker*. The amount by which the competitive power of a party diminishes per mile movement away from home is the *loss-of-power gradient*. If this is high, mutual survival is easy, games of ruin are unlikely, and a large number of parties can exist in a given field. As the loss-of-power gradient falls, conflict is likely to become more acute, games of ruin ensue, and the number of parties decline until there are few enough parties that they can be far enough away from each other to avoid games of ruin; beyond a certain point in the decline of the loss-of-power gradient, only a single party is viable in the field. As we shall see, this principle is of enormous importance in international relations.

The viability model stands out with peculiar sharpness in the case of the conflict of firms because here there is a clear concept of the payoff in terms of profit or net return. In the conflict of individuals, groups, nations, and so on, the payoffs are harder to identify and usually cannot be expressed in such simple quantities as dollars and cents. Nevertheless, in all conflict patterns, payoffs of some kind exist, whether these are psychological satisfaction, national self-esteem, or simply a generalized field concept called utility. The payoff may have more than one dimension, as may happen even in the case of the firm where decisions are made on the basis of prestige, reputation, and so on, and monetary reward may be sacrificed to these goods. In this case, the problem becomes more complicated, and we may have to rely on some larger utility concept that orders the field of payoffs. In these circumstances, the survival boundary may not coincide with a payoff contour; there may be terms on which we do not want to survive. This does not destroy the concept of a survival boundary, but it does mean that we must exercise some care in carrying over the analysis from the firm to more complex cases.

5

THE INDIVIDUAL AS A PARTY

TO CONFLICT

Up to this point, we have treated the party to conflict as an abstract entity, though, for purposes of exposition in the previous chapter, we treated him (or it) as a firm. Parties to conflict, however, may be individual persons or they may be organizations or groups. Organizations and groups are made up of persons, and the character and behavior patterns of their constituent persons will certainly have something to do with their behavior as collectivities. The problem of organizational and group behavior we shall defer to later chapters and deal here with the individual person in his role as a party to conflict. This does not necessarily involve us in a complete theory of individual behavior. Even though a certain view of human behavior as a whole is inevitable in discussing any particular aspect of it, it may be possible to abstract from the totality of individual behavior those aspects which are most relevant to behavior in conflict.

The economist looks at the problem of individual behavior in a rather different way from the psychologist, and it is instructive to explore these differences, even though they may amount to no more than a somewhat different way of looking at essentially the same phenomenon. The economist thinks of the individual as seeking that position in his field of possible choice which maximizes his utility or which stands highest on his preference scale. Thus, the economist perceives the individual as looking out over a field of potential futures, ordering these according to some scheme of valuation, which means simply labeling each element in the field "first," "second," "third," etc., and then choosing the one labeled "first" if that one is unique and proceeding into that particular future. The psychologist, by constrast, tends to think of the individual as moved by a number of specific drives and as directing his behavior toward certain specific goals. The two approaches can, of course, be reconciled formally by simply supposing that the goal of the psychologist is equivalent to the point of maximum utility of the economist. Movement toward the goal, then, is interpreted as a movement toward positions of higher utility or preferability in the value field. Thus, in Fig. 1.1, we might suppose that B is the ultimate goal of the individual and that he moves constantly as far as possible toward higher and higher indifference curves or utility contours.

The major contribution of the psychologist to the economist's view of behavior is perhaps to point out that there may be negative goals that repel the individual as well as positive goals that attract him. This is the basis of an important theory of conflict within the personality developed by Lewin and Miller. Lewin thought of the goal as exercising an attractive force on the individual if positive and a repulsive force if negative.[1] These forces pull him toward attractive places in the field and repel him from the unattractive ones. When an individual is in an equilibrium of forces in a part of the field that is not in some sense optimum for him, he is said to be in conflict. Thus, suppose, in Fig. 5.1, an individual is situated halfway between two equally attractive goals. This is the famous problem of Buridan's

---

[1] See K. Lewin, *Resolving Social Conflicts: Selected Papers on Group Dynamics*, New York, Harper, 1948. It is paradoxical that Lewin should have called his theoretical scheme *field theory*, for the main object of field theory in the natural sciences is to get away from the concept of force and replace it with the concept of equations of motion in a field. See also N. E. Miller, "*Experimental Studies of Conflict*," in J. McV. Hunt, ed., *Personality and the Behavior Disorders*, New York, Ronald, 1944.. For a summary and bibliography of the topic see J. S. Brown, "*Principles of Intrapersonal Conflict*," *Journal of Conflict Resolution*, (June, 1957), 135.

ass between the two equally attractive bales of hay. H_1 and H_2 are the bales of hay, and A is the ass halfway between them, with the arrows representing the direction and, by their length, the strength of the attractive forces. This equilibrium of conflict at A, it should be noticed, is different from the economist's equilibrium, which would be either an equilibrium at the goal, say, at either H_1 or H_2, at which the force disappears altogether because the goal has been reached,

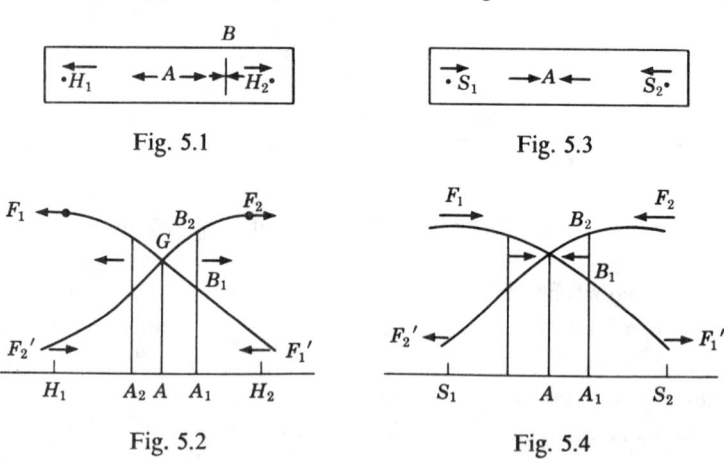

Fig. 5.1

Fig. 5.3

Fig. 5.2

Fig. 5.4

or would be at equilibrium at a boundary imposed by a kind of Newton's third law, action (the force impelling towards the goal) being opposed by an equal force of reaction at the boundary. Thus, if there were a boundary fence at B, the ass might smell the hay on the other side of it and move toward it but would be stopped by the equal and opposite reaction of the fence.

The scholastic question as to whether the ass will starve to death is easily answered, for though there is an equilibrium at A, it is clearly unstable. If chance fluctuations impel the ass slightly toward one bale, this bale will smell a little sweeter than the other, assuming that the attractive force increases as we get closer to the goal, at least right up to the goal itself. This is formalized in Fig. 5.2, where we measure the attractive forces in a vertical direction: $F_1 F_1'$ shows the attractive force toward H_1 at each point of the field H_1H_2, and F_2F_2' shows it for H_2. Then, even though it is true that, at A, the attractive forces AG are equal, a slight movement, say, to the right to A_1, will make A_1B_2 larger than A_1B_1, and the ass will move to H_2; similarly, a slight movement to the right moves the ass to H_1. The ass, therefore, will go to one bale, and, having eaten that, will presumably go to the other bale for his dessert.

Now, however, let us place the unfortunate ass between two skunks. This is what Neil Miller calls an avoidance-avoidance conflict, by contrast with the approach-approach conflict of Fig. 5.1. This is shown in Figs. 5.3 and 5.4. Here, the goals S_1 and S_2 are negative goals from which the subject is repelled by a force that declines as he moves away from the repellent object. The repulsive forces are shown by the lines F_1F_1', F_2F_2' in Fig. 5.4. There is again an equilibrium at A. A divergence from equilibrium, however, say, to A_1, means that the repulsive force from S_2, A_1B_2, is greater than the repulsive force from S_1, A_1B_1, and the subject, therefore, is driven back to A. As our unfortunate ass moves toward either of the skunks, the smell becomes stronger, and he is driven back to the middle position of equilibrium. He is in a stable psychological conflict, or *quandary*, from which he can escape only either by jumping over one of the skunks or by going off at right angles in another dimension. If he is completely boxed in, his behavior will become disjointed and random, and he will soon have a nervous breakdown. The unity that constitutes and organizes him as a behavior unit will eventually cease to exist.

A third situation is the approach-avoidance conflict, shown in Fig. 5.5. Here we suppose a positive and a negative goal in the line of movement of the subject. The skunk is sitting on top of the bale of hay or perhaps standing in front of it. The ass is repelled by the skunk but attracted by the hay at the same time. He may reach an equilibrium quandary, as in Fig. 5.6, where, at A, the two forces are equal. We see that, in the figure, this is a stable equilibrium. HH' shows the strength of the attractive force and SS' of the repellent force. At A_1, therefore, the repellent force is stronger than the attractive, and the subject is driven back to A. Similarly, at A_2, the attractive force is stronger, and the subject is again driven back to A. If the line HH' is above the line SS', the attractive force will be

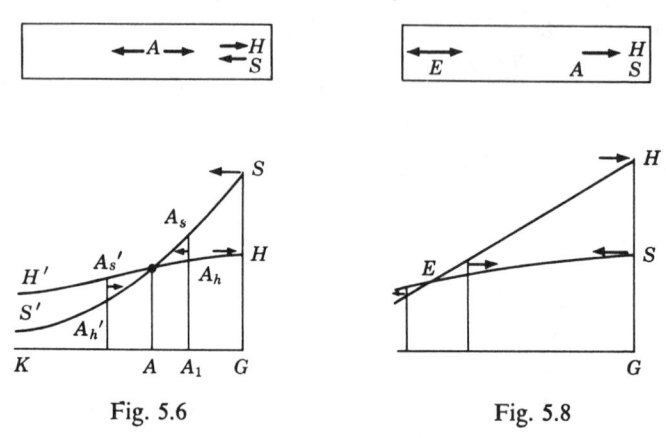

Fig. 5.6

Fig. 5.8

stronger, and the subject will move toward the joint goal at G. If SS' is above HH', the subject will move away from G. The equilibrium at A in Fig. 5.6 is clearly stable; the ass moves toward the joint goal from, say, K, but as he approaches it, the smell from the skunk rises faster than the aroma from the hay until, at A, the repulsion from the skunk just equals the attraction from the hay, and the ass remains in a quandary, again with the inevitable result of frustration, aggression, and breakdown. If, however, as in Figs. 5.7 and 5.8, the attractive force of the hay is greater than the repulsive force of the skunk between the ass and the goal, he will proceed with nose averted right to the hay and will eat it. The equilibrium E in Fig. 5.8 is clearly unstable.

It is not difficult to interpret these situations in terms of the value-field theory developed in the preceding pages. In Fig. 5.9, H_1 and H_2 are the two bales of hay, and A is the ass between them. For each position on the line H_1H_2, we suppose the ass has a value ordering, or utility, given by the curve H_1EH_2. We adopt the convention that

THE INDIVIDUAL AS A PARTY TO CONFLICT 85

a lower position on the vertical scale is an order of preference—first, second, third, etc. We see that the point E is a point of unstable equilibrium; a slight tip one way or the other will move the donkey to either H_1 or H_2, which are optimum points. In Fig. 5.10, on the other hand, S_1 and S_2 are the two skunks, and A again is the ass. We see that he remains firmly at A unless he can summon up courage to get over the hills at S_1 or S_2 and so get on the other side of the skunks. Why, however, we may ask, should the ass not be perfectly comfortable at A? It is clearly a preferred position to any in the immediate neighborhood, though if he succeeded in getting

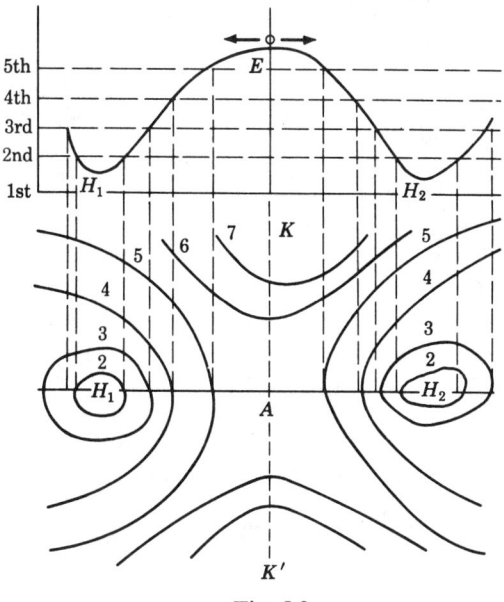

Fig. 5.9

over the hill he might reach a still better position. What, in other words, is the difference between a simple equilibrium as the economist understands the term and a conflict, or quandary, as the psychologist understands it? The answer to this question is found

86   CONFLICT AND DEFENSE

in the concept of acceptability, which we used in Chap. 1 in discussing the bargaining situation. Let us suppose, for instance, that, in Figs. 5.9 and 5.10, the fifth degree of valuation is the limit of acceptability; that is, anything better than this, e.g., the fourth, third degree, etc., is acceptable, and anything worse than this is unacceptable, in the sense that, in an acceptable position, the individual is, if not happy,

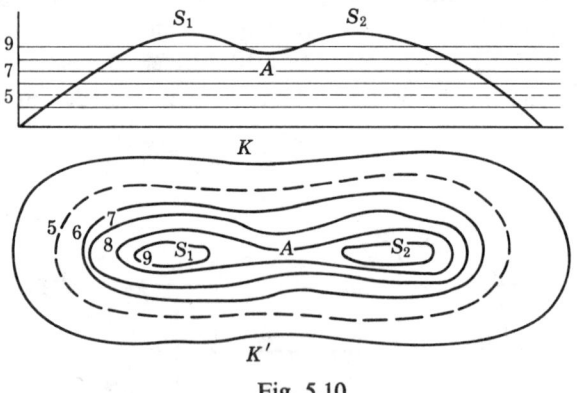

Fig. 5.10

at least content with the situation and not wasting energy in fretting and fuming. Then, the individual in Fig. 5.9, even though his position at E is unacceptable, will soon find acceptable positions at either H_1 or H_2. The individual in Fig. 5.10, however, at A will be in a position that is both unacceptable and stable. This is what the psychologists mean by a conflict.

In the lower portions of Figs. 5.9 and 5.10, we see the same figures expressed as indifference contours in a two-dimensional field. Thus, if we visualize the surfaces above the plane of the paper represented by the indifference contours, we see that the upper half of each figure is the section of this surface through the horizontal line through A. In the lower part of Fig. 5.9, we see that there is a line of unstable equilibrium, or psychological conflict, KK'. A ball confined to this line will descend to A. The slightest deviation from the line however, will carry the ball to either H_1 or H_2. In the lower part of

Fig. 5.10, we see that A is stable only as long as movement is confined to the line S_1AS_2. If movement is permitted in other parts of the field, the individual will move either toward K or toward K', thus removing himself from the skunks. In both figures, A is what is known topologically as a saddle point. It is like the top of a mountain pass—the highest point across the pass, and the lowest point along the ridge. By contrast with the two-person game, in an individual value ordering, saddle points are unstable positions of equilibrium: the individual will run off down the pass if there is the slightest variation in his position. Only true troughs are stable, as at the bottom of a bowl, where movement in every direction leads to less favorable positions.

The approach-avoidance conflict is harder to interpret in terms of value-ordering theory. Here, the goal is supposed to have both positive and negative values to the individual, so that he is ambivalent toward it; he both likes and dislikes it, is attracted to it and repelled by it at the same time. This seems inconsistent with the principle that each position in the field can have only a single value order attached to it. A given position cannot at the same time be fifth and fifteenth on the value ordering, though if it is what mathematicians call a weak ordering, there is nothing to prevent two positions tying for fifth place. All that the value field can represent is the *net* value ordering, which results from balancing the desirable against the undesirable elements in each position of the field. The net value, then, is the difference between the positive and negative values. We could, for instance, postulate a value field in the case of Figs. 5.6 and 5.8 that exhibited a maximum utility or preference at A in Fig. 5.6 and at G in Fig. 5.8. If we merely look at the net value ordering, however, we may be overlooking an important aspect of the situation. Two positions may have the same net value, and yet one may be the result of an excess of a high positive over a high negative value, whereas the other is an excess of a low positive over a still lower negative value. $1000 - 995$ is the same figure as $10 - 5$, yet, for some purposes, there may be important differences in these two situations. This is especially likely to be true in uncertain situations: the excess of a small gain over a small cost may be more secure than the equal excess of a large gain over a large cost. This means that the economic approach to behavior through preference fields frequently needs to be supplemented by the psychological approach through the dynamics of goal seeking or avoidance.

The above analysis throws a good deal of light on the genesis of certain personality variables that are of significance in conflict situations. We have seen, for instance, that, in the Richardson process, the position, or even the existence, of equilibrium depends greatly on the initial hostility of the two parties as well as on the reactivity. In the analysis of duopoly in Chap. 4, we saw that the position of equilibrium depended on the ability of each firm to act against its apparent short-run interests and that long-sightedness usually paid off through a deliberate manipulation of the reaction function. It is not unreasonable to look for personality characteristics that lead in the individual to high initial hostilities and to high reactivities, for not only are these important in person-to-person conflict, but, in so far as the character of the individual components affect the behavior of organizations, they are important in conflicts between and within organizations.

Modern psychological theory, and especially psychoanalytic theory, has laid a good deal of stress on the close connection between frustration and aggression. The connection is a good deal more complex than Freud, perhaps, supposed; nevertheless, some connection in broad terms exists. The constantly frustrated individual, whether rat or human, develops high initial hostilities and high reactivities that lead him constantly into Richardson processes that proceed to boundary breakdowns in fights, or even in irrational behavior of a violent nature like screaming, shouting, or thrashing around and cursing. Frustration, however, is not a simple, single-valued variable, nor is aggression; there are many types of both, which a careful analysis must identify. There is a world of difference, for instance, between what might be called rational aggression, in which a party deliberately plans a movement into the field of another, or even plans a game of ruin against him, in the sober expectation of being better off as a result, and irrational aggressiveness, in which the party thrashes around wildly without any real hope of planned gains but simply as an expression of an otherwise intolerable frustration. Similarly, there may be several types of frustration, ranging from the sober acceptance of impotence in a well-appraised situation, leading to a careful and rational search for new fields and new solutions, to the panic and mental collapse of the individual placed under a burden too great for his capacity.

The analysis of the different types of psychological equilibrium throws some light on the problem of the nature of different types of frustration. It is tempting, for instance, to suppose that there are two ideal types of personality, one of which makes decisions by moving toward what he likes whereas the other makes decisions by moving away from what he dislikes. The first might be called the approacher and the second the avoider. The approacher will be able to resolve conflicts of goals easily; he is like the ass between the bales of hay. If, at any time, he is faced with two equally attractive goals he may hesitate for a short while between them, but as random fluctuations take him toward one, that becomes more attractive than the other and he goes towards it. His equilibriums, therefore, are likely to be boundary equilibriums; that is, he will proceed to positions in his field of possible futures that have greater and greater utility until he reaches some boundary beyond which he cannot go. This is impotence but it is not necessarily frustration in the classical psychoanalytic sense. He cannot go beyond the boundary immediately; he may, however, work on the boundary and he may devote present effort to extending it. Thus, a man who cannot afford something now may devote himself to increasing his income so that he can afford it later. This is a rational reaction to impotence rather than an aggressive reaction to frustration.

The avoider, on the other hand, constantly finds himself in quandaries, like the ass between the two skunks. As he moves away from one of his negative goals he is pushed toward the other. Note that he always moves away from, never toward. Consequently, he finds himself not in a boundary equilibrium like Fig. 1.1 but in a trough equilibrium like Fig. 5.10. In a trough equilibrium, there is likely to be less sense of being able to change the situation by slow changes through the future. A boundary may be pushed back gradually; a trough requires a desperate leap to jump over the skunk into a more promising part of the field. Consequently, trough equilibriums or quandaries, are likely to lead to erratic, violent, and aggressive behavior rather than to cool, rational, and purposive choice. Economic man, we should notice, is an approacher to the core and enjoys perfect mental health. This is probably why economists have never even noticed this problem. They have always assumed implicitly that there was no real difference between maximizing utility and minimizing disutility, and no economist, to my knowledge, has ever even noticed the possibility of a quandary. Economic man always maximizes utility and hence resolves his psychological conflicts and goes coolly and rationally to his frequently undistinguished goals. It is interesting to speculate whether the great sociological difficulties and conflicts associated with labor markets may be connected with the fact that labor is a discommodity and the laborer is engaged in minimizing the disutility of labor rather than in maximizing the utility of consumption.

The situation of *ambivalence*, where a positive and a negative goal are located close together, in the field or at least both in the line of travel of the subject, is also likely to give rise to frustration. This is the approach-avoidance conflict noted in Fig. 5.6. This can be interpreted in two ways. We can think of ambivalence as consisting in positive and negative values attached to the same goal or as a region of high value that is surrounded by a region of low value that must be traversed by the subject in order to reach the high-valued goal. The first situation is analogous to Fig. 5.8. As long as the good in the goal certainly outweighs the bad, no psychological conflict is likely to arise, the individual being moved by his net preferences straight to the goal. Difficulties might arise in this case, as we have noted, where there are uncertainties. If, for instance, the goal involves a chance of gain and a chance of loss, if we play a maximin strategy we will be moved more by the fear of loss than by the hope of gain. This does not necessarily mean that we will be an avoider; we can move toward the position of least possible loss rather than away from the position of greatest possible loss. One may venture a tentative suggestion, however, that the constant employment of the maximin strategy on the part of an individual may lead to a fearful, loss-avoiding attitude toward life that will eventually turn him into an avoider. This may be a psychological hazard of an otherwise quite rational strategy and may explain in part why this type of strategy has a bad press historically.

The second situation is the very common one of the optimum in the small that is not a maximum in the large. Thus consider the situation of Fig. 5.11, which is like that of Fig. 5.6 except that the SS' curve intersects the HH' curve twice. This may be interpreted by supposing that, as we get really near the skunk, he somehow does not seem to be quite so bad as when we contemplated him from farther away, whereas the hay smells even nicer as we get close to it. The point E_2 is an unstable equilibrium: to the left of E_2, the subject falls back to E_1, but, to the right of it, he goes on to G. In Fig. 5.12, we see the corresponding utility or preference curve; there is a trough at E_1. If, however, the subject can get up enough steam and courage to push over the pass at E_2, he can roll down to G, where his position is much better than at A_1. Frustration at E_1 may arise not only because of the generally frustrating situation of a trough, where any unsuccessful effort to get out of the situation merely rolls one back into it again, but also because of a sense of the existence of a superior position at G, coupled with the inability to get up enough dynamic to roll over E_2.

Frustration does not always result in aggression; it may result in apathy. The subject simply gives up and adjusts his level of aspiration or of tolerability and decides to endure what he cannot cure. In

Fig. 5.11

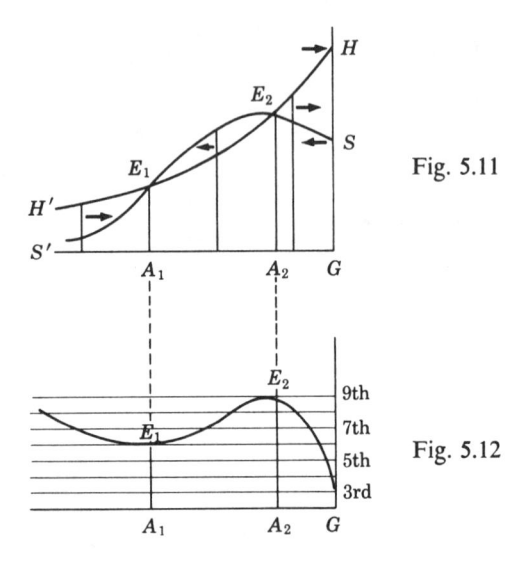

Fig. 5.12

the extreme case, this may lead to catatonic states in which the subject withdraws from the real world altogether. For frustration to result in aggression, there must be some faint hope remaining that action might produce desirable results. The problem can perhaps be illustrated by a payoff matrix, as in Fig. 5.13. Suppose the subject has two strategies or choices—a little effort on the one hand, or a big effort on the other. Nature we suppose, has two states, which we describe as lucky and unlucky. If the subject makes little effort, it does not matter whether he is lucky or unlucky; whatever happens he gets a payoff of 2. This is a position like E_1 in Fig. 5.12. If he tries a big effort and nature is unlucky, he is actually worse off (1), he rolls up the hill toward E_2 and rolls back again; the effort has cost him something, and he has gained nothing. If he makes a big effort and nature is lucky, he rolls over the hill at E_2, and his payoff is large (10). The maximin

	Little Effort	Big Effort
Unlucky	2	1
Lucky	2	10

Fig. 5.13

strategy here is little effort if nature plays an unknown pure strategy. It is reasonable to suppose that nature plays a mixed strategy, meaning by this that sometimes the subject will be lucky and sometimes unlucky, and there is no way of telling which in any one play, but that we may know how many times out of a thousand the subject will be lucky. In this case, it might be thought that the subject should also play a mixed strategy. In fact, however, a game against nature like this does not follow the minimax dynamic of an ordinary two-person game, because nature's strategies can be assumed independent of the subject's strategies. The actual strategy that is rational for the subject to adopt depends on the chance of each of nature's strategies. We can, for instance, calculate the expected value of either of the subject's strategies; if nature's strategies are 50 percent each, the expected value of little effort is 2 and of big effort is 5.5, assuming that the payoffs are comparable, and it will be rational to adopt the big effort. This assumes, however, that there can be a large number of moves that can be averaged.

What the subject will do actually depends a great deal on what he has learned from past experience. Suppose, in a succession of small, similar cases, he has made a big effort and failed. He is likely to interpret this as a strategy on the part of nature; he is unlucky, and once he has learned this, he will always make little effort, especially in this case, where if he makes little effort, there is no way to find out whether he has been lucky or unlucky, as he gets the same return in each case. Suppose now that the return on little effort is very unsatisfactory. The subject cannot stay in little effort and he may have no faith in big effort. The result is a great accumulation of tension that manifests itself either in apathy or even catalepsy or in wild or uncoordinated aggressiveness.

The above is a mere outline sketch of an enormously complicated phenomenon. We should notice further, however, the phenomenon of displacement. We saw earlier that the ass between the two skunks might escape if he could find another dimension. This is frequently a source of escape from the frustrations of human existence, even if the dimension is an imaginary one. This may take the simple form of daydreaming, which at one extreme turns into literature and art and at the other extreme becomes schizophrenia and paranoia. A society faces a very real dilemma here: a high level of general frustration may be necessary for the development of creativity, for creativity, whether in the arts, science, religion, politics, or business is precisely the attempt to find previously unexplored dimensions of organization and experience that promise escape from an existing frustration; on the other hand, a high level of general frustration may likewise lead to high levels of mental breakdown in the individual and to political conflict and instability in the society.

We can perhaps distinguish several different forms of displacement. We have first the displacement of *feeling* from one object to another. This is the familiar phenomenon of the man who cannot express his hatred of his boss and so comes home to kick the cat and bully his wife and children. This is an important element in the Freudian scheme, and it clearly corresponds to an element in everyday experience. The feeling that is displaced is frequently a feeling of self-hatred, which is just as inadmissible to the person as hatred of the boss, so that it becomes displaced on to others. It is sound psychology that we cannot love our neighbor until we have first loved ourselves. Hatred of parents and of others in power positions over us in childhood is likewise a powerful source of generalized aggressive feeling.

In the second place, there is the displacement of *activity*. In its extreme form, this takes shape as the compulsive behavior of the neurotic or the psychotic. In its benign form, it takes shape as art, science, religion, and creative enterprise. It frequently takes the form of *ritual*, that is, a stylized activity that is repeated over and over again in forms that derive a good deal of their value from the mere fact of repetition. Wherever, indeed, man is faced with a fundamentally insoluble problem he tends to develop ritual as a substitute for its solution. This is not perhaps the only function of ritual in a society but it can be a very valuable one; it can prevent the disintegration that is all too likely to result from merely random aggressiveness. Even such an apparently rational activity as accounting turns out upon examination to have large elements of ritual within it; the basic problems of the accountant are fundamentally insoluble, as they involve information about the future that is not accessible to him. A great deal of accounting technique, therefore, is an attempt to ensure that all accountants come out with the same answer, whether this is the right answer or not. The ritual element in sport is very pronounced and perhaps is derived from the necessity for simplifying human interaction. The ritual element in social intercourse, in taking food and drink together and in conversation, is likewise very pronounced and may be interpreted as a device to protect us from the awful fate of having to know one another. Triviality is the ritual that protects us against the abyss of love. The ritual element in religion is a very large part of the total activity and may likewise be interpreted as a psychological answer to the impossible epistemological problem of the knowledge of ultimate truth. The danger of ritual is that it may sometimes be too good a substitute for the solution of a problem and may actually prevent its solution. Ritual is fine for insoluble problems but it is very bad for soluble problems. Magic may have useful psychological functions and may help to hold a society together in the face of the great unknown, but it does not help us much to penetrate the great unknown itself.

Up to this point we have been considering the character of the individual party to conflict still in very general terms, as possessing certain abstract qualities such as hostility, aggressiveness, touchiness, and so on. For some purposes, however, we must face the fact that there is a content to the mind or image of an individual; he is hostile, aggressive, touchy, or the reverse, about something. Conflicts are not merely the result of generalized aggressiveness; they too have content, and they too are about something. I have elsewhere[2]

[2] Kenneth E. Boulding, *The Image*, Ann Arbor, University of Michigan Press, 1956.

called the content of the mental structure of an individual his *image*; this is his view of the universe and of himself as part of this universe. The image is a result of a growth process; we need not at this point go into its physical substratum, for the essence of the image is information, which is structure or arrangement. The question of what is structured or arranged can be left to the physiologists, just as it is immaterial whether a particular message is structured in neural nets, sound waves, electrical impulses, or marks on a piece of paper. The image grows partly as a result of the genetic process by which the genes build up the pattern of the phenotype out of nutritive substance. In the human being, however, the image grows mainly by the receipt of messages, partly from the outside world through the senses and partly from messages that are internally generated by the organism itself (the imagination). These messages may come from other persons or from nonpersonal sources. The messages from the senses build up a picture in the image of our immediate environment. Messages from persons, however, may be more than signs of an immediate environment; they may be symbols. Thus, if I hear someone talking behind me, I interpret this as a sign that another person is in the room. The tone of voice may convey other signs: it may tell me whether the person is angry or composed, upset or at ease. The content of the language, however, is symbolic; it may create changes in the hearer's image of things that are remote in time and place from the actual conversation. The voice may, for instance, be telling me something about Australia, where I have never been, and may modify my image of this place of which I have had no direct experience. Even more symbolically, the voice may be telling me about heaven, or loyalty, or entropy, or the square root of minus one, all of which noises or shapes convey meaning to me and perhaps again affect my image of ideas and relationships.

The symbolic image is of enormous importance in the understanding of human conflict, mainly because so many conflicts both between persons and between groups and organizations are about symbols. Even conflicts that seem at first sight to be about simple material objects like land or property are almost always deeply associated with symbolic elements like prestige, respect, and so on. These symbolic elements, however, are very difficult to handle in abstract form, mainly because they inevitably involve what William Blake calls *minute particulars*. It is hard to reduce an insult to mathematical form, for the reduction has to be so great. Through the course of history and human experience, certain things, forms, and places acquire symbolic value far beyond their value in the currency of rational behavior. One thinks, for instance, of the enormous impact that the symbolic character of the Holy Land had had on human history, from the days of Joshua to the Crusades and on to Zionism and the establishment of the state of Israel, or the extraordinary impact on history of symbols like the cross or the flag.

The systematic study of the power of symbols is still poorly developed, and no well-established body of theory or of empirical studies exists. Nevertheless, one may hazard a guess that the power of symbols is closely related to two factors: the first is the degree of concentration that the symbol represents, and the second is the degree of ambivalence in attitude toward what it symbolizes. A symbol is always a shorthand: it evokes from the recipient more than the literal or narrow meaning of a message. The more of human experience is concentrated into the symbol, the more it can evoke, and the more powerful it is. All symbolization, whether this is the statistical processes by which, say, a price index or a regression coefficient is obtained or whether it is the process by which human experience is distilled into poetry or art or religious symbols, is a process of condensation—of the loss of information in such a way that what is lost can be evoked if necessary. It is this evocative property of symbols which not only gives them a great deal of their power but is the source of misunderstanding, for the same symbol may evoke very different expansions in the minds of two different people, depending on what their images and life experiences have been like. The image that is evoked by the symbol of the father, for instance, depends very much on what experience a person has had with his own father, and this will vary greatly from person to person. The study of the process of evocation, or deconcentration, from abstract symbols, as in the Rorschach test, is a valuable clue to the nature and history of the person.

Generally speaking, then, we can suppose that highly concentrated symbols that have high evocative power are more powerful than symbols of low concentration and evocative power. The price-level index is a less powerful symbol than the flag partly, at least, because it represents less and hence evokes less: a price index evokes only the possible list of prices from which it was derived, whereas the flag evokes a colorful and poetic image of centuries of national history.

Concentration, however, is not enough to account for the emotional power of symbols or for their importance as a field of conflict. The multiplication table, or even a single abstract number, is an enormously concentrated symbol that abstracts from a vast field of experiences of quantity. Nobody, however, has, to my recollection, ever quarreled much about the multiplication table or about the abstract number "three," though there have been some fine, bloody quarrels about the Trinity. To account for the emotional power of symbols, we must appeal to another property—the degree of ambivalence both in fact and in value toward what they represent. For a symbol to be a source of conflict, there must be uncertainty in its connotation, and there must also be ambivalence in attitude toward what it represents. It is the things that we both hate and love at the same time that exert such extraordinary power over the human imagination, simply because they place us in a quandary from which there is no escape. Why, for instance, should an act of desecration arouse such instant and such fierce hostility? If anyone doubts that it does, just let him wipe his feet on the flag on some public and patriotic occasion, or spit on a crucifix, or insult motherhood! An obvious answer is that the act of desecration is an overt expression of hostility toward an object toward which most persons feel a suppressed hostility as well as a perfectly genuine and open affection. The great symbolic value of parenthood arises from the fact that we both hate and love our parents (this is one of Freud's greatest insights) but that the payoffs of our society induce us to express the love and repress the hatred. Consequently, when anyone insults our parents, or even the abstract ideal of parenthood (consider, for instance, the disproportionate emotion produced by the expression "son of a bitch)," he is doing something that, with one part of our constitution, we would like to do but dare not admit that we would like to do it, even to ourselves. Consequently, we release on the insulter the hostility that we dare not release on the subject of the insult. This is the phenomenon of displacement already noticed. The intensity of the emotion varies directly with the degree both of love and of hatred that are involved in the ambivalent relation. Something toward which we have mild feelings of both attraction and aversion will not stir us deeply. We do not get excited (in Western culture) about the avuncular relationship, nor about township government, nor about the International Postal Union, even though there may be some things that we like and some we dislike about these institutions. Where, however, there is both strong love and strong hatred toward the same object, its symbolic value will be high.

The strong symbolic values of both nationalism and religion arise in part out of the ambivalence we feel toward their objects. A man's country and his church stand somewhat *in loco parentis;* he feels toward them both genuine affection and genuine hatred. His country gives him his formal education and it provides, through social security, for his old age and guards him against many of his misfortunes. It also, however, taxes him, conscripts him for war, and involves him in the cruelty and insecurity of a system of national defense. It ties him to a great deal of policies and programs of which he may not approve, especially if he is part of a minority opinion, and it constantly stands as a potential threat to him through the system of law, police, and courts. Like the parent, the nation at the same time rewards and threatens, and it generates the same kind of ambivalent response. The church frequently does the same; it portrays God as both an angry judge and a loving redeemer, and so creates ambivalence towards Him even in the minds of the most devout. It is this very ambivalence, however, which is the source of the strength of the institution and of the symbols that it embodies. It is ambivalence that makes objects interesting. Things that we simply love, or toward which we are attracted, are either attained, in which case, they no longer attract us, or they eventually bore us. Things that we simply hate we flee from and escape. It is the things that we both love and hate which hold us in a quandary and which interest us. We can neither escape them, because we love them, nor can we attain them, because we hate them, so that they interest us continually, and it is the degree to which it continues to attract interest that is perhaps the best single measure of the strength of a symbol.

Because of our strong interest in them, we are likely to be touchy about things of high symbolic value; that is, we may respond to messages coming in from outside, and also to the internal messages of our own imagination, by sharp readjustments in our basic attitudes, both overt and covert. This means that Richardson processes are likely to be set off for both attitudes in an ambivalent feeling: if we have ambivalent attitudes with small degrees of love and hate, the ambivalence tends to create a touchy situation in which we respond to loving messages from the object with an increase in love and to hostile messages with an increase in hate, so that both love and hate grow together, thus increasing the symbolic value. Thus there is some tendency for objects to have either very high symbolic value or very little: we react strongly to objects like the cross and the flag and to mother or father symbols, but there is a whole host of objects—chairs and tables, the multiplication table and the arithmetic mean, which has little symbolic significance and toward which we have little ambivalence.

One of the striking characteristics of symbolic systems is their occasional great instability, not only in the individual but even in mass populations. This phenomenon is of great importance in history; occasionally we see the overthrow of old symbols and their replacement by a new set. This happens in the conversion of an individual to a religious or political faith. It happens sometimes on a mass scale, as in the rise of new religions or political movements. We shall examine this phenomenon in more detail in the following chapter. Meanwhile, we may conclude this very brief survey of a large problem by noting that, in the explanation of the instability of symbolic systems and also in the explanation of many apparent irrationalities of human conduct, it is useful to postulate two elements in the person's image and attitudes: an *overt element*, which he acknowledges to himself and to the world, and a *covert element*, which he keeps hidden. The covert image may again be divided into two parts: that which the person keeps hidden from others, or the *conscious covert*, and that which is hidden even from himself, or the *unconscious covert*. Perhaps Freud's greatest contribution to the understanding of man and society was his emphasis on the great importance of the unconscious, that vast reservoir of thoughts, memories, emotions, and attitudes which is not accessible to the ordinary processes of recall but which frequently plays a large part in determining our behavior. The human image is an iceberg, which hides much of its content below the surface of conscious recall. From the point of view of the social system, conscious covert images and attitudes may also be of great importance, especially in explaining sudden social reversals. A society imposes certain conscious attitudes on its members by its system of rewards and punishments, but these may lead only to outward conformity, not to inner consent. Where the overt and covert elements either in an individual or in a society follow dynamic paths of their own, as they often do, there is always a possibility of dramatic overturn or revolution by which the previously covert becomes overt and the previously overt, covert. This almost literal revolution (through 180°) is particularly likely to be suffered by symbolic systems with objects of high symbolic value, for here, as we have seen, our attitude toward these objects is almost bound to be ambivalent, with one polar attitude dominating the other as the overt element and the other being suppressed as the covert. Then, dramatic reversals may occur as the dynamics of the situation affects one more than the other. Thus, in a marital situation, we suppose that each partner has a somewhat ambivalent attitude toward the other that may be written $\frac{\text{friendly}}{\text{hostile}}$. Each of these attitudes—the first one overt, the second one covert—is subject to a dynamic of its own: friendly messages from the other party increase the friendliness; hostile messages increase the hostility. If one party takes the other for granted and ceases to send friendly messages (endearments), the covert hostility in the second party may grow relative to the overt friendliness until one day there is a reversal, and the hostility becomes overt and the friendliness covert. The same thing may happen in people's attitudes toward a religion, a government, or a nation. A regime in power may neglect acts of friendliness toward its supporters, as it takes them for granted; as a result the covert hostility grows until finally there is a reversal in a revolution.

Changes in symbolic systems are highly complex and cannot, of course, be reduced to simple reversals of attitudes. We might distinguish roughly three types of change in symbolic systems. There are *conversions* or *revolutions*, which involve the rejection of a previous symbolic system and its replacement by a different one. The heathen tribe throws away its idols and becomes Christian; the Russians reject the tzar and accept the Bolsheviki. This happens when the suppression of the hostile attitude toward the old system is very effective and complete, so that people remain overtly friendly even under pressure of great covert hostility because of fear of the repressive powers of the system. When the system is finally overturned and hostility toward it becomes overt, this hostility is so great that the old system is largely swept away and replaced by a new one.

The second type of change is the *reformation*. Here there remains a strong element of friendliness as well as of hostility toward the old, so that, even when the system is reversed, the covert friendliness toward the old system is strong. Under these circumstances, there is a strong tendency to idealize the revolution as a reformation or purification of the old system rather than as a destruction of it. Then, the new system can harness the friendliness that existed toward the old through the device of attempting to get rid of the bad elements in the old system, which are generally thought of as accretions, while retaining the good, which are thought of as original. Thus, reformations in religion generally take the form of an appeal to a return to the pure religion of an earlier day and a rejection of more recent accretions. The residual friendliness that persists toward the old religion can then be harnessed to the service of the new, and the elements that caused hostility can be diminished.

The third type of change in symbolic systems is the *accretion of new elements*, either borrowed from other systems or developed spontaneously from within. This may happen simply because symbolic systems have inner laws of development; they cannot remain stationary. Change is forced on them by the playfulness and inventiveness of the human imagination, which constantly wants to do something that has not been done before. Or there may be contact with other cultures, which almost inevitably leads to cultural borrowings of certain elements. Thus, Christianity borrowed the Christmas tree from the Germans and Christmas from the Saturnalia of the Romans, the adoration of images and of saints from more primitive tribal religions, and so on. If the accretions become too great, the culture may become so diverse as to arouse covert hostilities; then it is in danger of reformation.

The history of aesthetic taste provides some nice examples of these three types of change in symbolic systems. At any one time, a certain system of taste tends to dominate—gothic in the Middle Ages, baroque in the seventeenth century, and so on. Each system has a certain tendency to move in the direction of self-elaboration or of accretion from outside. Thus, Gothic moves from the simplicity of Early English to the complexities of the Perpendicular and flamboyant styles; the Renaissance style, which succeeded it, moves from the simplicity of the Palladian to the over-ripeness of rococo. When there is much contact with other cultures, styles tend to become eclectic, as in the nineteenth century. Sometimes the revolution takes the form of a reformation—a return to an earlier style, which is really what happened in the Renaissance—or it may be a true revolution, as in the modern style of today.

We cannot get very far with the prediction, or even the perception, of the course of conflict situations unless we develop means for probing the covert levels of hostility and friendliness, as well as the overt. An exclusive concentration on overt expressions may be extremely misleading and is likely to lead to some disagreeable surprises. The nature of the information system also profoundly affects the dynamic course of hostility and friendliness. Where attitudes are covert, the individuals who are affected by them are often not able to deal with them, simply because they are not aware that there is anything that needs to be dealt with. The development of better information systems, therefore, is likely to diminish the frequency of revolutions, for if the growth of what would otherwise be covert hostility is perceived, the sources of this hostility may be corrected in time.

6

THE GROUP AS A PARTY TO CONFLICT:

THE ECOLOGICAL MODEL

We may usefully distinguish three levels of conflict as defined by the nature of the parties. At one extreme, we have simple conflict among persons acting on their own behalf and not in any representative capacity. This is how we visualized the party to conflict in the previous chapter. We see this in sibling rivalry, schoolyard quarrels, personal feuds, and, in its extreme form, the duel. At the other end of the scale, we have the conflicts of organizations, that is, between well-structured groups with clearly defined roles and constitutions. We see this in conflict between nations, between trade unions and employers associations or corporations, between firms, and even between athletic teams. This will be the topic of Chap. 8. In an ill-defined middle ground between the person and the organization lies the *group*, the unorganized subpopulation of persons that exists as a social fact because of its presence in the image of the persons concerned as a significant classification of the total population. A group, in this sense, is a subpopulation within some larger population with which individual persons may be identified, either as included in it and belonging to it or as excluded from it and not belonging to it. Thus, a particular person may or may not be a Negro, an American, an Iowan, a Latin American, a Catholic, a Mason, a professor, a farmer, a Republican, an alumnus, a criminal, a woman, a widow, a chess player, an alien, a Philadelphia Biddle, a Navaho, a workingman, a pauper, a General Motors employee, or a teen-ager. These are all groups in the sense that there are at least some individuals who could answer the question, "Are you a Negro, American, etc.," by a simple "yes" or "no." Some groups are at the same time organizations, and many groups have some kind of organization associated with them, though not necessarily coterminous with them. Some groups, however, have no organization associated with them, though there is a strong tendency for organizations to form when there is a strong group identification and there is a tendency, also, for organizations to create groups. Thus, outside the pages of Sherlock Holmes, I know of no league of red-headed men, in spite of the fact that red-headed people form an easily identifiable group in the sense that most people could say at once whether they were in this group or out of it. On the other hand, there are many organizations, like the NAACP, that organize around the existence of a group, even though the organization is much smaller than the group. Workingmen felt themselves to be a class long before there were trade unions, and the development of national consciousness frequently precedes the organizational establishment of the nation.

The group is important as a party to conflict, in spite of the fact that conflicts between groups are vaguer and less well defined than conflicts between either persons or organizations. This is because the conflicts between organizations frequently arise out of and express the underlying conflict between the groups which comprise the members of the organization or the groups of which the organization is itself an expression. Thus, conflict between nations is not merely a conflict of diplomats, heads of states, and employees of government; it is a conflict that arises because the nation is not only an organization but a group, consisting of persons who think of themselves, for instance, as Frenchmen and as not Germans, for whom this affiliation is of great emotional importance. Similarly, industrial conflict is not only between organized labor unions and an organized employer or employers; it is a conflict that originates in a feeling of group identification with the boss or with the men.

Group conflict frequently exists without organization or with only loose, temporary, and informal organization. Racial conflict is often of this loosely organized character; it reflects itself in unorganized mass migrations and in individual prejudices and attitudes. Sometimes it manifests itself in temporary, loose organizations, like a rioting mob or a lynching party. Industrial conflict, likewise, exists long before its formalization by labor unions; slowdowns, cacanny, sabotage, and strong group pressure against the worker who cooperates too enthusiastically with the boss are all marks of unorganized or very loosely organized group conflict. Indeed, almost all the phenomena that are associated with the union-management relationship can also be found among unorganized labor. Religious conflict is frequently group conflict rather than organizational conflict. Nowadays especially, churches do not openly persecute and seek to exterminate the heretic, but there is a subtle and persistent undercurrent of conflict as expressed in social discrimination, avoidance, and individual religious prejudice or preference.

We shall not attempt here an exhaustive categorization of the groups in modern society; the following is intended merely to illustrate the richness and variety of groupings. We might distinguish first between *involuntary* groupings, which are mainly the result of the genetic history of the individual over which he has no control, and *voluntary* groupings, which are subject to change, where an individual has the possibility of changing his group. I shall distinguish five major types of involuntary group: (1) sex, (2) age, (3) race and physical type, (4) family position, and (5) kinship. The first three are almost entirely involuntary; change of sex is a curiosity, and change of age is impossible except by waiting, though rejuvenation is not wholly off the human agenda. Physical type is largely involuntary, though we do have plastic surgery. With race, we are moving more toward the social and voluntary and beginning to get away from the strictly genetic and involuntary, for race has largely a social definition, as the 40,000 or so Negros who become white every year in the United States testify. Family position has a twofold aspect: partly it is strictly genetic, like the parent-child or uncle-nephew relationship; partly it is social and voluntary, like the husband-wife status or the status of an adopted child or of a divorced person. The group of those who have the same family position—the group, for instance, of all parents or all grandmothers—is not usually very salient or important, though parents are organized in parent-teacher associations. Then, finally, there is the kinship group, which has been of great importance in human society. This again is partly genetic and partly voluntary through marriage or adoption. Even though kinship has a genetic base, the significance of kinship is a social phenomenon. There are some societies in which the relationship of a third cousin twice removed is of importance and is a salient relationship of which people are strongly aware; there are other societies in which even a first-cousin relationship goes almost unnoticed.

Seven additional types of more or less voluntary groupings can easily be added, and, no doubt, more could be adduced. We have (6) religious groups, which may or may not be coterminous with churches or church membership. There are several layers of group classification: thus, a man may think of himself as a Christian, a Protestant, a Methodist, a Wesleyan Methodist, a member of a conference, a circuit, a local church, and a group within the church. Then (7), there are social groups: lodges, clubs, hobby groups, music groups, athletic groups, almost *ad infinitum*. Then (8), there are political parties or faiths: Republicans, Democrats, Socialists, etc. Then (9), there are class groups: upper, middle, and working, or urban and rural; linguistic subgroups speaking class dialects might be added to this list. Then (10), there are civil-status groups: paupers, criminals, aliens, slaves, conscripts, and solid citizens. Then (11), there is an important class of economic categories: occupational groups, employee groups (defined as people having a single employer), customers of a single firm, and members of a cooperative society.

Then (12), there is the classification by past educational experience: high school graduates, university graduates, and so on; an important subgroup may be those who have graduated from a particular institution (alumni). Veterans groups might almost be included in this category. Last (13), and perhaps, in the modern world, the most important, there are national and local groups, ranging from the town (or even the ward) through the county, state, nation, empire, commonwealth or group of nations to the group of all humanity of which all the others are subsets.

Within each of these groups there are likely to be specialized functional subgroups—organizational hierarchies (popes, bishops, priests, deacons, laity), though these tend to be characteristic of organizations rather than of groups as such. The functional specialization of role, however, creates groups corresponding to each level within the organization, and their behavior as groups may be somewhat different from their behavior as individual role fillers. Once organizations get established covering and expressing the concerns and interest of a group, the organization itself develops functional subgroups that eventually get to have more in common with similar subgroups in other organizations than with other subgroups in what is supposed to be their own group. Thus, trade-union leaders, church leaders, and political leaders lose group contact with their followers and tend to find a lot in common with leaders in other groups. Indeed, one sometimes feels that the most important group classification of humanity is into the group that gets around and the group that does not. This tendency for the leaders to grow away from the led into a general leadership group may be the explanation of a good deal of long-run instability in social organization, for the leaders, as they become identified with the leadership group rather than with their followers, are in growing danger of being replaced from below by a new generation of rising leaders who are closer to the led. This happens in trade unions as the leadership acquires the attitudes of business leaders, it happens in churches as their leaders acquire the attitude of the political elite, and it happens in popular political parties as the leadership becomes more popular with the old elite than with the people they are supposed to represent. This process is akin to Pareto's famous principle of the *circulation of elites.*

Group conflict is complicated by the fact that each person belongs to many different groups. Consequently, the field of group conflict is not a simple conflict of groups for persons as members but a struggle for roles, or for parts of persons—for human time, energy, and attention, which may not be a closed field. Thus it is quite possible for some group to spring up that taps hitherto unused resources of human time and energy and hence does not compete with any existing group. On the whole, however, an expanding group expands into a field of human time and energy that has previously been devoted to other groups, and so conflict arises. This whole problem of the field of group conflict is surprisingly difficult.

An important distinction can be made, using the language of set theory, between groups that are *partitions* of some larger set, either of individual persons or of the vaguer field of human time and energy, and groups which are not partitions but which overlap. A set is said to be partitioned among subsets if each element of the set is included in one and only one of the subsets. The simplest partition is a dichotomy, in which the set is divided into two mutually exclusive subsets. There are some groups that are based on a partition of the total set of persons, so that each person can be identified as a member of one and only one group in the classification. Sex classification is a good example. The total population of persons is partitioned into men and women, and every person, if we except medical curiosities, can be unequivocally placed in one group or the other. Age classification is another partition. This can be done into as many groups or subsets as we wish. Thus we could partition the population into 2 age groups, say, under 30 and over 30, or we could partition it into over 100 age groups of 1 year each. Classification by race and physical type might be described as a vague partition. We can set up subsets and partition the set of all persons among them, for instance,

Negros, Jews, Chinese, and so on, but the boundaries will be indefinite and the definitions to some extent arbitrary. There will be many persons whose classification is in doubt—products of interracial marriages, for instance. If we pursue the process of classification far enough, we may end up with a group for each individual. Or we might even have a classification scheme with more boxes than there were individuals to fill them. The vague partition is a problem not confined to the social sciences. The spectrum of white light, for instance, is usually partitioned into colors—red, orange, yellow, green, blue, and violet. Nobody can say, however, exactly where the boundaries lie—at what exact point, for instance, does yellow turn into green—perhaps because the distinction is a convenience of our perceptive system rather than a property of light itself, which exhibits a continuum of wavelengths.

Kinship groups, in general, are not partitions, for one person may belong to several family groups through his various forebears. Relationship groups likewise are not partitions, for the same person can be both a father, a son, an uncle, a nephew, and so on. It is interesting to note here, however, that there is some tendency for family groups to be defined socially as partitions, in some societies, by a very elaborate system of clans, moieties, naming, and so on, so that each individual can be allotted to one and only one family group. We might even regard the custom of passing the surname through the male line as an attempt to reduce the hopeless network of kinship into a neat partition. Even though surnames form a partition of the total population into groups of like name (the Smiths, the Browns, and so on), these are not now kinship groups and are not usually conscious groups at all.

Most voluntary groups form a very complex set of overlapping partitions. Most individuals can be assigned to one and only one city, state, and nation. They can further be assigned to a religion or sect. Sometimes these classifications coincide; sometimes they do not. Thus, if a person is identified as a Spaniard, it is extremely likely that he will also be a Roman Catholic; if he is identified as a

Swede, it is likely that he will also be a Lutheran. If he is identified as an American (United States) or as a Dutchman (Netherlands), his religious identification is still largely in doubt, though, even in this case, he is not likely to be a Moslem or a Hindu. Political groups are yet another overlapping partition (a vague one, perhaps); so are class groups, civil-status groups, and educational-level groups.

Some voluntary groups, however, do not constitute a partition of the persons in a population, though they may constitute a partition of some more general field of time and energy. Social groups, for instance, are not necessarily a partition: a man can belong to a chess club, a tennis club, and a masonic lodge, and one does not exclude the other. As in the case of kinship groups, we may note a certain tendency to create partitions even here; the club becomes exclusive, creating a significant partition between those who belong to it and those who do not. Economic groups, also, on the whole, are not necessarily partitions. There is some tendency for occupational classification to be a partition, but this may be more an illusion of the census taker, who likes to have one and only one occupational pigeon hole for every person. Increasingly, in advanced societies, there is a tendency for people to have two or even more jobs, often in different industries. A man may, for instance, be a part-time farmer and a part-time factory worker, and the day is passing when a man could be identified unequivocally by his occupational niche. Employee groups consisting of all the employees of a single firm likewise are not necessarily partitions. The great difficulty that economists find in making an industrial classification of the economy reflects the lack of a clear partition by occupation. Does the steel industry, for instance, include the major users of steel; does it include the coal mines that produce the coal used in the making of steel; does it include the manufacture of competitive commodities like aluminum? We have a case here where some classification system is necessary but where not only are the boundary lines vague but the various subsets are overlapping.

An important distinction can be made between what might be

called *boundary* conflict on the one hand and *ecological* conflict on the other. There are some groups where the individual members are contiguous in the sense that they occupy a well-defined area in some kind of space from which members of other groups are excluded. Groups of this kind form what may be called a bounded partition; in the space that the individual members occupy, reasonably simple boundaries can be drawn that will divide the space into regions such that each region contains only members of one subgroup. Where there is conflict between groups of this kind, it is manifested in attempts to move the boundary line; it may, therefore, be called boundary conflict. Any such move of the boundary line in a fixed field of necessity makes some groups larger and some smaller and if these size redistributions are not acceptable to the parties concerned, a conflict is involved. International conflict is frequently of this type; so is the conflict of firms for market areas, as we have seen in Chap. 4. The most usual type of boundary conflict is in physical or geographical space; the concept, however, might be applied conceptually to any kind of vector space.

There is a second kind of group conflict in which the groups interpenetrate each other, either in physical or in social space, so that there is no line boundary between them and each individual of the one group tends to be in some sort of contact with individuals of the other group. This is the sort of group conflict that characterizes an ecological system of competing species, where the individuals of the various species interpenetrate the space and there is no central organization of the group. This is pure group conflict or the conflict of species; we may call it ecological conflict. The partition here is the partition, say, of the total mass of living matter that a given habitat can support among different species. Following the terminology of Chap. 1, we should perhaps call this competition rather than conflict, as it is not organized or conscious. Ecological competition, however, is an important background for the conflict of human groups, for where there is competition among groups, conflict frequently becomes organized among organizations. Even in the biological competition of species, we seldom find pure ecological competition of populations; a biological species such as a hummingbird or a birch tree has a distinct geographic pattern with a central region of highest density and a periphery where we can find something like a line boundary. The pure model of ecological competition, however, is a useful extreme case and throws a good deal of light on the forces that may lead to the rise or extinction of species.

Consider first a model of ecological equilibrium. Let us suppose only two species, or groups, A and B, and suppose that there is some equilibrium population of each that is a function of the actual population of the other. These functions are very much like the reaction curves of Fig. 2.3 and Fig. 4.3. The equilibrium of the whole system, if it exists, is at a combination of populations that represents the intersection of these curves or the solution of the simultaneous equations of these curves. Several cases are distinguished. In Figs. 6.1 to 6.5, we plot the number, or population, of species or group A on the horizontal and B on the vertical axis. In Fig. 6.1, we have the case of mutual competitiveness. If there are no members of B, there will be OA_1 members of A. As the number of B increases the equilibrium population of A declines, along A_1A_2, showing that B is competitive with A. At A_2, the number of B is so large that A cannot survive at all and is reduced to zero. Similarly, if there were no A, there would be OB_1 of B. If the number of A becomes larger, the equilibrium number of B declines, following B_1B_2; when $A = OB_2$, B is zero. Here there is a point of equilibrium at E. As in Fig. 2.3, we can use lines of dynamic path to study not only the dynamics of the system but the stability of the equilibrium. Here we suppose that a population below its particular equilibrium will grow, at equilibrium will be stationary, and above equilibrium

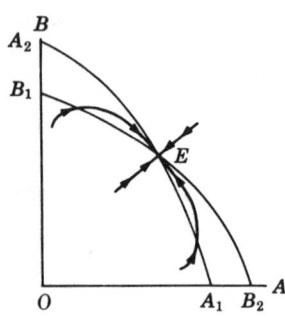

Fig. 6.1. Mutual competitiveness.

will decline. To the right of A_1A_2, therefore, A grows; on A_1A_2, it is stationary; to the left of A_1A_2, it declines. Above B_1B_2, B declines; below B_1B_2, B grows; on B_1B_2, B is stationary. The dynamic paths must be vertical at points on A_1A_2 where A is not changing but B is. They must be horizontal at points on B_1B_2 where B is not changing but A is. The dynamic paths in Fig. 6.1 show clearly that the equilibrium at E is stable.

In Fig. 6.2, we show mutual cooperation or complementarity. Here, the line A_1A_2 has a positive slope, indicating that, as B gets larger, the equilibrium value of A gets larger too. Similarly, B_1B_2 has a positive slope. In the figure, there is a point of stable equilibrium at E, as shown by the dynamic paths. This figure is strikingly similar to that of the Richardson process of Fig. 2.3. Here, again, if the slopes of the lines diverge, there will not be an equilibrium but indefinite expansion. This is never found in nature, though mutual cooperation is not infrequent; good examples are the symbiosis of

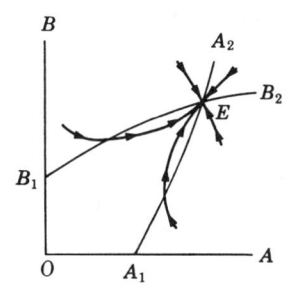

Fig. 6.2. Mutual cooperation or complementarity.

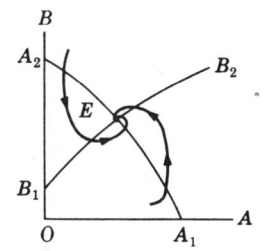

Fig. 6.3. Predation or parasitism.

the two forms of life in lichen, for instance, or of flowers and the insects that feed on them and fertilize them. Each symbiotic group, however, will be in competition with other species or will be limited by a physical habitat, and this will prevent their indefinite expansion.

Figure 6.3 shows the very interesting and common case of predation or parasitism, where, in this case, B competes with A (the more of B, the less of A) but A cooperates with B (the more of A, the more of B). B, in this case, is the predator or the parasite and A the prey or the host. The more wolves, the fewer rabbits; but the more rabbits, the more wolves. This also has a stable equilibrium at E. An interesting possibility here is that the dynamic paths exhibit a degree of circularity: they tend to spiral around the equilibrium point, even though they usually converge on it. Under

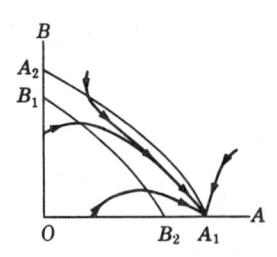

Fig. 6.4. Dominance.

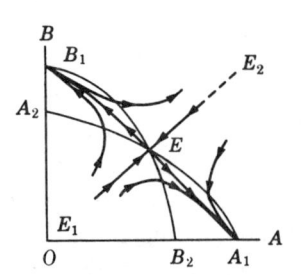

Fig. 6.5. Watershed dominance.

some dynamic conditions, however, they may well circle the equilibrium indefinitely. Certain predator-prey systems in very sparse environments like the arctic have been shown to exhibit circular, that is, cyclical, movements of this kind. In more complex systems, the movements tend to be masked by the sheer variety of relationship. There is a similarity here to the Richardson submissiveness case.

In Fig. 6.4, we see a case in which one group or species dominates the other in the sense that the dynamics of the system leads to the extinction of one species—in the case of this figure, species B. The equilibrium is at A_1, where $A = OA_1$ and $B = 0$. This is a boundary equilibrium which is not derived from the solution of the equations of particular equilibrium, as in the first three figures, but which arises because the dynamic paths of the system eventually reach a boundary (of zero population) beyond which they cannot go, because negative populations are meaningless. In Fig. 6.5, we see an even more interesting case of watershed dominance. Here we have a position of unstable equilibrium at E. From any point above and to the left of the line E_1E_2, the dynamic path through E, all the dynamic paths go to B_1; A dies out, and B is left in possession of the field. From points to the right of and below E_1E_2, all the dynamic paths go to A_1; B dies out, and A is left in possession of the field. The equilibrium E is unstable because slight variations to one side or the other set the system off on dynamic paths that lead away from E and end up at A_1 on one side or at B_1 on the other. Again, the similarity of these ecological systems to some of the Richardson process systems of Chap. 2 will be apparent; both, indeed, are cases of a general class of interaction systems.

The more species or groups are included in the model, the more complex the detailed analysis becomes, though the general principles remain much the same. If we have n species, it is easy to write n equations of equilibrium of the form $x_i = F(x_i, x_2, \ldots, x_n)$, where x_1, x_i, and x_n are the populations of the different species, and the equation gives the equilibrium value of the population of species i, given the size of all the other populations. There is no guarantee, of course, that this system of equations has a unique, or any, solution in which each species is given a positive equilibrium population, especially as there is no reason to suppose that the equations are linear; indeed, they are likely to exhibit some kind of diminishing-returns character.

The complexities of the multi-group model can be illustrated by a brief analysis of the three-group case. When we introduce the third group or species C into the model, it is clear that the particular equilibrium curves of Fig. 6.1 to 6.5 refer only to a situation where the population of C is fixed. As C changes, the curves of these figures will change too. For each figure, we can postulate four broad cases. A rise in C can either benefit or injure either A or B. A *benefit* is reflected in a shift of the partial-equilibrium curve outward and an *injury* by a shift inward. Thus, if a rise in C benefits B, the curve B_1B_2 will shift bodily upward, meaning that, at each level of A, a larger B can exist in equilibrium than before. If a rise in C benefits A, this shifts the curve A_1A_2 to the right, meaning that, at each level of B, a larger population of A can exist in equilibrium than before. Thus, in Fig. 6.6, we suppose that a rise in C benefits both A and B; the lines A_1A_2 and B_1B_2 shift outward to A_1A_2' and $B_1'B_2'$, and the equilibrium of A and B shifts from E to E'. Each point on the dotted

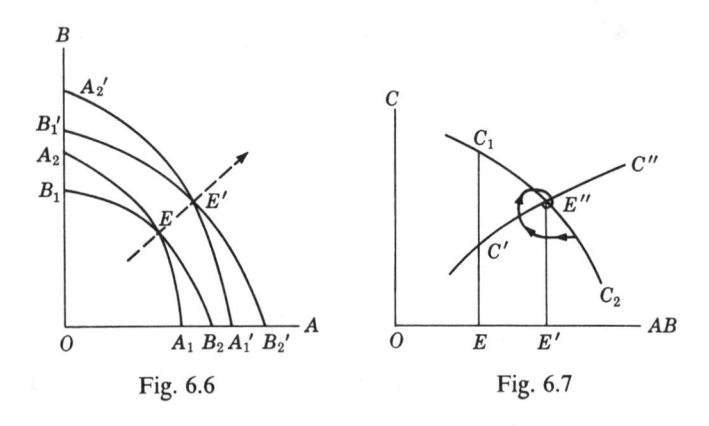

Fig. 6.6

Fig. 6.7

line EE', which is the locus of all the points of equilibrium of A and B, now shows an equilibrium value of A and B corresponding to values of C, rising in the direction of the arrow. Then, in Fig. 6.7, we spread the line EE' along the horizontal axis and measure C vertically. Each point on OEE' represents a certain combination of A and B given by Fig. 6.6. The line $C'C''$ shows the value of C that corresponds to the equilibrium of Fig. 6.6. Thus, when C is EC', the curves in Fig. 6.6 give the equilibrium of A and B at E. The line C_1C_2 shows the partial equilibrium of C for each of the values of A and B on EE'. Thus, when A and B have the values shown by E in Fig. 6.6, the equilibrium value of C is EC_1 in Fig. 6.7. The equilibrium of all three populations is at E'', where C is $E'E''$ and A and B are given by the coordinates of E' in Fig. 6.6. What we have been doing here, of course, is simply a graphic solution of three simultaneous equations. We could, if we like, express the whole system in a three-dimensional diagram with axes A, B, and C. We would then have three partial-equilibrium surfaces, the first showing the partial equilibrium of A for sets of values of B and C, the second the partial equilibrium of B for sets of values of A and C, and the third the partial equilibrium of C for sets of values of A and B. The first and second surfaces intersect in a line, the projection of which in the A–B plane is EE'. Figure 6.7, then, is a section of the figure vertically above the projected line EE'. CC' is the line of intersection of the A and B partial-equilibrium surfaces itself; C_1C_2 is part of the C partial-equilibrium surface vertically above EE'.

Dynamic paths for this system can be traced in the three-dimensional figure and may be quite complicated, as they will not usually be confined to a single plane. In Fig. 6.7, for instance, we may get circular or spiral dynamic paths, as in Fig. 6.3; it is not at all impossible that these might be divergent to a circular or cyclical equilibrium path. The general conditions of equilibrium of these systems, therefore, is a problem of great difficulty, and we must guard against assuming too easily that, merely because we have a system with an equal number of equations and unknowns, a stable-equilibrium solution of these equations exists.

Three additional cases, at least, can be developed from Fig. 6.1. In Fig. 6.8, we reproduce Fig. 6.7 except that we suppose that an increase in C injures both A and B, so that CC' now has a negative slope. The equilibrium at E'' is stable, on the analogy of Fig. 6.1. If, however, we increase the slope of CC' still more so that it cuts C_1C_2 from above, the equilibrium will be unstable, as in Fig. 6.5, and a watershed system will be set up leading to the extinction either of C or of both A and B. In Fig. 6.9, we reproduce the situation of Fig. 6.6 except that we suppose that an increase in C benefits A but injures B. Here, a rise in C shifts the A–B equilibrium from E to E' again, but the line EE' now has a negative slope. The sensitivity of the A–B equilibrium is likely to be great; quite small changes in C may lead to the extinction of either A or of B. Again, two cases can be distinguished corresponding to Fig. 6.7 and 6.8, depending on whether it is an increase or a decrease in C that moves the equilibrium of A–B from E to E'. I will not weary the reader by going through the corresponding cases derived from Figs. 6.2 to 6.5, we as are rapidly reaching the point where general conclusions are hard to come by and we wallow in a welter of individual cases. The main evidence for the possibility of stable equilibriums in systems of this

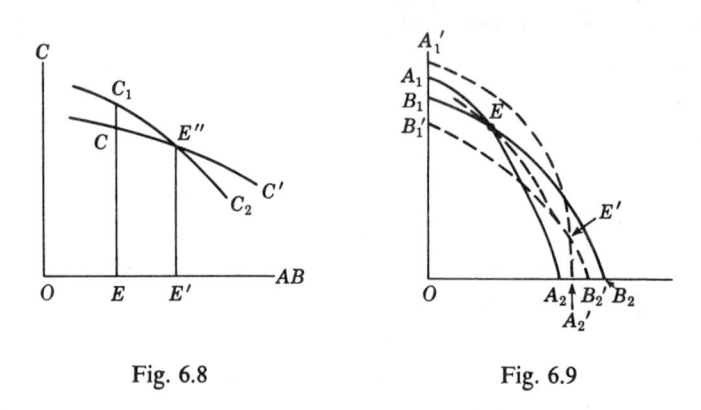

Fig. 6.8

Fig. 6.9

sort is that they exist in nature, and what exists must be possible. There are innumerable ecosystems in the pond, the field, the forest, the savannah, the river, the ocean, and so on, which exhibit a considerable degree of actual stability and which must represent, therefore, a stable multi-species equilibrium system of the kind outlined above. We can indeed think of the whole evolutionary process as a grand attempt to find stable solutions to these kinds of equations by an enormous game of trial and error; each mutation is a trial, and the vast majority of them are errors. Occasionally, however, a mutation introduces another equation into the system and upsets the old equilibrium, so that the system never returns to it but follows a dynamic path to some new equilibrium, perhaps with a totally different distribution of species or groups. The process by which states, churches, lodges, unions, firms, commodities, and industries rise and fall is strictly parallel to this general process of ecological succession. In part, it is mutation, the entrepreneurial function, that changes the equations. In part, however, the cumulation of irreversible processes that are thrown up in the course of the homeostasis of the system also changes the equations. Ponds and even seas fill up with mud and plant deposit, ice ages destroy themselves and are in turn re-created, knowledge accumulates irrevocably in a society, things get debunked on which great social systems depend, and cannot ever be rebunked, inconsistent images, however useful, eventually worry themselves into devastating conflict, and so time marches on.

Let us now look a little more deeply into the machinery of the ecological relationships of groups or species. A group grows if the *births* exceed the *deaths*; it declines if the deaths exceed the births. A birth is the addition of a new member to the group; a death is the subtraction of an old member from it. In the case of the element or individual member, the processes of birth and death do not generally involve immediate creation or annihilation. Even physical birth is merely one event in a long process of growth for the individual. Physical death is more abrupt and drastic a change, representing, as it does, a change from a homeostatic, self-maintaining physical system to a physical structure without powers of maintenance and subject to a continuous and irreversible process of decay. Even physical death, however, can be thought of as simply the most drastic and dramatic event in a long process of aging. Birth into and death out of social groups are a much less drastic process for the individual and merely represent the moments when he first begins and first ceases to conform to the definition of the element in the group. A birthday represents the death out of one age group and the birth into the next; joining a church, a club, or a political party means a birth into a group and a death out of the nongroup, or perhaps out of a competing group. Because of this, the competition and, therefore, the conflict of groups must be reflected in the influence that the size or nature of one group has on the birth and death rates of another. We see the same thing in the competition of species. If the growth of one species affects the equilibrium population of another adversely, it must be because it causes an increase in its death rate or a decrease in its birth rate. The dynamics of population change is complex, and we need not explore it here except to warn the reader that crude birth and death rates are often not very significant and that the age distribution of a population has an important effect on the crude birth and death rates. From the point of view of the growth or decline of a group or species, the most significant birth rate may be the net birth rate of those who survive to adulthood. Thus, an increase in infant mortality has much the same effect on the dynamics of a population as a decline in the birth rate.

In the case of the human group, the birth rate consists of two components: a *natural* component of children who are born into the group and a *conversion* component of people who join the group after birth or early childhood. Thus, people may be born Americans, or Catholics, or even Republicans, for children are usually brought up in the faith or social group of their parents. In a society like that of India, with strong occupational castes, a man may even be born into an occupation, for he has little chance of not following the occupation of his parents. On the other hand, there are also births into human groups after childhood; a man may become an American by naturalization and a Catholic or a Republican by conversion. Because of the powerful influence of the family on the children, however, there is a strong tendency for human groups to perpetuate themselves by natural birth. Catholics produce Catholics, Lutherans, Lutherans, and Amish Amish; Americans produce Americans and Germans Germans. If this were the only method of birth into a human group, conflict among groups would be confined to those arising out of differential reproduction; groups that grew more rapidly by natural reproduction would eventually begin to press for living space of some kind on groups that grew more slowly. Where groups can add to themselves and subtract from others by conversion, the dynamic processes are different and often very dramatic, and conflict between groups becomes more intense. This problem is considered in the next chapter.

7

THE GROUP AS A PARTY TO CONFLICT:

THE EPIDEMIOLOGICAL MODEL

In the preceding chapter, we drew attention to the similarity between the conflict of groups in human society and the competition of species in biological ecosystems. The competition of human groups, however, has many attributes that go beyond the simple model of ecological competition. The competition of biological species operates mainly by the impact that the number of one species has on the birth and death rates of other species. An individual element in a biological species can enter it only by being born and can leave it only by dying. Metamorphosis, where the caterpillar is apparently converted into a butterfly, may be regarded as an apparent exception to this, but, in spite of the great difference in their appearance, the biologist usually regards both caterpillar and butterfly as members of a single species, as they are identical from the genetic point of view.

In the case of the group in human society, as we have seen, additions and subtractions to the group may be made by conversion as well as by birth and death. This fact alone gives the human group a very different character and dynamics from that of the biological species. A lion never becomes a giraffe; but a Catholic does occasionally become a Protestant and vice versa, an Englishman occasionally becomes an American, and a healthy man gets sick and sick people get well. This shift from one group to another may take place for two very different reasons. In the first place, it may happen through some inner change or mutation in the dynamic processes of the person himself, quite unrelated to the outside environment. These mutational changes are probably rare in the case of changes in the image or mental structure; they may be commoner in the physical structure, where many degenerative diseases seem to be a product of the individual's own pattern of development rather than of any contagion from like cases outside him. The second type of group change is through contagion with one or more persons of another group. We catch the measles from someone who already has it. In a similar way, people catch religious or political views from people whom they meet.

Epidemiologists have developed interesting models of the process by which contagious diseases are spread through a population.[1] These models have a good deal of relevance to group conflict of the kind that is carried out by conversion. Indeed, the spread of an epidemic can be regarded as a special case of group conflict between the group of well people in the population and the group of sick people, or even, say, the group of people sick with a particular disease like mumps or syphilis. These groups are easily identifiable and form a partition of the total population, though they do not generally embody themselves in organizations and do not have much group consciousness. For this very reason, they are good examples of group competition without organizational admixture. Epidemiological systems, however, are not confined to physical health or disease. There is also an epidemiology of the image, that is, of the cognitive and affective structure of the individual, which may be of great importance in the interpretation of social movements, political and religious changes, and the shifting moods of belligerency toward one or another opponent that Richardson characterizes as *war moods*.

---

[1] See A. J. Lotka, *Elements of Mathematical Biology*, New York, Dover, 1936, chap. 8; and Lewis F. Richardson, *Arms and Insecurity*, Pittsburgh, Boxwood; and Chicago, Quadrangle, 1960, chap. 22.

THE GROUP AND CONFLICT: EPIDEMIOLOGICAL MODEL 125

It would be foolish to suggest that the simple epidemiological model is a sufficient explanation of phenomena as complex as a social movement. Nevertheless, the spread of Islam, or the Reformation, or Methodism, or Marxism, or Nazism in a society is a phenomenon not wholly unlike the spread of measles, and we may get some important insights from the simple models.

Let us begin, therefore, by postulating a society of n individuals, each of which can be characterized as either an h or a k. We might suppose that h stood for a healthy individual and k for a sick one. Then we suppose that, in each time period, there are a number of contacts between individuals, so that there are mn such meetings. m measures the congestion or degree of contact of the population; it is the average number of meetings per person. We can then suppose that sometimes, when an h meets a k, the h becomes a k: this is the phenomenon of *contagion*. We may suppose that contagion is less than complete: that only in 1 out of $1/g$ meetings of k and h does the h become a k. g then measures the contagiousness of the condition. We further suppose that a proportion s out of the mn meetings, totaling mns, are meetings of an h and a k; the others, $(1 - s)mn$, are either h meeting h or k meeting k, which is not significant from the point of view of the contagion. In each time period, then, there are $gmns$ cases in which an h becomes a k. The proportion s is some function of h and k. If this function is known, an expression can be obtained for the course of the epidemic, that is, the growth of k through time.

A graphic solution to the problem is shown in Fig. 7.1. We measure k vertically on OK, s to the left from O, time to the right from O. The curve $OS_0S_1S_2\cdots N$ is the s curve showing the proportion s of h–k meetings for various values of k. The function must have the property that $s = 0$ when $k = 0$ and also when $k = n$ ($h = 0$), as obviously there cannot be any meetings of an h with a k if there is no h or no k. The simplest assumption is that the function exhibits a maximum somewhere between $k = 0$ and $k = n$, as in the figure, but we do not have to assume a smooth or continuous

Fig. 7.1

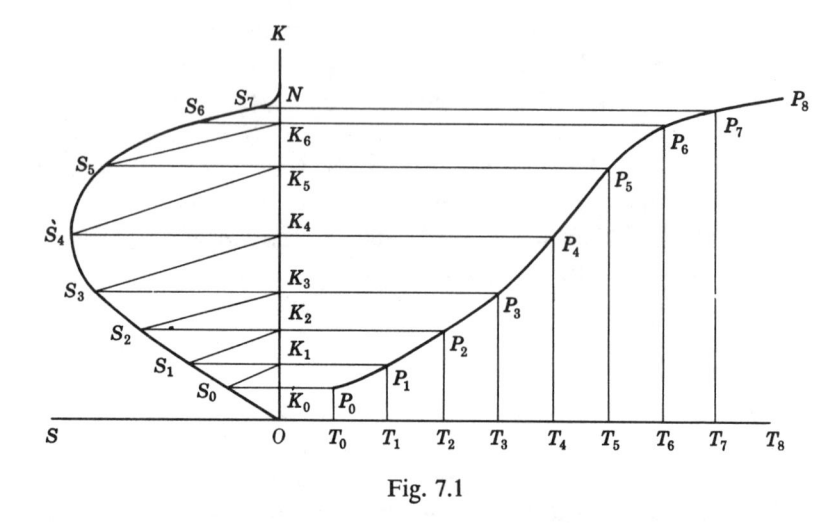

function. If the meetings of h and k are purely accidental and random, we should expect the maximum at the halfway point $h = k = n/2$. We do not have to limit ourselves to this assumption, however, and, in the figure, we suppose that h (the uninfected) makes a positive effort to avoid contact with k; in this case, the maximum will be shifted toward the point N, and the curve will be asymmetrical. Now given the s curve, we can construct the curve $P_0 P_1 \cdots P_8$, showing the time course of the infection as follows. Suppose we start from a given level of k, OK_0. (We must start from some positive level, for if there are no k individuals, there can be no contagion.) The number of persons infected in the next time period is $K_0 K_1 = gmns$. We have, therefore, $gmn = K_0 K_1 / K_0 S_0$, which is the slope of the line $S_0 K_1$. This we suppose to be a constant, so that, in order to find the position of K_2, we simply draw $S_1 K_2$ parallel to $S_0 K_1$, and similarly for subsequent points. The time course of the epidemic can then be plotted by laying off equal distances $T_1 T_2$, $T_2 T_3$, etc., on OT and erecting $T_0 P_0 = OK_0$, $T_1 P_1 = OK_1$, and so on. It will be seen immediately from the figure that, the bigger the slope of $S_0 K_1$, etc., that is, the bigger gmn, the more rapidly will the contagion spread; that is, the more contagious the condition and the larger the proportion of persons coming into contact, the more rapid will be the initial course of the epidemic—not a very surprising result but, still, one on which we can build. The final result, however, depends not at all on the contagiousness of the condition; if the system continues, eventually everyone in the population will be infected. Even if well people try to avoid contagion by avoiding the sick k's, as in Fig. 7.1, this merely means that the epidemic will be slower at first but will eventually reach the same degree of infection. The evil day is merely postponed.

Let us now modify the model by supposing that people recover spontaneously; that is, after an h has become a k, in a given period of time t, he reverts to h again. We suppose again that there are no births or deaths, and we suppose that there is no immunity; having had the condition k gives a person no protection against catching it again. The common cold seems to be not far from this condition. Then, in Fig. 7.2, we reproduce the construction of Fig. 7.1. Beginning at K_0, we proceed to K_3 as before. Following Fig. 7.1, we would then go to K_4, but we now suppose that those who were infected in the first period now recover, so that the total increase in k in the fourth period is not K_3K_4 but K_3K_4', where $K_4'K_4 = K_0K_1$, the number infected in the first period. We assume here a four-period course of the condition; that is, after having had the condition k for four periods, a person reverts to h. From K_4', we go on as before, with $K_4'K_5$ new cases of k, and K_5K_5' $(= K_1K_2)$ recoveries, the net increase being $K_4'K_5'$. It is clear that, at K_4, there is a sharp check to the spread of the disease and that, in fact, the number infected will reach an equilibrium short of the whole population, unlike the first model in which the whole population eventually becomes infected. The equilibrium will be reached at a point K_e, where the new infections K_eK_e' are just equal to the number of new infections of t periods back, in this case, K_dK_d' or $K_4'K_5$, where t is the time it takes to recover. We notice that K_e and K_d must lie on opposite sides of the maximum s, with gmn constant. The point of equilibrium, therefore, will be beyond the point of maximum s by an amount that depends directly on the duration of the disease in the individual; that is, the longer the duration of the disease, the more people will ultimately be affected. This is not surprising, but a surprising and paradoxical conclusion follows. It is that the equilibrium proportion infected is likely to be less, the closer the maximum of the s curve

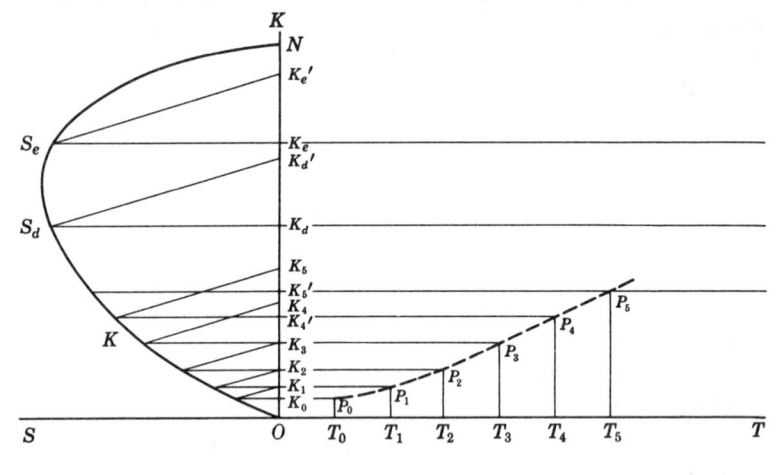

Fig. 7.2

to $k = 0$; that is, the less people try to avoid infection, and the more they actually go out of their way to meet infected people, the fewer will be infected in equilibrium. The rationale of this conclusion is that, if people try to avoid infection, this merely delays the spread of the disease at first, but eventually a larger proportion of the population will have to be infected before the new infections just balance the recoveries.

Now let us introduce doctors into the population. This means that, when a k meets an h who is a doctor, instead of the h becoming k, the k becomes h, with a given degree of probability; that is, out of r significant meetings of an h and a k, rg h's will become k, and rd k's will become h. The net result is that $r(g - d)$ h's will become

k. The proportion d depends on two further factors: the proportion of doctors in the population and the chance of a doctor effecting a cure. The important conclusion, however, is that the introduction of doctors into the population merely affects the contagiousness of the disease; it does not affect its equilibrium incidence unless $d \geq g$, in which case the contagion is that of health rather than of sickness. In terms of Fig. 7.1, the introduction of doctors simply lowers the slope of lines such as $S_0 K_1$. As long as this slope is positive, however, indicating a positive net coefficient of contagion, the growth of k will continue; all that the decline in the coefficient of contagion means is that the curve $P_0 P_1 \cdots P_9$ becomes flatter. It takes longer for the population to become infected, but as long as any remain uninfected, the epidemic will continue. If the coefficient of contagion falls to zero, which will be the case if $g = d$, the epidemic will stop at whatever point it has reached. If the coefficient of contagion becomes negative, a growth curve in the opposite direction, with h growing at the expense of k, will be set up. In Fig. 7.1, this would eventually carry the population to $k = 0$, i.e., to complete health. In Fig. 7.1, therefore, either the population moves to complete health or to complete sickness; there is no equilibrium possible at any halfway position unless $d = g$. Whether the introduction of doctors does any ultimate good or not, therefore, depends on whether d can reach the critical value g. If it cannot, then the coefficient of contagion remains positive, and doctors merely delay the transformation of the population from health to sickness; they cannot stop it. The moment d becomes greater than g, however, nothing can stop the population from becoming completely healthy. When d is in the neighborhood of g, therefore, a very slight improvement in medicine may make an enormous difference to the equilibrium health of the population.

Fig. 7.1, of course, is very unrealistic. In Fig. 7.2 again, so long as d is greater than g, the number of sick will continue to grow to the equilibrium value of K'_e. An increase in d merely slows up the growth of sickness; it cannot reverse the process until d becomes greater than g. What happens, then, depends on the assumptions of the model. We might assume, to make the model symmetrical, that a healthy person will become sick again after a certain time interval t_h by spontaneous processes, e.g., aging, quite apart from contacts with others. If this is the case, then even if the coefficient of contagion is negative, the system will move to an equilibrium somewhere below the level of k that corresponds to the maximum s. The larger t_h, the smaller will k be in the equilibrium; that is, if it takes a long time for a well person to become sick again by spontaneous processes, there will be many well people and few sick people in the equilibrium position, but if it takes only a short time for a well person to become sick, the equilibrium will be close to the maximum s. Thus, in Fig. 7.3, we show some possible growth curves: K_0K_1, K_0K_2, and K_0K_3 are the growth-of-sickness curves for successively

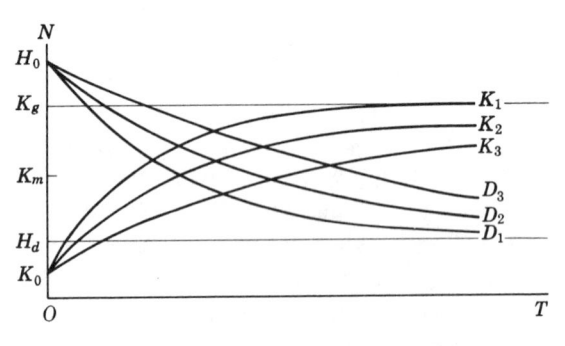

Fig. 7.3

smaller values of the positive coefficient of contagion; all the curves move to the equilibrium volume of sickness, OK_g. If K_m is the point of maximum significant meetings, s, K_mK_g depends directly, though not linearly, on the period of sickness, t_s. Similarly, H_0D_1, H_0D_2, and H_0D_3 are growth-of-health curves from the position H_0 for successively larger negative coefficients of contagion. These, too, reach an equilibrium at a volume of health equal to NH_d, where K_mH_d varies directly with the period of spontaneous health. If d

THE GROUP AND CONFLICT: EPIDEMIOLOGICAL MODEL 131

and g fluctuate with time around the value $d = g$, the system will fluctuate somewhere within the two equilibrium boundaries: when d exceeds g, it moves toward H_d, and when g exceeds d, it moves towards K_g. In this system, doctors do either a great deal of good or no good at all.

One further complication must be introduced into the model. Up to now, we have assumed no births or deaths in the population, and we must relax this assumption. The simplest model that includes births (additions to the population) and deaths (subtractions from the population) is obtained by assuming first an equilibrium population, so that the number of births in any period is equal to the number of deaths, and second, that deaths are all from the sick part of the population and births are all healthy. This means simply that, in any period, a certain number of k (the deaths) are replaced by an equal number of h (the births), without regard to the processes of contagion. The case, therefore, is very similar to Fig. 7.2 except that, for the moment, we consider the number of spontaneous recoveries (replacements of k by h) as constant. Thus, suppose, in Fig. 7.2, that we start again at K_0; K_0K_1 is the number of new cases of sickness. If now the number of births (and deaths) B, is equal to K_0K_1 the system will return to K_0 and K_0 will be an equilibrium position. If however, B is less than K_0K_1, the system at the end of the first period will be at some point between K_0 and K_1, and a process of contagion will start. It will continue past the maximum s to the point K_r, where $K_rK_{r+1} = B$, at which point an equilibrium will be established. If B is greater than K_0K_1, the system at the end of the first period will be below K_0 and will move toward $k = 0$. At some point here, this model breaks down, because we cannot maintain either the assumption that the number of births and the number of deaths are constant or that all the deaths are from the sick population; otherwise, when we get to $k = 0$, there will be no sick persons left to die, and deaths would fall to zero. Models with changing population are complex and would carry us beyond the purposes of this analysis. It is clear, however, that the introduction of births and deaths into the models increases the possibility of healthy equilibrium positions where k is small, if the coefficient of contagion is small enough.

In the case of social groups, a somewhat different model is appropriate here in regard to births and deaths. Social groups generally, though not always, tend to perpetuate their kind; children of Catholic parents, for instance, are usually brought up as Catholics and only become members of another religious group, including, for this purpose, atheists and agnostics among religious groups, by conversion. Consequently, in our model, children of the h's will tend to be h's also, and children of the k's will tend to be k's also. The processes of birth and death, therefore, do not discriminate so so much in favor of one group as they might do in the sickness-health case. Each group may be assumed to have its own natural rate of growth, which may, of course, be zero or negative, through the excess of its births over its deaths. If the total population is in equilibrium, of course, any excess of births over deaths in one group must be balanced by an excess of deaths over births in the other; this would not have to be true in a growing population. In an equilibrium population model, we may suppose some change in the number of each group due to the balance of births and deaths; unless there is a marked difference between the groups in their birth and death rates, however, this factor will be very small and will not much affect the dynamics of contagion or conversion. There are cases, however, where the differential rates of natural increase of different groups is an important source of tension in a society, especially where the contagiousness of the groups is extremely low, so that there is practically no conversion from one to the other. One thinks, for instance, of the Catholic-Protestant ratio in the Netherlands or the proportion of Negroes to East Indians in Trinidad or British Guiana.

The effect of mixed marriages, in this regard, is also interesting. A group may be dominant in marriage in the sense that the children of a mixed marriage will tend to belong to the dominant group. In this sense, Catholics tend to be dominant in Catholic-Protestant marriages, where the children are usually brought up as Catholics, and, in the United States, especially in the South, because of the social concept of race, Negroes are dominant in Negro-white unions. It is a curious paradox that the group that is most concerned about its purity is least likely to be dominant in the genetics of group perpetuation and transmission, and this may be a real handicap to it in group conflict.

The fact that conversion, of necessity, involves a rejection of the cultural group of the parents creates psychological hazards in many areas of group conflict at the adult level and accounts for a good deal of the intensity of group conflict by conversion as against group conflict by family transmission. We see this phenomenon in fields as diverse as religious conflict and economic development. It is hardly too much to assert that conversion can only take place where there is deep and uncomfortable ambivalence toward the parents or toward the culture of the parents. This may be inherent in the parental culture itself, especially in its child-rearing practices. There seems to be a distinct relationship between repressive child rearing and revolutionary attitudes in the adult, on the one hand, and permissive child rearing and conservative attitudes in the adult, on the other. Too much stress should not be placed on this relationship, however; if the culture of the parents is challenged by a much stronger and more successful culture, as in China, then even a culture with relatively permissive child-rearing practices may produce revolutionaries. One of the deepest problems related to economic development under any system is that inevitably it involves a group conflict between the group that keeps to the old ways and the group that adopts the new ways, and this frequently involves a parent-child conflict that puts deep psychological strains on the society. The parent-child relationship is perhaps the most intense of all human relationships and the most important in the psychological dynamics of the individual. The intensity with which aspersions on the quality of one's mother are rejected in almost every culture is a testimony to the intensity of this relationship. Any deep group change in adulthood, whether this is the kind of change involved in economic development and the shift from subsistence agriculture to modern industry (in the field or in the town) or whether it is the change involved in adopting a new political or religious faith, involves persuading the convert that his mother was all wrong. This can only be done at some psychological cost and may account for some of the violence and excesses of behavior that characterize every revolutionary period.

Another property of epidemiological systems that is of great importance in diseases of the body is the property of *immunity*, that is, the case where recovery from the disease greatly lessens the chance of reinfection. There are parallels to this phenomenon in the conflict of groups and in changes in the individual image. A person who has been a Communist, or almost anything, and repented is very unlikely ever to return to the fold. Childhood indoctrination, likewise, often seems to play a role almost like that of vaccination: a child brought up in a heavily religious atmosphere, for instance, seems often immune to the infection of currently fashionable religious movements. We must beware of stretching the biological analogy too far here; the transformation of the image is complex and often unpredictable. Nevertheless, in the over-all dynamics of social groups, the phenomenon of immunity to certain ideas, groups, or movements is not to be neglected.

The equations of an epidemic with developing immunity are rather complicated, mainly because we can no longer assume a constant s function, the proportion of significant meetings now depending on the proportion of immune people, which grows constantly in the course of the spread of the infection. It is a little hard to illustrate, therefore, with our simple graphic technique, though the general pattern can be visualized. We now have three classes in the population, for we must add i, the number of people who have recovered from being k (sick) and, therefore, are immune to infection. The proportion of significant meetings s is now a function not simply of k and $n - k$ but of k and $n - k - i$ ($= h$, the infectable part of the population). Thus, suppose, in Fig. 7.4, ON is the total population, and we start with OK_1 sick (k), K_1B_1 infectable but well (h), and B_1N immune (i). Then, the s curve must run from O to B_1, not from O to N, as before, for there could be no significant

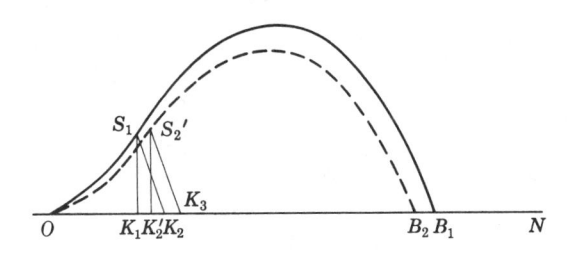

Fig. 7.4

meetings if the number of sick were equal to the total population less the number of immune. Starting from the position K_1, K_1S_1 is the number of significant meetings, K_1K_2 the number of new infections, and K_2K_2' the number of recoveries from infections t periods before, so that we start the next period from K_2'. The number of immune, however, has now increased from B_1N to B_2N, where $B_1B_2 = K_2'K_2$. There is now, therefore, a new s curve, dotted in the figure, from O to B_2; this we may expect to be lower than the previous curve. The number of significant meetings in the next period, then, is $K_2'S_2'$, and so we go on, with the s curve falling and shrinking in each period. It is clear that k will grow up to a maximum and will then decline as the number of immune grows.

If there are no births and deaths and if immunity once achieved is perpetual, it is clear that this process will go on until the whole population is immune and, therefore, healthy ($h = n$, $k = 0$). If immunity is not perpetual but only persists for a given time after recovery from infection, the downward movement of the s curve may eventually come to a halt when the number of new immunes is just balanced by the number who have lost their immunity. At this point, there may be an equilibrium of the type of Fig. 7.2, where the number of new infections is just balanced by the number of recoveries from past infection. This may not coincide, however, with the point at which the s curve ceases to decline, and an interesting possibility of cyclical movements opens up. The k group may first rise, reach a maximum because of developing immunity, decline with increasing immunity and the fall of the s curve, and then begin to rise again as the fall of the s curve is arrested by the increasing loss of immunity with the passage of time. Such cyclical movements are not infrequent in the incidence of infectious diseases, and cycles in taste and fashion may be related to this kind of phenomenon. A new fashion, for instance, expands rapidly into the population; there is no immunity against it. There is, moreover, a certain antagonism toward the old fashion simply because it is old, and the new fashion at first, therefore, is highly contagious. Eventually, however, the new fashion becomes old, and people become immune to it; and a still newer fashion takes over till eventually, perhaps, we are back at the old fashion again. We may note that we could treat the phenomenon of immunity as a simple loss of contagiousness, that is, a decline in g, which would be reflected in Fig. 7.4 as a continual steepening of S_1K_2 as the infection proceeded, without any change in the s curve.

The introduction of births and deaths into the model does not change it materially as far as an equilibrium population is concerned, for the birth and death process also operates as a continual loss of immunity in the population. We may suppose, for instance, that the newly born are not immune and that deaths are divided between the immune and the nonimmune. If the disease itself is not fatal and does not affect the expectation of life, then we could assume that deaths are divided between the immune and the nonimmune in the proportion in which they exist in the total population. In an equilibrium population, therefore, where births equal deaths, there will be a net increase in the nonimmune part of the population as a result of the birth-death process, for only part of the deaths are nonimmune and all the births are nonimmune. The case differs from that in which there is simple loss of immunity after a period of time in that, as the infection proceeds and a larger proportion of the population becomes immune, there will be more immune and fewer nonimmune among the deaths, and, hence, the excess of nonimmune births over the nonimmune deaths will increase; this effect, therefore, is larger, the more people are immune. Here again, there is an interesting possibility of cyclical movements: a disease of the body or a fashion of the mind sweeps through a nonimmune population but is checked and eventually reduced by the rise of immunity; the replacement of the old population by new births, however, eventually creates a new nonimmune generation, and the stage is set for the resurgence of the old disease or fashion. We may note that the assumption that the disease in itself affects the death rate makes the whole analysis much more complicated, as we cannot now assume an equilibrium population without very farfetched assumptions about offsetting movements in deaths that are not caused by the disease. The analysis of nonequilibrium populations, however, would carry us beyond the needs of this chapter.

In applying simple mechanical models such as we have explored in this and in previous chapters to the enormously complex dynamics of conflict in society, we should look for insights rather than for exact correspondences. We really know very little about the dynamics of the human personality, and it is on these individual processes of immense complexity, resting, as they do, in the tortuous field of symbolic systems, that group and other conflicts of society ultimately depend. When we reflect, for instance, on how little we really know about the phenomenon of conversion, or even about the absence of conversion, that steady replacement of parents by like-minded children that is the major source of group and cultural stability, we should be hesitant to place on these very simple mechanical models more weight than they can bear. Nevertheless, the simple model can often symbolize or capture some essence of a much more complex process, and as we observe the actual processes of social dynamics, we shall often be reminded of the behavior of the simple models that we have been discussing.

Let us consider as an example the general quality of hostility or friendliness of a society. This is a quality not easy to measure but clearly meaningful to recognize. We notice a difference even from city to city within a fairly homogeneous society like the United States: some cities seem to be racked with factional conflict—labor-management relations are bad, party strife and religious divisions are bitter, and racial feeling is high—whereas other cities, often in the same general vicinity, seem to avoid excesses of conflict and relations are generally good-humored even where there are sources of real conflict. As we move from culture to culture, the differences are even more striking, as shown, for instance, in Mead's classic studies of the belligerent and quarrelsome Mundugumor in contrast with the gentle Arapesh or by the even more striking extremes of the Dobuans and the Zuni.[2] Even within Western culture, we find some countries that seem to be in a perpetual internal turmoil, whereas, in others, life is placid to the point of boredom. Much work needs to be done on this problem; nevertheless, the models of this chapter provide some explanatory insights. Thus, suppose we could partition a population into two groups, which we might call hostiles and friendlies. This is a great oversimplification, as, in fact, there is not only a continuum of personality types, but it is very doubtful whether this continuum can be expressed in any single, one-dimensional scale such as the hostile-friendly scale. Nevertheless, this heroic assumption has the virtue of enabling us to apply the models of this chapter. Let us suppose, for instance, that we give away our value presuppositions by classifying hostiles as sick (k's) and friendlies as healthy (h's), while begging the question whether it is not occasionally good to be hostile, for our model knows no moral distinction between the h's and k's. We suppose that, when a hostile meets a

---

[2] See Margaret Mead, *Sex and Temperament in Three Primitive Societies*, London, Routledge, 1935; and Ruth Benedict, *Patterns of Culture*, New York, New American Library, 1946.

hostile, both simply remain hostile (we are not here considering degrees of hostility), and likewise when a friendly meets a friendly. When, however, a hostile meets a friendly, a conflict of images is set up, and there is a chance of change in the image. If the friendly is merely a publican of a previous chapter, there is a chance g that the contact will infect him with hostility, so that, from the k–h meeting, two k's emerge. If the friendly is a saint, who corresponds, in our previous model, to the doctor, there is a chance that the hostile may be converted, and the k–h meeting produces two h's. So far, the model is identical with our model of Fig. 7.1. If g, the proportion of k–h contacts that results in two k's, exceeds d, the proportion that results in two h's, the number of hostiles will increase at a rate dependent on the coefficient of contagion until the whole population is hostile; if d exceeds g, then the number of friendlies will increase until the whole population is friendly. The end position of the population depends solely on the subtle balance between saints, devils, and publicans. If there are not enough saints, the rest of the population will become entirely hostile; just as a few more may make the difference between highly hostile or highly friendly end positions of the dynamic process.

As in the case of bodily disease, so with the diseases of the image, there may be a curative operation of the sheer lapse of time. There may be a certain time interval after which a hostile becomes a friendly, if he has not been reinfected with hostility meanwhile. Our model of Fig. 7.2, therefore, has important implications in explaining equilibriums of hostility or friendliness; if the phenomenon of healing through lapse of time takes place, this leads to equilibriums short of total hostility. One might, I suppose, take an extremely gloomy view of human nature and argue that friendliness likewise, in some cases, depreciates through lapse of time until it is transformed into hostility. This would simply mean, however, that a dynamic process of increasing friendliness will culminate in an equilibrium short of 100 percent friendliness. The introduction of births and deaths into the model presents some features that may differ from the model of physical disease. Friendly people may live longer than hostile people, but the evidence for this is doubtful, and, in any case, the differential is small. On the whole, therefore, we can again assume that death removes both friendly and hostile at random, so that both friendly and hostile die in about the same proportion. Births, however, are not neutral, for if we consider the significant population as consisting only of adults, a child being born into the adult population only when he reaches maturity, hostile parents tend to produce hostile children and friendly parents friendly children, simply through the interactive processes within the family. If the birth rate of friendlies exceeds the death rate of friendlies, if, for instance, friendly parents have more children than hostiles or if children have a natural tendency to be friendly in spite of the hostility of the parents, the birth and death processes tend to dampen the growth of hostility and to produce equilibriums even in a process of dynamic increase of hostility that is short of total hostility. If birth and death rates of friendlies and hostiles are equal, this factor does not affect the process of infection either toward increasing hostility or toward increasing friendliness. If the birth rate of friendlies is less than their death rate, which implies, if total births and deaths are equal, that the birth rate of hostiles is greater than their death rate, then the birth-death process adds hostiles in each period and moves the equilibrium toward the hostile end of the scale.

It may be objected to this analysis that we have so far assumed a simple black or white picture of the personality: persons are either hostile or friendly in the above models, and nothing in between. In fact, of course, persons exhibit many grades and dimensions of hostility and friendliness; a person may be hostile toward one person and friendly toward another, or even may feel both hostile and friendly toward the same person. Ambivalence is a most important element in the human personality. In the simple quasi-mechanical models of this chapter, we cannot, of course, take account of all these complexities. Nevertheless, the complexities by no means destroy the insights gathered from the simple models. Thus, the fact that a person may exhibit various degrees of hostility or friendliness can be incorporated in the model by the simple device of supposing that each person consists of, say, 10 character units, any number of which from 0 to 10 can be counted as hostile and the remainder as friendly. The total population is then considered as $10n$ character units rather than as n people. The s curve of Figs. 7.1 and 7.2 will probably be more complex; it may, for instance, be bimodal, for if most people are neutral (with 5 friendly and 5 hostile character units), there may be few significant interactions. There may also, however, be complex interactions within the personality; there are internal interactions between the friendly and the hostile elements of the individual character that may have a dynamics of their own, leading to a dominance of one or the other. There may, therefore, be different s curves for different distributions of the character units among the individuals. The model is a highly artificial one, and there is no point in pressing it too far. It is not unreasonable to suppose, however, that the basic dynamic processes of infection and recovery still obtain even for a system of character units, so that our previous analysis is not seriously modified. If the s curve is bimodal, the possibility of equilibrium positions in each half of the curve develops, so that both a predominantly hostile and a predominantly friendly equilibrium might exist; which the system reaches depends on where it starts.

These epidemiological growth systems are instructive in the study of general levels of hostility or friendliness in particular populations. They are not well adapted to situations in which there are sudden changes, such as the outbreak of war, or sudden conversion to a new religion or political faith. Richardson pioneered in the discussion of these systems in his article on war moods.[3] The simple epidemiological theory of the preceding pages cannot account for the extremely rapid rise in hostility at the outbreak of a war nor for the often

[3] Lewis F. Richardson, "War Moods," *Psychometrica*, XIII (1948), 147–174, 197–232.

equally rapid decline at its close. Here we suppose that the population is again divided into two groups: k, which is in favor of war with a specified country, and h, which is not in favor of such a war. At the outbreak of a war, k usually rises with startling rapidity, perhaps from a low level to nearly 100 per cent of the population within a matter of days, or even hours. This happened in Britain, for instance, in the first few days of August, 1914, and, again, in September, 1939; it happened in the United States within a few hours after the Japanese attack on Pearl Harbor. These very sudden changes in public sentiment cannot be accounted for by any epidemic-like spread of hostility from one person to another; they are too sudden and dramatic. Richardson's own explanation is that the person is inhabited by two attitudes, one being conscious and dominant and the other being unconscious and repressed. There is evidence for this assumption, of course, in psychoanalytic theory and in the success of psychotherapy based on it. This can be symbolized by writing the dominant mood on top of the repressed mood. Thus, a mood that is overtly friendly but unconsciously hostile would be written $\frac{\text{(friendly)}}{\text{(hostile)}}$. The possible course of a complete cycle of international relations is then outlined below:

$$\text{Peace} \to \text{Arms Race} \to \text{War} \to \text{Attrition} \to$$
$$\frac{\text{Friendly}}{\text{Friendly}} \to \frac{\text{Friendly}}{\text{Hostile}} \to \frac{\text{Hostile}}{\text{Friendly}} \to \frac{\text{Hostile}}{\text{War-weary}} \to$$
$$\text{Armistice} \to \text{Postwar} \to \text{Peace}$$
$$\frac{\text{War-weary}}{\text{Hostile}} \to \frac{\text{War-weary}}{\text{Friendly}} \to \frac{\text{Friendly}}{\text{Friendly}}$$

We are considering the relations of two nations, or one nation vis-à-vis the rest of the world, and considering the attitudes of a single nation. We begin with a state of peace in which both the overt and the underlying attitudes are friendly. We now suppose an arms race or some similar Richardson process in mutual interaction that leads to a deterioration of the underlying relationship from friendliness to hostility, while the overt relationship remains friendly. At the outbreak of war, there is a sudden reversal of this order; we may compare the situation to that of an iceberg that tips over into a new position. There is some critical point in the growth of covert hostility at which the covert and overt attitudes are reversed; this can happen very suddenly and marks the outbreak of open hostilities. Richardson then introduces a third attitude, that of war weariness, somewhat intermediate between hostility and friendliness, and supposes that, as the war proceeds, the covert attitude gradually changes to increasing war weariness and that, at a certain point (the armistice), there is again a reversal of covert and overt attitudes, the war-weary attitude dominating the hostile attitude. Then, in the postwar period, the underlying hostility, assuming now a Richardson process of increasing friendliness, gradually changes to friendliness, and we end up at a condition of peace again.

Richardson's account of the war cycle has obvious limitations, though it is illuminating and suggestive. The distinction between overt and covert attitudes is important and undoubtedly accounts for the explosive nature of many conflict situations, not only in international relations but in industrial life, in family affairs, and in domestic politics. The Richardson processes of mutually increasing hostility may go on, for instance, at the covert level, while, superficially, an appearance of harmony is maintained, until suddenly the pressure of covert hostility becomes too great, and the situation flares up—into a strike, or a family quarrel, or even a civil war.

A factor that Richardson neglected is the impact of the mass media of communication on the spread of attitudes of hostility or friendliness. Epidemics of ideas, attitudes, and fashions are not only carried by the simple contagion of face-to-face communication but are air-borne by the swift dissemination of messages in newspapers, radio, television, and so on. The rapid spread of hostile attitudes, for instance, at the outbreak of a war may be attributed not to simple contagion but to the fact that almost everyone is in the same state of mind of a precarious balance between overt friendliness (or neutrality) and covert hostility and almost everyone receives the same information at the same time through the press and the radio, which tips the balance and causes a large-scale reversal of attitudes. At this point, simple epidemiological models are not particularly helpful, for what are involved are the symbolic aspects of the national image.

Richardson's covert-overt model may throw light on a good many dramatic phenomena in history—mass conversions, mass defections, and revolutions. Sometimes, the existing social group retains the overt loyalty and support of the people at the same time that, covertly, this support is being eroded away. This is particularly likely to be the case where the fear of violent consequences is an important element in the support of the existing group or regime. It is hardly too much to say that every group that attracts support by violence and terror will suffer an erosion of its covert support and that, if this goes on long enough, the group will be suddenly overthrown by a mass transfer of allegiance to another group. The relative impermanence of particular tyrannies is clear testimony to this principle, even though the problem of replacing a tyranny by a better system rather than by another tyranny involves a deeper level of social dynamics that is not always achieved.

8

THE ORGANIZATION AS A PARTY TO CONFLICT

There is a strong tendency in human society for the unorganized group to develop organization and for organizations to develop even where there has been no consciousness of a group previously, in which case the organization itself creates the group that it expresses and embodies. Consequently, group conflict tends easily to pass over into organizational conflict, and the growth of organizations themselves may create conflict where no previous consciousness of conflict existed. Furthermore, the perception of conflict with other organizations is frequently an important and sometimes a dominating factor in determining the behavior of a particular organization. Organizations frequently organize themselves against something, and, in the absence of a perception of conflict, their reason for existence is weakened or disappears, and they suffer from internal disorganization or even dissolution. Conversely, the perception of conflict is frequently heightened by the existence of organizations that are specialized for conflict. The existence of weapons predisposes both animals and men to fight, the existence of specialized conflict agencies such as armed forces predisposes nations to war, and whereas one would not want to accuse the profession of law of promoting litigation, there can be no doubt that familiarity with the law promotes litigiousness. By far the most impressive conflicts are those of organizations. Duels are less impressive than war, private lawsuits are less impressive than legislative struggles between parties or organized pressure groups, and a debate between two individuals is less impressive than the mighty clash of conflicting (and organized) ideologies or religions. I use the word "impressive" rather than "important" because I am not sure how to evaluate the importance of a conflict, but there can be little doubt that, by and large, the conflict of organizations makes more impression on the world than merely private quarrels.

Group conflicts either tend to be below the surface of consciousness, in which case they approach the condition that we have called competition rather than explicit conflict, or if they do rise to the surface of consciousness, they frequently produce organizations and, hence, transform themselves into organizational conflicts. These organizations may be temporary, like the informal organization of a mob under a leader or of industrial conflict among unorganized workers. There is a tendency, however, for groups to develop more formal organization, as we see it, for instance, in the development of churches out of religious movements, trade unions out of a labor force, or corporations out of informal partnerships and of nation-states out of national groups. We shall not go far wrong, then, in supposing that organizational conflict is the dominant form. Before examining its properties, however, we must take a brief look at the nature of organization and organizational behavior.

An organization is a structure of units that are called *roles*, a role being that part of a person's behavior and potential behavior that is relevant to the organization. These roles, more exactly, the persons who occupy the roles in their capacity as an occupant, are connected by lines of communication and by mutual compatibility of expectations. Thus, in a business enterprise, we have the roles of president, vice-president, controller, accountant, general manager, plant manager, sales manager, production engineer, foreman, operative, janitor, and so on. The role is a job; the nature of the

THE ORGANIZATION AS A PARTY TO CONFLICT   147

job to be done, to a very large extent governs the behavior of the person doing it. We expect a manager to behave like a manager and a janitor like a janitor, no matter who occupies the role. It is true, of course, that the personality of the occupant makes some impression on the role itself. This is particularly true of the higher and more responsible roles. Nevertheless, for most roles and for most occupants, the nature of the role itself exerts a predominant influence on the behavior of the occupant in the role.

Roles may be classified according to a hierarchical, or *line*, classification or according to a division of labor, or *staff*, classification. Any organization will have some kind of hierarchy, formal or informal. There will be some communications within it that take the form of orders or instructions, and these invariably pass from higher to lower members of the hierarchy. The familiar rankings of pope, cardinals, archbishops, bishops, priests, or commander-in-chief, generals, colonels, majors, captains, lieutenants, sergeants, corporals, privates, or president, vice-president, dean, department chairman, professor, or president, general manager, branch manager, superintendent, foreman, operative are all examples of the universal pattern of line organization. Each role in a hierarchy, except the highest and the lowest, will have a number of roles beneath it to which it issues instructions and will be a member of a group of roles of equal status that receives instructions from a higher role.

Not only instructions, however, but information passes both up and down the hierarchy. A *decision* in any role is made as a result of information received as well as instructions. Instructions always have to be more general than the situations in which they have to be carried out. They set limits for the behavior of those who receive them but do not prescribe the exact behavior to be employed in all circumstances. To try to do this would be to destroy the whole purpose of organization, which is to enable the higher members of the hierarchy to control broad lines of behavior without having to channel through their minds the enormous amount of information that would be necessary to prescribe behavior in detail. The hierarchy, therefore, operates as an information filter upward, with each level of the hierarchy only passing up to the next such information as is considered relevant. The president of the corporation does not want to know that a particular machine in plant X needs oiling; the pope does not want to know the troubles of a particular parish priest in Bolivia; the general does not want to know the feelings of a particular private. The organization is thus an apparatus mainly set up to shield the executive from information. Similarly, on the downward flow of instructions, the higher the level, the more general the instructions. The president of the corporation does not want to tell a particular operative what to do with his machine; the pope does not pass on the plans for a new church building in the Philippines; the general does not set the menu for Thursday's dinner in camp X.

The simple hierarchical model is rarely adequate to describe an organization. In addition to the line organization, there is almost always a staff that is auxiliary to a particular position in the hierarchy or to some group within the organization. The main task of the staff is to collect and transmit information outside the line channels, which will give the executive in the upper ranks of the hierarchy some independent check on the general state of the organization. This is the main function of accountants, statisticians, market research men, spies, intelligence officers, stool pigeons, secret police, papal legates, ambassadors, and so on. The need for these staff sources of information is twofold. In the first place, there is need for information about the environment of the organization beyond what is received by members at the end of the line. It is usually by its humblest members that an organization directly touches its external environment, for these members constitute the social surface or the extremities of the organization. Thus it is the salesclerks who are the contacts with the selling-market environment of a great department or chain store; it is the parish priest who is the chief contact of the Roman Catholic Church with its parishioners; it is the private soldier who is most likely to come into contact with the enemy. These sources of information may be likened to the touch receptors of the body: they inform the executives or upper members of the hierarchy about its immediate environment, or the conditions at the surface. They do not, however, bear much information about the larger environment, or conditions away from the surface. Just as the body has developed information sources in the eyes and ears that inform the "central agent" about matters at a distance through utilizing the wave motions of sound and light as information carriers, so organizations develop information sources in the staff to inform the central executive about matters at a distance. The image that the executive has of the organization and its environment, then, is built up from two sources of information: information that is filtered up the line from the lower members of the hierarchy at the surface of the organization and information that is funneled through a staff organization specialized in the detection of conditions at a greater distance.

The second function of staff organization is to check on the information received up the filter of the hierarchy. One of the difficulties of hierarchical organization is the dependency of the lower members of the hierarchy on the upper members. This dependency almost inevitably tends to distort the information that passes from lower to higher members of the hierarchy. The lower members tend to tell the higher members what they think will be acceptable rather than what they know to be true. This is particularly likely where the upper members are domineering, aristocratic, or proud and look down on the lower members as inferiors. Such executives, whether they are monarchs, barons, dictators, or movie magnates, tend to surround themselves with yes men. Their information systems, therefore, are subject to distortion, even to the point where a totally false image of the organization and its environment is created. These false images not infrequently result in disastrous policy decisions. The greater independence of a staff organization reduces the probability of distortions of information due to dependent personal relations, especially where the staff participates in a larger professional community and develops professional, peer-judged standards of conduct. Even in the case of staff organizations, however, the problem of dependence arises. One solution of this problem is the development of independent staff organizations that sell their services to many different clients, thus ensuring themselves and the clients against undue dependency on any one of them. Thus, the auditor is an independent check on the accountant and the management consultant on the junior executives and the research staff. Similarly, the Willmark operative checks up on the salesclerks of a store, and private detectives have frequently been employed to detect disaffection among employees. The United Nations secretariat performs something of this function of an independent outside agency in the information processes of its constituent states. This function, using again an analogy from the biological organism, might be called the *proprioceptive function*. Just as the body has information receptors that inform it directly as to the position of the limbs, so an organization needs information sources to give it an image of itself as well as an image of the environment.

The fundamental principle of behavior is much the same whether we are considering an individual acting on his own behalf or a person acting in an organizational role. In each case, the behavior unit has some image of the state of things of himself and his environment and especially some image of the possible alternative situations or positions that this state might take under various possible lines of behavior. A decision consists of a choice among alternative states. Involved in any decision, then, are two properties of the image. There must be a set of alternatives; that is, there must be some distinction between possible and impossible states of the relevant universe in the mind of the decider. Then there must also be an ordering of these possible states at least adequate to permit identification of the state at the top of the ordering. This best state is, of course, the one that is selected. This is frequently regarded as if it were a theory of rational behavior only. This, however, is too narrow a view. All behavior, in so far as the very concept of behavior implies doing one thing rather than another and, therefore, choosing one state rather than another, falls into the above pattern, even the behavior of the lunatic and the irrational or irresponsible and erratic person. The distinction between rational and irrational behavior lies in the degree of self-consciousness and the stability of the images involved rather than in any distinction of the principle of the optimum. We must not suppose that it is only the self-conscious parts of the image that govern behavior. The image both of the state of things, of the alternatives, and of the value ordering lies partly in the conscious and partly in the unconscious. Even the most stupid and irrational behavior always involves some kind of image of the state of affairs, and the behavior that is selected is that which seems best at the moment. Thus, the difference between rational and irrational behavior must be found in the broader, more consistent, and truer images of the rational behavior rather than in any difference in the principle of behavior itself. The rational person builds up an image of the relevant state of the universe that is reasonably consistent, responsive to suitable modifications from information received, organized with the information receptors into a coherent system, and valued according to a consistent though not rigid value ordering. The irrational person has a view of the relevant universe which is partial and incomplete, or false in the sense that behavior according to this view leads to unexpected results, but which also may be rigid, not subject to modification by information received, and valued by inconsistent and constantly shifting orderings, so that one state is preferred at one moment and a contrary state at another.

With this very brief sketch of a theory of organization and behavior, let us now return to the main theme of conflict, and consider the nature of a conflict system between organizations. For conflict to exist between two organizations, the following conditions must be fulfilled. First, each of the organizations must be present in the image of the responsible decision makers of the other. For simplicity, let us suppose that each organization has a single responsible decision maker, whom we will call the executive, whose decisions govern the role behavior of every member of his organization. In the minds of each of the executives, then, there must be an image of his own and of the other organization both as to their respective states and as to the value ordering that is imposed on relevant alternative states. Two organizations that are quite ignorant of each other obviously cannot be in conflict, though they might be in competition, in the sense that the actions of one might unknowingly affect the state of the other in a direction that it would value as worse. The second condition of conflict is that a decision on the part of either executive must affect the state of both organizations in value-significant directions. Two organizations that do not affect each other cannot be in competition and, therefore, cannot be in conflict. The third condition is that a decision on the part of either executive must affect the image of the state of the other in a direction that he regards as unfavorable. If every decision on the part of one produces a change in the state of the system that the other regards as favorable, that is, higher on his value scale, then there is no conflict between them.

The concept of the relevant state of the universe in the image of each organization is, of course, a complex one. It will include an image of the *extent* of both organizations and also probably an image of the power, or potential extent, of each organization. It also includes a dimension of hostility or friendliness or identification of each with the other. When two organizations, A and B, are hostile, then a movement to a state that A regards as worse for B is regarded as better by A, simply because it is thought to be worse for B.[1]

---

[1] We should perhaps distinguish between malevolent and nonmalevolent hostility. Malevolent hostility exists when A values positively his image of the worsening of B's position, simply because it is a worsening of B's position, without regard of its subsequent effects on A himself. Nonmalevolent hostility exists when A values positively a worsening of B's position, but only because of A's image of the consequences of this for A's own position; that is, the worsening

It should be observed that hostility is related to the image of the other in each organization, not to the self-images. Thus it is possible for A to like a certain move because A thinks that this injures B, whereas B might regard the move as beneficial to him. This would still indicate hostility.

In all cases of conflict, we have identified the field of conflict as that set of relevant variables within which conflict movements may occur that make one party worse off and one better off in their own estimation. In the case of the organization, a very important aspect of the field of conflict is the extent of the organization. The extent of an organization may have dimensions; it may be measured, for instance, by membership, or by income, or by territory. Wherever two organizations are expanding into a common field, so that possession of part of the field by one excludes the other, conflict is possible. Thus, two churches or two trade unions may be competing for members; two nations may be competing for territory; two corporations may be competing for sales and income. As long as both organizations wish to expand into the same field, conflict is almost inevitable. Much depends here, however, on the self-image of each organization. The existence of potential conflict in a field of expansion does not necessarily involve actual conflict, if the self-images of the organizations make them content with the existing situation. Thus, two nations may be content with their common boundary, like the United States and Canada, even though each could only expand across this boundary at the expense of the other. Similarly, two trade unions may be content with their respective

---

of B's position is valued only because it leads directly to a bettering of A's absolute or relative position. In the case of malevolent hostility, A may move to a position that weakens or injures himself, as long as it weakens and injures B sufficiently. In nonmalevolent hostility, A will never move to a position that weakens or injures himself, though he may move to positions that weaken or injure B. Hitler's attitude toward the Jews could almost certainly be described as malevolent hostility; two firms in competition are usually in nonmalevolent hostility, for neither desires injury to the other as such but only as a means to some other end. We might even push farther up the scale and notice the possibility of *benevolent hostility*, a situation where "this hurts me more than it hurts you"; A is forced to be hostile to B regretfully because of B's impact on A.

jurisdictions, even though each might possibly expand into the jurisdiction claimed by the other. Similarly, an employer and a union may stake out a boundary of rights and responsibilities that neither wishes to invade.

The condition that turns potential conflict into actual conflict might be described as *expansion pressure*; where the self-image of the organization attaches a high value to its expansion, or increase in extent in some field, whether membership, income, or territory, the possibilities of conflict are high. We can measure the expansion pressure by some desired or homeostatic rate of growth of the organization; that is, we suppose that there is some rate of growth that satisfies the self-image of the organization. If the rate of growth is below this ideal, the organization will be dissatisfied and will seek to expand faster; if it is above the ideal, the organization will slacken its efforts and not try to expand so fast. We can now make a weighted sum of the ideal rates of growth of all the organizations in a field. This we may call the no-conflict rate of growth for the whole field. If the field itself is growing at this rate, all organizations in it can achieve their ideal rates of growth, and there will be no conflict among them, at least, no conflict due to expansion competition. This assumes that the field is homogeneous and that each organization can expand into any part of it. In the case of spatial expansion, this is not so; each organization can usually expand only into that portion of space that is contiguous or at least convenient to it. This modification, however, does not, affect the fundamental principle.

If, then, the rate of growth of the whole field is less than the no-conflict rate, there will inevitably be conflict among the competing organizations, in the sense that all of them together cannot satisfy their ideal rates of growth, and, therefore, if one attains or moves toward its ideal rate, this can only be done at the cost of preventing some other organization or organizations from expanding at their ideal rates. The success of one, in this case, means failure of another. If, on the other hand, the growth of the field equals or exceeds the no-conflict rate, each organization can expand at its ideal rate, and the expansion is no occasion for conflict.

There are many historical occasions that at least have the appearance of being illustrations of the above principle. Thus, when the labor movement is expanding in total membership into the field of the unorganized, the intensity of jurisdictional disputes between unions is observed to decline, for each union can expand by organizing the unorganized rather than by trying to obtain jurisdiction over the members of another union. On the other hand, in periods like the 1920s, when total union membership was stationary or declining, the intensity of jurisdictional disputes was high, for the expansion of one union frequently took place at the expense of others. It is tempting also to attribute the relative peace in Europe between 1815 and 1914 to the fact that the more aggressive European powers were busy carving themselves empires in other parts of the world and so were able to expand at the expense of the weak non-European powers rather than at the expense of each other. By 1914, however, this process had come to an end, partly because the process of exploration and seizure of the unorganized parts of the world was almost complete and partly because of the rise of non-European powers like Japan and the United States. The belligerency of the twentieth century in Europe by contrast with the nineteenth may in part be due to this cessation in the expansion of the field. The diminution in religious strife in Christendom in the nineteenth century may also in part be attributed to the fact that a great part of the energy of the more belligerent and expansion-minded sects was diverted into the task of missionary activity in non-Christian areas (organizing the unorganized) rather than to mutual competition for members at home.

We must be careful, of course, not to erect what is at best an insight, or a partial model, into a universal principle. It is not always true that an expansion of the field leads to a diminution of conflict among the organizations that seek to occupy it. The ideal rate of growth of an organization is not a stationary magnitude; it can and does vary with the history of the organization. Frequently, a dangerously unstable situation arises because the experience of a little growth whets the appetite for more. Thus, a situation in which the field has been stationary for a considerable period and in which the organizations in it have adjusted themselves to zero or to very small rates of growth may be disturbed by a sudden expansion in the field, so that organizations now revise their ideal rates of growth sharply upward and may collectively overestimate the potential growth of the field, so that an acute conflict situation may develop from what originally was an expansion of the field, which normally one would expect to diminish conflict.

It is clear that the problem of the determinants of the self-image of organizations and especially the determinants of their image of the ideal rate of growth is quite critical for the theory of organizational conflict. Unfortunately, this is a vast and little-explored field, and only a few tentative suggestions can be made at this point. Reverting to our skeleton theory of the organization itself, we can postulate that the contrast between a conservative, timid organization with a low ideal rate of growth and little expansion pressure and an aggressive, expansion-minded organization with a high ideal rate of growth depends to a considerable extent on the nature of the persons who occupy the critical executive roles; that is, this is a characteristic that is person-determined rather than role-determined. The higher we go in the hierarchy of an organization, the more important become the person-determined aspects of behavior relative to the role-determined aspects. The operative or the private soldier has little opportunity for stepping outside his prescribed role, that is, for the exercise of individuality and initiative. The leader of a great state, the president of a university, or the head of a church has a less clearly prescribed role, even though the extent of his freedom to mold the role can easily be exaggerated. Consequently, the inevitable succession of persons in the top roles brings changes to the character of an organization that are the result of the personality of the occupant rather than that of the role structure itself. In looking at the larger dynamics of an organization, then, we must look carefully at the processes by which the top roles are filled. Where the occupants of top roles are drawn from a small, self-perpetuating oligarchy, the character of the organization is likely to be fairly stable, because as each place in the group falls vacant, say, by death or retirement, the surviving members are likely to select a new occupant who has characteristics much like the old. Where, however, the occupants of top roles are selected by processes in which chance plays a large role, it is quite possible for the role to be occupied by a succession of very different personality types, each of which will give his distinctive stamp to the role and, therefore, to the whole organization. The self-image of the organization, therefore, depending, as it does, to no small extent on the personality of the occupant of the dominant role or roles, may undergo radical shifts, from, say, passive to active or peaceable to aggressive, as chance places aggressive or peaceable individuals in the key roles.

Two highly contrasting processes of selection of the occupants of upper roles have this common property of having a large element of chance. One is the hereditary principle, and the other is democratic election. In neither of these, of course, is the selection of the occupant of the upper role a matter of pure chance, as it almost seems to have been in those Greek republics which chose their officials by lot. The eldest son is likely to inherit at least some of the qualities of his father and will certainly receive an important cultural inheritance to build him up into the role that he is to occupy. Nevertheless, in the accidents of human heredity, chance plays an important part, and cases have been numerous where strong, vigorous fathers have been succeeded by weak, timorous sons and, perhaps somewhat less numerous but still not uncommon, where weak fathers have produced strong sons. In democratic election, likewise, the process is not one of pure chance, less so, in fact, than when the succession of role occupants is determined by the hereditary principle. Nevertheless, it must be admitted that chance factors are important both in the selection of candidates and in the final election. In both the hereditary monarchy and in the representative democracy, a certain principle of alternation may frequently be observed. A vigorous and aggressive king is succeeded by a son who has grown up under that shadow of his father and who reacts by a contrast to become a less aggressive character. Similarly, in democratic states, an aggressive and militaristic government is often suceeeded by a quiet and peaceable one, and vice versa, as the policies of one lead to exhaustion or of the other to apparent weakness or to a humbling of national pride.

We have looked here at the impact of the occupant on the role; we must not neglect, however, the equally important, perhaps more important, impact of the role on the occupant. We have noticed that, this impact is likely to be stronger, the further down the hierarchy we go. Nevertheless, it is frequently very strong even at the upper levels. This is especially true in large organizations where each of the upper roles is the nucleus of a large inner organization of staff. To a very large extent, the staff creates the role that it serves, because of its control over the information that reaches the occupant of the role and especially because of the atmosphere of valuation that it creates. If no man is a hero to his valet, still less is he a hero to his staff, and, by subtle and often not so subtle judgments on the decisions of a boss, the staff molds his image of the role to its own. This provides continuity even in those roles where chance plays a large part in the selection of the occupant. We see this, for instance, in the basic continuity that guides the policies of great nations in spite of wide divergence in character and even in the overt policies of the occupiers of the top roles. This continuity comes in very large part from the staff—the civil service, the career diplomats, and the foreign office or department of state, which act in many ways as self-perpetuating oligarchies.

The staff may provide continuity, but what determines the nature of these continuous policies? This is a difficult question to answer, for the basic character of an organization is a product of its whole history. Nevertheless, the influence of the environment of the organization is powerful, especially the influence of the other organizations that form usually so important a part of that environment. Frequently, indeed, the character of an organization is determined by the nature of its enemies, for its enemies are the most important part of its environment. Thus we often find that corrupt or aggressive unions face corrupt or aggressive employers, that aggressiveness in one nation produces aggressiveness in its neighbors, or even that one hostile or aggressive family in a neighborhood can set the whole neighborhood to quarrelsomeness. The more cheerful converse of this gloomy picture is that generous and responsible attitudes on the part of employers and unions reinforce each other and that nations, like Canada and the United States, frequently are able to live together for long periods in mutual trust and security. We do not explain much, of course, by saying that the character of an organization is determined by its environment, especially by the other organizations that surround it, unless we know what determines the character of these other organizations. There is danger of being involved in circular reasoning here. Nevertheless, we can appeal to something like a generalized Richardson process of character action and reaction that moves a group of interacting organizations either toward aggressive and corrupt characters as each reacts to the other or toward peaceable and responsible characters. As in all these dynamic processes, it may frequently be a hairbreadth at the beginning of the process that determines whether the end product will be good or bad; this is the watershed principle that we have noticed earlier. In this characterological dynamics, the influence of the saints and the devils may be of importance. The saints are those organizations which react to bad characteristics of their surrounding organizations in such a way as to improve them. Similarly, the devils react to good characteristics of the surrounding organizations in such a way as to worsen them. Because of the watershed principle, a few saints or devils may at times exercise a quite disproportionate influence on the final result.

Beside the external influences on the character or self-image of an organization, there are also important influences that arise out of the internal structure of an organization. One of the most acute problems in the perpetuation of an organization is that of maintaining internal cohesion. The larger an organization grows, the more tendency there is for factions and dissident elements to grow within it and for the organization ultimately to split or to fall apart. We see this happening in a perfectly regular and creative way in the splitting of the cell. We see it happening in irregular and disorderly ways in civil war and wars of independence, in religious schisms, in trade-union splits, and so on. The problem here is that of maintaining a consistent structure of roles that can be filled by reasonably satisfied occupants. If the organization consists of a structure of roles which nobody can be found to fill or for which only dissatisfied occupants can be found, then it is in grave danger of dissolution. We may distinguish perhaps between a situation of factionalism, where there is competition for the top roles among those who occupy the roles immediately below the top, and the revolutionary situation, in which there is dissatisfaction among those who occupy the lower roles sufficient to disrupt the organization or to displace those who occupy all the higher places in the hierarchy.

The problem of internal stability in an organization thus resolves itself into that of the rewards of the role: generally speaking, an organization with rewarding roles will be internally stable; one with unrewarding roles will be internally unstable. The rewards of a role may in turn be of two kinds: external rewards, such as wages or salaries or other perquisites, which are granted to the individual as an inducement to occupy the role and internal rewards, which consist in the satisfaction derived from the performance of the role itself. Some roles, like that of the honorary secretary, are so rewarding internally that they need no external inducements; most jobs, however, need external rewards before incumbents can be found to occupy them. Practically all roles involve a mixture of both internal and external inducements: by and large, the greater the one, the smaller need be the other.

The power of an organization to offer external rewards to its role occupants depends mainly on its ability to attract revenue of some kind. This it may do by producing and selling goods and services, like a business firm, or by attracting voluntary contributions, like a church or charitable institution, or by being able to exact involuntary contributions (taxes), like the state. Its power to offer internal rewards depends to a great extent on the significance for the value systems of the participants of the over-all task and function of the organization and on the extent to which the roles themselves are felt to be significant in the larger purposes of the occupants. An organization that is felt to have mean and unworthy purposes will find it hard to offer internal rewards, and if this is to survive, it must, therefore, find itself in a position where it can attract sufficient revenue to pay the necessary external rewards. An organization, on the other hand, that is felt to have noble purposes with which the participant wishes to be identified can offer large internal rewards. The ability of states, churches, armies, and religious orders to attract devoted service with very little in the way of external reward is an important factor in the survival and in the competitive strength of these organizations.

An important element in the internal strength of large organizations is their ability to capitalize on loyalties that are generated toward smaller groups within the organization. It is often the small face-to-face group that commands the deepest loyalties, especially in difficult or dangerous situations. A man dies for his buddies rather than for his country, and the large internal rewards that have to be generated by states at war are frequently aroused by exploiting for the benefit of the larger group loyalties that are generated by putting small groups to difficult or concentrated tasks, in which success or failure is easily measured. One of the problems of large organizations is that it is difficult to keep large purposes before the minds of small people. Consequently, organizations frequently devise a system of minor goals for individuals and smaller groups which altogether may fit into the larger purpose but which is close enough to the individual and to his levels of aspiration to be powerful as motivators. So we have courses and grades in school and college as aids to the broader objective of the increase in knowledge, we have production quotas and group productivity tests in both socialized and in private industry as aids to the larger ends of the organizations, and so on. Degrees, titles, orders, medals, citations and suchlike claptrap of life are part of the same process.

It seems to be a fact that most organizations can increase the internal rewards of their role occupants by putting the organization in a situation of strain or conflict. There are several possible reasons for this. One is that a situation of conflict heightens the sense of the larger purpose of the organization and so augments the internal rewards that come from a feeling of participation in these larger purposes. A conflict usually simplifies the purposes of an organization, simply because the objective of winning or surviving the conflict comes to dominate over all others. Thus, a nation in peacetime has a diversity of purposes and objectives. It is harder to achieve a sense of national unity under these conditions, and factions and diverse interests within the nation tend to pull it apart. A strong enemy, however, is a great unifying force; in the face of a common threat and the overriding common purpose of victory or survival, the diverse ends and conflicting interests of the population fall into the background and are swallowed up into the single, measurable, overriding end of winning the conflict. We see this principle operating most clearly in alliances: the threat of Hitler, for instance, produced an alliance between the Western powers and Russia that fell apart as soon as the common threat disappeared. In many ways, organizations are creations of their enemies, and it is through a common hatred of the enemy that they establish their internal unity. We see this not only in nations—where George III's England created the United States, Napoleon's France created Germany, and so on—but in labor unions, where the enmity of the employer frequently creates a solidarity of feeling that no mere common interest could create, and even in churches, where a sect often establishes its internal unity by battles against the heretic and the unbeliever.

THE ORGANIZATION AS A PARTY TO CONFLICT

It is, therefore, a very serious question for the theory of conflict whether there are circumstances under which conflict is necessary for the internal stability of organizations. We need perhaps to distinguish three cases. Case 1 is where we have organizations existing in contact but without conflict, or at least without serious and organized conflict, because neither their internal stability requires an enemy nor are their self-images inconsistent with the maintenance of the *status quo*. Case 2 is where we have organizations existing in stable conflict, where either because of the requirements of internal stability or because of the incompatible self-images of the organizations, conflict is a necessary part of the system but does not proceed to the extinction of the organizations or of the system. There is just enough conflict to maintain the internal unity of the organizations and not enough to destroy them. Perhaps the best example of such a system is an athletic league. The whole purpose and internal unity of the teams would disappear if there were no conflict, for conflict with other teams is almost the sole purpose of the organization. Nevertheless, the conflict is limited by a larger organization and by a set of rules that prevents or at least limits the destruction of the constituent organizations. Case 3 is that of unstable conflict, where conflict is a necessary part of the system for much the same reasons that prevail in case 2 but where the absence of an over-all organization, or any limits on the conflict, or mutual viability of the constituent organizations makes the system unstable, so that some or all of the organizations are destroyed and the system disintegrates. Examples of all three cases can be found in history. Thus, in international relations, the United States and Canada, at least since the mid-nineteenth century, are an example of case 1. Enmity toward Canada is in no sense necessary to the internal unity of the United States; a somewhat covert enmity toward the United States is of more importance in the national unity of Canada, but it apparently is sufficient for this enmity to remain covert. The self-images of the two nations are compatible: Canada does not have the power and the United States does not have the will to upset the present arrangement of frontiers and the existing mutual disarmament. The international system of, say, the eighteenth and nineteenth centuries approximates case 2: the self-images, for instance, of Britain and France were inconsistent over most of the period, and rising nations like the United States and Germany needed wars to create their internal national unity. The system as a whole, however, was fairly stable; the various nations were probably mutually viable, and the conventions of limited war for the most part prevailed. International relations in the twentieth century probably illustrate case 3: nations are neither mutually viable, nor do they have consistent self-images; and a desperate state of peril results.

One of the phenomena observed in organizational conflict is the possibility of sudden shifts in the character of one or more of the parties as new occupants get into top roles, as new factions within an organization rise to dominance, or as old bosses get new ideas. The character of organizations is probably much less stable than the characters of persons, and an important element in organizational conflict consists in attempts by one organization to change the character of another in a direction that the former regards as favorable. Communists, for instance, indulge in a good deal of boring from within in the attempt to remake the character of organizations with which they are in potential conflict. It is not unknown for one nation to foment a revolution in another. This technique is rare in the case of conflict among corporations or firms, unless we interpret the merger movement along these lines. The whole vast art of persuasion, however, whether expressed in advertising, missionary work, government propaganda, or political-party campaigning, can be interpreted as attempts on the part of some organizations to affect the behavior of other organizations favorably to the first, even though these organizations are not necessarily in conflict. A constant source of error and ineptitude in conflict situations is a result of an *image-lag*, the failure to recognize changes in the nature of the enemy or even of the friend. We build up our images slowly and often painfully, and it is painful to change them: contradictory evidence is at first rejected or may even be twisted to support the image, as every act of the outside world, for instance, no matter how friendly, is interpreted by the paranoic as hostile.

We are now perhaps in a position to evaluate more carefully the similarities and differences between individual and organizational conflict. In spite of the greater complexities of organizational conflict, the similarities bulk larger than the differences. The clue to the character of any conflict system is the self-images of the parties. In the case of an individual, this may be a fairly simple, unified image; in the case of an organization, we must consider the images of its many participant members, and the chain by which information reaches these members and modifies the images is longer, more diffuse, and correspondingly more capable of false transmissions. Even in the case of large organizations, however, the image of certain key persons occupying top roles is of dominating importance, and even though the processes by which these images are created and modified is more complex, it is not essentially different from that by which the image of an individual is created and modified. Whereas we must be careful to avoid a certain oversimplification that is involved in the personification of organizations, it is not inappropriate to regard such broad concepts as character and personality as having applicability both to persons and to organizations. Much of the theory of conflicting organizations, therefore, applies equally well either to organizations or to persons. The main difference lies in the greater capacity of organizations for growth and, therefore, for incompatability in their self-images. Persons are sharply limited in extent by their biological structure; organizations are much less limited in this way, though, even here, the biological limits on the capacity for the receipt of information and for the elaboration of images may be important. For this reason, organizational conflict is likely to be more extensive, more diffuse, and perhaps more dangerous than the conflict of persons. It is not, however, an essentially different system.

9

CONFLICT BETWEEN THE INDIVIDUAL, THE GROUP, AND THE ORGANIZATION

In previous chapters, we have considered conflict between individuals, between groups, or between organizations. Some important aspects of social conflict, however, are missed if we concentrate solely on these conflicts between parties of the same organizational type. Very interesting conflicts arise in society between individuals and groups or between individuals and organizations. It is hard to think of examples of conflict between groups and organizations, mainly because as soon as unorganized groups get into conflict, they tend to become organized so that a group-organization conflict will pass over quickly into an organization-organization conflict. Even within the conflict of organizations, however, we may wish to distinguish two types of conflict with very different properties: conflict between organizations of like character or purpose, on the one hand, and conflict between organizations of different character or purpose, on the other. The first might be called homogeneous organization conflict—wars between states, quarrels between sects, and jurisdictional disputes between unions. The second might be called heterogeneous organization conflict—the struggle of a state with a church, of a union with a corporation, or of a university with a state government or a church authority. In general, we may call conflicts between different types of parties heterogeneous conflicts, to distinguish them from homogeneous conflicts, where both parties are of the same type.

Perhaps the most interesting kinds of heterogeneous conflict are those in which one party is an individual person and the other party is a group or organization. Such conflicts arise where the role that is imposed on an individual by reason of his membership in a group or organization differs from some role or pattern of behavior which he prefers and which he thinks he is able to perform. To some extent these conflicts are inevitable; they are created by the very fact of an individual's membership in a group or organization the formation of which he does not control. The mutual relationships of the individual and his groups and organizations, however, are extremely complex, for the character of the individual is in part formed by the groups of which he happens to be a member at the same time that his individuality rebels against the very group that is forming him.

The earliest and perhaps, ultimately, the most important conflict between an individual and group or organization is the conflict between the child and the family in which he grows up. The process of *socialization*, by which the child becomes a member of a culture, is a constant process of conflict. The child comes into the world with a simple but firm value structure. It likes food, warmth, and embraces and it dislikes hunger, cold, loud noises, and insecure positions. This elementary value structure is presumably largely innate, that is, built into the structure of the newborn baby's image by the work of the genes, though we do not know much about how far these values may be determined by prenatal experience or even the experience of birth itself. Psychoanalysts have made a good deal of the birth trauma and the unconscious desire to return to the womb. To my knowledge, however, little empirical work has been done on the relation of difficult or easy births to subsequent personal character, and, in the present state of knowledge, the total processes making for the formation of personal character are so little understood that propositions in this area inevitably have a speculative character. It is not unreasonable to suppose, however, that conflict may begin even in the womb (one recalls the Biblical story of Esau and Jacob), and it is also not unreasonable to interpret the birth experience as a source of inner personal conflict and as a type of the conflict between security and adventure that frequently dominates adult life.

Once the child is born and begins to experience the impact of parents and siblings, the conflict processes are more clearly observable. There is a struggle first with the mother for the competing demands on her time; children cannot always be fed when they are hungry, or changed when they are wet, or reassured when they are insecure, simply because mother has so many other things to do. This is particularly important for children after the first-born, and the larger the family, the more important is this source of conflict. Because the other claims on a mother's time and energy frequently involve other members of the family, conflict for alternative uses of the mother's attention often gets translated into sibling rivalry, and the intensity of conflict among siblings is probably related to early experiences of deprivation of maternal attention. The difference in character between the youngest child, who has never been displaced by a younger brother or sister, and all the other children is frequently remarked, and, in cultures like that of the Navaho, where displacement of the currently youngest child by a new baby is sharp and painful, the child who does not go through this experience is observed to have a markedly less aggressive character as an adult than most of his generation.

Sibling rivalry, of course, is not all a matter of competition for parental attention; there are plenty of opportunities for direct conflict in play and other activities. The fact that children of the same family, with the exception of twins or adopted children, have to be of different ages is important in structuring the type of conflict; the older child usually has a certain advantage, and the younger child may constantly be in the position of relative inferiority. A good deal here depends on the spacing of the children: if their

THE INDIVIDUAL, THE GROUP, AND THE ORGANIZATION   169

ages are sufficiently disparate they hardly enter into competition at all. It is when they are only one or two years apart that conflict between them is likely to be the most acute.

The problem of the general level of tension within the family group deserves a great deal more study. We can think of this general level as built up by a complex series of Richardson processes between various individuals or subgroups within the family, in which an *encounter*, that is, a specific act of hostility or friendliness, is the basic component. We have seen that the equilibrium of a Richardson process depends on two main factors: the initial hostility and the touchiness of the parties. Initial hostility is itself a function of the equilibrium level of tension, so that what we have is a complex dynamic system that usually exhibits cyclical fluctuations of a fairly irregular character. One of the great unresolved problems here is the exact relation between frustration and aggressiveness. Aggressiveness itself has at least the two dimensions we have previously noted of initial hostility and touchiness. A person may be basically hostile but not very touchy, in which case the equilibrium level of tension may be not much above the basic hostility level; a person may, by contrast, have low basic hostility but be very touchy, with a high reaction coefficient, and, here, in spite of the low basic hostility, the equilibrium level of tension may be quite high.

It is extremely obscure what kinds of frustration experience produce what kind of aggressiveness. Furthermore, it is not even clear that frustration necessarily produces aggressiveness at all. Frustration in the sense of reaching a possibility boundary with a perceived but unattainable preferred position beyond it is an absolutely universal experience. It can produce three broad types of reaction. First, the individual can simply accept the situation as given and maximize his satisfactions, like economic man, subject to the constraints of the possibility boundaries. Second, the individual can refuse to accept existing boundaries but can direct his activity rationally toward changing the boundaries, pushing them out in the direction of his preferred positions. A man who is frustrated because he is poor can set about making himself richer. A man who is frustrated because he is ignorant can set about making himself knowledgeable. Third—and it is this which seems to catch the attention of the psychologists—the individual can refuse to accept existing boundaries but refuse also to set about changing them; he then becomes irrationally aggressive, beating his head against the boundaries and raising his level of emotional tension. The emotional tension thus aroused can easily be displaced on to other objects, especially if the expression of hostility toward the original boundary results in punishment, that is, in disagreeable or low-valued events that are associated with the expression of hostility. The child cannot go out to play because mother forbids it; mother, then, is perceived as a boundary that prevents the child from reaching a preferred position. The child can either accept this, or try to persuade mother to change her mind, or go into a tantrum. Overt expressions of hostility toward mother are likely to be punished, so that child suppresses these, but frequently directs a displaced hostility on to a pet, a toy, or another child.

All this is a commonplace of psychoanalytic theory. The weakness of this type of analysis is that it does not define with sufficient accuracy the social system within which the dynamics of the individual personality develops and, in particular, does not define it as a system of interaction and conflict processes. The same or highly similar childhood experience may produce entirely different consequences for different individuals. The Freudian system, therefore, is a good example of an incomplete system, in that, whereas it works well as an explanatory system sometimes, it does not work always, indicating that there are important variables that have been left out of it. These variables may be in part genetic, though we know very little about the genetic factors involved in resistance to stress. They are certainly in part group-interaction variables, in that the character of the individual is hammered out in his conflict with the primary groups in which he happens to be placed. One hopes that the concept of an equilibrium level of general tension or hostility may be a useful one here. One hopes also that some progress can be made toward identifying the determinants of the three main reactions to frustration—apathy or acceptance, constructive activity, and random aggressiveness. The second of these is so obviously more desirable than the other two that we need to know much more about how to encourage it.

An important element in the pattern of individual-group conflict is the role of the *conflict absorber*. This is the person whose reaction to a perceived hostile act on the part of another has low hostility or even positive friendliness. As we have seen in the study of Richardson processes, the saint, who returns good for evil, has a great power over the final position of equilibrium of the system. Similarly, in the interaction processes within the family or within any small face-to-face group, the final equilibrium and the nature of the personalities that emerge from the melee may depend a great deal on the presence of one or more conflict absorbers in the group. In the family, this is often the mother, sometimes the father, sometimes even one of the older children who play this role; if it does not exist at all, the tension level of the group is likely to be very high.

The preceding discussion illustrates a dilemma that is often encountered in discussions of groups. We have here discussed the interaction of an individual with his primary group not in terms of the character of the group as a whole but rather as a system of action and interaction with individual members of the group. Does the concept of the group, then, really disintegrate when we try to make a system out of it, and does the group, then, become simply a generic name for a process of personal interaction? Does the interaction or conflict of an individual with his family, for instance, simply break down into a series of successive interactions with his father, mother, sisters, brothers, and other relatives? In a sense, it must be admitted that the group is an abstraction, a mental construct, and that the reality is indeed a complex series of person-to-person interactions. Nevertheless, where the interactions with a number of individuals have the same general character, as, for instance, in the case of a child and its parents or older siblings, the various individual interactions can often usefully be summarized in the concept of the interaction of an individual with a group.

This group concept applies particularly well to the socializing process by which the child learns to be a conforming member of the culture in which he grows up—the process by which the Chinese child learns to be Chinese and the American child to be American. The child faces a group of people all of whom, for instance, usually speak the same language to him, reprove or chastise him for fairly similar misdeeds, praise him for similar acts of virtue, and so on. Considering the essentially conflictual pattern of the process, most of which consists of forcing the child to do things he does not want to do, it is remarkable that it is so universally successful and that the end product is usually an acceptance of the frustrations that belonging to a particular culture implies. There can be little doubt, however, that some cultures manage the acculturation of the child with less stress and strain than others and that this may be reflected in the character of the culture itself. A culture with strong taboos, for instance, that go against the grain of certain instinctive drives is also likely to be aggressive, simply because the process of acculturation of the child sets up such severe internal strains within the individual personality. A culture that is easygoing and permissive both in child rearing and in its taboos is likely to produce nonaggressive personalities and to have nonaggressive ideals. Generalization is dangerous here, however, because frequently a society has at least two cultures, an overt culture that contains the official rules and prescriptions and ideals and a covert culture which is not outwardly acknowledged but which provides opportunity for the release of drives that may be denied by the overt culture.

Another important element to look for in the individual-group conflict is the distinction between the peer group and the hierarchical group. The peer group, consisting of individuals of like age and status in the community, is frequently a more important socializer than the hierarchical group. A child is more strongly influenced, for instance, by other children of about his own age than he is by parents, teachers, preachers, and so on, who stand in a relationship of superior age, wisdom, and experience to him. The *American Soldier* studies[1] clearly indicated that the buddies were more important in determining a soldier's behavior than all the hierarchy above him. The phenomenon of overt versus covert culture is frequently found in contrasting the peer-group behavior of an individual with his behavior when faced with hierarchical superiors. Children give one set of responses to the teacher, because they have learned what responses pay off best in this situation; they may give a totally different set of responses to each other in the schoolyard. This is a serious problem in social-anthropological research. It takes a great deal of living with a people before an anthropologist becomes one of their peers and it may be questioned whether he ever becomes one in their eyes. If he does not, however, one suspects that people reserve part of their behavior for the anthropologist and another part for when he is not around to observe them.

Conflict of the individual with a peer group may be much more painful that conflict with a superior or inferior group. The child who is constantly in trouble in the classroom may be secretly, or even publically, supported by the other children. The child who is rejected by his peers receives a hurt that is not assuaged by being teacher's pet or mother's darling. The tension between the desire for approval by the peer group and the desire for approval from some superior group is a potent source of conflict within the person. One can argue indeed that the peer group is so dominant that a person will reject his present and immediate peers only if he hopes to find another peer group and a higher level of status. Much of the personal and social disorganization that is traditionally associated with upward social mobility may be traced to the rejection of lower peer groups that is involved. The ambitious and upwardly mobile youngster has to reject his earlier playmates and companions who are content with

[1] S. A. Stouffer and others, *The American Soldier*, Princeton, N.J., Princeton University Press, 1949-1950.

a lower level of achievement if he is to rise in the social scale himself, and there is always the chance that the rising individual, having rejected his old group, fails to find acceptance in the higher status group and so becomes a social isolate, and usually an unhappy one. The dilemma is particularly poignant when it involves rejection of the family group that has nurtured the individual. The light Negro who passes into the white community at the cost of breaking off all contact with his darker family, the scholarship boy whose newfound professional skills cut him off from the peasant or working class home from which he sprang, the second-generation immigrant who rejects and despises the language and culture of his parents—these are all types of human tragedy. This is not to say that the cost involved may not be adjudged worth the gain in moving to a richer culture, but the cost is often very high.

The socialization conflict that may cause a person to reject his family also may cause him to reject his society and his country and to become either a revolutionary or an emigrant. A revolutionary is one in whom the socialization process has failed. This may be simply because of a failure within the family group and a rejection of undue parental authority, which is then displaced on to the father image of the state, the capitalist boss, or the communist dictator. Not all revolutionaries are such, however, merely because they hate their fathers. There may be real failure and breakdown in the social system around them that causes them to reject the acculturation process not merely because of the psychological strains set up but because the culture to which they are expected to conform is itself a failure, failing to provide security, decent living, moral allegiances, or enough of the basic needs of the human organism. Even where there are valid reasons in the failure of a culture for a rebellion against it, the rebellion almost inevitably induces strong internal psychological conflicts within the rebel; it is not surprising, therefore, that so many revolutions have been violent and that the popular stereotype of the revolutionary is that of a man with a smoking bomb. The violence of revolutions probably does not help them;

indeed one can argue that by far the most important revolutions in the state of man have been accomplished quietly with little violence, and almost unnoticed at the time, and that violent revolutions lead often to the old thing in a new dress—the French Revolution, for instance, replacing Louis XVI by Napoleon, and the Russian Revolution, replacing the tzar by Stalin. Nevertheless, the violence of revolutions arises out of deep psychological forces, and it takes a strong counterideology, as in the case of Gandhi, to counteract them.

The struggle of the individual against the group that is trying to socialize him is often perceived most clearly in the period of adolescence, a period that is often identified by the name of adolescent revolt. In part, this revolt is an inevitable part of the process by which the individual finds his identity within a culture; it may not be a revolt against the culture, and, in most cultures, this process of finding an adult identity is in some degree formalized and ritualized. At some point in the development of the individual, he must cease being identified as so-and-so's boy or such-and-such's girl and must develop a name and identity in his or her own right. Marriage is in most societies the clearest landmark of the attainment of the adult role; it is at this point that the man or woman leaves the home and family of his parents and sets up an establishment of his own. In the case of women in Western society, the change is particularly striking, as the woman takes the name of her husband, which symbolizes very clearly her new status in a new family. The period of adolescent revolt is often considered as a preparation for marriage and is the period in which a marriage partner is sought. The whole ideology of the adolescent subculture revolves around marriage or some equivalent partnership as an end. Marriage, furthermore, is supposed to put an end to this period; this is when the young man or woman settles down and becomes a conforming member of society. There are some, of course, who never settle down and who remain in the stage of adolescent revolt all their lives. Sometimes this is a fairly unpleasant spectacle, though sometimes it is creative; there must be something of the adolescent about the poet, the artist, the actor, the prophet, or any creative personality.

The problem of finding an identity for the individual often resolves itself into that of finding which group to join; that is, an individual finds an identity not by remaining outside groups or organizations but by joining them. Our identity is found in identification with something, and the something is usually a group. This may be a religious group, a national group, an occupational group, or any of the innumerable groups to which men give some sort of allegiance. Frequently, an individual has many identities, as he belongs to different groups; thus he may be an American, a Baptist, an optician, a Rotarian, a member of a family or clan, and so on. The struggle of an individual with a group can usually be interpreted as dissatisfaction with the identity provided by the group to which he currently belongs and the search for a more satisfactory identity that would be conferred by another group. Leaving the parental home to set up another household, emigrating from one country to find a home in another, leaving one church or political party to find another that is more congenial are all examples of the quest for the most satisfactory identity.

Even a quite superficial knowledge of the social structure suggests the interesting question as to whether there is any equilibrium distribution of identity types and, therefore, of types of groups in society. Every society must provide a variety of roles to suit different personality types. Whether these types result ultimately from the distribution of the genetic material of the society or whether they are themselves determined in a complex process of environmental reaction of individuals with various groups is a question that cannot be answered in the present state of knowledge. On the whole, the smaller and more primitive the society, the more exacting is the conformity that it demands from its members; a child who grows up among the Trobrianders only has a relatively limited number of roles that he can fill, and if his temperament does not suit him for any one of these roles, there is not much he can do about it. In a complex society with extensive division of labor, as Durkheim[2] pointed out, there is room for much greater tolerance of subgroups and subcultures, and the individual has a much greater freedom of choice in his search for an identity and a group to identify with. Great strains can develop in a society, however, where the socialization and educational process produces a distribution of personality types and role expectations that cannot be satisfied by the existing distribution of jobs and roles. Thus, an educational system that is geared to produce dainty-fingered gentlemen in a society that needs dirty-fingered engineers is likely to produce a good many square pegs in round holes and will have a high level of general tension.

There are interesting parallels between adolescent revolt and the search for identity in the revolt against colonialism and the rise of nationalism. An individual who is a member of a colonial society in a sense lacks an independent identity: he is not a full member of the imperial society, and the colony of which he is a full member is only half a society. It is not surprising that, once a certain stage in development of self-consciousness is reached, there is a demand for breakaway from the parent country and a desire for independence. One of the great problems of the world society and one reason why a sense of world unity is so difficult to achieve in spite of its desperate necessity is that the national societies form a partition of the human race, so that an individual must have one national identity or another. A man must be either an American or a Russian or a Chinese; the option of being a world citizen as an alternative is not open to him. It may well be that the world society will never come into being until this option is provided so that the identity of belonging to the human race is a real alternative to the narrower identities.

So far we have considered mainly conflicts between the individual and the group. Groups, however, as we have seen, have a strong tendency to pass over into organizations, and the relation of the individual to an organization possesses properties that are not found

[2] Emile Durkheim, *The Division of Labor in Society*, trans. George Simpson, New York, Macmillan, 1933.

in the looser relationship of an individual to a group. An organization, as we have seen, is a structure of roles tied together by lines of communication. It can exist only if it can fill the roles, that is, attract individuals who will occupy the various jobs that constitute the organizational structure and who will perform the jobs according to the specifications laid down by the organization or, more accurately, according to those principles which will lead to the survival of the organization.

We noted that, in speaking of the conflict between the individual and the group, we were really using a shorthand notation for a complex series of interpersonal interactions within the group. Similarly, when we speak of conflict between the individual and the organization in which he serves, we are also using a shorthand notation for an even more complex system of interactions. Nevertheless, because of the more formal and structured nature of an organization, the shorthand is highly descriptive of the reality. Organizations develop personalities that are somewhat similar to the personalities of individuals. It is not an accident that the law regards a corporation as a fictitious person. Thus, organizations have constitutions, rules, procedures, precedents, organization charts, balance sheets, and formal structures that are analogous to the body of a natural person. They have habits of behavior and traditions that are largely independent of the persons occupying the role. Indeed, it is argued that, if the role is sufficiently well defined, the role itself largely creates the behavior of the person occupying it. In this sense, the notion of a conflict between the person of an individual and the personality of an organization becomes something more than a figure of speech. The organization, by reason of its history, habits, and constitution, may impose a role on an individual to which he does not consent. He visualizes the conflict as one between his own interpretation of the role that he wants to play and the definition of the role that is implied in the constitution and habitual behavior of the organization. As we saw in the case of conflict of the individual with the group, there are three main possible types of

THE INDIVIDUAL, THE GROUP, AND THE ORGANIZATION 179

reaction to a conflict situation of this kind. The first is acceptance; the individual, after a few kicks, simply accepts the role that the organization imposes on him. Acceptance, however, is often bought at the cost of apathy. We should, therefore, distinguish between two kinds of acceptance reaction: the apathetic reaction, in which the individual does not identify with the organization but simply performs his assigned task in a mechanical and uninterested manner, and the identification reaction, in which the individual identifies himself with the organization as a group and, therefore, finds some meaning and personal significance in his job. In the latter case, the individual is likely to adapt his performance to the actual environment and situation in which he finds himself rather than merely obeying instructions mechanically and to the letter.

This latter type of acceptance reaction merges into the second class of role reaction, which might be called the role-changing reaction. In this, the individual does not simply accept the role as given to him by his superiors in the hierarchy but seeks to influence the role itself, either by making adjustments that are either unknown to the hierarchy or are tolerated by them or by attempting to influence the image of his role in the minds of his hierarchical superiors and so redefine the official interpretation of the role. An important variant of the role-changing reaction might be described as the job-changing reaction. The individual who is in conflict with his role as prescribed to him by his job niche in an organization usually has the right and the power to quit and look for another job, either within the same organization or in another organization. This indeed is the meaning of the labor market.

The third general type of reaction to role conflict is the hostility or aggression reaction, in which the individual develops strong feelings of hatred toward the organization as such and actively tries to injure it through nonperformance or malperformance of his assigned role. In extreme cases, this takes the form of deliberate sabotage of the organization's objectives. The factory worker who dropped his sabot (or monkey wrench!) into the machinery gave rise to the name, of course, but the phenomenon is widely observed. The diplomat or civil servant or general who sells out his country, the Communist or the labor spy who betrays the trade union; the teacher or the preacher who deliberately undermines the faith or the doctrine that he is supposed to impart, and the parent who corrupts the mind and morals of his children are all specimens of this disease of society. We may want to distinguish two subtypes of this reaction also. There is the simple, nonideological saboteur, whose reaction is one of mere irrational aggression in a frustrating role. One suspects that the role has to be extremely frustrating to produce this reaction and that the commonest reaction to a role frustration from which no exit seems available is the apathetic reaction. One would expect to find, for instance, that, in the case of the saboteur, as opposed to the merely apathetic role occupant, some further frustrations and aggressions outside the immediate job situation were being projected and displaced on to the employing organization. The saboteur may really be fighting an aggressive father or a domineering wife as well as his employer. We do not understand much about the circumstances, however, that give rise to the difference between apathy and aggressiveness, and all generalizations in this area are of necessity speculative.

The ideological saboteur or traitor is a more complex case. Sometimes the individual actually joins an organization for the purpose of undermining its existing structure and purpose. This is the boring from within of the Communists, the union activity of the labor spy or *agent provocateur*, and the undercover work of the cloak-and-dagger man. Here we have a distinction developing between the overt and the covert role: the individual may have an overt role in one organization, such as a trade union, at the same time that he has a covert role in another, such as the Communist party. The covert role may be in a peer group rather than in an outside organization. In this case, we might have a genuine example of conflict between a group and an organization. The informal work rules of unorganized workers are an interesting example of this phenomenon. We may make a distinction here perhaps between the folk ideology of the unorganized group, as reflected in a purely oral tradition of wise saws, words of advice, verbal threats to dissident members, and so on, and the secular ideology of a sect or a party, which is embodied in written language and transmitted by more formal training.

Now let us look a little more closely at the kind of role conflict that is implied in the job, the type of membership in an organization that consists of being hired to occupy a role that the organization itself specifies, either through its hierarchy or its written rules. It is interesting to contrast the approach of the economist with that of the social psychologist at this point. The economist looks at the phenomenon of the job as an exchange: the employer pays out money in return for labor, and the worker, in a larger context, receives utility of the things that can be bought with money in return for the disutility or sacrifice that is involved in doing the work. Disutility here is a blanket term for the role conflict, that is, the conflict between what the individual would rather be doing with his time and what the job requires him to do. The economist generally assumes rising disutility with rise in the amount of labor performed, at least after a certain point. The measurement of the amount of labor performed is a difficulty that is usually passed over lightly. The number of hours worked per day is a good rough measure, but when we try to measure intensity or disagreeableness of labor, grave difficulties arise. The economist, then, usually assumes that the individual will willingly increase the number of hours worked as long as the utility of additional income or reward is greater than the disutility imposed by the additional work. As the number of hours worked increases, however, the additional utility of the additional reward (marginal utility) falls, and the marginal disutility from an additional amount of labor rises. At the number of hours worked where these two quantities come to equality, the individual is no longer willing to increase the amount of labor supplied. There is no sense of conflict here, though there is limitation on the power of the individual to do as he pleases; economic man, however, simply makes the best of whatever situation he finds and accepts it. If there is a better situation somewhere else, he goes to it; he does not, at least in the textbooks, try to lessen the disutilities or raise the utilities of an existing situation but accepts these functions as given.

The economist's abstraction is useful in pointing out that a job situation is not necessarily highly conflictual or that, even if there is conflict, this can be resolved by acceptance, that is, by unilateral decision, on the part of the employee. The social psychologist is likely to take a different point of view and to stress the conflictual elements in the situation, sometimes almost to the exclusion of that fact that, in most jobs, after all, people accept what they have to do for what they get with a minimum of fuss and feathers. Nevertheless, the social psychologist is right in pointing out the essential complexity of the labor transaction. The worker does not simply sell a homogeneous commodity called labor; he sells a slice of his life, time, status, and group relationship. Consequently the economist's disutility is not a simple function of physical effort but a complicated psychological magnitude that depends not only on the character and personality of the worker himself but also on the way in which the role is defined both by the employing organization and by the small group of workers, foremen, straw bosses, and so on, with whom the worker is in face-to-face contact. It is the underlying theme of personnel management that the disutility of work can be diminished by creating a work environment in which the worker feels accepted and with which he can identify as a group. If the job situation is such that the worker is treated with dignity, regarded as a person and not just as a hand or as a commodity, and made to find a personal pride and identification in his membership in the work group, then, the argument goes, people will work harder and more efficiently, and the conflict between the goals of the individual and the goals of the organization will diminish. There is much of value in this approach, though there is also a danger of cant and sentimentality. Personnel management can too easily become the art of pushing people around without their knowing enough about it to dislike it. If the genuine concern for human dignity, which is the essential moral core of personnel management, is lost, a very disagreeable art of manipulating people for the advantage of the large organization takes its place, and this will produce an inevitably unfavorable reaction. There is, therefore, value in the economist's recognition that work involves disutility, that this disutility has to be overcome by offering utilities of some kind as a reward or inducement, and also that this conflict can be resolved on the fairly matter-of-fact basis of paying enough to make the worker accept the role conflict. We shall return to this subject in a later chapter.

The conflict of an individual with an organization frequently revolves around the various mechanisms of control by which the upper members of a hierarchy seek to impose their will and image on the lower members. There are many of these control mechanisms. Of these, the most important perhaps is the budget, which is a planned schedule of disbursements for various purposes within a given time. This is particularly important for controlling subdivisions and departments of a larger organization; a department or division survives in a larger organization only if it can get funds from the larger body through a budget organization. If the upper members of the hierarchy disapprove of doings lower down, one very effective method of control is through a threat to cut off funds. A closely related method of control is the right to hire and fire. Within a private organization, this is the ultimate sanction. Within public organizations like the state or its subordinate municipalities, there are what seem to be, on the surface, at least, more severe sanctions such as imprisonment or even capital punishment, mainly one suspects because exile or deportation, which is the equivalent, at this level, of the right to fire or expel, from private organizations is hard to handle on the international or even municipal scale, perhaps because of the traditional inalienability of native-born citizenship.

Another important part of a control system is the audit, information about the organization supplied not by the hierarchy or even by its own staff but by an outside agency. The concept of the audit can easily be widened from its traditional use in accounting to include all types of outside information gathering from labor spies and Willmark operators to public-opinion polls. Then, finally—and this is the Achilles heel of control systems—much of the control is done on the basis of reports passed up the hierarchy from its lower to its upper reaches. The larger the organization, the more its product as far as the hierarchy is concerned comes to be reports. Reports, however, do not always reflect reality, and one may venture on the hypothesis that, the tighter and more rigid the control system, the less reality will be reflected in the information flow as it passes up the channels of the hierarchy. Any organization faces a dilemma here. If its control system is too tight, so that the lower members of the hierarchy feel themselves to be operating in a very restricted role, with little trust placed in them and a constant fear of being spied on, the identification of these members with the organization will be low, morale will be low, the apathetic reaction, if not actual sabotage, is likely to prevail, and productivity will be adversely affected. At the other extreme, a control system that is too loose destroys the sense of integrity and purpose of the organization itself; there may be strong identification with the organization and high morale, but the identification is not with anything very clear or important, and the morale dissipates itself in good fellowship rather than in getting on with a job. For every organization, there is an optimum degree of trust of its members or employees, and the cost of mistrust, in terms of too tight and costly controls, may be even higher than the cost of misplaced trust. One suspects that the costs of mistrust are likely to be underestimated, being less spectacular and less easily identified than the costs of misplaced trust, and that, therefore, there will be a tendency for organizations to be on the tight side of the optimum.

A good deal has been made in recent literature of the vices of organization man and of the dangers that beset the dignity of the person as a man tries to adapt himself to the ways of large organizations and climb up the slippery ladders of organization hierarchy.

Here perhaps is a real conflict between the individual and the organization that becomes of increasing importance as the organizational revolution leads to increase in the size of organizations. In the larger organization, it is argued, the individual is depersonalized, he becomes merely a number in an IBM machine file, his opportunity for spontaneous creativity is limited, and if he is to succeed, he has to conform to a slimy kind of culture in which most effort is directed toward ingratiating oneself with the immediate superiors, in which the appearance of efficiency is much more important than its actuality, and in which nobody does an honest day's work for an honest day's pay but everybody has to involve himself in a vast process of toadying that eventually engulfs not only the man himself but also his wife and family. At the other extreme, of course, stands the independent yeoman, cultivating his acres in righteousness and independence, or the sturdy village blacksmith, who is the pride and joy of every passing poet. The general argument bears relation to the long dispute between Babylon and the Prophets, between the advocates of rural peace and virtue and the defenders of urban excitement and civilization.

Literary breast-beating about the woes of man caught in the toils of large-scale organization may have been excessive, and the romantic affection for the peasant and the artizan glosses over a good deal of plain hardness and crudeness of life; but there still remains a real problem of how to defend the integrity and dignity of the individual against the organizations with which he is involved—not only the corporation but the educational system, the church, and the state. There are two very different kinds of answer to this problem: one is given by the market, that is, by the right to quit, and the other by constitutionality, which is the right to argue. The market is the economist's baby and has been much neglected by the political scientists; conversely, constitutionality is the darling of political scientists and has been neglected by the economists. In an over-all view of the problem, however, we should see these two as coordinate pillars of individual freedom. The right to quit an organization is a powerful check on the power of its hierarchy. The right to quit one firm and join another is a check on the arbitrary power of the boss; the right to quit one university and join another is a powerful force making for academic freedom; the power to quit one church and join another is a major limitation on the power of a spiritual hierarchy; the power to divorce a wife or husband is a check on the potential tyranny of marriage; the power to quit one country and emigrate to another is a powerful implied criticism of national governments; the power to quit one seller and trade with another is the essential competitive check on monopoly.

On the other hand, the power to quit may be absent or may be empty, or quitting may have too high a cost for the individual. The individual gets deeply involved in his organizational roles; his job is part of his life, and shifting employers, conversion to another faith, divorce, emigration, or even changing from a favorite store are costly and often traumatic experiences, involving a deep uprooting of the individual from his previous setting. Where there is unemployment, the right to quit an employer may be empty, for there are no other jobs to go to; where no other country offers asylum, the right to emigrate may likewise be empty. The greater the difficulty or cost of quitting an organizational relationship, the more important it becomes to develop constitutionality, that is, previously agreed upon and socially sanctioned procedures and rituals by which grievances of the individual against his organizational role can be dealt with. In the case of the firm, we see constitutionality developing in such things as the union contract and grievance procedure. In the case of the state, constitutionality is the essential component of democratic as against totalitarian institutions, in which the individual has certain constitutional rights as against the state. In the case of marriage, there are internal rituals within the family; there may also be marriage courts and marriage counselors and an apparatus of outside constitutionality, as yet rather poorly developed. In the case of commercial relations, there is an elaborate framework of arbitration and legal procedure. And over the whole of society broods the great constitutionality of the law, providing generalized procedures for everybody's grievances against everyone and everything for those who can afford it.

There is an obverse to the defense of the individual against the organization—the defense of the organization against the individual. As the obverse of the right to quit, there is the right to fire; as the obverse of the individual's constitutional right to procedure, in the settlement of his grievances against the organization, there is the organization's constitutional right to proceed against an offending individual. We arrive here at one of the most ancient and difficult problems involved in the relations of the individual to society and where an old conflict between two different philosophies still continues in the world. At one extreme, we have the individualistic, democratic, Athenian position that an organization and, indeed, society itself are assemblages or structures of individuals and that the rights of the individual must be paramount over the rights of organizations, organizations being mere conveniences or machines, without souls or rights in themselves except in so far as individual rights are expressed through them. At the other extreme, we have the authoritarian, organic, Spartan position that the reality that resides in the society or the organization is at a higher level than that which resides in the individual, for persons come and go, but the role goes on forever—"The king is dead, long live the king!" Hence, individual rights must be strictly subordinate to the preservation and health of the organization, especially, of course, the organization of the state, which is the chief expression of the whole society. This ancient controversy continues today in the struggle between individualistic democracies and totalitarian states, whether of the right or of the left. Its ultimate resolution may be a long way ahead or may be closer than we think. There are clearly two extreme positions, which we might stigmatize as anarchy on the one hand and tyranny on the other, that are to be avoided, and the truth lies somewhere in between; but just where the mean is golden is not easy to discover. That clearer view of the nature both of persons and of organizations which one hopes will be the fruit of social science may help us also to narrow the limits of argument on this vital subject and find modes of organization that neither impoverish the life and freedom of the individual nor enable the individual to threaten the life and freedom of others.

10

ECONOMIC CONFLICT

Up to this point in the argument, we have been trying to formulate general principles of conflict and conflict processes that are common to all or to most conflict situations; that is, we have been developing an abstract model of a conflict situation or a conflict process that applies no matter what the setting, who the parties, or what the issues. In the previous four chapters, we have moved from the most general analysis to some more specific discussion of types of parties and the conflicts that are appropriate to each type. We still, however, have left the matter at a very general level: the processes that we have described hitherto are applicable equally, with some modifications, to industrial conflict and strikes, international conflict and war, family conflict and divorce, legal conflict and a judgment, race conflict and a riot, and political conflict and an election. Now we want to take a closer look at the differences between different kinds of conflict situations. It is a major argument of this work that all conflicts have common elements and general patterns and that it is in the search for these common elements that we are most likely to understand the phenomenon in any of its manifestations. A major corollary, however, is that all conflicts are not alike; there are important differences between, say, industrial and international conflict or between intrafamilial and interracial conflict. For a complete understanding of the phenomenon, we must understand these differences as well as the similarities. Otherwise, we shall be misled by analogy and will try to find elements in international conflict, for instance, that are really peculiar to industrial conflict. A strike is not a war, a divorce is not a riot, and so on. We may note that these differences appear most striking in what might be described as the *boundary process*. The processes by which relations go from bad to worse are rather similar in all cases; these are the familiar Richardson processes. It is the crisis, or the overt breakdown of relationship into combat, that differs most from situation to situation.

In our drive toward the specific cases, let us first look at the peculiar characteristics of economic conflict. At first sight, economic conflict looks like a fairly simple example of field conflict in which two or more parties are trying to occupy a limited field and in which the field is not large enough to satisfy the preferred amount of occupancy of all the competing organizations or persons. The field, in this case, is commodities—goods and services. Whether these are thought of as a stock or a flow, as capital or an income, the same principle of scarcity holds; there is not enough of these things to satisfy all demands for them, which is what the economist means by saying that these things are scarce. Out of the fact of scarcity arises both exchange value, or the price system, and economic conflict. The conflict arises because of a famous law that I have sometimes called the Duchess's law, from one of the morals of the Duchess in *Alice in Wonderland*—"The more there is of yours, the less there is of mine." If there is only so much pie to go around and if demands cannot be satisfied by any distribution of pie among the claimants, economic conflict inevitably arises, in the sense that, if one gets more, everybody else taken together must get less and that the "more" and the "less" are significant to the parties. If everyone could be satisfied with existing supplies, of course, there would be no conflict, but this happy state of affairs is still far off in spite of economic development and technical progress.

The poorer the society and the scarcer commodities are in general, the more intense will be this conflict. The intensity of economic conflict in this general sense can be measured hypothetically by the marginal utility of income, that is, by the significance to the individual of a unit increase or decrease in real income. There are difficulties of measurement here that we shall ignore, as they do not destroy the general validity of the concept. In a very poor society, a little more income may be a matter of life and death; here, the conflict is acute, for my life may perhaps be bought, in extreme conditions, only by your death. In a famine, for instance, the richest and most powerful part of the population survives literally by depriving the rest of the means of life. As society gets richer, the significance to the individual of additions to income presumably grows less and less: this is the famous principle of the diminishing marginal utility of income. Galbraith has argued that, in the affluent society, economic conflict virtually disappears, for who can get excited about another square foot of chrome on the tail fin when all major needs are satisfied? In most of the world, of course, we are still a very long way from affluence, and even the United States is not as affluent as Galbraith seems to imply; but the general point is well taken.

Economic conflict of the kind discussed above may be called the *personal distribution conflict*, as it is concerned primarily with the distribution of the total economic product of society among persons. It takes on a very different appearance in a progressive society, that is, a society in which per capita real income is rising, from what it does in a stationary society, where per capita real income is not changing. In a stationary society, the conflict is perceived as an acute one. If one gets more, then, automatically, the rest of the people together must get less. The luxuries of the rich are literally paid for by the destitution of the poor. It is little wonder that such societies tend to generate acute class conflicts that occasionally burst forth into violent revolution. In a stagnant society, the only road to relieve the poverty of the poor seems to be to expropriate the rich and divide up the proceeds. The popularity of killing landlords remains unaffected by the economist's timid reminder that, in a poor society, people would still be very poor even if all incomes were equal.

In a progressing society, the situation takes a very different turn, especially under conditions of rapid progress. Here, the rich can get richer without the poor getting poorer; indeed, anybody can get richer, up to a point, without anybody else getting poorer. There is still economic conflict, in the sense that some get richer faster than others. This is very different, however, from the conflict in a stationary society, where one only rises by pushing another down. This is the difference, of course, between the positive-sum game of the progressive society and the zero-sum game of a stationary society. In the negative-sum game of a declining society, the conflict is even more acute: here, one can only succeed in staying where one is by pushing someone else down. The negative or zero-sum game, as we have seen, is pure conflict, the positive-sum game is a mixture of conflict and cooperation, especially if cooperation can increase the positive sum. There is cooperation in increasing the pie and competition in sharing it, but if each man gets the increase for which he is cooperatively responsible, the conflictual element is reduced to the vanishing point.

An interesting example of the mixture of conflict and cooperation that is found in a positive-sum game is observed in the very phenomenon of free exchange itself, which is the core of economic life and organization. In a free exchange, both parties must benefit by the fact of the exchange; otherwise, the exchange will not take place. Some economists, especially Marx, have worried about how this could be so, especially as, in pure exchange, nothing seems to be created, for there is only a reshuffling of the ownership of commodities or exchangeables among the exchangers. The marginal-utility school cleared up this problem and showed how exchange could increase the total utility of each party, in spite of the fact that it represented only a redistribution of exchangeables, because each party gave up something that was less significant to him in return for something that was more significant. This could take place partly because of differences in tastes (some people like nuts more than apples, and some like apples more than nuts, even if everybody has the same quantity) but mainly because of differences in specialization and in distribution of stocks of goods before exchange; everybody gives up what he has too much of in return for what he has too little of. Specialization, however, increases the total product, at least up to a point, according to the famous principle that the jack-of-all-trades is master of none. Exchange, therefore, up to a point, is a positive-sum game even in commodities as well as in utilities.

This is not to say, of course, that specialization cannot be taken too far. Even Adam Smith himself has a much neglected passage in which he denounces the division of labor as a creator of stupidity and torpor of mind.[1] Overspecialization can put a limited horizon on economic development both for an individual or for a region, and it exposes the specialist to the winds of changing taste and techniques in a way that the less specialized person or society avoids. There may be, therefore, a case for the restraint of specialization, and many of the economic arguments for protection, for regulation, and for discriminatory taxation rest on the fear of too great specialization. The point of optimum specialization is not easy to find; up to this point, however, specialization is clearly a positive-sum game.

In exchange, the peculiar combination of cooperation and competition that is characteristic of the positive-sum game takes the form of cooperation in the fact of organization of exchange and competition in regard to the *terms* of the exchange, that is, the ratio of exchange. For any act of exchange, there will normally be a range of exchange ratios within which both parties benefit and a free exchange will take place. Within this range, however, the distribution of the benefit depends on where the actual exchange ratio lies. At one extreme, all the benefit goes to one party, and, at the other extreme, all goes to the other party. Thus, in an exchange of wheat for money, there is a price of wheat that is so low that the seller receives no advantage, and all the gains of the exchange go to the buyer. There is another price that is so high that the buyer

---

[1] Adam Smith, *The Wealth of Nations*, New York, Modern Library, 1937, Book V, chap. 1, p. 734.

receives no advantage, and all the gain goes to the seller. Within this range, exchange benefits both parties, but the higher the price, the more of this gain goes to the seller, and the lower the price, the more of this gain goes to the buyer. Here, there is clearly a conflict that has to be resolved by a bargain, and the settlement of the conflict depends on a mysterious magnitude known as bargaining power. We shall return to this concept later.

In the model of perfect competition, where there are large numbers of buyers and sellers in contact and no loyalties to divert individuals from the serious business of maximizing individual gains, it should be observed that the conflict element in the act of exchange tends to disappear. This is because, with large numbers of buyers and sellers, the range of prices at which any particular pair of exchangers can trade with mutual advantage shrinks, simply because of the alternative buyers or sellers who are available. Thus, if we have only a single buyer and a single seller in the wheat market, the buyer might be willing to pay as much as $4 a bushel rather than go without, and the seller might be willing to get as little as $1 a bushel rather than not sell. There is a wide range of mutual advantage and much scope for conflict in bargaining about the price. Suppose now, however, that there are a considerable number of other buyers and sellers and that some sellers are selling at $2.51 while some buyers are buying at $2.49. This automatically reduces the range of mutual advantage of our original pair of exchangers to $2.49 to 2.51, for our original buyer will not buy from the original seller at any price above $2.51, for he can buy in the market at that price, and our original seller will not sell to the original buyer at any price below $2.49 for he can sell in the market at that price. The range of bargaining, then, is only 2 cents, and the conflict between the original pair is very small. In the absolutely perfect market of the economist's imagination, the range shrinks to zero, and there is no conflict between any particular pair of bargainers at all, simply because there is no range of bargaining.

Even in perfect competition, a change in price will make some people better off and some people worse off. Even though, therefore, there is no conflict in the bargain in perfect competition, there is competition, in the sense that circumstances over which no individual has any control may make one group of people gain and another group of people lose. In general any change in the structure of prices will cause extensive redistributions of wealth and of income among the persons of a society. If one price rises relative to others, the people who hold this commodity, security, or whatever the exchangeable happens to be will gain in the relative distribution of the total market value of assets, relative to those who do not hold it: people who hold much of it will gain more than those who hold little. Because of the vast interconnectedness of the price system, however, and the fact that it is almost impossible to change one price without setting off a vast reverberation among other prices, the ultimate effects of the change of a single price may be very different from its immediate effects. This means that the nature of economic competition, that is, the actual effects on the distribution of wealth and income of any particular change, is very obscure, and as long as this is the case, the lines of real economic conflict remain even more obscure.

Generally speaking, the short-run effects are more apparent; the long-run effects are more obscure because of the difficulties of tracing the dynamic consequences of any particular change. Some examples will illustrate the problem. Consider, for instance, the effect of an increase in the import duty on a particular commodity, say, watches. The immediate result is that foreign producers who have previously been exporting are probably harmed and that domestic producers are benefited, as they can sell their watches dearer or can sell more of them. Domestic purchasers of watches are probably harmed, as they have a narrower choice and may have to pay more for their watches, and as people were purchasing the imported watches before the raise in duty, the inference is that these were preferred by some people to the domestic product. Foreign purchasers of watches may be benefited, as watches that previously went to the original market are now diverted to others, where they will probably be sold cheaper than before. If we confine ourselves to these short-run effects and to the comparison of an equilibrium position before the change with an equilibrium after it, it is not difficult to show that, on fairly plausible assumptions, the net benefit to all concerned is likely to be negative, though there may be important exceptions to this rule.

Though, in the short run, it is fairly easy to allocate gains and losses, at least qualitatively, in the long run the position is much more obscure. Suppose, for instance, that there is no monopoly and that there is complete freedom of entry into the domestic watch industry. The benefits that are the result of the increased duties attract new producers, and it will not be long before the profits in the industry are down to normal; the net long-run result is that there is a larger domestic watch industry than before, but the industry will be no more profitable than before. If the unusual profitability of the industry attracts an excessive number of new producers, as is not impossible, there may be a middle period in which the industry is actually abnormally unprofitable before the final adjustments are made. In the long run, therefore, the net gain to a competitive protected industry is dubious and may even be negative. The long-run impact on purchasers of watches depends on the consequences of expansion of the domestic industry. If there are what the economist calls external economies, so that the expansion of the industry makes it more efficient as a whole and reduces its costs per unit, prices to the purchasers of watches may actually be reduced, and the purchasers will be better off. If, however, the expansion of the industry means that less suitable resources have to be drawn into it, its costs per unit will rise, and purchasers will ultimately be somewhat worse off. The long-run effects on the foreign industry are equally obscure, depending on the nature of the long-run-cost curve.

The above analysis is merely one example of a large class of problems that illustrates the great difficulty of assessing the long-run effects on the distribution of wealth and income of any particular policy. We shall see later that wage policy involves exactly the same difficulties; it is very difficult to assess the long-run effects, for instance, of a given increase in wages. Similarly, it is by no means clear who is benefited and who is injured in the long run by subsidies to particular industries, such as agriculture. Indeed, one almost is forced to the cynical conclusion sometimes that an almost sure way to harm people is to try to help them. Subsidies to farmers, for instance, by encouraging them to remain in a low-income, declining industry when, otherwise, they would have got out into an advancing sector of society, may actually harm them as persons. Technical assistance, like the introduction of the potato in Ireland in the eighteenth century or the rapid spread of malaria control in the tropics since 1945, may set off a population explosion that makes the final condition of the assisted people worse than before. Aid to dependent children may create a subculture within the larger society in which children are raised to perpetual dependence. Pension plans for workers may tie them to their jobs and weaken their bargaining power. Conversion to a higher faith may disorganize the life of a primitive people, so that they can follow neither the old ways nor the new. Independence and self-government may cut a small country off from the world centers and leave it eventually to fester in misery and disorganization. These deplorable consequences are not, of course, necessary, and one does not want to abandon the desire to do good merely because its practice is difficult. Nevertheless, the social scientist has a certain duty to point out that it is hard to do good and hard to establish justice and that, the more we know about the intricate processes of social dynamics, the better chance we shall have of doing those things which will, in fact, promote human welfare and social justice.

In spite of the complexity of the problem of economic conflict, there are one or two fairly simple things than can be said about it. One is that the impact of any given change on an individual depends on his adaptibility and mobility. Suppose, for instance, that we have a fall in the price of a single commodity, say, coffee. This will lower the income of almost all those engaged in the coffee industry. The first impact will be on the owners of coffee estates, whose profits will be reduced; the impact will soon be transmitted, however, to workers on these estates, through either lower wages or unemployment, and to small coffee growers. If there is absolutely nothing else for coffee growers to do but to grow coffee, their lot is hard indeed; there is no way that they can escape from this reduction in income, and if it is severe enough, they may be driven to destitution. If, however, they are adaptable, if the coffee growers can easily turn to some more profitable crop, and if displaced coffee workers can easily find opportunities for employment elsewhere, the injury done to them is slight, and the conflict implied in a shift in relative prices is small.

A second proposition is that the impact of any given change on a group depends on the mobility of people into it or out of it and that, hence, the severity of economic conflict among groups depends on the mobility of their individual members. Where it is very hard for an individual to leave the occupational or cultural group to which he belongs or to join another, a reduction of the price of the group's product, or, as an economist would say, the worsening of its terms of trade, is likely to be long-lasting and unresponsive to any attempt at corrective behavior on the part of the group itself. Conversely, favorable movements, likewise, may have lasting effects if the group can prevent entry of new members. Where groups are mobile and shifting, so that individuals can easily shift from one to another, a disadvantaged group soon loses members to more advantaged groups, and this shift of membership normally tends to equalize the advantages of the two groups. Under these circumstances, group competition is ephemeral, strong group loyalties and identifications are not likely to develop, and group conflict will be slight. When, however, there is no mobility between groups, group identification and loyalty are likely to be strong, and conflict, therefore, is likely to be acute. There is a curious problem here in the dynamics of development of immobility and group loyalties, for the immobility that generates group loyalties is intensified by these loyalties themselves.

A group may begin by being quite open to ingress and egress, but if mobility is low enough to begin to generate group self-consciousness and group loyalties, this fact in itself makes ingress and egress harder, and this, in turn, intensifies the group loyalties. One suspects that the development of nationality obeys a dynamics of this kind; similarly, the development of strong class consciousness, say, among factory workers, tends to prevent upward mobility into the managerial or professional group, and so the class consciousness may be increased by the very immobility that it generates.

A good example of a potential group conflict that is constantly being undermined by mobility is the conflict among age groups. The competition among age groups, especially in unstable times, can be very severe. It is reflected at a particular moment of time in the competition of the young, the middle-aged, and the aged for the product of society. By and large, it is those in the middle-aged groups between adolescence and senility who produce the product of society. They have to share it, however, with the young, who must be fed, clothed, sheltered, and educated in the nonproductive years, and also with the aged, who must also be supported when they are not producing anything. The conflict is a very real one; the more of the product goes to one group, the less is currently available for the others. Fine schools and generous old-age pensions mean smaller current real incomes for those in middle life. The conflict occasionally breaks out into the open in the form, for instance, of a struggle about school appropriations, refusals to pass school bonds, debates about old-age pensions, old-age political movements like the Townsend Plan, and revolutions of young insurgents against the (presumably) corrupt old men in positions of power. In spite of the very real nature of the competition, however, age-group conflicts tend to be sporadic, disorganized, and unstable, and they soon peter out. Age-group organizations, in which the common interests of a given age group are the only bond, likewise, are sporadic and have difficulty in maintaining themselves. Youth organizations are generally maintained by the middle-aged in a framework of some larger organization: it is not the young, after all, who run schools, universities, boy scouts, or even youth movements, and where students, for instance, do take over the administration of a university, the results are not always too happy. Organizations of the old, likewise, are likely to peter out as they find it difficult to replace leadership as it dies off.

The reason for the instability of age-group organizations is, of course, that this is the one group that has perfect one-way mobility through the mere passage of time. The young get middle-aged, the middle-aged get old, and the old die. Consequently, the young always have at least one eye on the group to which they are soon going to join, and likewise with the middle-aged. By the time a youth group has succeeded in winning something from the middle-aged, its members are likely to be middle-aged themselves and suffering from their own earlier success. The middle-aged are willing to support the old, as a matter of principle, because they will soon be old themselves, and supporting the old eventually pays off for anybody who does not die first; and if he does die first, he presumably does not have to worry anyway.

The conflict between the age groups is a very interesting example of an economic institution which is only partially in the exchange system and which involves gifts or support. If we look at the economic system in strictly current terms, it is clear that a good deal of income is, in fact, derived not from production but from support (transfers). The consumption of the young, of the old, of the sick, and of the indigent is received as a kind of gift from the productive sectors of the population, in the sense that the recipients of this real income do not give anything currently for it in return. There is, therefore, an interesting economic conflict between the supporters and the supported that is not a conflict about terms of trade or the price system but is a conflict about how much should be given in support of the currently nonproductive. The tax system is a particularly important arena of this conflict, because a major function of the tax system is precisely that of financing support—taking money away from those who derive income from the production and sale of goods and services and giving it to those who currently produce nothing.

When we take a longer time perspective, a good deal of income that looks like support in a short time period is seen as long-term exchange. Thus, when the young and the middle-aged save for their old age, they are purchasing future consumption by sacrificing present consumption. Their sacrifice of present consumption may, in fact, represent a transfer to the current group of aged, but it can be represented as in a sense a bargain with the future. In a large and rather vague way, we can regard the support that the middle-aged give to the young and to the old as a bargain across the generations: the middle-aged support the young now in return for an implicit bargain that in twenty-five or thirty years the young, who will then be middle-aged, will support the middle-aged, who will then be old. The support that the middle-aged give to both the old and the young can then be thought of as two bargains: the support given to the young is the first part of a bargain that will be fulfilled one generation hence, and the support given to the old is the second part of a bargain made one generation ago. Thus we have moved away from support conflict into bargain conflict; there is, then, as we have seen, community of interest in the fact of the bargain but conflict about its terms.

The rate of interest in one of its many functions is an expression of the terms of the bargain between the generations. If the rate of interest is high, the middle-aged will support the old generously, and if the young have borrowed for their support and education, the middle-aged will likewise be supporting the young generously. The savings of the middle-aged will accumulate at a high rate of interest, and when this generation is old, it will be able to live better than if the rate of interest had been low. Similarly, if the middle-aged have borrowed when young, they will have to pay a high interest on these borrowings.

The problem of age-group conflict is greatly complicated by the introduction of fluctuations and dynamic disequilibriums. The rise and fall of birth and death rates, for instance, may substantially change the proportion of the population in different age groups. In the 1930s, for instance, the number of people of working age in most developed countries was unusually large; birth rates had been declining, so that the middle-aged came from a larger cohort than the children, and the rise in the expectation of life had not fully worked out its influence on the number of old people. In a rising population, in any case, the old come from a smaller cohort than the young or the middle-aged. In the 1960's on the other hand, the proportion of people of working age is much smaller; the birth rate has been rising sharply in most countries, so that there is a large cohort of children and young people, and the rise in the expectation of life is now being felt in an increasing number of old people. The burden of current support of the young and old, therefore, is much greater than it was a generation ago, and the burden is likely to increase.

Another aspect of the same problem concerns the age-specific character of the labor market and the size of the cohorts coming onto it. Normally, there is a rough distribution of jobs available by the age of the worker, and when there is a sharp distortion in the size of the cohorts coming onto the market, labor shortages or surpluses may result. Thus, in Britain, there was an acute youth problem in 1935, as the large generation of 1919, when the end of the first World War raised the birth rate nearly 50 percent, left school at 14 and came onto the labor market. Conversely, in the United States in the 1950s, the unusually small cohorts of the 1930s were coming onto the labor market, and it was very easy for them to get jobs. In the 1960s, the much larger cohorts of the 1940s (almost twice the size) will be coming onto the labor market; and it may, therefore, be quite difficult to place them, and a sharp rise of unemployment among the young may be expected. Similarly, in many tropical countries, there was a large reduction in infant mortality following the health revolution of the late 1940s, and an acute youth problem may be expected very soon as a result.

The business cycle and the war cycle, likewise, cause acute disparities in the experience of different generations. The generations, for instance, that came to maturity during the two world wars or during the Great Depression, had a much harder time of it than generations that came to maturity in times of peace and of prosperity. The generation that graduated in 1933, for instance, never really recovered from the experience of coming onto the labor market at the depth of the Great Depression. Similarly, the generation that was in its 20s in 1914 or in 1939 suffered not only war casualties but missed economic opportunities in a way that veterans legislation only partly compensates. The young farmer who bought a farm in 1919 at the peak of prices was almost doomed to fail no matter how great his abilities; even if he survived the agricultural depression of the 1920s, he was almost sure to lose his farm in the Great Depression of the 1930s. A young man, by contrast, who bought a farm, a business, or a house or who went into debt for almost any purpose in 1934 was likely to succeed no matter how inefficient he might be.

These conflicts among the generations are perhaps the most acute sources of real economic competition in the sense of group benefits and misfortunes. Nevertheless, they do not result in a strong sense of conflict, and only rarely do they develop organization for conflict. No greater demonstration could be made of the proposition that it is not mere homogeneity or similarity of fortune that makes an economic group or that sets the lines of organized economic conflict. A group may be very heterogeneous from the point of view of economic conflict, in the sense that, whatever happens or whatever the organized group does, some of its members will benefit and some will be harmed; and yet the group may have a strong sense of identity, and some of its members may support policies as members of the group that, in fact, injures them as individuals. Group consciousness is more important in setting the lines of conscious conflict than group interest. We shall run across the same phenomenon in the discussion of international conflict.

The two main types of self-conscious economic groups are the commodity or service groups—occupational, industrial, or professional—on the one hand and the class or cultural groups on the other. The occupational and industrial groups have perhaps the clearest common interest; almost all people in agriculture, for example, are interested in a high price for agricultural products, and all people in the steel industry are interested in a high price for steel. These commodity groups, therefore, tend to form political pressure groups to extract laws and regulations from the state with the object of making their product scarcer. Tariffs are one aspect of this conflict, and we have seen how dubious a benefit this is likely to be. Subsidies are another aspect. Restriction of entry and licensing is a third important aspect. Of these, only those legal restrictions which give the commodity or service groups the right to exclude would-be members—which is the essence of monopoly power—give much hope of benefiting the group in the long run. Nevertheless, the pulling and hauling of commodity groups is perhaps the largest business of any legislative assembly.

Agriculture presents such an important special case and has so many peculiarities that it deserves special mention. In most societies, agriculture is in trouble; agriculturalists have a strong group consciousness, wield a political power frequently out of proportion to their numbers, and have usually succeeded in getting the state to intervene in the price system and in the system of support gifts and transfers, ostensibly with a view to shifting income toward agriculture and away from other sectors. The reasons for this pattern are complex, though they operate in nearly all modern societies. Agriculture does tend to have lower per capita incomes than other occupations, especially in a rapidly developing society. This is mainly because of technical improvement in agriculture itself, paradoxical as this may seem. Technical improvement in agriculture in the sense of greater output of food and fibers per man inevitably means a relative decline in the agricultural labor force, because of the inelastic demand for most agricultural products. With medieval techniques, it took about 80 percent of the people to feed the population; with modern techniques, we can grow all we need with less than 10 percent of the people. In the course of this transition, there must be a constant decline in the proportion of people engaged in agriculture, and this can be achieved only by making agriculture less attractive than other occupations. How much the differential must be depends on the mobility of resources out of agriculture and into other vocations. If agricultural resources are very immobile, large differentials in income must develop before resources will move out of it. If resources are mobile, the transition can be achieved relatively painlessly.

Unfortunately, the problem has usually been conceived in terms of a static justice rather than in terms of dynamic adjustment. Hence, the remedy has been sought not in facilitating the adjustment and in speeding the movement from agriculture into industry but in trying to raise agricultural incomes by creating artificial scarcities of agricultural products or by giving direct subsidies. These measures, however, tend to prevent the inevitable adjustment and so frequently prolong the agony. Price supports have led to unwanted accumulations of surplus products, subsidies tend to feed on themselves and require constant increase until they become unmanageably burdensome, output restrictions either have defeated themselves, as acreage restrictions usually do through the increase in yield per acre, or where they are effective as in the case of marketing quotas, they tend to be capitalized in the rents of quota-bearing land or in the market value of the quota itself where this is salable and, hence, benefit only the generation that happens to be in the saddle when the quotas are imposed, thus leading to further injustice between the generations. The basic fallacy behind much agricultural policy is the attempt to do justice to a commodity rather than to people. Thus, agricultural policy is frequently sold, politically, even in countries with predominantly urban populations, by an appeal to social justice; farmers are poor, the argument goes, and should, therefore, be helped. What actually gets helped, however, is wheat or corn, and when this is done, only some farmers get helped, and these are usually the richer farmers. The paradox of trying to cure agricultural poverty by raising agricultural prices is that poverty in agriculture is mainly due to small farmers and subsistence farmers having so little to sell. When we raise prices, we do little for the man who has little to sell; we do much for the man who has much to sell.

The other type of economic conflict that has received attention is the class conflict. This is, of course, particularly associated with the Marxist ideology. Here the classification of society is not by commodity groups but by income groups; the class conflict, roughly speaking, is the conflict of the poor and the rich, of the privileged and the unprivileged, or of the dominant and the dominated. Like all other group conflicts, this conflict is likely to be more acute, the less mobility there is between the groups and the more self-conscious of their identity and distinctiveness the groups become. The most acute case of class conflict is where the rich and the poor have totally different cultures, perhaps even different languages, and where there is no mobility from one group to the other. In rich and fluid societies, where there is a continuum from the rich to the poor through the middle class, where there are no sharp breaks in the income distribution and there is a good deal of mobility between income groups, with some individuals or families getting richer and some poorer, and where there is a common language and a widely diffused common culture in spite of income differences, class consciousness will be low and class conflict unimportant.

Underlying the whole problem of class conflict is the problem of what really determines the distribution of wealth and income. This is a problem of such complexity that one despairs of reducing it to simple terms. The distribution of wealth is the result of a long historic process of inheritance, saving, capital gain and loss, marriage, taxation, expropriation and redistribution, and so on. We can point to certain institutions that will make for a movement toward greater equality in distribution, such as inheritance taxes, equal distribution of estates among children, public education, and so on. Similarly, we can point to institutions that make for inequality, such as primogeniture, regressive taxation, caste, and so on. Inflation and deflation are great redistributors of wealth: inflation tends to discriminate against settled and customary payments, fixed money incomes, bond-holders, and so on; deflation discriminates against profit makers, farmers, the unemployed, and so on. The very complexity of these processes, however, makes it hard to draw clear lines of conflict. The decisions that affect the dynamic process of distribution are not usually taken with any clear notion of consequences in mind; they are taken or are often not taken as a result of events, pressures, and images that have nothing to do with their ultimate or even their immediate consequences. Both deflation and inflation occur as a result of a failure to do things rather than as a result of doing things; they are seldom planned deliberately. Tax structures, likewise, which may have a profound effect on distribution, are often thrown together out of the exigencies of a period of war or crisis finance and remain to have profound but unsuspected repercussions on subsequent decades.

This is not to deny the existence of class conflict; the class struggle has been and still is a powerful symbol, and a good deal of history can be interpreted in terms of the rise and fall of classes. What must be emphasized, however, is that the class struggle is a much more complex phenomenon than the simple struggle of the poor to take from the rich and of the rich to defend themselves against the poor and more complex also than the struggle of the workers against the capitalists, as we shall see more fully in the next chapter. This is because the struggle is not a static conflict about a fixed aggregation of wealth or income but a conflict about an immensely complex dynamic process in which it is very hard to trace causes and effects. The class conflict is not like two dogs struggling for a bone in which, if one gets more, the other gets less. It is much more like the evolutionary conflict of species, in which temporary advantages often lead to ultimate defeat. We shall pursue this theme in more detail in later chapters.

11

INDUSTRIAL CONFLICT

By industrial conflict, we mean the conflict between employer and employed. Each of these parties may be individuals, unorganized groups, or organizations. Industrial conflict arises as soon as the employer-employee relationship emerges in the course of economic development. In primitive societies, it is rare, simply because specialization of function has not proceeded to the point where specialized employers or employing organizations have emerged. In a society of independent hunters, small family farmers, and individual shopkeepers and craftsmen, the employer-employee relationship hardly exists. Each family derives its income from the sale of some product that it produces or trades in, and work for wages is a rarity. The army with hired soldiers was probably the first example of an employer-employee relationship on a fairly large scale. In the ancient empires, much of what today is done through an employer-employee relationship was done through slavery, which is a different kind of relationship. Even in ancient times, however, wage labor was known; there are many references to it, for instance, in the Bible. It was not, however, until the so-called industrial revolution that wage labor began its swift rise to dominance. Today, in most advanced countries, wages and salaries comprise about 60–70 percent of the national income; that is, about two-thirds of total income is derived from the sale of labor to an employer rather than from the direct production and sale of commodities. It is little wonder that industrial conflict has risen to proportions where, at times, it seems to be the major internal problem of advanced societies.

The term *industrial conflict* is perhaps something of a misnomer, for it is the conflict arising out of the employer-employee relationship or the earning of wages, which are the cases in point, and this can and does exist in agriculture just as it does in industry. The employer-employee relationship is not very different, for instance, in a sugar plantation from what it is in a steel mill. It is still true, however, that, in many parts of the world, agriculture remains the major region of family enterprise and nonwage labor, so that the term "industrial" as applied to the employer-employee relationship is understandable.

The key to the understanding of industrial conflict is the examination of the wage bargain itself as an exchange. We have already examined the type of conflict that is involved in exchange, and we have seen that this has the characteristics of a positive-sum game in that there is both a community and a conflict of interest at the same time between the parties. The wage relationship, however, has peculiarities that are not found in simple commodity exchanges. These peculiarities are so great that they have occasioned rhetorical attempts to deny that labor is a commodity at all; Samuel Gompers, the founding father of the American Federation of Labor, was particularly insistent on this point, and it was even written into the charter of the International Labor Office that "Labor should not be regarded merely as an article of commerce."[1] For all these protestations, labor is something that is bought and sold, enters into exchange, and has a price, which is the wage, all of which properties are characteristic of a commodity. However, even if it must be admitted that labor is a commodity, it is certainly a very peculiar one, and its peculiarities single it out for special treatment both in theory and in practice.

The basic peculiarity of the purchase and sale of labor is that here

[1] Treaty of Versailles, June 28, 1919, Part XIII (Labour), Sect. 427.

we have an exchange in which the exchangeables appear very differently to the two parties. When wheat is bought and sold for money, neither the wheat nor the money appears very different to the buyer and to the seller, though they will have a somewhat different significance, or exchange will not take place. The wheat that the seller gives up is much the same wheat that the buyer receives, and the money that the buyer gives up is much the same money that the seller receives. The exchange of labor for money, however, looks very different from the side of the employer, or buyer of labor, from the way it looks to the worker or seller of labor. For the employer, the transaction is significant in so far as it is an exchange of money or liquid assets for the product of the work. Thus, suppose an employer hires a man to weave yarn into cloth for a week. The result of this operation is that the employer at the end of the week has less money and less yarn but more cloth than he had at the beginning. If the value of the cloth gained is more than the value of the money and yarn (and possibly other things) given up, the transaction was presumably worthwhile. The transaction, however, appears as essentially an exchange within the balance sheet; money and yarn are exchanged for cloth, and it is the cloth that matters, not the labor or human effort that the money went to pay for. From the point of view of the worker, the transaction looks very different. He gains, it is true, the money that the employer gives up; this is the wage. The significance of this, however, will be different for the worker and for the employer. The money that the employer pays in wages represents an opportunity foregone to buy other things—a machine, for instance. The money that the worker receives in wages represents the opportunity to buy those goods and services which constitute the worker's real income. It is not the money that is of interest to the worker but what the money will buy. Thus, a rise in the price of *wage goods*, which workers buy with their money, will reduce real wages even though money wages remain the same and possibly even though the significance of the money wage payment to the employer does not alter. When we look now at what the worker gives up in return for the money wages, this appears directly as time, eight hours a day, or, more exactly perhaps, as time and energy, for hard work may be in some sense more labor per hour than light work, or, more exactly yet perhaps, as time and disutility, for unpleasant work may be more labor per hour than pleasant work. Indirectly, the time signifies alternative uses of life: it is what the worker could have done with the time and energy that he sells which is what he really gives up and which also helps to determine the supply price of his labor. A man who has attractive and remunerative alternative uses of his time will only sell his labor dear; a man who has no alternative but idleness and destitution will sell it cheap.

It is this fact that what the worker gives up is something very different from what the employer receives and what the employer gives up has a different significance to him from what the worker receives that gives rise to most of the peculiarities of industrial conflict, for we have here not only the usual economic conflict about the terms of an exchange but conflict of mutual misunderstanding about exactly what is being exchanged. The employer is really exchanging commodity (or money) for commodity; the human aspect of the transaction, however much he may recognize it indirectly, is not directly relevant to the transaction. The worker is exchanging life for income; the transaction involves him in status, prestige, his standing in the eyes of his family and of the community, and his whole position as a man. The job role not only takes more of his actual waking time and energy than any other but, to a large extent, dominates his other roles; his friends, associates, and clubs, and even his religion, may be determined in part by the job he works at. It is not surprising, therefore, that, between the worker and the employer, there descends a thick wall of cultural misunderstanding. The buyer of wheat may be a seller the next day, and, in organized markets especially, there is no sharp group or cultural distinction between the buyer and the seller. Once the labor or industrial relationship is firmly established, however, there is only a small chance that the employee of today will become the employer of tomorrow, even though this does occasionally happen. The worker is on one side of the exchange for life, and the employer likewise. Consequently, they find it hard to empathize with each other or to see each other's points of view. To the worker, the employer seems remote and impersonal, quite unable to appreciate the deeply personal nature of the transaction in which life is exchanged for money. To the employer, the transaction is in commodities rather than in life, and the worker is an instrument, and often a rather unsatisfactory and overcomplex instrument, in this transaction. It is not surprising that class consciousness develops; the employers and the workers become two noncommunicating groups in society, neither meeting with each other nor getting to know each other outside the narrow limits of the labor transaction. Consequently, the worker is incapable of feeling what it is like to be an employer. He never gets a sense of the problems that beset a man responsible for a great enterprise, or indeed a sense of being part of an enterprise; he does his work and gets his money, and that is all. The employer, on the other hand, likewise finds it hard to feel what it is like to be a workman—giving up so much of one's life for what seems often a pittance and so desperately dependent on the arbitrary good will of the boss, or even of the straw boss, not only for one's livelihood but for one's whole status in the great scheme of society. The stage can easily be set for cultural conflict and mutual misunderstanding that may be much more of a problem than the actual economic conflict involved in the wage bargain. I have drawn what is no doubt an extreme picture. As the industrial relation matures, this cultural conflict diminishes; the employer comes to see that his relationship with his employees is much more than a commercial relationship (labor is more than a commodity) and involves personal and domestic relationships that cannot be handled on a strictly commercial basis. Likewise, the employee comes to see that his own status and welfare is intimately bound up with the financial success of his employer. This, however, represents the ultimate resolution of the cultural conflict, and much, if not most, of the industrial conflict in history arises out of the cultural difference that is implicit in the basic exchange of labor for money.

The distinction that has been made earlier between the three types of parties—individuals, groups, and organizations—can be used to outline a typology of industrial conflict. Both the employer party and the employee party can be either an individual, a group, or an organization, which gives us nine possible types, as shown in Fig. 11.1.

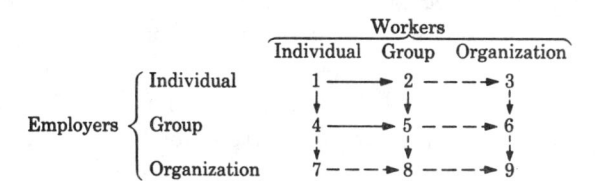

		Workers		
		Individual	Group	Organization
Employers	Individual	1 →	2 --→	3
	Group	4 →	5 --→	6
	Organization	7 --→	8 --→	9

Fig. 11.1

Type 1, where an individual worker hires himself to an individual employer, is still an important type in spite of the rise of organization. The hired man on the farm, the shop assistant in the corner grocery, the doctor's nurse, and the lawyer's clerk add up to a considerable labor force that may even be expanding as the tertiary industries rise in the course of economic development. As in the case of simple exchange, the limits of the bargain are set by the competitive opportunities on both sides. If these are many and well known, the range of bargaining is small and the conflict correspondingly low, as we saw in the previous chapter. If the hired man has many potential employers to choose from and if the farmer has many potential workers, the bargaining range will be limited to the alternative opportunities; if the hired man finds the work too hard or the pay too little, he can skip off to another employer; if the farmer finds the work too little and the pay too much, he can fire his man and hire another. The alternative opportunities that are relevant may even be far away and in another occupation; the situation in agriculture is very different when there is full employment in the towns.

Even in the relatively simple relationship of an individual employer to an individual worker, the social and psychological complexity of the relationship often emerges. The relation between a farmer and a hired man is not purely economic; the man is not selling a simple commodity in return for simple money. The money wage is very far from expressing the true rate of exchange in the transaction. The worker may be selling humiliation, dependence, and self-respect as well as plowing and hoeing; the farmer may be buying domination, power, and the exercise of a quasi-paternal authority as well as plowed fields and gathered crops. On the other hand, the worker may be buying a certain status and security along with his wages; the farmer may be selling worrying responsibilities for a difficult, dependent family along with the money wage and the perquisites and fringe benefits that go along with it. Whether the relationship between the employer and the employee is friendly and agreeable or hostile and conflictual depends more perhaps on these nonmonetary elements in the bargain than it does on the monetary terms of employment. A man may pay high wages and yet be hated by his employees if he uses them as a vehicle for his personal aggressions and discontents. There is a certain similarity here between the industrial and the domestic relationship; in both, the exchange element is heavily overlaid with a complex pattern of psychological gains and losses.

The second type of industrial relationship, where a group of employees faces a single employer but where the employees are not organized is of great interest. The interest of the case arises out of the fact that the employees are a group and develop a subculture of their own rather than out of the fact that they face a single employer: types 2, 5, and 8 of our figure illustrate this relationship and are essentially similar. There have been several important studies of the subculture of unorganized work groups[2]. Their images and patterns

---

[2] See especially Stanley B. Mathewson, *Restriction of Output Among Unorganized Workers*, New York, Viking, 1931; and Elton Mayo, *The Social Problems of an Industrial Civilization*, Cambridge, Harvard University Press, 1945.

of behavior differ, of course, from industry to industry, for the character of the work sharply influences the character of the work group. Some jobs do not permit much communication among the workers; some do. Some jobs are repetitious and do not demand much of the worker's capacity; others demand his full and constant attention. Some groups are teams, in which the effort is that of the group as a whole and in which a careless member may endanger the productivity or even the lives of the whole group; some groups are collections of individuals each performing his own task without much dependence on the others. Wherever groups work together, however, they are likely to develop norms of behavior and attitude; a newcomer entering the group is indoctrinated by the other members into what they regard as correct behavior, and if he does not learn to conform, either he must find a niche as a tolerated nonconformist, or life will be made so unpleasant for him that he will be forced to leave the group. The persistence of the group subculture depends a great deal on the turnover of the group; the more people are leaving and joining, the harder it is to impress the newcomers with the old patterns, and the more likely are the newcomers to bring their own patterns of behavior and so gradually transform the culture of the group. A declining group with few newcomers is much more likely to develop a peculiar subculture of its own than is a rapidly growing group, which has to absorb many newcomers.

A very common work group subculture is built about the idea of *job rationing*. This pattern is especially likely to emerge in industries that are subject to severe fluctuations in output and employment. Work descends mysteriously on the group from unknown sources; it fluctuates irregularly. It is not surprising, therefore, that an elaborate system of restriction of output develops in order to conserve employment opportunities. The good Joe does not work too hard, does not set too hard a pace for the others, and spins the available work out as far as possible without incurring the employer's wrath. It can easily be seen that this pattern of behavior leads to a sharp conflict of interest between the employer and the workers' group. The problem arises because, in the labor bargain, the quantity of labor that is given in exchange for the wage is not a simple physical thing like a bushel of wheat but is a complex pattern of human action and interaction. Even though the wage may be measured in hours, what is important to the employer is not the hour spent in work but the product of the work. The employer who pays for an hour wasted in substandard activity or even devoted to sabotage of the productive effort is not likely to be well pleased.

Attempts are frequently made to overcome the problem of the measurement of the amount of work paid for by instituting various forms of payment by results. These are frequently resisted by the work group, who see these schemes, often quite rightly, as a threat to their existing pattern of life; this is an important source of industrial conflict. The work group often looks at piecework, for instance, as a device to break up the solidarity of the group. Under piecework, each individual is encouraged to work as an individual, not as a member of the group. Furthermore, the more successful a single individual, the more likely, in the opinion of many work groups, is the group to suffer through the imposition of higher standards or lower rates. For this reason, among others, the more sophisticated attempts to devise methods of payment by results often use group performance as the measure of individual reward.

When tension between a work group and an employer reaches some limit of toleration, overt conflict breaks out, usually in the form of a strike. The strike is an open withholding of labor on the part of the whole work group. It takes place occasionally among unorganized work groups; even there, however, it is almost always a prelude to organization. We have seen in general how unorganized groups tend easily to become organized, especially if they develop a sense of common purpose. Typically, therefore, the strike is associated with types 3, 6, and 9, in which an organization of workers faces some kind of an employer. The unauthorized, or wildcat, strike is an interesting example of action by unorganized or very loosely and temporary organized groups within a labor organization, and the persistence of this phenomenon is a useful reminder of the basic character of industrial conflict as group conflict rather than as organizational conflict. If the organization does not embody and reflect the underlying group, it will be bypassed.

The strike as a social phenomenon has received a good deal of study. In terms of its actual cost to society as measured, say, in workdays lost, it is relatively insignificant; in the United States, for instance, workdays lost in strikes seldom amount even to 1 percent of the total days worked and usually amount to less than 1 day in 400. Sickness and unemployment are very much more important as a source of lost workdays than strikes, and it can be argued that some, at least, of the workdays lost by strikes may be made up in higher employment after the strike. Nevertheless, the strike is a salient phenomenon. It symbolizes, moreover, a breakdown in the industrial relationship, and this underlying condition may be of more importance than the strike itself. A strike, like a divorce or a marital separation, is sometimes the only apparent answer to an intolerable situation in rising tension, and, in this sense, the strike may even be an agency of conflict resolution, in that it releases previously accumulated tensions and enables the parties to start afresh. Often, however, the fresh start is a poor one, with unresolved bitterness left over from the strike itself.

The strike cannot be treated as the economist might like to treat it, as a rational phenomenon, in which each side nicely calculates the expected benefit of another day's strike and weighs this against an equally nicely calculated loss. It is, in part, a catharsis, a release of tensions, but it is also a drama, something that brings excitement and a sense of high purpose into otherwise humdrum lives. The labor movement appeals to the heroic as well as to the economic in man. This aspect of the strike is more important to the workers than it is to the employers. Employers are actors; they move men around, they organize great processes of production, and they are likely to find in the high decisions and risk taking of business the danger and excitement that help to satisfy the heroic element in man as well as the financial rewards that assuage his economic yearnings. The strike to them, therefore, is a meaningless interruption of the grand drama of enterprise; it is like a rebellion in the middle of a war, and they react to it with distaste and alarm. The workers, however, sense very little of the drama of enterprise; they make no high decisions, nor are they conscious of the excitement involved in keeping an organization alive and thriving in a dangerous world. The strike to them may be their only chance to participate in what seem to be dramatic and important events and to take sacrificial risks in the hope of future betterment.

As industrial relations mature, the strike often becomes ritualized. In the American coal industry, for instance, it became customary to have a strike in the spring, when coal stocks were high and workers were tired and wanted to go fishing; nobody suffered very much, and the strike at least provided workers with a little drama. In many industries, strikes have become rarer and rarer as skill in industrial relations has developed, largely through the institution of grievance procedures, which release tensions bit by bit, instead of allowing them to build up. We must not necessarily assume, however, that, with the maturing of the industrial relationship, industrial conflict will become a thing of the past. Better techniques can be devised for handling it, but a certain basic conflict of interest remains that cannot be wished away by better personnel management. Then again, strikes that start off as ritual strikes, like the American steel strike of 1959, develop a dynamic process of their own and become real and bitter struggles without anybody perhaps intending this.

The labor organization or trade union has developed two functions that are not necessarily consistent: one is the actual conduct of strikes and industrial warfare, and the other is the administration on a day-to-day basis of the industrial relationship and the prevention of open strife. These functions may be compared to those of the armed forces on the one hand and the diplomatic organization of states on the other. Perhaps one of the greatest differences between industrial and international warfare is that, on the international scene, these two functions are sharply separated into two distinct types of organization, whereas, in a labor organization, they are combined in a single labor union. There is nothing in the labor union to correspond to the standing army, if we except the occasional goon squad and bodyguard, which are an instrument of internal warfare more analogous to police than to military. Consequently, there is a strong tendency for the diplomatic aspect of unionism to dominate the military aspect. Unions that were purely "military," like the IWW, were not able to survive. The IWW rejected collective bargaining, labor contracts, and anything that looked like compromise and treating with the enemy; it was interested in industrial warfare and in that alone. Consequently, it could move in and conduct a strike where the situation was ripe for one, but it had no capacity to consolidate a victory even if the strike were won. It failed to recognize that war cannot be the normal state of society, no matter how frequent it is, and that war must somehow be followed by peace. The business union, on the other hand, has increasingly become an agency for the negotiation of contracts and for their day-to-day administration. A large proportion of its activity is taken up with grievance procedure, so that it becomes, in effect, a kind of advocate for its members in a quasi-judicial process of which the contract is the constitution and law. The militant types that frequently rise to leadership in the early days of a union when it is fighting for recognition often find it hard to make the transition to the more legalistic system and are replaced by more diplomatic and legal types. Often, this process goes on to the point where the union can no longer satisfy the demands of its followers for militancy, and it suffers from wildcat strikes or even militant revolts from below against its leadership. The trend of development, however, is always against militancy, simply because militancy cannot win anything or cannot retain anything it has won without being transformed into diplomacy.

Continuing now our typology of industrial conflict, we come to those in which the employer party is a group. These are not common cases, and it is significant, perhaps, that the nature of the employee party differentiates the types of industrial conflict much more sharply than does the nature of the employer party. Nevertheless, there are occasions on which it seems possible to speak of employers as a group and to differentiate types of conflict on this basis. Thus, Adam Smith observes that "Masters are always and everywhere in a sort of tacit, but constant and uniform combination, not to raise the wages of labor above their actual rate. To violate this combination is everywhere a most unpopular action, and a sort of reproach to a master among his neighbors and equals."[3] Employers form a subculture just as much as workpeople do, and a set of values and norms of behavior quickly develops in it; these may not be always so rigid or so inimical to wage increases as Adam Smith suggests, but they can impose sharp limitations on what a single employer feels free to do. The employer group is, of course, a tighter and better defined subculture in an old homogeneous country like Scotland than it is in a new, heterogeneous country like the United States; in the United States, a tight labor market is much more likely to be broken by some outside employer failing to hold the line and trying to attract workers away from his fellow employers by offering higher wages. Nevertheless, everywhere employers tend to belong to the same stratum of society, and employers in the same trade are likely to meet socially. An outsider who does not abide by the customs of the group is soon made to feel uncomfortable, and strong social pressures may modify his conduct unless he has another group of his own to which he can retreat.

There may, therefore, be a real difference between type 1 (individual employee facing individual employee) and type 4 (individual employee facing a group of employers), in the sense that, even though the individual employer may be making a wage bargain with an individual employee, the other employers of the same trade or district are, as it were, looking over his shoulder, and his freedom

---

[3] Adam Smith, *The Wealth of Nations*, New York, Modern Library, 1937, Book I, chap. 8, p. 66.

of action is correspondingly limited. Even, therefore, where we have something that looks like a competitive labor market with individual workers working for individual employers, the situation, on further examination, is likely to look more like type 5 (groups related to, or in conflict with, groups). We can also hazard a guess, at least, that types 1, 2, and 4 tend to move toward type 5, simply because of the strong tendency of men in the same boat to form groups. Workers of the same trade are, in some sense, in the same boat, and the same is true of employers in the same industry.

Groups, however, as we have also seen, tend to pass over into organizations, so that we might expect to end up with type 9, organizations of workers dealing with organizations of employers. There is some tendency for this to happen, though not a universal tendency. The group-group relationship is often surprisingly stable, and the advantages of organization do not always seem paramount. There are still substantial areas of economic life, for instance, where unorganized labor prevails. Indeed, in the United States the proportion of the labor force that is organized into unions seems to have stabilized itself at about 25 percent. Industry-wide bargaining among employers is still, in the United States, rare enough to be almost a curiosity, although the group pattern of following the leader is not uncommon. In some industrial countries like Sweden, the industry-wide organization of employers and industry-wide bargaining are common, but this may simply reflect the smallness of the country. The arrows in Fig. 11.1 reflect these tendencies—the strong tendency for individual parties to form groups and the weaker tendency for groups to form organizations.

An important question, which, however, is not easy to answer, is that of the limits on the field or range of industrial conflict, especially in the wage bargain. This closely affects the power of organizations in the field, for if the range of the field is small, the advantage of organizing is likewise small. A long debate has gone on among economists almost from the time of Adam Smith on the question whether trade unions can really raise wages. The classical economists thought, on the whole, that they could not, although, of all the classical economists, Adam Smith was probably the most sanguine in this regard. There is fair agreement among economists that a trade union can raise the wages of its members if it has some degree of monopoly power and can also prevent free entry into the occupation that it controls. Thus, if a trade union controls all the workers of a certain trade, so that the employer can only hire workers with the consent of the union, then it does not even have to bargain: it can simply raise the wage at which its members are willing to work, and the employer has no recourse short of finding substitute methods of getting the same thing done, which he often does. The power of the union to raise wages, then, depends on the elasticity of demand for its particular kind of labor, that is, the amount by which employment declines as the wage is raised, and on the willingness of the members to suffer unemployment or the ability of the union simply to expel from the occupation those who cannot find work at the wage it sets. It is highly significant that the first successful unions were not great omnibus organizations like the Knights of Labor but small craft unions, for instance, in printing, in the building trades, and in metalworking, that were able to exercise a certain monopoly power because of the very smallness of the craft. These craft unions were the foundation of the American Federation of Labor in the 1880s. The industrial unions of the Congress of Industrial Organizations were only successful in the 1930s, when the legal and political climate was much more favorable to labor.

It is one thing for a small craft union to have monopoly power, however, and quite another thing for the labor movement to be able to raise wages as a whole. The monopoly power of the union also gives monopoly power to the employer, for the restriction of the entry of labor, likewise, restricts the output of the industry. Consequently, the gains of monopoly unionism tend to be made not from the employer but from the purchaser of the product, who may easily be a worker in some other industry. The losers from unionism may also be the unorganized workers or the workers in other fields who would be attracted into the union's occupation if there were not barriers imposed. One doubts whether these gains and losses in any case are very large. The studies that have been made of this question are significantly inconclusive. There is no doubt that wages of organized workers follow a different pattern through time from those of unorganized workers: they tend to rise in boom and to be stable and fall very little in depression, whereas the wages of unorganized workers rise very sharply in a boom and fall sharply in a depression. There does not seem to be much difference, however, in the long-run trend. It is hard to avoid the inference that the great movement of inflation and deflation is a much more important determinant of the distribution of income between labor income and nonlabor income than any rise or fall of labor organization. In the period in the United States, for instance, from 1933 to 1943, when the number of organized workers rose from under 4 to about 15 million, the proportion of national income going to labor declined from 74 to 63 percent. This, of course, was due to the recovery of profits from the depth of the Great Depression. The rise in total income was so great that aggregate labor income, likewise, rose, and labor was absolutely better off, in spite of its smaller share; but it is clear that, in this period, any gains in money wages were more than passed on to the purchasers of the product.

An important aspect of industrial conflict is that of unions among themselves. The jurisdictional dispute, in which two unions claim the same group of workers as members by reason of the jobs that they hold, is the characteristic form of this conflict. Jurisdictional conflict is much more like international conflict or the competition of firms than is the employer-employee conflict. The field of operation of the union is not so much workers as jobs. The union does not usually care very much who holds the jobs, and, in any case, job occupants come and go; but the job persists as a role defined by an organization. The organization that defines the content of the job role, however, is not the union but the employer; hence there is a curious symbiotic—one might even say parasitic—quality about the union-employer relationship: the employer creates the jobs that the union then organizes. It is only a slight exaggeration to say that a union organizes jobs rather than men, for even though its members are men, they are members only because of the job role they occupy or might occupy. A union usually carries a number of job seekers (unemployed) on its books, but only if they are seeking the jobs that define the field of the union. We can think of the field of the labor movement, therefore, as a set of jobs to which the different unions (about 200 in the United States) lay claim. It is not difficult for two unions to claim the same job, just as two nations may claim the same piece of territory or two firms the same customer. Even among the crafts, the craft lines are not clear, and a large and powerful union frequently is interested in making them still less clear; the carpenters, for instance, lay claim to any job that has ever been done at any time past with wood, so that they run into stonecutters and metalworkers and all kinds of seemingly unrelated trades. The machinists and the teamsters are willing to organize almost anybody, and, at one time, the United Mine Workers set up its famous District 50 with the avowed intent of organizing everybody. In the jurisdictional domain, therefore, the unions look not unlike jealous nations, each surrounded by Alsace-Lorraines. The federations, of course, provide a judicial framework within which jurisdictional disputes can be mediated, but it is a very loose framework, looser even than the United Nations, and the warfare sputters sporadically.

It is not the purpose of this chapter to cover the vast field of the labor movement; we are interested, rather, in picking out those aspects of it which are of particular interest in developing a general theory of conflict. We may, therefore, take a brief look at some institutions in the labor field which might claim to be conflict-reducing. As we have seen, the recognition of unions in the contract and the development of a body of industrial jurisprudence itself tend to substitute orderly legal procedure for open strife. An interesting aspect of union contracts is *union security*, that is, provisions in the contract by which the employer assists the union to maintain and discipline its membership. The checkoff of dues, the closed shop, the union shop, and maintenance of membership are all devices of this kind. They have been restricted somewhat in the United States, by the Taft-Hartley Act of 1947, though, in one form or another, they are still important. Nothing illustrates better the peculiar character of the industrial relationship than to imagine, for instance, one country making a treaty with another in which one country undertakes to collect taxes for the other and to discipline its citizens. The advocates of union security, often on both sides of the fence, argue that these provisions remove from the union the necessity of constant militancy in order to keep its members and enable the union to make the transition easily from the militant to the judicial and diplomatic stage of maturity. The danger one fears is that a union that is too secure eventually loses the interest and support of its members and will be replaced by a militant upheaval from below. This arrangement, however, seems to be able to persist for a long time. An instructive analogy is that of the state church in the problem of the conflict of church and state. This conflict has sometimes been resolved by church security and a kind of checkoff: the state collects a tax for the church and perhaps even compels people to belong to it, and, in return, of course, the church is not usually too troublesome. The history of state churches indicates, however, that this arrangement is not very healthy, especially for the church, and it may be that those unions also will maintain their vigor longest who do not rely on this method of ensuring membership and funds.

The problem of state intervention into labor conflict is again very instructive as an example of the attempt to control conflict through the imposition of forms of organization that transcend and include the contending parties. The justification of state intervention is simply that both employer and employee are citizens and that, in this role, they have an interest in seeing that their conflicts do not get out of hand and so threaten the fabric of the society in which both find themselves. The forms of state intervention in this field have been various. Some countries, like Australia, have experimented, not too successfully, with compulsory arbitration. Most industrial countries have set up apparatus for mediating disputes and have various limitations on the right to strike. Most countries limit the terms of the labor bargain in some way by minimum wage laws, factory acts, health regulations, and so on. Many countries provide a legal framework under which unions can organize, such as the Wagner and Taft-Hartley Acts in the United States, which provide for the holding of elections among employees and for compulsory recognition of, and bargaining with, unions by the employer under certain circumstances. In totalitarian countries of any stripe, unions tend to be brought rigidly under the control of the state and become agents of state policy rather than independent instruments of the will of the members. Even in democratic countries, the public and government encouragement of unions is a fairly recent development, which nowhere goes back further than the early years of the twentieth century. In the eighteenth century, labor organizations were almost universally made the subject of strong legal attack, and they have had to fight their way to power and respectability against constant opposition from the constituted authorities.

Perhaps no very clear conclusion emerges out of all this experience. Nevertheless, on the whole, one feels a modest optimism. Here we have an area of life in which conflict seems to have become less violent and less disruptive and in which institutions for handling it creatively have been forthcoming. This is a great contrast to the sad condition of international relations. The difference may, of course, merely be due to the difference in the difficulty of the problem. Industrial conflict is, as we have suggested, a curiously ambivalent affair, closer to the domestic battle of the sexes than to the clash of armies. Consequently, it is not difficult to build on the positive-sum or cooperative aspects of the game and to develop institutions that express this aspect. This perhaps is why the union, which may have been originally devised to prosecute conflict, in many cases becomes an instrument to resolve it in a way, for instance, that an army never does. This, however, brings us to the next chapter.

12

INTERNATIONAL CONFLICT:

THE BASIC MODEL

Today, international conflict dominates all other. It has always been the most spectacular form of conflict. It comprises a large part of what gets into history books. In the long run, if there is a long run, it may not loom so important as the slow, evolutionary conflict of species, ideas, and techniques. At the moment, however, international conflict threatens to put a stop to civilization and perhaps to all life on earth, so that it is not surprising if it dominates our attention.

There are problems involved in the definition of the party to international conflict. There is a gradation from tribal conflict through feudal conflict and imperial adventure to full-scale conflict of great powers. The nature of the conflict depends as usual on the nature of the parties. We can distinguish roughly the following types:

1. *The Tribe.* Organization is loose, and the unit is small, numbered in thousands at the most. There may be a specialized class of warriors; usually, however, there is no specialized full-time armed force. When overt conflict breaks out, the warriors are organized to meet the occasion on a temporary basis; in the intervals of peace, they return to other occupations. Hunting or food gathering is most

characteristic of this stage of development, and not many resources can be spared from basic subsistence-producing activities.

2. *The Agricultural, or Feudal, Society.* Settled agriculture yields a food surplus that can be used to support full-time armed forces and urban craftsmen. The walled city, paradoxically enough, is the prime expression of the agricultural society. Sometimes this is a city state (Athens, Tyre, etc.) depending on trade and merchandizing for its food supply; sometimes it is the capital of an agricultural empire (Babylon, Nineveh, etc.).

3. *The Universal Agricultural Society.* In the course of the rise and fall of agricultural empires, one may rise to predominance (Rome) to the point where, for a time, it has no serious competitors.

4. *The Industrial Power.* The early stages of the technical revolution both in agriculture and industry and in weaponry produce a type of nation that is very different from the agricultural society. Standing armies and navies can now be afforded on some scale. The nineteenth century great powers (Britain, France, etc.) are good examples.

5. *The Superpower.* In the mid-twentieth century, two superpowers, the United States and Russia, emerged, maintaining very large standing armed forces.

6. *The World State.* This has not yet emerged; yet it seems to be in process of formation as a result of the onrush of technical change.

Leaving out the sixth type as not yet relevant yields us 15 conceivable kinds of international conflict as defined by the different types of party. Of these, the conflicts of type 3 with anything larger than the tribes at its edges can be ruled out. We are left, then, with three major categories: (*A*) conflict between equals—(1-1) tribe against tribe, (2-2) feudal state against feudal state, (4-4) industrial power against industrial power, and (5-5) superpower against superpower; (*B*) conflict between the unequal—(1-2) tribe against feudal state, (2-4) feudal state against industrial power, and (4-5) industrial power against superpower; (*C*) conflicts between the hopelessly unequal—(1-3) tribe against empire, (1-4) tribe against industrial

INTERNATIONAL CONFLICT: THE BASIC MODEL   229

power, (1-5) tribe against superpower, (2-4) feudal state against industrial power, and (2-5) feudal state against superpower. We may notice a certain discontinuity between types 3 and 4. The universal empire is the culmination of one line of development; the industrial power represents the first stages of a new line of development that leads logically to the world industrial state. This discontinuity is a profound historical reality; it represents the transition, in which we are still living, from the folk society to the scientific society.

As one of the parties of an earlier stage begins to rise into the next stage above it, the conflict between equals tends to be transformed into a conflict between unequals. The rising feudal state gobbles up its neighboring tribal neighbors, for the amateur warrior cannot survive against the professional with superior technique. The tribe can be defended only by inaccessibility and tends to survive, therefore, only in mountains and jungles, where the larger, better organized, but perhaps clumsier forces of civilization cannot get at it. A successful feudal state will have ambitions to become a world empire and may absorb rival states in this process. With pre-scientific technique, the world empire seems to be too large to be stable and breaks up into smaller feudal states. The rising industrial states found it easy, as in India, to conquer feudal empires, where they were not opposed by other industrial states. Two of the industrial states became superpowers because of their unique advantage in being able to expand into a large land area occupied for the most part by people at the tribal level; this is where we are today. Around the two superpowers are clustered a group of smaller industrial powers, with two or three potential superpowers—China, Brazil, and India—among them. The feudal state survives, if at all, only as a protected anachronism; the tribe, likewise, is rapidly disappearing before the march of economic development.

The key to this long process is found in the theory of viability as developed in Chap. 4. We want to find the conditions under which one state can conquer or overcome another. This is a problem formally similar to that of the conditions under which one firm can overcome another. Thus, suppose, in Fig. 12.1, we have two states, A and B, with the home bases located at A and B respectively. For the moment, we shall suppose that their home bases are points rather than areas, but this assumption can easily be relaxed later. $AB \, (= s)$ is the distance between the two states. We suppose for simplicity a world that consists only of the line AB and its projections.

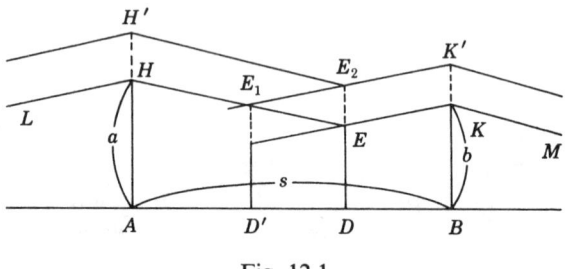

Fig. 12.1

Now let us suppose a variable called *national strength* or, more simply, strength. The measurement of this is a difficult problem. Military strength is a multidimensional quantity, composed not only of the number of men in the armed forces and the equipment that they carry but also of subtle psychological variables such as the will-to-fight. For the present argument, however, we shall suppose that some index of strength can be constructed, the only condition being that at any point where A can beat B, A's strength must be larger than B's, and vice versa. We shall then suppose that each nation's strength is a maximum at its home base; this we call its *home strength*. It is measured by AH for A and BK for B in Fig. 12.1. We suppose, furthermore, that each nation's strength declines as it moves away from its home base, following the lines HE and HL for A and KE and KM for B. In the figure, we assume these to be straight lines; their slope may be called the *loss-of-strength gradient*, a very important quantity, which we might name for short the LSG. In fact, the strength lines will not always be straight, and the LSG will vary from place to place even under the most ideal conditions, as is shown in the appendix to this chapter; however, this is a minor amendment, as the deviations from linearity are not likely to be great. The law of diminishing strength, then, may be phrased as *the further, the weaker*; that is, the further from home any nation has to operate, the longer will be its lines of communication, and the less strength it can put in the field.

In Fig. 12.1, then, with home strengths $AH (= a)$ and $BK (= b)$, there is a boundary of equal strength at D, where the strength lines intersect at E. To the right of D, B is dominant and is stronger than A; to the left of D, A is dominant and is stronger than B. The analogy with Fig. 4.1a is exact: the home-strength concept corresponds to the *mill price*, or the minimum average cost of the firm, and the LSG concept corresponds to the cost of transport per unit mile of the firm's product. Indeed, the LSG is a cost of transport of strength, whatever strength is. In the case of the firm, of course, the higher the price charged, the less its competitive strength, so that the strength lines in Fig. 4.1a slope upward; they still represent, however, an LSG. The area where each country is dominant may be called its *sphere of influence*. Suppose now that country B is not satisfied to have so small a sphere of influence and wishes to push the boundary of equal strength farther away from its home base. It may be able to do this by raising the amount of resources devoted to the means of coercion, so that its home strength rises from BK to BK'. The boundary of equal strength is pushed from D to D'. If now A is not satisfied with this position, A may likewise increase its home strength by devoting more resources to arms, and the point of equal strength is moved back to D again (E_2). This is the pattern of the arms race and also of the price war. Following its distinguished theoretician, we have called this a Richardson process. It was discussed in Chap. 2.

Considering now merely the statics of viability, we see, as in the case of the firm, that both nations will be unconditionally viable only if each is stronger than the other at home. This is clearly the case in

Fig. 12.1. In Fig. 12.2, however, A is dominant, and B is only conditionally viable, for A is stronger than B even on B's home base. The condition for unconditional viability of both nations is that

$$\frac{b-a}{s} < c > \frac{a-b}{s} \qquad (12.1)$$

where c is the LSG per mile, s is the distance between the two power centers, and a and b are their respective home strengths. As before, therefore, two nations are likely to be unconditionally viable with

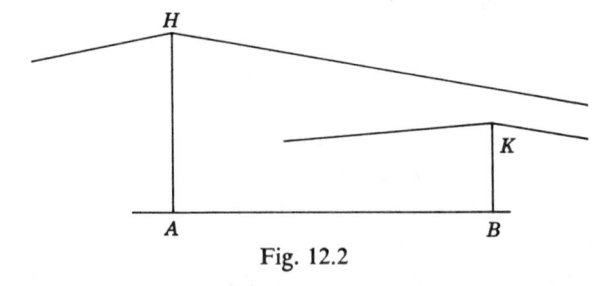

Fig. 12.2

respect to each other if the distance between them is large, if the LSG is steep, and if the difference in home strengths is slight. As the distance becomes smaller, the LSGs less, and the differences in home strength greater, the chance of unconditional viability diminishes.

There is a concept of maximum home strength that corresponds to the economic concept of minimum average cost. This maximum home strength depends much more directly on the absolute size of a nation than does the average cost on the absolute size of a firm. It may be measured roughly by the total number of men who can be devoted to war. This depends first on the total population and second on the proportion of the population that can be devoted to war. This latter ratio depends mainly on the general level of technique of the nation and especially on its efficiency in the production of food and other basic necessities. A nation that must devote 90 percent of its people to food production in order to feed itself obviously cannot devote more than a small proportion of its manpower to war without disaster from starvation. A nation that can feed itself, like the United States, with 10 percent of its population can devote a much larger percentage of its labor force to war. The efficiency of the war industry is also an important element in the home strength; 100 men well equipped may be worth 10,000 men without equipment. The factor of morale is also of enormous importance; there must be a will-to-war before resources can be devoted to it. These factors, especially the latter, are strongly susceptible to fluctuation. Nevertheless, under given circumstances, the concept of a maximum home strength is meaningful. These are the significant a and b quantities of Eq. 12.1.

The problem of *returns to scale* presents peculiar difficulties in the case of the nation-state—difficulties that are by no means absent from the firm but seem to be less pressing. One difficulty is that the area of influence, that is, the area within the nation's boundary of equal strength, may include two parts: the nation proper and its dependencies. The situation of the nation, therefore, is more complex than that of the firm, where the expansion of its field of influence simply means an extension of its market and its sales; the customers are not thought of as part of the firm. In this sense, all the firm's field of influence consists of dependencies. In the case of the nation, however, the distinction between the core of people who identify with the nation and the dependents, who are merely subjects of the nation, is an important one. The subjects, if they are dissident enough, may be a source of weakness to the nation rather than a source of strength and may diminish rather than increase its home strength. As a nation expands its field of influence, then, it is almost certain sooner or later to run into diminishing returns to scale, that is, a decrease in its home strength with each successive increase in the field of influence. This phenomenon may have a different set of causes from the somewhat similar phenomenon that is observed in the case of the firm, where it arises mainly out of the difficulties of maintaining communications systems and a good decision making process as the scale of the enterprise increases. This factor applies also to the nation or the empire, but there is, in addition, the further factor of heterogeneity and conflicting loyalties. This may sometimes come into the picture of the expansion of a firm as it develops new products; there are diseconomies of heterogeneity in the firm as well as in the state, but they are peculiarly striking in the case of the imperial state.

These effects can be analyzed with an apparatus similar to that of Chap. 4. Thus, in Fig. 12.3, we plot the home strengths of the two nations, a and b, along the horizontal and vertical axes respectively. We may note that, by contrast with Figs. 4.3 to 4.9, the competitive strength of the party increases as we move away from the origin. To make these figures comparable with Chap. 4, they must be rotated through two right angles. In Fig. 12.3, we then postulate two viability boundaries, $U_a U_a'$ and $U_b U_b'$, with equations $b - a = sc$ and $a - b = sc$. These are analogous to the market extinction lines of Chap. 4. Only within these lines is Eq. 12.1 fulfilled. Above and to the left of $U_a U_a'$, nation B is stronger than A at A's home base; below and to the right of $U_b U_b'$, A is stronger than B at B's home base. Now let us suppose that, for each nation, there is a maximum level of home strength, OM_a for A and OM_b for B, dependent on their resources, their will-to-strength, and so on. In this figure, we suppose that this maximum home strength is constant and that it is independent of the area of influence of each nation and, therefore, independent of the home strength of the other nation. We have, therefore, maximum-home-strength boundaries $M_a M_a'$ for A and $M_b M_b'$ for B. A is not viable anywhere to the right of $M_a M_a'$, and B is not viable anywhere above $M_b M_b'$.

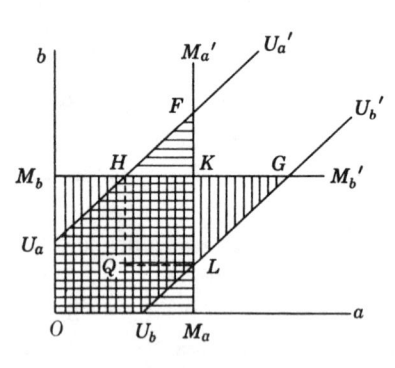

Fig. 12.3

INTERNATIONAL CONFLICT: THE BASIC MODEL

These boundaries now define viability areas for each nation. The viability area for A is the horizontally shaded area OM_aFU_a, shaded horizontally to suggest that A can move horizontally by its own choice but not vertically. Similarly, the viability area for B is the vertically shaded area OM_bGU_b. The crosshatched area OU_aHKLU_b, where these two viability areas overlap, is the area of *mutual viability*. Then we have two triangles U_aM_bH and LKG where B is viable but A is not and two triangles U_bLM_a and HKF where A is viable and B is not. In the unshaded area, neither party is viable.

These boundaries do not, of course, give us any equilibrium solution to the home strengths. This depends, if it exists, on the Richardson equations and the Richardson processes outlined in Chap. 2. If the Richardson processes of arms-race reaction give an equilibrium within the area of mutual viability, this presumably is a stable condition as long as the assumptions and coefficients underlying the equations remain constant. There are strong reasons in the case of Fig. 12.3 for supposing that, in fact, the Richardson process must result in an equilibrium within the area of mutual viability. Suppose, for instance, that the equilibrium of the Richardson process is in the triangle HKF, where B is not viable; B can always move vertically downward into the area of mutual viability. Similarly, from any point outside the area of mutual viability, one or other of the parties has the power to move within it. Unless, therefore, one or other of the parties deliberately seeks suicide, the Richardson process must be limited to the area of mutual survival. Where, within this area, the equilibrium will lie depends on the initial hostilities and reactivities of the two parties. If we have two very hostile and reactive parties, the probability is that, in the absence of the restriction placed on the Richardson equations by the necessity for reaching a solution within the area of mutual viability, there would be either no equilibrium or an equilibrium somewhere beyond K. In this case, the equilibrium is likely to be at K, where both parties are at their maximum home strength. If the parties are somewhat less irrational and quarrelsome, the position Q is a kind of minimax, which would represent a solution imposed by a condition that might be called that of rational quarrelsomeness. Thus, if the parties are at K, it may occur to B that, if he reduced his home strength from M_aK to M_aL, he is really no worse off militarily, as A still cannot really beat him, and he may be better off economically, as he does not have to waste all these resources on defense. The same thing may occur to A, in which case he moves to H, and the joint move lands the parties at Q. Below Q, B might feel uneasy, as A could move him into the area U_bLM_a, where he would be wiped out; similarly, to the left of Q, A might be uneasy over B's power to move him into the area U_aM_bH.

The most advantageous situation of all, of course, would be an equilibrium at O. This might be called the equilibrium of rational cooperativeness, as it is the position at which both parties are clearly best off on condition that they can trust each other. If they cannot trust each other, however, the position may be unstable, for, at this position, each party could wipe out the other by an appropriate move.

Consider now what will happen in this model if the viability boundaries U_aU_a' and U_bU_b' move closer together, as they will if either c, the LSG, or s, the distance between nations, diminishes. We recall that $OU_a = OU_b = cs$, so that a decline in c or s reduces OU_a and OU_b without changing the slope of the lines. The area of mutual viability becomes smaller and slenderer: H, L and Q move towards K. If the home strengths of the two nations are not exactly equal, then, at some point, either H or L will coincide with K, which will then be the minimax. As c or s declines farther, we have a situation, as in Fig. 12.4, where there is no longer a minimax and the weaker party, in this case, A, is no longer unconditionally viable. B can establish a level of home strength greater than M_aF against which A has no recourse: there is no level of home strength available to A at which B is not stronger than A at A's home base. This does not mean that A may not survive and may not be conditionally viable. The equilibrium of the Richardson process may lie in the area of mutual viability OU_aFLU_b. This, however, is either because

INTERNATIONAL CONFLICT: THE BASIC MODEL 237

B wills to keep A alive and presumably feels better off within this area than outside it or because B is rather unreactive and has low initial hostility.

Now let us relax the very unrealistic assumption that the home strength of each nation is constant. In Fig. 12.5, we suppose that the

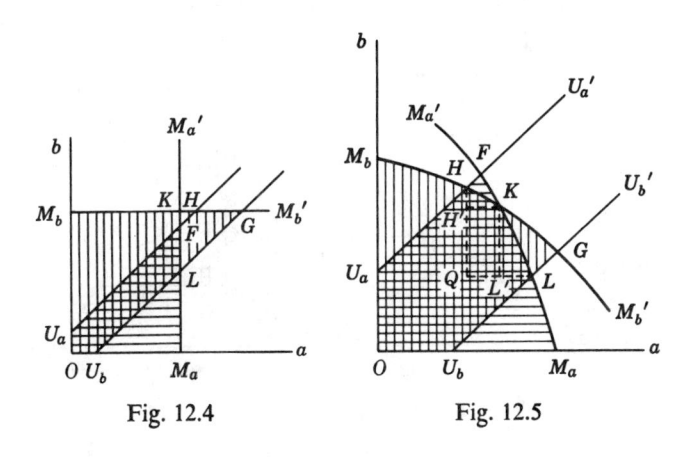

Fig. 12.4

Fig. 12.5

home strength of each nation is at a maximum at its greatest extent of influence where the home strength of the other is zero. Then we suppose that, for each nation, as the home strength of the other nation rises, the maximum home strength of the first declines. We have, therefore, a maximum-home-strength curve for A, $M_a M_a'$, and a similar curve for B, $M_b M_b'$. There will again be a viability area for A, shaded horizontally, $OU_a F M_a$, and a similar area for B, shaded vertically, $OM_b G U_b$. Where these overlap is the area of mutual viability $OU_a H K L U_b$. The analysis is not very different from that of Fig. 12.3. There will be a minimax solution at Q, for, below Q, either country can be wiped out by an appropriate move of the other into region $U_b L M_a$ or $U_a H M_b$ respectively. Now, however, we notice a certain difference; if B ventures above H', A can render him nonviable by moving into the area FHK, where A is viable but B is not. Similarly, if A ventures to the right of L', B can move into KLG.

We have, therefore, a kind of minimax quadrilateral $QL'KH'$, within which neither party can move to ruin the other without ruining himself. If we suppose that the parties try to get away with the least amount in defense expenditures while still remaining within this safe area, we shall end up at Q as before. In Fig. 12.3, of course, the minimax quadrilateral is $QLKH$.

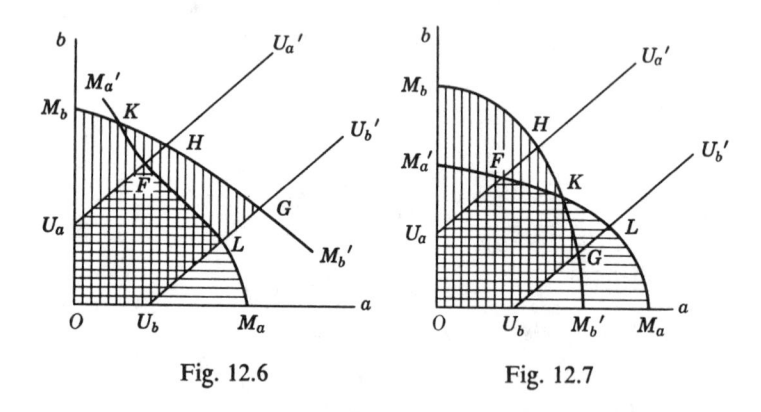

Fig. 12.6

Fig. 12.7

Now suppose that we rotate the line $M_a M_a'$ counterclockwise, indicating that the loss of home strength with loss of dominated area operates more strongly than before. The point K approaches H; the minimax quadrilateral shrinks until, when K and H coincide, it has disappeared. Beyond this, we get a condition like Fig. 12.6. Here, A is no longer unconditionally viable; if B increases its home strength above F, there is no move that A can make that can make it stronger than B at home. There is no minimax; A's only hope for survival is the lack of will on B's part to exterminate it. This lack of will may be rationally based, in which case we have the secure conditional viability noted in Chap. 4, or it may be a result of ignorance and inertia.

If both home strength curves bend steeply, we may get a situation like Fig. 12.7. This is, in fact, a not implausible system. The assumption is that the maximum home strength of any country

INTERNATIONAL CONFLICT: THE BASIC MODEL   239

diminishes very rapidly in the neighborhood of the viability boundary with increase in the home strength of the competitor. What is happening here is that the enemy is pushing its dominance deep into the home territory; the weaker power has less and less resources to draw upon, and its ability to resist rapidly disintegrates as the enemy pushes in. This situation is assumed to hold for both countries. We then get a situation in which neither country is unconditionally viable. There is an area of mutual conditional viability, OU_aFKGU_b, but, from any point within this area except K, either country can take a move that will eliminate the other. A can move to the right into the area KGU_bM_aL, or B can move upward into the area KHM_bU_aF. The point K is a curious kind of quasi-equilibrium. If the parties are actually at K, they are likely to stay there; neither party can increase its home strength, and if either decreases its home strength, it exposes itself to extinction from the other. On the other hand, if the parties are not at K, there is no sure way of getting there, for, below K, there is no sure way of preventing one of the parties from expanding its home strength to the point where it can overcome the other. It is possible, of course, that a Richardson process might yield an equilibrium at K, but this would be a pure accident; there is nothing inherent in the nature of the system that would give this result. This is, therefore, a very unstable relationship; it will almost always result in one of the parties gobbling up the other.

The instability of this situation may be resolved not only by conquest but by changes in the home-strength boundaries. Suppose, for instance, that A is able to make things very difficult and costly for B as B tries to advance close to A's home base. As we approach A's viability boundary, U_aU_a', B's home strength, then, will diminish, as in the curve M_bHK' in Fig. 12.8. This means, in a sense, that A is concentrating on defensive weapons close to home. Not surprisingly, this restores A's unconditional viability. At any level of A's home strength within the area FHK', B can only move, vertically, we recall, to points of mutual viability or to points where B is not viable. In

Fig. 12.8, however, B is only conditionally viable. At any level of B below K, A can move horizontally from the area of mutual viability into the area KGU_bM_aLK and so can exterminate B; at any level of B above H, A can exterminate B by moving into the area FHK'. We may note that, if the line M_bHK' is somewhat less steeply sloped, indicating a smaller degree of effectiveness of A's defensive measures,

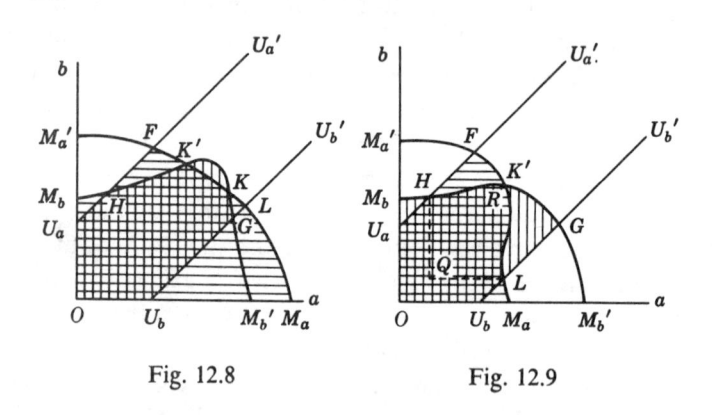

Fig. 12.8

Fig. 12.9

the point H may be above the point K, in which case we get the rather surprising result that a defensive measure on the part of one country restores unconditional viability to both, as there is a minimax area restored in which values of a and b can be found in which neither party can exterminate the other.

In Fig. 12.8, we suppose that only one party took these highly defensive measures; usually, however, what is open to one is also open to the other, so that Fig. 12.9, where both parties take highly defensive measures, is likely to develop out of Fig. 12.8. Here, as either country approaches the viability boundary of the other and penetrates into the other's home territory, the home strength of the invader declines, as it has to absorb a dissident and hostile population and defense measures reduces its capacity for inflicting damage. In Fig. 12.9, then, we have an area $QHK'L$ which is a minimax area, within the area of mutual viability in the sense that, within it, neither power can move to a position where it alone can survive. Suppose, for instance, from a position such as R, A tries to lure B into the area HFK' by disarming; B can always extricate itself and move into the area of mutual viability by disarming itself. In a similar way, A can always extricate itself from the area $LK'G$.

In these models, we have assumed implicity that the various boundary lines and functions were independent and that, for instance, the unconditional-viability boundaries were not affected by the position of the system on the home-strength boundaries and that the home-strength boundary of one country was not affected by the position of the home-strength boundary of the other. In fact, this assumption may not be true, and the models should be modified accordingly, even though the detailed analysis of this type of modification requires mathematical analysis well beyond the scope of this volume. We noted in Chap. 4, for instance, that a fall in the cost of transport would affect not only the viability boundaries but also the boundaries of minimum net return, which correspond, in the case of the firm, to the home-strength boundary in the models of the present chapter. Similarly, we must recognize that home strength is not a simple quantity but a complex of many factors and that a change in the structure of the defense organization of one nation may affect the home-strength boundaries of both nations. In simple cases, it is not too difficult to make the appropriate modifications in the present models, and, in any case, these interrelationships are likely to be of a second order of magnitude and do not affect the usefulness of the first-order models.

In all these cases, it is clear that a decline in the LSG (c) or in the distance between the national centers (s) will bring the two viability lines closer together and will lessen the chances for a stable solution. A further condition of stability can now be added: the less powerful the principle of increasing returns to scale, or of increasing home strength with increase of area dominated, and the more powerful the opposite principle of diminishing returns to scale, the more likely are we to find stable equilibriums of national defense. The recipe for stability is to have high cost of transport of violence, countries a long way apart, and rapidly diminishing efficiency with increase of scale. It is because of a failure of all three of these conditions that we face an acute breakdown of the system of national defense in the world of today.

The question of the number of firms that, in a stable system, can occupy a given closed area such as a sphere has been discussed in Chap. 4, and the solution given there is generally applicable to the problem of how many nations can stably occupy a similar closed surface such as the earth. The problem does not seem to be capable of simple mathematical solutions without introducing extremely limiting assumptions; however, the broad lines of the solution are clear. The stability of the system depends on the attainment, for each contiguous pair of nations, of a certain critical value of cs. This critical value depends in part on the shape of the maximum-home-strength functions, in part on the nature of the Richardson process equations, and in part on the preference functions of the nations themselves. Given this critical value of cs, however, it is clear that any decline in c must increase the minimum value of s, the distance between the national centers, at which a stable system is possible. On a circle, the relation between s and n, the number of nations, is very simple: on a circle with circumference k, we have $n = k/s$. The larger s, the fewer nations there can be. On a homogeneous sphere, the mathematical relation is much more complicated, as we noted earlier; however, with the possibility of unimportant exceptions, the same rule follows: the farther apart the national centers, the fewer nations there can be. With every diminution in the LSG, therefore, the maximum number of independent national units consistent with stability of a system of national defense diminishes. The only possible exception to this principle would be if a diminution in the LSG resulted in a diminution in the critical value of cs. This might happen, for instance, if a general decline in the cost of transport enabled more people to travel abroad and so led to a decline in xenophobia, a more tolerant and sympathetic attitude toward other countries, and a general spirit of live and let live. Even though a decline in the cost of transport will almost always cause a decline in the number of countries that can coexist in unconditional viability, it may also lead to an increase in the stability of conditional viability. This is not, one should add, a certain result; sometimes better communications corrupt good manners and travel makes people all the more self-centered and hostile to foreigners. It is, however, a possible result that should always be considered.

In this model, we have thought of the earth as a uniform globe, which, of course, it is not. The geographical heterogeneity of the earth's surface, however, in no way destroys the value of the model we have developed; indeed, as we shall see, it can be used to develop some important interpretations of the course of history.

We should not leave this theoretical model without calling attention to the modifications that may be introduced into it by the recognition of the dynamic character of the processes involved. Up to this point, we have assumed that the home strength of a nation is a function only of its area of dominance and, therefore, of the home strength of the competing nation. In fact, of course, the home strength is also a function of time. If it is below the maximum value, it can grow only at a certain maximum rate. It takes time to raise armed forces, supply them with equipment, and train them. Furthermore, a nation may be able to maintain a level of home strength for short periods that it cannot maintain indefinitely. This is somewhat analogous to the distinction made in the theory of the firm between average variable cost, which must be covered by average revenue if the firm is to survive in the short run, and the (greater) average total cost, which must be covered if it is to survive in the long run. By putting forth a great national effort, a nation may be able to sustain a very high level of home strength for a while, but the effort will exhaust it, and, inevitably, as weariness and exhaustion set in, its home strength will decline. The static theory that we have been elaborating in this chapter is essentially a theory of the long-run equilibrium of national defense; in the short run and in the dynamic course of the system, we cannot assume given levels of home strength and given boundaries of equal strength.

Nevertheless, the static theory illuminates the dynamic process. At the beginning of a war, for instance, one nation is frequently better prepared, that is, with its home strength at a higher proportion of the maximum, than its opponent. Consequently, it is able to drive deep into what previously had been its enemy's territory or dominated area. As it advances, however, the great law of diminishing strength with distance (the further, the weaker) not only comes into play to weaken the invader at the boundary of contact of the two forces but serves to strengthen the defender. Now, however, the dynamics of the situation comes into play; if the initial push of the invader is not sufficient to reach the defender's home base, as time goes on, the defender is able to mobilize his resources, and his home strength rises faster than that of the invader, who is closer to his maximum and has fewer unutilized resources to mobilize. If the invader has been exceeding his long-run home strength, then, as time goes on, exhaustion and weariness will set in, and his home strength may even decline. If his will-to-invade depends on the success of the invasion, then, if the initial push is halted and a stationary front established for a while, the morale element in his home strength will diminish. The defender's morale, on the other hand, is likely to increase; the halting of the invasion is a sign that the defender is, in fact, viable—something that must be a little in doubt while the invasion is proceeding—and he will have a positive image of the outcome of the conflict, with the invader repulsed and humiliated. As the invader's home strength declines and the defender's grows, the temporary equilibrium gives way; the invader starts to retreat, and, once this process begins, it may lead to a disastrous collapse in the invader's morale. It is true that, as the invader is pushed back, he gets closer to his base and his lines of communication get shorter; however, he may still be operating in hostile territory, which is a source of weakness rather than of strength, and his lines of communication can be harried by the defender's people, while the defender's lines, being in his own territory, are quite secure. Once the invasion turns back, then, it is likely that the retreat will continue right back to the old frontiers and beyond; the retreat may even turn into a rout. If the countries are big enough, of course, the erstwhile invader may rally himself as he is pushed back into his own country, as in the model of Fig. 12.9. Now it is the other country who is the invader and who suffers the disadvantages of invasion, and it will not be surprising if the war ends with the parties in much the same relative position in which they started.

The inference is that the static solution may be a fairly stable one, in the sense that it can survive large disturbances, if the countries are large and are both unconditionally viable. If the countries are small and close together, the static theory may give little clue to the dynamic course of history, for an initial aggression may be total, in the sense that the defending country is overrun and subjugated before it has time to reach its maximum home strength. Once this has happened a country that is potentially viable may be suppressed or may never come into existence because of the dynamic factors in the situation. There may be an initial hump that the country finds impossible to get over by its own efforts. A general war, however, in which the dominant countries weaken each other may lower the threshold of formation of a dormant country and permit its reformation as an independent state. Some historical examples are suggested in the next chapter.

APPENDIX TO CHAPTER 12:
THE LOSS-OF-STRENGTH GRADIENT

The forces that determine the actual LSG of a nation, i.e., the degree to which its military and political power diminishes as we move a unit distance away from its home base, are complex in the extreme and depend on a host of geographical, psychological, and organizational factors. Nevertheless, we can construct one or two very simple models that illustrate some of the essential features of the problem. Let us suppose that the home strength of a nation is measured by the number of man-hours or, more simply, men, that it can devote to coercive purposes. Let this number be a. Then let the strength at a distance from the home base s be measured by the number of men that can be spared for direct coercive action, h. The number $k\,(=a-h)$ we suppose is required to maintain the lines of supply. At any point not at the home base, we divide the total strength in manpower, a into two parts: a part h, which is the effective coercive force at this point, and a part k, which is necessary to maintain the lines of supply.

Let us suppose first that k is proportionate to both s and h; that is,

$$k = qsh \qquad (12.2)$$

That is, the more people have to be supplied at the front, and the longer the supply lines, the more men have to be engaged in supply. q is a basic constant of the system; it is the number of men that has to be employed in supplying one man at the front for each mile of distance. We have also

$$a = h + k \qquad (12.3)$$

From Eqs. 12.2 and 12.3, we get

$$k = qsh = a - h$$

or

$$h = \frac{a}{qs + 1} \qquad (12.4)$$

The LSG, then, is

$$c = \frac{dh}{ds} = \frac{aq}{(qs+1)^2} \qquad (12.5)$$

From Eq. 12.5, we see that the LSG continually declines with increase in s.

This is just a first approximation, because the supply lines themselves have to be supplied with secondary suppliers. This further diminishes the proportion of total forces that are at the front, the further the front extends. The secondary suppliers have to be supplied by tertiary suppliers and so on, to an infinite converging series. In the following table, we suppose that suppliers are located at each milepost of the road to the front. Suppose there are five such mileposts, the front being at the sixth. The table following, then, shows how many primary, secondary, etc., suppliers must be located at each mile:

s (miles)	1	2	3	4	5
Primary suppliers	qh	qh	qh	qh	qh
Secondary suppliers	$4q^2h$	$3q^2h$	$2q^2h$	q^2h	
Tertiary suppliers	$6q^3h$	$3q^3h$	q^3h		
Quaternary suppliers	$4q^4h$	q^4h			
Quintary suppliers	q^5h				
Sum	$qh(1+q)^4$	$qh(1+q)^3$	$qh(1+q)^2$	$qh(1+q)$	qh

INTERNATIONAL CONFLICT: THE BASIC MODEL 247

The primary suppliers supply the h men at the front; there are qh at each mile, qhs altogether. The secondary suppliers supply the primary suppliers in front of them; the first one, therefore, supplies the $4qh$ primary suppliers at the second, third, fourth, and fifth mileposts, the second supplies $3qh$, and so on. The tertiary supplier at the first mile supplies the $3q^2h + 2q^2h + q^2h$ secondary suppliers in front of him, and so on. The coefficients are those of the binomial triangle. The columns are binomial expansions; the sum of all the suppliers, k, is the sum of the geometric series $qh[1 + (1 + q) + (1 + q)^2 + \cdots + (1 + q)^{s-1}]$. We have

$$a = h + k = h + qh \frac{(1 + q)^s - 1}{(1 + q) - 1}$$

that is,

$$h = \frac{a}{(1 + q)^s} \qquad (12.6)$$

We can write this $\log h = \log a - s \log (1 + q)$.

The loss-of-strength curve, thus, is linear on semilogarithmic paper, and the linear diagrams we have been using for cost of transport, where $h = a - sq$, can be used equally well for the more complex phenomenon. An arithmetical example will illustrate the importance of the principle of supplying the suppliers. Let $q = 0.1$ and $a = 1000$. Then we have for successive value of s:

s	0	1	2	3	4	5	6	7	8	9	10	20
$1 + sq$	0	1.1	1.2	1.3	1.4	1.5	1.6	1.7	1.8	1.9	2.0	3.0
$h_1 = \dfrac{a}{1 + sq}$	1000	909	833	769	714	667	625	588	556	526	500	333
$h_2 = \dfrac{a}{(1+q)^s}$	1000	909	826	752	685	621	535	488	443	401	365	148

Thus, at a distance of 20 miles, out of 1000 total men, only 333 can be put into the field if we consider supplying only the men in the field; if we consider supplying the suppliers, only 148 can be put in the field.

13

INTERNATIONAL CONFLICT: MODIFICATIONS AND APPLICATIONS OF THE BASIC THEORY

The basic theory of the preceding chapter is common to many conflict situations wherever parties are competing in some kind of a field in any element of which one or the other parties may be dominant. Thus, in Chap. 4, we developed the theory in regard to the competition of firms for a market, and, in Chap. 12, we showed how it could be applied to the competition of states for territory. Generalized models of this kind inevitably involve a degree of simplification to the point where the peculiarity of particular situations may be overlooked. The historian or the reader trained in international relations especially must now be straining to point out the many peculiarities of international conflict that the general model does not cover. Some of these peculiarities we must now attempt to deal with, even though their full exposition would require another volume. The basic model relies heavily on certain similarities between the competition of firms and of states and, indeed, of any organizations such as rival labor unions or churches that are competing in a given field. This basic similarity is fundamental to the approach of this book. Nevertheless, the differences between the various types of conflict are also very important and must be carefully examined lest we fall into the trap of making false analogy.

It is one of the major tasks of science in any field to detect similarities in superficially different situations and to detect differences in superficially similar situations.

One of the most striking differences between the conflict of firms and of states (and, in this respect, the conflict of rival unions or churches is more like the conflict of states) is that the competition of firms in a market field is continuous but the competition of states is marked by a dramatic alternation of peace and war. This alternation of two contrasted forms of conflict—covert conflict of threats, promises, and pressures during peace and overt conflict in war—is not confined to international relations. It is found, as we have seen, in industrial relations, where a period of covert conflict is sometimes followed by a strike; it is found in family relations, where covert conflict may be followed by divorce or separation; it is found in factional or ideological conflicts within an organization, where a period of covert conflict within an organization such as a church or a political party is followed by a split or schism. Nevertheless, the covert-overt pattern as a standard and almost regular cycle is found in its most developed form in international relations. Clausewitz's famous remark that war is an extension of diplomacy is a recognition both of the unity of the system of diplomacy and war and of its two sharply contrasted patterns. What we have really is two systems—one, diplomacy, and the other, war—each of which moves to a point where it gives rise to the other, so that we have a constant though not necessarily regular alternation between them. I have used the word "diplomacy" rather than "peace" to describe the covert-conflict system of international relations partly because peace is a much overworked and ambiguous word but also because one must distinguish sharply between that system of covert conflict between states which has a strong probability of ultimately passing the system boundary into war and that condition of genuine peace, or political integration, in which the agencies for the nonviolent resolution of conflict are adequate to maintain the system without either the threat or the actuality of war.

There are certain instructive analogies between the diplomacy-war international cycle and the boom-depression business cycle which again must not be pushed too far but which help to illuminate the nature of the system involved. In both cases, we may distinguish two processes: a *worsening* and a *bettering* process. Each of these processes proceeds to some kind of boundary or turning point, after which it is either succeeded directly by the opposite process or by an intervening *crisis system*, especially in the case of the worsening process. Thus, in the business cycle, we have a process of deflation, increasing unemployment, decreasing investment and output, and so on—the familiar vicious spiral. This may go on until it produces a crisis, a panic search for liquidity and debt repayment, with widespread business failures and bankruptcies. After the crisis, the betterment spiral of increasing employment, investment, and output usually begins; this also may go on to a crisis, usually in the form of a sharp fall in speculative prices, that often inaugurates a new process of worsening. Similarly, in international relations, within the general system of diplomacy, we can have a worsening process in which relations seem to go from bad to worse and in which arms races develop, feelings are exacerbated, and fears increase. This frequently leads to a crisis in the form of a war. War, of course, is a much more elaborate and long-drawn-out process than an economic crisis; however, it has something of the same element of a breakdown in relationships. War is frequently followed by a regrouping of powers into a more stable formation, as an economic crisis is followed by reorganizations of assets and firms, and a period of betterment follows in which things go from bad to better rather than from bad to worse. The period of betterment may be ended by a shock to confidence, an internal change of government or revolution, and a reverse movement from bad to worse is inaugurated. In both cases, the betterment crisis, which ends a period of betterment, is usually much milder than the worsening crisis, which ends a period of worsening. Thus we see war as a prolonged worsening crisis and diplomacy as capable of two states: betterment or bad-to-better and worsening or good-to-worse. The scheme is illustrated in Fig. 13.1, with the economic cycle[1] on the top line and the international cycle on the bottom. Oddly enough, there seems to be some tendency for these two cycles to move in opposite directions, with international relations worsening in an economic boom and improving in an economic depression, but the correspondence is not close.

An important point, here, is that the turning points of the system do not necessarily involve crises, especially if the amplitude of the

```
                    Betterment
                     crisis
                                 Worsening
         Betterment      Worsening  crisis    Betterment

         Boom       Break  Depression    Crash     Boom
         Bad-to-better Break Good-to-worse War   Bad-to-better
```

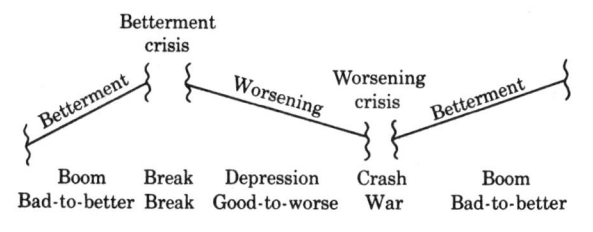

Fig. 13.1

system can be held down and the turning points can be introduced before the movement gets out of hand. We see this particularly in the business cycle. With increasing skill in the handling of financial institutions and in the development of general stabilization policies, liquidity crises in the sense in which they took place regularly in the eighteenth and nineteenth centuries have become vanishingly rare. One even hopes that the amplitude of the cycle has now been reduced to the point where it is no longer seen as an intractable social problem. This is largely because of the development of countercyclical instruments—some of them automatic, like the tax and social security systems, and some of them matters of policy, like monetary

[1] Strictly speaking, the word "cycle" is inappropriate for a system of this kind: it is not a *pendulum* type of system, in which movement in one direction constantly increases the force making for movement in the other; it is rather a *billiard ball between two parallel cushions* system, in which a continuous movement goes on persistently until it is interrupted by a shock. However, the word "cycle" is so well established in the case of the business cycle that it seems impossible to find a substitute.

and fiscal policy, which throw inflationary forces into the system when it is gathering deflationary momentum and deflationary forces when it is gathering inflationary momentum. This, incidentally, makes the system much more like a pendulum and less like a billiard ball. In the case of the diplomacy-war cycle, these countercyclical instruments are still very poorly developed. The United Nations takes cognizance of gathering war clouds and may be able to do a little to prevent their breaking, but, up to now, the instruments of real countercyclical action in the diplomacy-war cycle are very inadequate. Their very inadequacy, however, points up an important line of thought in solving the problem of war. If we think of war as a crisis in a cyclical system, this is likely to be much more fruitful of remedies than if we think of it as something wholly unpredictable and nonsystematic. In economics, we have been accustomed to thinking in terms of cybernetic, or stabilizing, institutions, and the exercise has been enormously fruitful. It is not too much to hope for a similar result from a similar mode of thought about war and peace. The problem, here, is first, how to identify a worsening movement and then, how to throw counterforces into play.

Although the time pattern of the diplomacy-war cycle may resemble that of the boom-depression cycle, there are important differences between the two systems and sets of processes. The business cycle is largely unconscious except in so far as deliberate countermeasures are taken. The interactions that bring it about are interactions of very many decision makers, each largely unconscious of the other decisions but reacting because of some neutral information carrier, such as sales, prices, and so on. The interactions of the diplomacy-war cycle are interactions among relatively few decision makers: they are much more like the relations of oligopolists than like the generalized and impersonal relations of the competitive market. Indeed, as we have seen, oligopolistic price wars and arms races are both examples of Richardson processes. This means, however, that conscious reactions are much more important. We live in a world here not of reactions to impersonal movements of sales or prices but of reactions to threats, promises, statements, bluffs, treaties, alliances, and so on, most of which represent not actual data or phenomena but attempts to change expectations of the future.

This brings us to a second peculiarity of international conflict. The importance of war as a social phenomenon is not merely that it represents a system boundary of worsening diplomatic relations, a lashing out when the tension of diplomatic relations becomes intolerable for one party or the other; it also represents an ever present threat in diplomatic relations themselves. One could, indeed, classify the nature of diplomatic relations as peaceful or warlike by the extent to which the threat of war was used an an instrument in the conduct of diplomatic relations. Thus, in Canadian-American relations, the threat of war is extremely remote and plays virtually no part in the day-to-day relationships and negotiations. In American-Russian relations, unfortunately, the threat of war is never very far from the surface.

The threat (or promise, since a threat is simply a negative promise) is a very complex phenomenon. Only recently has there been any attempt to reduce it to theoretical analysis, and the quantification of the concept still remains very rough. A threat may be defined as an act that creates a conditional expectation of damage, conditional on the performance (or, perhaps, nonperformance) of some other act; it typically has the form, "If you do (or do not do) A, I will do B." A threat may be conscious and explicit, or it may be merely implied in a situation. The significance of a threat lies wholly in the way it is perceived by the parties. This opens up the possibility that what looks like the same threat or situation may be seen quite differently by the various parties. Something that I may regard as a purely defensive act you may regard as a threat to your very existence. On the other hand, I may perceive myself as having made a very serious threat, which you may not believe or take seriously at all. The image of the threat in the minds of the parties depends partly on the perception of the means to carry it out and partly on belief about the will to carry it out. Threats that do not have the means of execution are clearly empty, though there is an important area here of creating a false perception of the means; from this point of view, the appearance of power is just as good as the reality. The most difficult cases to judge are those in which the means are clearly available but the will to use them is in doubt. Here, the belief about the will-to-use depends partly on the perception of the range of choice that faces the threatener and partly on the image of his past history of carrying out threats or promises. A parent, a union, or a nation, as a result of its past history, gets a reputation either as a stern executor of promises and threats or as a bluffer whose threats and promises are not to be believed because they have been so often unfulfilled.

Schelling has pointed out in his brilliant analysis of this problem that, in so far as bargaining power depends on the ability to make convincing threats or promises, the apparently weaker party frequently has the greater bargaining power, simply because his range of choice is so limited, and is perceived by the opponent to be so limited and that there is really no will involved and, hence, no doubt about the nature of the threat.[2] Thus, the aged, the sick, and the indigent, in effect, say to society, "Support us or we shall die," and the threat has to be believed. When a nation threatens war or a union threatens a strike, however, it does not have to be believed because it has some freedom of action; it does not have to go to war or to strike, and the problem, then, is whether its past history justifies belief in its word. The more powerful the party, the more freedom of action it possesses, and the more the dubious element of the will-to-carry-out is involved in its threats. One of the great problems of the powerful threatener, therefore, is how to get into positions in which he gives up his freedom of action so that his threats must be believed.

The very problem of the image of the reputation of the threatener, however, points up a weakness of a threat system like diplomacy and

[2] T. C. Schelling, "Prospectus for a Reorientation of Game Theory," *The Journal of Conflict Resolution*, II, no. 3 (1958).

leads to the conclusion that diplomacy must almost inevitably end up in war, even apart from the tendency of Richardson processes within the system of diplomacy to carry relations from bad to worse. If a threatener is to avoid getting a reputation as a bluffer, which would undermine the value of his threats, then, if the threatened party does not change its behavior to conform with the threat, the threat must be carried out, at least with a certain probability. To make threats effective, it is not necessary that they always be carried out, but they must be carried out on a sufficient proportion of occasions so that the party threatened will take them seriously.

A curious problem arises here about the dimensions of a threat. The importance of a threat in the mind of the threatened, that is, the likelihood that it will make him change his behavior in the manner desired by the threatener, has two dimensions: one, the magnitude of the threat itself, that is, the prospective disutility to the threatened party if the threat is carried out, and the other, the subjective probability in the mind of the threatened party that the threat will, in fact, be carried out. We could presumably define these quantities so that the importance of the threat was equal to its magnitude multiplied by its subjective probability. Now, however, we face the possibility that these two factors are not independent and that, beyond a certain point at least, the bigger the magnitude of the threat, the less its subjective probability. This means, however, that there may be a maximum value of the importance of the threat and that increasing the magnitude of the threat beyond this point actually diminishes its importance.[3] The mother who says angrily to her child, "I'll kill you if you don't stop that noise," is seldom likely

---

[3] Suppose we measure the subjective probability of the execution of the threat, p, along Op and the magnitude of the threat, M, along OM. The curve pM, then, relates p to M: it may have a rising sector, as small threats are too trivial to be believed, but it will eventually decline. At a magnitude OB the importance of the threat ($T = pM$) is the rectangle $OBKA$. This is at a maximum at some value of M between O and M, where $dt/dm = M(dp/dm) + p = 0$, or $p/M = dp/dM$.

to meet with a successful response; the threat is of such magnitude that the subjective probability is zero, and its importance is likewise zero. A smaller threat is likely to have a greater effect. We must beware, of course, of taking threats too literally; frequently, a convention develops by which big threats are discounted by everybody, simply because everybody knows they are meaningless, and are interpreted as threats of much smaller magnitude. "I'll kill you" presumably means, to both parties, "I am annoyed enough to spank you hard."

In international conflict, there are roughly three kinds of threats: the threat of punishment, the threat of conquest, and the threat of annihilation. As between two unconditionally viable nations, the threat of punishment is the only significant threat, as neither can conquer nor annihilate the other. One nation can, however, make things uncomfortable for another by military action and so may be able to sway the policies of other nations in its own favor. The difficulty with punishment, of course, especially as between relative equals, is that the traditional plaint of the angry parent, "It hurts me more than it hurts you," though rarely believed by the victim, has many grains of truth in it. The infliction of punishment is costly for the punisher as well as for the punished, quite apart from any retaliatory action, and the threat of punishment is correspondingly less effective as its cost increases. The Crimean War is a good example of a threat that turned into a war of punishment; the British and French presumably had no thought or hopes of conquering Russia, but, by making things unpleasant, they hoped to dissuade her from extending her power toward Constantinople. In the course of making things unpleasant for her, however, they also made things very unpleasant for themselves, or at least for their armies.

When a nation is no longer unconditionally viable, the threat of conquest becomes possible, and, in the expansion of empires, this threat has generally been used with powerful effect. Its use requires a situation of conditional viability for the threatened nation, where the threatening power can conquer it but, for some reason, prefers to withhold its hand. It is frequently advantageous to a powerful country to surround itself with a ring of subservient but nominally independent buffer states that can be kept in order by the threat of conquest. The attempt to absorb them into the empire of the dominant power may actually weaken it through heterogeneity, and, hence, that power may prefer to let its weaker satellites manage their own internal affairs, provided that they maintain a firm alliance and a friendly posture. The British Empire at its height was a masterly example of the use of the threat of conquest to organize a vast heterogeneous domain. In India for instance, a mosaic of princely states in the matrix of British India (directly governed by the representatives of the Crown) testified to the effective use of a combination of actual and threatened conquest. Indirect rule in Africa was an example of the same basic pattern.

The threat is not always one of conquest by the dominant power; sometimes it is of allowing the threatened country to be conquered by a rival dominant power. This seems to be the case today, for instance, in Western Europe. The Western European countries have little or no fear of conquest by the United States, because even though they may not be unconditionally viable with regard to the United States, they enjoy secure conditional viability; the United States has no wish to absorb them into its political structure. Nevertheless, because these countries do have a very real fear of conquest or of domination by Russia, the threat of withdrawal of defense by the United States is a very effective one. It is interesting to note that this threat is not very effective against the traditional neutrals, Sweden and Switzerland, whose reliance on a mixture of historical habit and physical geography has so far been effective. In the case of the Russian satellite countries like Poland and Hungary, the threat of conquest, by Russia, is very real; there is the additional complication that the existing regimes face substantial internal opposition and rely on the support of Russia to prevent their overthrow from within.

The third threat, that of annihilation, is not altogether new (one remembers Carthage and Jerusalem), but it has reached a new intensity with the development of nuclear weapons capable even of destroying all life on earth. This has altered the nature of the threat of war so completely that the present situation must be regarded as so different in degree from that prevailing under earlier forms of weaponry as to be different in kind. The peculiar danger consists not so much in the destructiveness of the modern weapons but in the rapidity of their application and their world-wide range. Carthage was destroyed just as completely, indeed, more completely, than Hiroshima. This, however, was at the end of a long process. Today, the world might destroy itself in a few hours, perhaps as a result only of an accident or a misinterpretation of information received at some obscure station. A threat system of this kind, especially when the powers of annihilation are mutual, is intolerable and introduces a condition of desperate instability into international relations. We are all sitting under the sword of Damocles; it is not surprising that some desperate attempts are being made to strengthen the thread.

This brings us to a third important peculiarity of international conflict—the distinction that can be made between offensive and defensive armaments and actions. In the case of the competition of firms, there is little defense but attack: if one firm cuts its price, almost the only response of the other firm is to cut its price also. Product differentiation, selling cost, and product innovation may be thought of as defensive in the sense that they may not injure the aggressor firm; these things, however, are closer to flight than to defense. In the case of conflict between nations, however, there is a distinction between defensive organization and weapons, which are aimed at preventing the enemy from doing harm but not at harming the enemy, and offensive or retaliatory organization and weapons, which do not lessen the capacity of the enemy for doing harm but which are aimed at harming the enemy directly. The distinction is not always easy to draw, but it clearly represents an important difference. Thus, a shield, a city wall, or a bomb shelter are purely defensive armaments: they lessen the capacity of the enemy to harm but can in no way harm him. A fighter plane or a submarine chaser has a somewhat intermediate status. Its main objective is to destroy agents of the enemy that are engaged in injurious activities, so that it has a defensive aspect; on the other hand, its defense is not passive like that of a bomb shelter, as it is aimed at injuring the aggressive agents of the enemy. A bomber or a missile is a clearly offensive weapon designed mainly to injure the enemy, even though this may have indirect effects in weakening the enemy's power to injure. This distinction is important in distinguishing a possible pattern of response to threat; the threat of injury may be followed by defensive action, which simply diminishes the power of the threatener to injure, or it may be followed by offensive action, which increases the power of the threatened party to injure the threatener. This latter is the retaliatory response to threat. Between these two extremes, as before, we may notice an intermediate reaction—the offensive defense, which aims to injure the threatening agent of the threatener but not the threatener himself.

It is a commonplace of military history that military technology has usually exhibited a race between the offensive and the defensive armaments: each new offensive weapon has rendered obsolete the old defensive armament but has, in turn, stimulated the development of new defenses. The arrow and the spear produced the shield and the wall; the cannon and the rifle eventually produced the tank and the ironclad. The increased technical efficiency of offense generally seems to precede that of defense, perhaps because the payoffs to the innovator are greater in the case of offensive weapons. This is because offensive weapons always have a defensive aspect, through their power to destroy the offensive weapons of the enemy, whereas defensive weapons seldom have an offensive aspect. For the innovator, therefore, the development of a more efficient offensive weapon kills two birds with one stone: it makes his own threats more effective, by increasing his capacity to injure his enemy, and it makes the enemy's threats less effective, for it diminishes the enemy's power to injure by reason of the increased power of the innovator to injure the enemy's offensive weapons. The improvement of a defensive weapon from a situation of rough parity with the offensive weapons has, by contrast, very little payoff; it may slightly diminish the power of the enemy to injure the innovator, but it does little or nothing to increase the power of the innovator to injure a potential enemy. It is not surprising, therefore, that the dynamics of weapon development has always favored a constant increase both in the power and the range of offensive weapons and that the improvement in defensive weapons, where it has taken place, has been a catching up rather than a leading change.

In terms of the basic model of the previous chapter, a unilateral improvement in offensive weapons is likely to lead to a situation like Fig. 12.6, where the lagging party is deprived of unconditional viability.

If, now, the innovator does not take immediate advantage of his opportunity to conquer the other party, this party will imitate the innovation, and we shall have a situation like Fig. 12.7, in which neither of the parties is unconditionally viable and a very unstable situation results. Now there is a strong incentive to develop defensive weapons, even for one of the parties, as in Fig. 12.8, as this may restore his unconditional viability, and if the other party follows suit, as in Fig. 12.9, this may restore unconditional viability for both parties.

The distinction between defensive and offensive weapons can also be made in terms of their effects on the LSG. Thus, in Fig. 13.2, as in Fig. 12.1, *AH* is the maximum home strength of country *A* and *BK* of *B*. If there are uniform LSGs, as in the lines *HTL* and *KEM*, country *B* is clearly not unconditionally viable. Now suppose that *B* can develop defensive weapons that will change *A*'s strength line from *HTL* to *HTES*. The effect of *B*'s defensive weapons is to increase *A*'s LSG as *A* approaches *B*. If the effect is sufficient, there will be an equilibrium of mutual viability and a boundary of equal strength at *E*. It is difficult to translate changes in the loss-of-strength line into the infinite-game matrix figures of Figs. 12.3 to 12.9. A little device, however, easily solves the problem; instead of supposing that the defensive weapon alters the loss-of-strength line, we suppose that it creates an equivalent loss of home strength with constant, linear, loss-of-strength lines. Thus, the strength of country A at B with the loss-of-strength curve $HTES$ is BS; it would be the same if its home strength were AH' and its loss-of-strength curve were $H'S$.

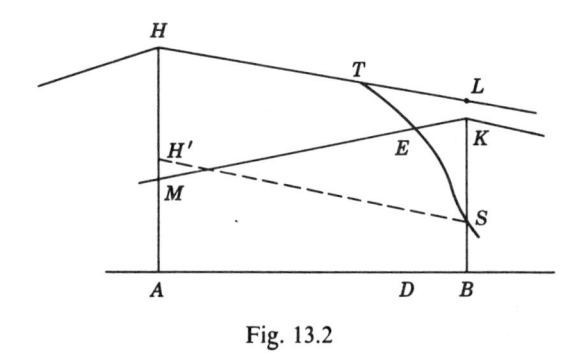

Fig. 13.2

Assuming a decline in home strength of A from AH to AH', moving from T to S with a fixed imaginary LSG is equivalent to the actual decline in the strength curve from T to S. This is essentially, the approach of Figs. 12.8 and 12.9; these can be interpreted as implying either a loss in its real home strength as one nation invades another's heavily defended territory or an increase in the LSG, which is the slope of the loss-of-strength curve, as the invasion proceeds, with a corresponding decline in the virtual home strength such as AH'.

This leads to a very important distinction that corresponds roughly, though not exactly, to the usual distinction between offensive and defensive weapons. This is the distinction between innovations that diminish one's own LSG (aggressive) and innovations that increase the opponent's LSG (defensive). The first type of innovation has the effect of making existing nations less viable and the existing equilibrium, if it exists, more precarious; the second has the effect of increasing the viability of the existing nations and

262   CONFLICT AND DEFENSE

system. We have seen, however, that, from a situation of equilibrium, the aggressive innovation is much more likely to pay off to the innovator, especially if he can take advantage of it quickly before it is imitated. This is one reason for the observed phenomenon of the secular decline through history of the LSG and the secular rise in the minimum size of the viable nation; defense weapons are always

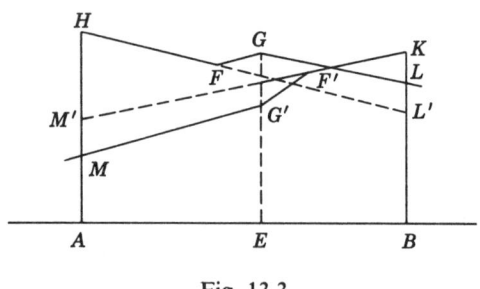

Fig. 13.3

fighting a rearguard action. In addition, there is the phenomenon of technical development in general making for cheaper transport; the payoffs for improvements in transport are high in all fields, whereas there are seldom payoffs for increasing costs of transport except through highly artificial means like tariffs, which appear in this analysis as a thoroughly defensive weapon. General improvement in means of transport are nearly always reflected in a decline in the LSG, simply because the transport of violence always involves the transport of men and things.

The possibility of reversing the LSG, at least for a certain distance, is illustrated in Fig. 13.3. This is the problem of the effect of *bases*, or secondary centers of home strength. By establishing a base at G, the country A may actually raise its on-the-spot strength between F and G, and this raises it above what it would have been everywhere beyond G. The naval bases of Britain and the air bases of the United States are good examples of the attempt to overcome the factor of loss of strength with distance. In the special sense in which we have

INTERNATIONAL CONFLICT: MODIFICATIONS 263

used the terms, the off-territory base may be both defensive and offensive. In so far as it raises the country's strength line, as in *FGL* of Fig. 13.3, above what it would have been without the base (*FL'*), it is clearly an offensive weapon, making mutual viability more difficult. A base may also have the effect of lowering the strength line of the opponent. With *A*'s base located at *E* in Fig. 13.3, *B*'s loss-of-strength line may well be *KF'G'M* instead of *KM'*. The base requires an effort to circumvent, and this reduces *B*'s strength at all points beyond it; the reduction, in fact, probably begins as soon as the effective range of the base is reached at *F'*. In this sense, therefore, the base is defensive. It is this offensive-defensive character of a base which makes bases so touchy a subject in international negotiations; it is easy for the owner of a base to see only its defensive aspects and for the other party to see only the offensive aspects.

This model also serves to illustrate the theory of the buffer state. Thus, in Fig. 13.4, suppose we have a buffer state C_1C_2 between the two main centers of power. The strength gradient of each of the two main centers dips as it passes through the buffer state, indicating that

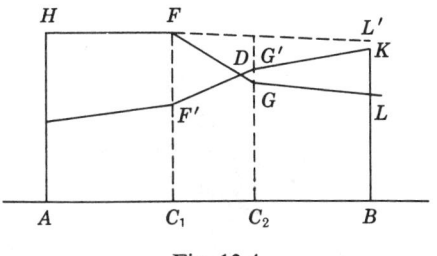

Fig. 13.4

the organization of the buffer state is enough to reduce the power of main centers in its territory, even though the buffer state itself may not be unconditionally viable. The buffer state, therefore, may restore unconditional viability to the main centers; thus, without the buffer state in Fig. 13.4, *A*'s strength gradient would be *HL'*, and *B* would no longer be unconditionally viable. It is clearly in *B*'s interest, therefore, to establish a buffer state. It may be less in A's interest, but if the dynamic situation is such that the positions of A and B might be reversed at some future date, the maintenance of the buffer state may be in B's interest also. The fact that the point of equal strength (D) between A and B may lie within the boundary of the buffer state also may reduce tension, as there is less gain to either party in trying to move the position of D. Hence, there will be less chance of an arms race, and the whole situation is more stable than it would be in the absence of the buffer state. The buffer state must, however, have enough inner coherence in its own right not to be dominated by either of the major powers; otherwise, fear of domination by one may lead the other to extinguish it or lead the major powers to divide it. Poland in the eighteenth century was a good example of a buffer state that failed; Belgium, Holland, Luxembourg, and perhaps Switzerland are examples of states which have perhaps never been unconditionally viable but which have survived because of their buffer situation.

Yet another difference between international conflict and the competition of firms is the much greater importance of geographical boundaries in international relations. The firm competes in a market area where boundaries are shifting and ill defined and where effort is spread over the whole area rather than being concentrated at the boundary. In international conflict, by contrast, the boundaries of nations tend to be very sharply defined, any violation of a boundary is regarded as a matter of gravest concern, and the efforts for survival or expansion of nations are highly concentrated on the boundaries between them. It is so difficult to change international boundaries by diplomacy that it is tempting to interpret the diplomacy-war cycle in terms of a concept of strain on boundaries. During peace, that is, international conflict by diplomacy, it is impossible to make any but the most minor and insignificant adjustments in international boundaries; because of the slowly changing relative power of nations, however, the existing structure of boundaries gets more and more obsolete and is subject to greater and greater strain. Eventually, the strain gets too great for the system of diplomacy and war breaks out. War creates a fluidity in national boundaries that did not exist under diplomacy, and the war ends when the parties think that the adjustments in boundaries that will come out of it are not damaging enough to the weaker parties to make it worth their while continuing the war. This is presumably what winning a war means. In the treaty that follows the war, a new set of boundaries is drawn, presumably corresponding more than the old set to the structure of national power that the war has revealed. The strain on the national system is thereby reduced, and diplomacy is once more feasible as an international system; the peace treaty that re-establishes diplomacy, however, also has the effect of freezing the boundaries, and the cycle starts all over again.

The legal boundary of a nation, however, is not always its most significant boundary. We need to develop a concept of a *critical boundary*, which may be the same as the legal boundary but which may lie either inside it or outside it. The systems of Figs. 12.7 to 12.9 suggest that a nation will have some critical boundary, not perhaps so well defined as its legal boundary but of great importance in understanding its policies and behavior, that is something like the skin of a living organism. The penetration of an alien organization inside this critical boundary will produce grave disorganization, perhaps on the part of the invader as well as on the part of the invaded. War, therefore, is only useful as a defense of the national organism if it is carried on outside the critical boundary. This makes the distinction between defense and aggression very hard to make in practice; frequently, a nation operates outside its legal boundary in order to establish what it regards as a critical boundary. Britain was defended for hundreds of years on every soil but its own.

The concept of a critical boundary can be extended to include a series of shells of boundaries of varying degrees of importance. At the extremity, we may have a vague sphere of influence, violation of which may call forth little more than a diplomatic protest. As we get closer and closer to the home base of a nation, we pass boundaries of increasing degrees of importance, until the final critical boundary cannot be violated without war. Thus, the European powers were prepared to jockey for overseas colonies, and clashes over outlying imperial territories might produce nothing more than an incident. It has been a cardinal policy of Britain, however, for centuries to regard the Low Countries as within her critical boundary, in spite of the fact that they have never been within her legal boundary, and she has fought every country that threatened to dominate or subdue them—first Spain, then France, and, in the twentieth century, Germany. The United States had a similar critical boundary in Hawaii or perhaps now has one in Formosa and Japan—but not in Hungary.

The concept of the critical boundary is related to another important magnitude in the war system, and, therefore, potentially in the diplomacy system, that has no counterpart that I have encountered in any other form of conflict. This is the *range of the projectile*. War as a system can be defined roughly as men throwing things at each other with malicious intent. It starts with rocks, and it advances to spears and arrows, to cannons and rifles and machine guns and bazookas, to poison gas and airplanes with bombs and guided missiles with nuclear warheads. In all this "progress" the range of the projectile has been increasing to the point now where it is many thousands of miles and soon will be as much as half the circumference of the earth; any greater range than this is of no significance as far as earthly warfare is concerned. The range of the projectile, then, determines the distance between the throwers. With a range of a few feet, we have hand-to-hand combat; with a range of anything beyond the range of sight, we have invisible enemies hurling anonymous projectiles at each other. It is not enough, of course, merely to hurl projectiles at random. There must be a receptor system to convey information about whether the projectile has reached its mark, and a cybernetic control system to guide the projection of the projectile in such a way that it does reach its mark. In hand-to-hand combat, where the projectile is a fist, a knife, a bayonet, or even a hand grenade, the receptor-control system is the human nervous system and is managed by direct perception. The longer the range of the projectile, the more difficult the receptor-control problem becomes; it becomes more difficult, that is, to know whether the projectile has reached its intended mark and correspondingly more difficult to aim it with a high probability of reaching the mark. As in the case of a threat, increased range and size of a projectile do not always increase its effectiveness, because there may be a corresponding diminution in the chance of its hitting the target. Besides the range and the damage power, or charge, of a projectile, there is, therefore, a third variable—its accuracy, or the probability of its hitting the target. Effectiveness is a function of all three things; up to a point, inaccuracy may be compensated by increasing range and charge, but only at an appalling cost in useless destruction.

The longer the range of a projectile, however, the more important it becomes to extend the critical boundary of a nation beyond its legal boundary in order to control the sites of potential missiles. No nation can now feel comfortable if rocket-launching sites are within several thousand miles of its vital centers.

It is the increase in the range of the projectile that has come with the airplane and the missile (the airplane, after all, is in a military sense mainly a manned projectile with a detachable warhead) that has caused the dramatic breakdown in the system of national defense as we see it today, even though the long, slow historical decline in the LSG prepared the way for this breakdown. For national defense as a system to possess any kind of equilibrium and for nations to be unconditionally viable under a system of national defense, each nation must be able to preserve an area of peace within its critical boundaries even if it has to maintain this area of peace by fighting wars outside it. Each nation must also be stronger than its potential enemies, or even any reasonably probable combination of them, within its critical boundaries, and it must be weaker than its enemies within their critical boundaries. This condition, as we have seen, is most likely to provide for a large number of nations in reasonable equilibrium when the LSG is high and, now we may add, when the critical boundaries lie close to the legal boundaries of the nations. If, because of the increasing range of projectiles, the critical boundary must now extend far beyond the legal boundary in order to give any kind of security, the chances of a viable system of national defense fall to zero. Violence can now jump any boundary, and the ancient concept of defense symbolized by the wall, whether of the walled city, the Great Wall of China, the Maginot line, or even the DEW line, has crumbled in ruins.

One feature of international and, especially, of military relations that we have neglected hitherto is that there may be many varieties of strength, which is not a one-dimensional quantity, as we have assumed, but a multidimensional structure. Some of these varieties may have larger LSGs than others; hence, we may have a situation where, for instance, one nation is dominant over another by air power but not by land power, or by military power but not by ideological or moral power. It is a common observation, for instance, that nations are often conquered culturally by the people they conquer militarily; we have seen a certain Japonification of American taste, for instance, and a certain Prussianization of American foreign policy since the Second World War. These types of change are not necessarily always for the worse. A problem that is perhaps peculiar to the modern world is that the LSG for air power is very much less than it is for land power; this changes the dimensions of war in ways that are highly unpredictable, especially as these different forms of power have somewhat different functions. The power to destroy from the air is not the same as the power to occupy with an invading army, even though all forms of military power are closely related. If we identify conquest with occupation, a frequent though not a necessary identification, we may run into the paradox that nations can be destroyed without being conquered.

It should be instructive before we leave the subject of international conflicts and systems to take a very brief view of the course of historical development of these systems to see how far the models that we have developed throw light on historical realities. History, of course, is a system immensely more complex than our simple mathematical models. Nations are born, grow, fight, conquer, are conquered, become empires, and rise and fall on the great stage of physical geography and human passions and knowledge, not on the homogeneous white planes on which we draw our diagrams. Nevertheless, the model does serve to interpret history and enables us to see the basic simple patterns that underly the baroque embellishments of the actual course of events. Thus, the model suggests that savage cultures resting on food gathering find it difficult to establish political organizations of any size. The tribe tends to be the basic unit; and this is small, and its LSG is very steep as it moves away from its usual hunting grounds into those of other tribes. With agriculture and civilization comes the possibility of larger political units. Even these, however, are sharply dependent on the means of transportation. It is no accident that the earliest empires developed along the great navigable river valleys, which provided not only opportunity for agriculture but also a means of transportation by which agricultural surpluses could be collected and transported to feed both cities and armies. Along the rivers, for river transport is both easy and cheap, an army could move far from home without suffering a fatal loss of strength due to the lengthening of its lines of supply. Egypt, therefore, developed along the Nile; Sumeria, Assyria, and Babylon developed along the Tigris and Euphrates; the ancient civilization of Mohenjo-Daro and Harappa was a creation of the Indus; and the ancient Chinese civilization rested on the Hoang-Ho and the Yangtse. These ancient civilizations were never able to extend their power securely beyond their own river basins, though Egypt and the successive Mesopotamian civilizations made forays from time to time into each other's territory. The empire of Alexander was much too large for the land communications that it involved and broke up almost on his death into the ancient river-bed patterns. The Greeks and the Romans, however, represent the rise of another kind of communication—island hopping and coastwise sea travel. The Roman Empire is the culmination of the Empire of the Inland Seas, that is, of the Mediterranean and the Black Seas. By adding Roman roads to the sea routes, the Romans were able to extend their empire some hundreds of miles inland from the Mediterranean, as far as Britain, Dacia, Central Anatolia, and Upper Mesopotamia, but they never could master the German forests, the Persian uplands, or the Russian steppes. Even the Roman Empire proved ultimately too large for the means of transport at its disposal, and it was gradually eroded by barbarian invasions and finally replaced by the Arab and then by the Turkish Empire, which, at its height, had almost exactly the boundaries of Justinian's empire. The invention of the rudder and better methods of navigation liberated seagoers from the coast and, by the end of the fourteenth century, had opened up the seven seas to Europe, which pioneered in this development. The Portuguese, Spanish, French, Dutch, and, finally, the British Empire were the results. Sea transport, both of commodities and of violence, is fantastically cheap compared with land transport. Between Vasco de Gama and Mahan, any nation that commanded the seas commanded the coasts of the whole world and might even command the navigable rivers too. From the coast, one could command territory far into the interior if opposition were primitive or disorganized, as in America, though one could not do so, as the Crimean War showed, if the opposition were even moderately well organized.

The growth of the Russian Empire is an interesting special case. The expansion from Moscow down the Volga and the Don to the south looks like a typical river empire. The vast geographical expansion across the land mass of Siberia, even as far as Alaska and California by the end of the eighteenth century, is a more surprising phenomenon. Some of this is coastwise shipping in the summer along the Arctic seaways; some of it is to be accounted for by the relative ease of winter travel across the snowy, treeless plains by sled. Partly, also, the expansion is due to the lack of any effective opposition and the fact that no potential competitor was geographically in a position to expand into northern Asia. The Russian expansion reached a certain natural, and symbolic, boundary when it got as far as Alaska, and the Russians were easily persuaded to move out of North America.

The nomadic empires radiating out of Central Asia and Arabia form an interesting special case. The nomad has a certain advantage over the agriculturalist and the city dweller in that he is less tied to a home base, simply because he carries his home base with him. His hard, open-air life makes the arts of war attractive to him, and he can devote a large proportion of his total surplus resources, above what is needed for his maintenance, to warlike pursuits. Consequently, he has a low LSG and, under favorable circumstances, can expand his power over very large areas, especially as the arid plains on which he lives make for relatively unhampered travel by horse or camel. The desert to the nomadic empires is what the Mediterranean was to the Romans—the great central highway where they suffered little loss of strength and from the edges of which they could make forays into the forested or settled regions that surrounded them. This accounts for much of the success of the Huns, of the Golden Horde, of the Tartars, and of the early Moslem Arabs. The nomad empires, however, were usually short-lived; the very military qualities that gave rise to them also led to constant internal faction and secessions, and their long lines of communication across the deserts were even more vulnerable than the sea lanes of the Romans.

The railroad effected a substantial revolution in the ease and costs of overland travel and probably reduced the differential in cost between land and water transport, though the application of steam and, later, oil power to water transport led to a similar decline in costs there. The railroad, therefore, played an important part in the unification of the continental countries such as the United States, Canada, Australia, and Russia. The Civil War in the United States is some evidence that, had it not been for the railroad, the United States might easily have broken up into several countries, like the

Spanish Empire in America. The railroad may have come too late to prevent the Civil War, but it played an important part in saving the Union. Even as late as the late nineteenth century, however, as Mahan pointed out so eloquently, the overseas empire and the viability of a seacoast country depended to a very large extent on the command of the seas. The American Revolution was probably successful only because it happened during the few years when the French wrested command of the seas from the British, and, by the time the British had regained this command after Trafalgar, the United States had a solid continental base and could be harried but not destroyed by the British in 1812.

The airplane and now the missile have brought about a revolution of quite unprecedented dimensions, as we have suggested earlier. For the air-borne carrier or weapon, the world is an almost featureless globe: coasts, mountains, deserts, and forests hardly exist as long as there are landing strips on the other side of them. The intricate geographical structure of national power, therefore, which rests on the combination of seapower with a very low LSG and landpower with a much higher LSG, has largely been swept away as far as air power is concerned. Everywhere now is accessible to everybody; there are no nooks, corners, or retreats left, and no snugly protected centers of national power. The great continental heartlands are just as exposed to aerial warfare as are the coasts to naval bombardment. The result is a sudden and dramatic collapse of unconditional viability. The Second World War showed that powers the size of France and Germany were no longer unconditionally viable and that, under modern conditions, they had no more significant depth in defense than Belgium or Luxembourg. Whether the superpowers are now also no longer unconditionally viable is a matter of quantitative fact that cannot be settled unequivocally; it is highly probable, however, that, even now, their unconditional viability has been destroyed, and the paradox is that, the greater their efforts in the perfection of missiles and warheads, the more likely is their unconditional viability to vanish.

Under these circumstances, the problem of conditional viability becomes of great interest, for the question whether we can continue to have a world of independent states or whether sovereignty, by the sheer logic of international systems, will have to be surrendered to a world government, by agreement, as we hope, or by conquest, as we fear, now resolves itself largely into the possibility of a system of conditional viability. We can only continue to have a world of separate nations if none of them wants to upset the existing structure, for none can really be defended, against a nation that wants to conquer them, without destroying the whole world. This question, however, is a matter of future rather than of past history and will be discussed in a later chapter.

APPENDIX TO CHAPTER 13:
KAPLAN'S THEORY OF INTERNATIONAL SYSTEMS

Attempts to reduce the complexities of international relations to theoretical models have been very rare in the past. Within the last few years, however, one major effect has been made in this direction by Kaplan, whose *System and Process in International Politics*[4] is an ambitious attempt at system building in this area. For the orderly progress of ideas, therefore, it seems wise to outline briefly what seem to be the relations between Kaplan's theory and the approach of the present volume.

Kaplan's basic theoretical bias is sociological and taxonomic, by contrast with my own economic and topological bias. He distinguishes first six possible types of international systems: (1) the balance of power system as exemplified roughly in the world of the eighteenth and nineteenth centuries, in which a number, say, six or seven, nations of roughly equal size and strength fight occasional wars, form shifting alliances, and jockey for position; (2) the *loose bipolar* system, roughly what we have today, in which two superpowers are surrounded by a cluster of smaller satellites and neutrals; (3) the *tight bipolar* system, in which the neutrals disappear and only two power blocs are left; (4) the *universal actor* system, in which the world political organization, such as the United Nations, is powerful

---

[4] Morton A. Kaplan, *System and Process in International Politics*, New York, Wiley, 1957.

enough to prevent war but in which nations still retain their individuality and jockey for power within the framework of the universal actor; (5) the *hierarchical international* system, or world state, in which one nation has absorbed all the others. These clearly form a progression, but the sixth system stands somewhat apart; it is (6) the *unit veto* system, in which any nation however weak can destroy any other.

These six categories fall comfortably into the theoretical framework of the present work. The balance of power system is possible and may even have a rough equilibrium, constantly disturbed, as far as particular nations are concerned, by chance forces but maintaining a fairly stable system as a whole, as long as the LSG and the other essential variables of the system are such as to give unconditional viability to a fair number of countries. As we have seen, however, technical developments tend to destroy the viability of this system, and it passes into the loose bipolar system simply through the loss of viability for any but the very largest powers; this is where we were in the Second World War. Whether there is any dynamic process leading from this to the tight bipolar system is not clear; Kaplan himself is more interested in the taxonomy of systems than in their dynamics. One may guess, however, that this depends on the stability of conditional viability, which is characteristic of the smaller powers in the loose bipolar system. If the conditionally viable powers are very different in culture from the superpowers, conditional viability may be quite stable, and there will be no tendency to pass over into the tight bipolar system. If, now, the superpowers themselves become no longer unconditionally viable, as seems to be happening, the instability and danger of such a system creates a pressure either for type 4, the current disarmament discussions are a tentative movement toward this—or, failing this, for type 5, which, however, in view of the great cultural and ideological heterogeneity of the world, is hard to visualize in the near future. The odd unit veto system, which might develop if the small nations developed the H bomb, rests on the assumption of the extension of the critical boundary of national defense to include the whole world, simply because of the increase in the range of the dominant projectile. Thus, I think I can claim that my functional models give a dynamic interpretation to the purely taxonomic structure of the Kaplan theory.

The economist cannot help being struck by the analogy between the states of the market as developed in economic theory and Kaplan's six international systems. The balance of power system corresponds roughly to perfect competition: the size of the competitor is small relative to the market, most competitors are unconditionally viable, and the system as a whole is stable in spite of the rise and fall of particular firms. A fall in the cost of transport or the development of economies of scale, however, leads to a reduction in the number of firms and an increase in their average size, and this goes on until we are left with perhaps only two big ones (duopoly). This is an unstable situation and either leads to collusion, cartels like the United Nations, or gentlemen's agreements (conditional viability), or it may lead to monopoly (conquest), which corresponds to Kaplan's type 5. The curious and frightening unit veto system corresponds to a system of absolutely perfect oligopoly under zero costs of transport where any firm, by shading its mill price only slightly, can take away the entire market of any other firm.

The bulk of Kaplan's book is concerned with developing a taxonomy of types of *national actor* (nations) and a taxonomy also of *patterns of choice* within the complex decision-making process of the national actor itself. These considerations might be described as second-order modifications of the basic models of the present work, which essentially abstract from the processes by which decisions are made, concentrating on the great forces that effectually limit the field of decision. We have deliberately neglected, therefore, many of the processes that Kaplan stresses—the processes by which false images, misunderstandings, rash decisions, accidental mistakes, and so forth, serve to modify the mechanical processes of our models.

One concept to which Kaplan devotes some attention and which I have perhaps neglected is that of the *national interest*. A great debate has raged among students of international relations between the *moralist* (tender) and the *realist* (tough) schools, the first stressing the importance of higher values, for instance, propagating democracy, in international relations and the second stressing the overriding importance of crude, selfish, national interest. Kaplan attempts to resolve this debate by pointing out the complexity and the moral or at least the valuational foundations of the concept of national interest, which cannot be separated from national values,(what people think is better or worse). I am sympathetic to this view, especially in so far as I stress the importance of symbolic systems in explaining the particular drives of nations toward expansion or defense, toward alliances or enmities and toward a high morale and will-to-conflict or a low morale and subserviency. It is tempting to look for a concept of national interest in the models of the past two chapters by analogy with the net revenue, or profitability, concept in the theory of the firm, such a concept might not only define the boundaries of maximum home strength, as the minimum-profit contour defines it in the case of the firm, but might give a greater rationale to the Richardson processes in terms of reaction moves being always to positions of higher interest. One must be careful of this analogy, however. One essential element in the national-interest concept is that it is vague and ill defined or is defined only at certain salient points; it is not a clear and unidimensional concept like profitability. It is clearly defined qualitatively, however, at the boundary of maximum home strength; this is the level of survival, and it is possible to postulate this as a basic value. Values of national interest either more than or less than survival, however, are difficult to define. What must be emphasized is that national interest is not a clearly defined quantity like a physical magnitude; it is a psychological magnitude that may be drastically changed by internal shifts in power or by changes in philosophy or value systems within the ruling hierarchy or even of the mass of the people.

14

IDEOLOGICAL AND ETHICAL CONFLICT

The study of conflict is by no means exhausted when we have considered the conflicts of individuals, groups, and organizations such as firms, labor unions, and national states. All these particular conflicts lie embedded in a matrix of a more general conflict—the great battle of ethical, religious, scientific, and ideological systems for the allegiance of men. At one level, of course, the conflicts of organizations can be discussed without any reference to the purposes or ideas that these organizations stand for or embody. The struggle between the United States and Russia, for instance, can be treated at one level quite legitimately as if it were simply a conflict of nation-states for relative strength, dominance, or defense and had nothing to do with the ideological positions of these two countries. This has been largely the approach of the previous two chapters, which have tried to abstract out of the complexity of international conflict that which was peculiar to it as a conflict of nation states.

Now, however, we must cast our net wider, for the conflict among organizations, almost without exception, has ideological overtones. The struggle between the United States and Russia is not merely a struggle of two superpowers; it is also a struggle of ideologies. When two organizations in conflict also have different ideological positions and when they come to symbolize these positions, the conflict is usually made sharper. Ideological similarities do not always make for organizational partnership in conflict, however, nor do ideological differences necessarily make for organizational enmity. Thus, in international conflict, religious ideology has ceased to be a factor of great importance, as it was, say, before 1648 in Europe. The First World War saw Protestant England, Catholic France and Italy, Orthodox Russia, and Shinto Japan aligned against Protestant-Catholic Germany, Catholic Austria, Orthodox Bulgaria, and Mohammedan Turkey.

The extent to which ideological differences result in overt conflict depends mainly on the extent to which these differences are embodied in organizations designed for conflict. Thus, the decline in wars of religion is not necessarily due to any decline in religious fervor, though this may have been a contributing cause, but rather to a gradual separation of religion from the state and its armed force as an organizer of conflict. As long as the church was identified with the state and regarded as an essential ideological organizer of a society, religious differences were embodied in the social system of interacting armed forces and became occasions for armed conflict. With the rise of the secular state and internal freedom of religion, religious conformity was no longer regarded as essential to the unity of society, which could be held together by purely political organization. Religion, therefore, ceased to be important as a source of international conflict. This is not to say that religious conflict ceased; it was simply removed to another arena.

The conflict of ideologies, therefore, is partly ecological and partly organizational. In so far as we regard an ideology as a population of adherents, the ecological and epidemiological models that we have outlined in Chaps. 6 and 7 are useful. The population of adherents grows partly by natural increase in the family: Catholic parents tend to produce Catholic children, Moslem parents Moslem children, and so on. It grows also by infection, that is, conversion. Likewise, the population of adherents of any one ideology declines by natural death and also by conversion to another ideology. Quantitative studies on this point would be interesting and, as far as I know, have not been made, as to the relative importance of family training versus adult conversion in the rise or decline of populations of adherents. There are some ideologies, like that of the Amish, that perpetuate themselves almost entirely by natural increase through family upbringing. For most settled populations of adherents, family upbringing is quantitatively more important than adult conversion, though the latter exists. Catholics, most standard Protestant churches, and Jews would conform to this description when considered as populations of adherents. In the very early stages of the development of a successful ideology, however, adult conversion is the only means of its spread, and we have studded through history examples of these true epidemics of ideological spread. The ecological and epidemiological models of Chaps. 6 and 7 also throw some light on these phenomena.

What the mechanical models do not illuminate is the process that Rapoport has identified by the name of *debate*.[1] This is one of the processes that underly the infectiousness of ideologies and the conflict between populations of adherents. The problem from the point of view of social dynamics is that of defining the circumstances under which an adherent of one ideology will shift to another. This may happen for reasons that have nothing to do with debate or argument; sometimes, for instance, people are converted to a particular ideology because they happen to marry an adherent of this ideology, or because they happen to reside among its adherents, or because the ideology carries prestige and power in their society. This cannot be the whole story, however; otherwise the spread and decline of ideologies would be a purely mechanical and stochastic process. Most people, perhaps all, would recoil from this view; we have a sense that ideologies are not arbitrary and accidental but that they conform to certain patterns of their own and are true or untrue.

We seem to need first, therefore, a concept of the power of an

[1] Anatol Rapoport, *Fights, Games and Debates*, Ann Arbor, University of Michigan Press, 1960.

ideology. The concept is hard to quantify, mainly because it is difficult to define standard conditions for the spread of an ideology, and where two ideologies of equal power confront each other, neither of them spreads. The concept has some analogies with that of the home strength of a nation; a weak ideology may spread rapidly and widely if it has no opposition, so that mere rapidity of spread is no measure of power. If, however, the conditions of spread could be standardized, the concept could be hypothetically measured by the rate of spread under standardized conditions. The analogy with home strength can also be extended to include the possibility of a reaction process or arms race. An ideology often increases its power because it runs into opposition, and two mutually opposed ideologies may reinforce each other, and each may even increase the power of the other by the modifications that it engenders.

The power of an ideology depends in large measure on its ability to organize a culture around it. An ideology is a view of the universe. It must give the individual a sense of the drama in which he is acting and the role that he has to play. It must be able to resolve doubts and bewilderments and to explain messages that apparently contradict it. It will be stronger and more persistent if the culture that it organizes contains structures, symbols, occasions, and agencies such as cathedrals, monuments, rituals, elections, churches, parties, and schools, that transmit and reinforce the ideology. One of the great puzzles in social dynamics is why one set of symbols seems to fire the imaginations of large bodies of people at a certain stage of history or in certain parts of a society and another set at another stage or another part. At one time and place, conceptual symbols like the filioque [the question whether the Holy Spirit proceeded from the Father alone or from the Father and the Son], or the Immaculate Conception, or the inward light, or *Liberté, egalité, fraternité*, or divine right, or surplus value, or free enterprise, stir and dominate the minds and hearts of men; at another time and place, these symbols seem empty and meaningless. At one time and place, physical symbols like Chartres, or the tractor, or the white cliffs of Dover, or the tricolor, or Old Glory move men to devotion and sacrifice; at another time and place, these are piles of stone, gadgets of iron, and wisps of cloth. Ideologies stand for centuries armed with a great panoply of priests and teachers, temples and rituals and mighty symbols: then one day the temples are empty, the priests and teachers fled. Some system there must be in this succession, but until we know more about the mysterious processes of symbolization in the human organism, we shall not understand them very well. The powerful symbol is that which condenses an enormous mass of information and experience in a single bit—there or not there, for me or against me, right or wrong. What it is, however, that gives this power to some symbols but not to others I believe we do not understand.

We may, perhaps, venture a hypothesis that the power of an ideology is made up of two factors, which we may call *intensity* and *appeal*. Some ideologies, like that of Jehovah's Witnesses, have high intensity in their adherents; they command great devotion and self-sacrifice and single-minded passion. Such ideologies can survive great persecution and, indeed, are often strengthened or at least intensified by this. On the other hand, they have but a limited appeal: they involve complex and seemingly unrealistic views of the world that appeal only to a limited group of people with somewhat the same personal backgrounds, experience, and personality as the adherents. By contrast, we have what might be called *worldly* ideologies of very low intensity but very wide appeal. Nobody preaches ordinary worldliness, and nobody carries banners for it or fights wars for it; yet it seems to have constituted the basic ideology of large masses of people in all ages. It seems reasonable to suppose therefore, that there is a negative functional relation between intensity and appeal: the greater the intensity, the less the appeal. Referring back to the figure in note 3 on p. 255, we see that, if this is a reasonably stable relationship and if we so quantify these concepts that power is the product of intensity and appeal, then there will be some intermediate level of both intensity and appeal at which the ideology has the greatest power. This explains, perhaps, why the most powerful ideologies seem to be those of moderate intensity and of moderate appeal. Nationalism, for instance, is a more intense ideology than common selfish worldliness and less intense than religious or political sectarianism. It has less intrinsic appeal than worldliness, because it does involve propagation and symbolization and people do have to be stirred up to make sacrifices for it, and it depends for its continued existence on the perpetuation of moderately untrue images of the world. It has more intrinsic appeal, however, than extreme sectarianism, which involves even more peculiar views of the world that have to be elaborately defended.

The conflict of ideologies is a dynamic process, and ideologies themselves constantly change through time. A very common pattern is for an ideology to emerge as the result of the rise of a charismatic leader. In its early years the ideology is intense and narrow in its appeal. It grows by separating out from the mass of the society a small subculture of dedicated people, who differentiate themselves very sharply from the mass culture and are frequently persecuted both by its official and by its unofficial representatives. If the power of the ideology is sufficient, however, it may develop to the point where it becomes a dominant ideology in the society. As it approaches this point, the character of the ideology changes: it becomes less intense and of wider appeal, reflecting a movement toward a maximum of power. Troeltsch's[2] distinction between the sect and the church is an apt illustration of this proposition: a religious movement that starts as a sect may end as a universal church. Similar patterns, however, are observed in political movements. The labor movement, for instance, begins as an intense movement of limited appeal. As it gathers strength, however, and cultivates ambitions for political dominance, it is forced to change its character to appeal to a larger and more middle-class clientele; it becomes less intense and has a wider appeal.

[2] Ernst Troeltsch, *The Social Teaching of the Christian Churches*, trans. Olive Wyon, London, Allen & Unwin, 1950.

An important element in the dynamics of ideological conflict is the formation of new ideologies. This seems to happen in two ways. It may happen by direct *mutation*, as when a charismatic leader founds a new movement, or it may happen by the mutual interaction of old ideologies that recombine certain of their elements into a synthesis. This latter type of ideology formation has a certain kinship with sexual propagation in the biological world, which develops new forms by the rearrangement of old genes. The biological analogy must not be pressed too far, though it is illuminating. In the course of the interaction of two competing and apparently opposed ideologies, there may take place mutation in the *elements* of the ideology, whatever these are, as well as the rearrangement of old elements. The elements of an ideology are not easy to identify, but the pattern of most ideologies exhibits sufficient regularity to suggest that the concept has some validity. A tentative and illustrative attempt to identify the elements of some major world ideologies is shown in the appendix to this chapter.

The interaction of old ideologies to form new ones is akin to the dialectical process associated with the names of Hegel and Marx. This is, of course, an old idea; the notion of a *tertium quid*, the third thing that emerges out of a conflict of two views, is at least as old as the Greeks. The idea that each ideology calls forth its opposite is perhaps more modern and also less true. The dialectical process is a good deal less tidy than either Hegel or Marx believed. The new ideology does not arise like a newborn child from the mating of the two old ones; it often comes through the mutual modification of the old ideologies to the point where they become almost indistinguishable or, at least, where they can coexist without overt conflict. A good example is the modification of American and European capitalism under the impact of the Marxian criticism. Such institutions as progressive taxation, inheritance taxes, social security, public health, conservation authorities, countercyclical fiscal and monetary policy, and the like, are in part outcomes of the socialist criticism of a pure market economy and in part the result of feedback of experiences and images of the society into the reform of its institutions. The Great Depression, for instance, did more to change the economic institutions of American society than did generations of socialist argumentation. Similarly, one sees the beginnings in the post-Stalin era of the impact of liberal criticism on Soviet society, and one hopes this process will go further. One certainly does not expect the two societies to end up with identical economic and political systems; it is not unreasonable, however, to hope that the dialectical process, or dialogue, between them will result in some mutually beneficial modifications and will at least lead to a situation of stable coexistence. The history of the religious wars also points in this direction. Catholicism and Protestantism have certainly not modified each other to the point of identity, but, in most parts of the world where they exist side by side, they have reached a *modus vivendi* within the framework of a secular state.

We should not suppose, however, that the pattern of *mutually convergent modification* of ideologies is universal. There are at least two other important patterns of ideological interaction. One is the pattern of *isolation or segregation*. Where an ideology is exposed to strong counterideologies in its environment, its adherents may resort to the defense of their ideology by withdrawing from the hostile environment into an insulated subculture where the ideology is continually reinforced by mutually supportive communications and where hostile communications from outside are simply cut off. This is possible in a complex society with extensive division of labor because the insulated group can support itself by simple commodity exchange with the larger society in contributing products to it, while, at the same time, there is no communication whatever between the two groups at the level of ideology. The Amish in the United States are an excellent example of such an insulated subculture that has managed to preserve not only an eighteenth-century pietistic ideology but even an eighteenth-century mode of speech, dress, artifacts, and habits by the simple process of having no contacts, apart from the minimum contacts of economic exchange, with the society around them. In a lesser degree, much larger and more important subgroups preserve their ideology by isolation. Thus, the Catholics in the United States, especially middle-class Catholics, may live and work among Protestant or secular neighbors and yet never discuss religion: they live their religious life in the isolated and encapsulated cell of church activities, and, hence, it rarely forms an arena of conflict with their non-Catholic associates.

A third pattern of ideological interaction is that of the *mutually divergent modification*. This is particularly likely to take place in the early days of the development of an ideology, when it is fighting to differentiate itself sharply from the world around it, but it is also likely to take place when enmity and hostility are important elements in the ideology itself. There are some ideologies, of which the military ideology and the communist ideology are perhaps the best examples, that organize themselves around the idea of conflict as a positive good and around the concept of the *enemy* as the main focus of thought and organization. Without an enemy, the whole dynamics and purpose of the ideology and of the organization that embodies it is lost. An armed force, for instance, must have an enemy, actual or potential; otherwise it cannot justify its existence. It has no internal reasons for existence as an organization. A church or a university, on the other hand, while it may have enemies and may be an instrument of conflict, can exist quite comfortably without enemies, as it has an ideology that gives it a purpose as an organization that is internal and not intrinsically dependent on outside conflicts, even though it may be affected, for good or for evil, by such conflicts.

The Communist ideology presents some curious paradoxes in this regard. It is not, like the military ideology, totally dependent on the presence of enemies. We can perfectly well imagine a Communist society devoting itself, like a church or a university, to the purely internal task of organizing the life of its people for their own supposed betterment, without any internal necessity for an outside enemy. In practice, however, Communist ideology has been strongly enemy-centered; almost everything is conceived of in terms of a struggle, either against external enemies, against internal enemies, or against nature. The problem of the identification of the enemy thus becomes a major exercise in Communist devotions. The reasons for this may be found partly in the character of the prophet of the ideology and partly in the necessity for any ideology to differentiate itself in its early stages from a hostile environment. Karl Marx was a man of deep inner hostilities who spent much of his life in bitter polemics. In terms of the theory of psychological conflict (p. 89), he may be diagnosed as an avoider rather than an approacher. His theoretical analysis is almost exclusively concerned with what is wrong with capitalism; he gives practically no attention to the problems of the socialist society that he believed would emerge. The Communists of capitalist countries seem very frequently to be of this personality type; communism is for them an ideology that legitimizes their inner conflicts and enables them to project on the society around them the hatreds that arise from the frustrations of their avoidance patterns.

Where communism is successful, of course, the personality type of the Communist may be expected to be different. There are real approach as well as avoidance elements in the Communist ideology; for instance, the organization of economic development, the encouragement of scientific and technical education, and the development of an integrated society from the benefits of which no class shall be excluded. The fact that these positive elements in the Communist ideology are not peculiar to communism but are also present in liberal capitalist ideology is a testimony to the drift of the two ideologies together and does not detract from their presence in either. The hangover from the revolutionary ideology of struggle and conflict, however, is a grave handicap to the Communists in the attainment of their positive goals, leading them to invent enemies where they do not exist and to couch developments in terms of struggle that would be better organized in terms of mutual cooperation.

Up to this point, we have treated the conflict of ideologies at the level of ecological conflict, regarding adherents as members of a species and the ideologies themselves merely as organizers of social species. We cannot let the matter rest there, however, because we must face the epistemological problem—in crude terms, that of the truth of an ideology. The conflict of ideologies is an important special case of the larger conflict of images, or cognitive structures. The images of different people may be inconsistent. I may think that the earth is round; you may think it is flat. If there is no communication between us, this inconsistency does not matter. If, however, we communicate, so that I have an image of your image and you have an image of mine, we each hold inconsistent images within the same cognitive structure. It is on this inner battleground that the conflict of images and of ideologies must be fought. The inconsistency of the images of different persons also becomes important when it results in conflicting behavior or a failure of expectations of behavior. In any organizational structure, behavior must follow a reasonably consistent pattern of role expectations. The role expectations, however, depend on the images of the role occupants. Breakdown in organization occurs when the communication system is not adequate to develop a consistent set of role images, so that orders at one level are translated into inconsistent actions at another and false information is fed back up the hierarchy.

The problem of the nature and test of truth has been worried by philosophers for a very long time, and we shall not pretend to solve it here. At the level of abstraction at which this analysis is being conducted, however, certain pragmatic tests of the truth of images are important. The image of an individual is modified continually by feedbacks of information, that is, by messages that have some previous pattern of expectations established for them from which they may diverge or with which they may agree. Thus I have an image of my house. I go there, expecting a certain combination of sense messages, and my expectations are fulfilled; this confirms the image. The more the expected messages agree with the perceived messages, therefore, the more confident I am in the truth of the image. There is one loophole: a false message may agree with a false expectation, so that the mere agreement of expectation with message is not proof of the truth of the image but is merely evidence. Similarly, if the message does not agree with the expectation, this shakes the image and calls it into question; but it is likewise not disproof of it, for either I may have made a false inference in drawing the expectation from the image, or I may have misread the message. We clearly have here a system with too many degrees of freedom, for both the failure and the success of expectations can be interpreted in three ways: as necessitating a revision either in the image, or in the expectation (inference), or in the message (experience). If there is to be any stability in the image and any sense of learning or of truth in the image, this system must be reduced to only a single degree of freedom; that is, two out of these three alternatives must be eliminated.

We can roughly distinguish three epistemological processes, therefore, depending on which two of the possible revisions are ruled out. These we may call the *authoritarian*, the *political*, and the *scientific* processes. In the authoritarian process, the image and the inference are stable, the image is sacred and not to be touched, and the authority is supposed to be capable of drawing the right inferences so that revisions can be made only in the perception of the message. If the message conforms to expectations, this of course confirms the image. If the message does not conform to expectations, the message is rejected as false. The schizophrenic or paranoic psychopath is an extreme example of this process. He has a fixed image of what the world is like and of what messages are to be expected. Thus, suppose his image of the world is one in which everyone is hostile to him. The inference (expectation), then, is that all communications express this hostility. Now, if he gets a communication that does not express hostility, his reaction is not to change his image but to reject the message: he interprets the apparent friendliness of the communication as insincere or as only a front to disguise a deep hostility. In extreme cases, even the messages of the senses are rejected or, rather, controlled by the nervous system, and the subject actually sees and feels the snakes that his imagination bodies forth. Not all authoritative epistemological processes are confined to people recognized as psychopaths; many political and religious images of sane and even of powerful people have the same degree of rigidity in the face of contradictory evidence and disappointment of expectations.

The political epistemological process is that in which the image is rigid and the messages are accepted as perceived at their face value, and all adjustments, therefore, are made in the inferences. If there is a disappointment, a failure of perceptions to agree with expectations, the conclusion is drawn that the expectation was wrong and that it was wrong because the wrong inferences were drawn from the basic image of reality; the image itself cannot be changed and the perceptions are trusted. I have called this political because it is peculiarly characteristic of political argument. Men tend to commit themselves to certain basic political images of the nature of social reality. They believe, for instance, in socialism, or free enterprise, or national defense. When expectations that they deduce from these images are disappointed, the tendency is not so much now to mistrust the perceptions, though this happens in political life too, nor to abandon the basic image, which is too precious and sacred to modify, but to say that we made the wrong inferences. Thus we cannot really believe that free enterprise will lead to depression, socialism to conformist tyranny, or national defense to ruinous war. We cannot abandon lightly the images around which we have organized our lives and expectations. In the political sphere, however, inferences are uncertain. The social system is very complex, and it is difficult, if not impossible, to assign specific events to specific causes. The tendency, then, is to associate unexpected events not with the rigid core of our image but with some peripheral and extraneous cause that makes it impossible to draw exact inferences. Thus, the depression could not possibly be the result of unregulated free enterprise; it must have been due to the aftermath of the last war, some specific unwise government policy, or international movements beyond our control. Similarly, Stalinist tyranny could not be due to socialism; it must have been due to accidental and extraneous forces in Soviet society. Similarly, war cannot be the result of the system of unilateral national defense; it must be due to inadequate defense or malevolent enemies. If the pursuit of a certain policy is followed by unexpectedly bad results, the conclusion is drawn that the policy was not pursued long enough or vigorously enough, not that the policy itself was mistaken in its conception.

In the third form of epistemological process, the scientific process, perceptions are trusted and are checked by the device of replication; what two men perceive independently is trusted more than what one man sees alone. Inference, likewise, is trusted, as it is supported by elaborate logical and mathematical systems that yield an almost unequivocal and universally agreed correspondence between the image (theory) and the predicted consequences. If, now, there is disappointment and if predictions are not fulfilled and actually do not agree with expected perceptions, the only thing that can be revised is the image itself. Thus, the essence of scientific method is carefully observed disappointments, whether noted by simple observation, as in astronomy and natural history, or deliberately contrived, as in the experimental sciences, leading to revisions in the basic theoretical image of the world rather than to rejections of the percepts or denial of the inferences.

When the matter is stated in this way, it can be seen clearly that all three epistemological processes may have some degree of validity. Not even in pure science can we be absolutely certain of recorded percepts, especially where the ultimate human observations are close to the differentiating capacity of the human senses. The scientist, like the artist, is trained by reward and punishment to perceive things in a certain way, and there is no guarantee that even his perceptions are always true. Even replication is not a perfect guarantee of accurate percepts, simply because perception is not entirely culture-free and most scientists are trained in the same kind of subculture. This is not to say that scientific observations are unreliable; they have very high but not perfect reliability. Then again, especially as we approach the complex systems of the social sciences, there is room for mistakes in inference. This is particularly likely to be the case where the systems with which we deal have strong stochastic elements in them, so that their exact future course is inherently unpredictable, even if the general nature of that course and perhaps some equilibrium position may be known. These stochastic elements may derive merely from ignorance, perhaps, however, from humanly incurable ignorance, simply because the simpler systems are subject to exogenous shocks from highly complex systems that we cannot predict. Thus, predictions about society or social organizations are constantly being upset by the fact that the dynamic course of society is in part dependent on human decisions, and the decision-making process of the human organism is so complex that it can be predicted only within fairly wide limits. The stochastic element in models of the social system may also derive from a true Heisenberg principle that the attempt to extract information about the system in itself changes the system. Suppose, for instance, that the act of observing a planet made it change its velocity by a random number; the astronomer's predictions would be no better than those of the social scientist. In the social sciences more than in the physical sciences, therefore, there is room for doubt in regard to inference, and there is some justification for what I have called the political epistemological process.

There are even some grounds for defending elements of the authoritarian process, even though this is the most likely to lead to pathological results. The very act of perception itself depends on the existence of a certain stability of the image in the face of apparently contradictory sense messages. Studies in perception have shown that the stability of the image is an important element in sifting truth from illusion. We do not believe that the approaching car is getting bigger, that the stick in the water is bent, or that the room changes as we walk about in it, in spite of the direct evidence of our senses to the contrary. Perception, far from being an immediate datum to the mind, is, in fact, a highly learned process in which we learn to see, hear, and touch the way we do because of certain payoffs. If, for instance, we interpreted the visual data to mean that we lived in a world in which objects of all kinds were constantly getting larger and smaller in fairly regular ways—and this is a perfectly legitimate, if somewhat Ptolemaic, way of interpreting the evidences of motion—we would soon find ourselves in painful situations.

We face here too the problem of self-fulfilling images in complex systems, especially in social systems. The paranoid whose image of the world is that everyone hates him will not only interpret all messages, however friendly, in this vein but will act in such a way as a result of his images that most people will come to hate him. By contrast, the saint who interprets even overt hostility as disguised friendship may behave in such a way as a result of this image that the hostility is actually converted into friendship. One does not suggest, of course, that this is always the case. There are rough facts of both physical and social systems that are highly resistant to modification by our image of them—like the law of gravity. The self-justifying phenomenon is important enough, however, to suggest that rigidity of the image in the face of apparent contradictory disappointments is not to be rejected out of hand.

In the light of this epistemological theory, crude as it is, we can now take a look at the function of argument or debate as a form of conflict. Changes in the epistemological structure take place not only as a result of direct messages from nature and the failure of expectations of direct sensory experience but as a result of talk, which is direct linguistic communication from one person to another. This capacity for the direct transfer of images by language is the faculty that most distinguishes man from the lower animals. Recorded language, whether in books or on tape, extends the range of this transfer enormously both in time and in space; people can communicate across the world, and the dead can communicate with the living through their writing or recorded speech, though this is strictly a one-way street. This direct communication of images, however, inevitably results in a conflict of images, simply because the images of different people are not alike. Out of this conflict of images, however, new images emerge. Thus I may think, as a child, that the world is flat, this being the obvious and immediate impression of limited experience. My teachers, however, assert that it is a globe. When I first hear this, I am presented with two contradictory images that cannot be reconciled; I must choose between one or the other. I may accept the word of my teacher simply because of the authority that he represents and of his power to make things unpleasant for me, or I may examine the evidence, still largely hearsay, that he presents and so be convinced in my own mind that he is right. Several stages in this process can be distinguished: (1) I start with "The earth is flat," (2) I go on to "I think the earth is flat, but teacher thinks it is a globe;" (3) I may pass through a stage of "I really think the earth is flat, but I shall pretend that I think it is a globe; otherwise people will think I am stupid, or I shall be punished;" (4) This may lead to "I used to think the earth was flat, but now I really think it is a globe;" (5) We might even pass to a still superior level of understanding: "The earth is a globe, but small portions of the surface can be treated as if they are flat because in the limit an infinite sphere is a plane." Here, in a sense, both earlier conflicting images are combined in a synthesis.

One can distinguish two extreme types of argument, or organized verbal clash of images. The first is based on the assumption that, where two images clash, one must be right, and the other must be wrong, and that the main business of argument, therefore, is to see that the right one wins. This is exemplified in the classical form of debate, in which two views are sharply contrasted and their proponents identified and in which one wins and the other loses, as decided by some ritual such as a vote or a judge's decision. The second is based on the view that conflicting images can eventually be understood as special cases of a larger synthesis, as suggested in the "flat earth" example above, and that, therefore, the search for such a synthesis is the main purpose of argument. The ideal type of this kind of argument is discussion, where points of view are modified in the course of the argument and a synthesis finally emerges that may then be recorded as a group decision. There is an underlying assumption here that there is a common search for truth rather than a struggle for power.

In practice, argument generally takes an intermediate form between discussion and debate. Without the element of discussion, debate becomes destructive of truth, as each side is forced into a Richardson process of increasing forensic chicanery and deception. Few discussions, however, are entirely free from elements of debate, nor should they necessarily be so; sometimes one side actually is right and the other wrong, though I suspect this is rare. Likewise, the element of personal power can seldom be ruled out by the realistic student of human affairs.

A problem that has attracted attention in recent years is that of how to prevent unnecessary disagreements by the use of semantic and epistemological processes that minimize misunderstanding. Argument I have already defined as the verbal clash of images; the arena for this clash is words. Between the image of one person and of another lie the words by which the one tries to convey his image to the other. This transmission process, however, is very complex. It is not only subject to noise in the information-theory sense, so that the message that leaves the one person may not be the same message that reaches the other, but it is subject to a massive barrier of assimilation to the image. The sender of the message frames the message in the light of his own image; the meaning of the message to him is the difference that it would make to his own image. Even if there is no noise in transmission and the identical message arrives at the image of the receiver, there is no guarantee that the receiver's image will be modified in the same sense that the sender's would be. The incorporation of messages into images is a process of great complexity involving most of the previous experience of the receiver. The situation is obvious when the sender and the receiver can only understand different languages: a perfectly clear English sentence will have no impact on the mind of a hearer whose past experience has not involved learning English and whose present image does not include a knowledge of English. In reality, however, every man speaks a language somewhat of his own, and even messages that are in languages that we think are mutual to the sender and the receiver get filtered, in fact, through the private languages of each individual. The exponents of general semantics have developed some useful prophylactics against misunderstanding. Their insistence that words do not have unambiguous referents, that words must not be mistaken for things, and that generalizations are good servants but bad masters certainly makes for protection against semantic confusion and misunderstandings. On the other hand, the process of image formation is so complex that it cannot be reduced to semantic formulas, and misunderstandings are by no means the only source of disagreements.

I should add a final word on ethical conflicts as a subset of ideological and image conflicts. Differences in value systems are among the most important sources of human conflicts of all kinds. Some, indeed, have despaired of finding any avenue to agreement at the level of basic values and have argued, for instance, like the logical positivists, for a sharp separation of judgments of fact which can be validated and about which agreement can always in principle be found and judgments of value which cannot be validated and which, therefore, have no sure roads to agreement; *de gustibus non est disputandum.* However, dispute about tastes and preferences continues briskly, as it always has done, and the mere difficulties of agreement in this area does not prevent the constant and often unsuccessful attempts of people to convert others to the preferences that they regard as right. My own view is that neither ethical nor factual judgments can be validated in any absolute sense but that both are subject to processes of validation (epistemological processes) that are not essentially different, even though these processes operate more easily at the level of the factual judgment. Our images of fact and of value grow together in inextricable symbiosis. Consequently, there is a great deal of use in disputing about values, if the dispute is carried on according to the rules of fruitful discussion, whatever they may be. Any revision of the image of fact inevitably produces strains on the image of value, and so does the verbal presentation of a contrary image of value. We are revising our value images all the time, therefore, under the pressure of these strains. The situation is complicated by what might be called *tied values*; we value something not for its own sake but because it is closely associated in our image with something that we value highly, and the bond of association cannot be broken. Conversely, we may value something negatively because it is associated with something else with a negative valuation. If we had a happy relationship with our parents, for instance, the values that they expressed to us become associated with the high value we place on their persons and affections and so resist strains and challenges that might otherwise undermine them. This is the basic reason for the genetic persistence of culture from one generation to the next.

An important but unresolved question is whether there are any basic values that are common to all mankind in the way that certain basic perceptions of the physical world are common. Almost all conscious values are instrumental, in the sense that we want A because it gives us B, we want B because it gives us C, and so on. Thinkers have sought the X that is the end of this regression—the *summum bonum*, utility, the general will, the will of God, and so on—with indifferent success. Nevertheless, there is a useful process of value analysis by which we resolve ethical disagreements by pushing toward the basic values. I prefer A_1 and you prefer A_2; we both want them, however, only because we find after discussion that they produce B. Then, the question is removed from the arena of value conflict and resolves itself into a (possibly) simpler question of relationship: does, in fact A_1 or A_2 produce B?

Most of the difficulty of resolving a conflict of values arises because, at some point in the process of moving from instrumental to basic values, we reach a multidimensional structure of semibasic values such as freedom, justice, democracy, economic growth, and equality that are hard to resolve into the still more basic value of the good. The very complexity of the structure of these semibasic values makes it difficult to obtain a clear image of them, especially as the description must be couched in semiquantitative and marginal terms like "How much justice will you give up for so much freedom?" rather than in the meaningless absolute "Do you prefer freedom to justice?" Consequently, it is hard to find out if, in fact, semibasic values differ and, if so, just what is the difference. Because of the insulation of the structure of semibasic values from effective description and discussion, the process of argument breaks down: either we find ourselves thinking that we disagree when, in fact, we agree, and we argue about nothing; or we may fail to perceive that we do disagree and drift along in an illusion of agreement that may be sharply shattered when it is put to a real test.

One of the main obstacles to discussion in this area is the confusion between the basic value or preference structure itself and the particular location in this structure given by our present condition and opportunities. Thus we may put a high marginal value on something—call it A—in the sense that we are prepared to make large sacrifices of something else (B) for it, either because A is valued highly in our over-all preference structure or because A is very scarce or B very plentiful; that is, we may think we want something very badly, not because it has a high intrinsic place in our value function, but simply because we have so little of it. "Like precious stones, his sensible remarks derive their value from their scarcity," as W. S. Gilbert observes in *Princess Ida*. Thus, an insecure society puts a high marginal value on security, a conformist society on liberty, and a loveless society on love. This is not, however, the whole story; there are societies which value liberty highly even when they have a great deal of it or which value security highly when they have a great deal of it. It is at this point that real value conflicts are most likely to occur.[3]

APPENDIX TO CHAPTER 14:
THE STRUCTURE OF IDEOLOGIES

The following table is an attempt to suggest the basic similarity in structure of some of the major ideologies of our day. It must be regarded as highly tentative and in no sense definitive; obviously the subtleties of a complex ideology cannot be expressed in a simple table. Some ideologies are also subconscious and implicit rather than conscious and explicit, though they may be important in determining behavior. However, they have to be deduced from the behavior, and this is a process strongly subject to error. With these reservations, however, the reader may find this table suggestive both of a possible pattern and also of further work that needs to be done. I distinguish three major ideologies of the Western world—Christianity, Marxism, and nationalism—and I subdivide each of these into an orthodox and a liberal wing. By way of comparison, I append what might be called the implicit ideology of worldliness, to show that even this falls into the same pattern of elements. It must be emphasized that these ideologies are models or ideal types which will not be found exactly in any actual specimen but which represent, as it were, model patterns. Thus, my division of Christianity into orthodox and liberal does not follow exactly any organizational division: both the Roman Catholic and Greek Catholic and the more orthodox Protestant churches

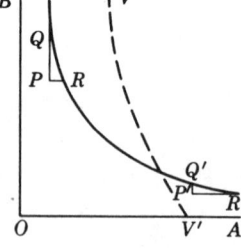

[3] The indifference-curve analysis illuminates this problem. Suppose we have two goods (which may be liberty and justice or ham and eggs), A and B, measured on the axes OA and OB. QQ' is an indifference curve, or contour of the preference function. The slope of this curve is the marginal value. Thus, between Q and R, we shall sacrifice PQ of B in order to get an additional PR of A and still feel as well off as before. When we have a great deal of A, as at Q', we shall only sacrifice a little of B ($Q'P'$) in order to get an additional unit $P'R'$ of A. Thus, the marginal value depends on the relative quantities of A and B. Suppose, now, we have a rise in our intrinsic valuation of A: this means a steepening of the whole indifference curve, say, to the position VV', where the marginal value is greater at every point than it was before.

IDEOLOGICAL AND ETHICAL CONFLICT 299

may be found in the orthodox pigeonhole, and many churches are divided into a more orthodox and a more liberal wing. Similarly, in my categorization of Marxism, neither orthodox nor liberal Marxism, as I have suggested it, corresponds exactly to the position of any particular Marxist sect or society, though Communists tend to be more orthodox and Socialists more liberal. I distinguish twelve elements in each ideology, not all of which are of equal importance and some of which may be grouped; more careful study, I am sure, will modify and extend the list.

ELEMENT 1. INTERPRETATION OF HISTORY

Christianity, orthodox	History a serial drama of fall and redemption, divided sharply into two eras (B.C. and A.D.) and ending in a catastrophic judgment.
Christianity, liberal	History a continuous drama of fall and redemption, with continual evolution of the good.
Marxism, orthodox	History a dialectical process of succession of classes, divided sharply into preconscious and postconscious eras at the nineteenth century (Marx), the process ending in a catastrophic revolution in which the proletariat succeeds to power.
Marxism, liberal	History a continuous evolution toward elimination of exploitation.
Nationalism, fascist	History has no meaning beyond the power of the state.
Nationalism, liberal	History is viewed from the perspective of the national state.
Worldliness	History begins and ends with the consciousness of the individual.

ELEMENT 2. IMAGE OF THE FUTURE, IMPLIED IN THE
INTERPRETATION OF HISTORY

Christianity, orthodox	Catastrophic supernatural eschatology: worsening conditions until the Second Coming and the establishment of the Kingdom of God.
Christianity, liberal	Evolutionary progress through time toward the establishment of the Kingdom of God on earth.

Marxism, orthodox	Catastrophic secular eschatology: worsening conditions of the proletariat through time until the revolution (the expropriation of the expropriators) and the establishment of the socialist society.
Marxism, liberal	Evolutionary progress toward the establishment of a socialist society.
Nationalism, fascist	Rise of the state to world dominance.
Nationalism, liberal	Continued preservation of the state, devolution of empire.
Worldliness	Continued eating, drinking, and being merry until death.

ELEMENT 3. NATURE OF IDEAL SOCIETY

Christianity, orthodox	Community of loving, redeemed souls in heaven; foreshadowed on earth only in communities separated from the world.
Christianity, liberal	Community of unselfish individuals, realizable in the world at some future time.
Marxism, orthodox	Classless society, achieved after the withering away of the state; foreshadowed by the Communist party.
Marxism, liberal	Classless society, achieved by social evolution.
Nationalism, fascist	The omnipotent state.
Nationalism, liberal	The well-defended, rich, and integrated state.
Worldliness	Any society that gives maximum opportunity to ego to satisfy desires.

ELEMENT 4. NATURE OF ULTIMATE REALITY (GOD)

Christianity, orthodox	Spiritual, purposive, interventionist, undetermined, anthropomorphic.
Christianity, liberal	Spiritual, purposive, bound by laws of nature, doubtfully interventionist and anthropomorphic.
Marxism, orthodox,	Material, determined, predictable, mechanomorphic, dialectical.
Marxism, liberal	Material, determined, doubtfully predictable, mechanomorphic, doubtfully dialectical.
Nationalism, fascist	The state as ultimate reality.

Nationalism, liberal	No clear view; frequently allied with theistic religion, but not necessarily so; the state as penultimate reality.
Worldliness	The satisfaction of individual desires as the ultimate reality for the individual.

ELEMENT 5. NATURE OF MAN

Christianity, orthodox	Predisposed to corruption because of a historic fall; redeemable by a catastrophic intervention of divine grace.
Christianity, liberal	Predisposed to goodness but liable to error; capable of improvement through education.
Marxism, orthodox	Predisposed to corruption through the institution of private property, created by a historic fall (primary accumulation); redeemable by catastrophic change in the social system.
Marxism, liberal	Predisposed to corruption by capitalist modes of production but capable of improvement through political evolution and education.
Nationalism, fascist	Nature determined by racial inheritance: those belonging to the wrong races are irredeemable.
Nationalism, democratic	All men capable of being educated as citizens.
Worldliness	Man seeks only to maximize his own pleasures.

ELEMENT 6. NATURE OF EVIL AND THE TEST OF GOODNESS

Christianity, orthodox	Self-will in opposition to will of God is basic evil; test of goodness is conformity to will of God.
Christianity, liberal	Self-interest in opposition to group interest is basic evil; goodness measured by extent of loving concern.
Marxism, orthodox	Self-will in preservation of private property, in opposition to the dialectical movement of history, is basic evil; goodness measured by progress toward socialism.
Marxism, liberal	Self-interest in quest for private profit is basic evil; goodness measured by extent of devotion to the cause of socialism.
Nationalism, fascist	Evil is the enemy of the state, external or internal; goodness is anything done by the master race.

Nationalism, liberal	Evil is anything that threatens the survival of the society; goodness is measured by the prosperity and security of the citizens.
Worldliness	Evil is pain or discomfort of the individual; goodness is pleasure.

ELEMENT 7. FORM OF WORSHIP (CENTRAL ACTIVITY CONSIDERED AS AN END FOR THE INDIVIDUAL)

Christianity, orthodox	Sacramental ritual, plus private devotion.
Christianity, liberal	Services of edification, plus private study and devotion.
Marxism, orthodox	Revolutionary agitation: agitprop.
Marxism, liberal	Political activity: propaganda.
Nationalism, fascist	Warfare.
Nationalism, liberal	Reluctant warfare.
Worldliness	Self-indulgence: excessive indulgence of the appetites for sex, food, drink, diversion.

ELEMENT 8. SACRAMENTAL DOGMA: DISTINCTION BETWEEN SUBSTANCE AND ACCIDENTS

Christianity, orthodox	Catholic: transubstantiation (substance of bread and wine in Mass is Christ, though physical properties are unchanged).
	Evangelical: vicarious salvation (substance of saved person is that of Christ, even though behavior is not).
Christianity, liberal	Sacramental dogma weak; individual may be transformed by his role in the religious community.
Marxism, orthodox	Surplus value (substance) not reflected in price (accident). Acts in themselves evil transmuted into good if committed in the service of the revolution.
Marxism, liberal	Sacramental dogma weak.
Nationalism, fascist	Acts normally evil are good if done by the master race.
Nationalism, liberal	The heroism and necessity of war justify the evil that is done in the course of it.

Worldliness	The need for self-expression justifies any extreme of self-indulgence.

ELEMENT 9. EMOTIONAL DRIVE

Christianity, orthodox	Love of God and fear of damnation, in various proportions.
Christianity, liberal	Love of mankind and need for self-esteem, in varying proportions.
Marxism, orthodox	Hatred and envy, with a dash of prophetic indignation.
Marxism, liberal	Prophetic indignation, love of the underdog, with a dash of hatred and envy.
Nationalism, fascist	Hatred of foreign elements, Xenophobia; some self-hatred and masochism; sadism.
Nationalism, liberal	Love of country, with a dash of hatred of the foreigner and the unfamiliar.
Worldliness	Love of pleasure and personal power; scorn of others.

ELEMENT 10. THEORY OF VALUE AND DISTRIBUTION

Christianity, orthodox	All values derived ultimately from God, but private property allowed under the doctrine of stewardship and paternalism.
Christianity, liberal	No clear theory; stewardship of property, but state encouraged to modify distribution in interests of equality.
Marxism, orthodox	All value derived from embodied labor; hence, all nonlabor income is invalid and unjustifiable.
Marxism, liberal	Value derived from labor and organization; hence, limited private property and market organization not necessarily unjustifiable.
Nationalism, fascist	No clear theory; all value and property ultimately from the state.
Nationalism, liberal	No clear theory as such. Liberal economic theory holds value derived from relative scarcity; private property has a positive function as an institution but may be modified.
Worldliness	Things only valuable if possessed by ego.

ELEMENT 11. THEORY OF SOCIAL ORGANIZATION

Christianity, orthodox   The church is divinely ordained body of Christ, hierarchical in organization and continuous through time. The state and other organizations can be sanctified and legitimized by the church. Authoritarian government is sanctioned in the interim.

Christianity, liberal   A church is a voluntary association of Christians. Other organizations, even the state, are likewise voluntary associations.

Marxism, orthodox   The party is the self-conscious instrument of the historical dialectic and is the embodiment at each time and place of the way, truth, and life involved in this dialectic. The state and other organizations must be guided and legitimized by the party. In the interim, there must be an authoritarian dictatorship of the proletariat through the party.

Marxism, liberal   The party is a voluntary organization as a political instrument of social change.

Nationalism, fascist   The single party is the instrument for transforming the state into an aggressive military power. No other party can be tolerated; economic and religious organizations may be distinct from state and party but must be guided by it.

Nationalism, liberal   All organizations, including parties, are voluntary and tolerate each other.

ELEMENT 12. CHARACTERISTIC FORM OF SOCIETY

Christianity, orthodox   Feudalism.
Christianity, liberal   Liberal capitalism.
Marxism, orthodox   Leninist-Stalinist communism.
Marxism, liberal   Social democracy; possible liberal communism.
Nationalism, fascist   National socialism (Hitler Germany)
Nationalism, liberal   Liberal democracy.

15

CONFLICT RESOLUTION AND CONTROL

This book has concerned itself mainly with the phenomenon of conflict as a social process that operates in many different contexts. The process clearly can be studied simply as a phenomenon of nature without any evaluation or practical conclusions. It must be confessed, however, that this study was not motivated merely by idle curiosity, even though curiosity about the nature and form of phenomena must be an important motive in any scientific and theoretical inquiry. We live in a day in which conflict, especially international conflict, threatens to get out of hand and destroy us. The theory of conflict, therefore, has practical implications, even implications about survival. We cannot leave the subject, therefore, without examining these practical implications, even though these inevitably involve us in ethical judgments.

In any given social situation or subsystem, we can perhaps postulate an optimum amount or degree of conflict. The concept is hard to specify, but it is of great importance. It relieves us immediately, for instance, from the illusion, if anyone ever possessed it, that conflict in any amount is either bad or good in itself. The evaluation of conflict has two aspects: quantitative and qualitative. In a given situation, we may have too much or too little conflict, or the amount may be just right. There is no simple operational definition of such an optimum; we must rely for our information on a complex structure of attitudes and evaluations. In a given situation, we may also have the wrong kind of conflict. Here again, there is no simple operational definition, but common speech has words that describe these qualitative differences: conflicts may be bitter and destructive, or they may be fruitful and constructive. We shall not argue here whether the qualitative difference can be reduced to quantity—whether, for instance, conflicts that are bad are so simply because there is too much or perhaps too little of them. In the absence of any clear index of the quantity of a conflict, this issue cannot be resolved. The best strategy would seem to be to go as far as we can with the concept of quantity but reserve the right to discover that conflict has more than one dimension and cannot, therefore, wholly be described in terms of simple "more or less."

We may think that a situation has too little conflict because it is dull and lacks drama. Drama is an important value in practically all cultures, and conflict is one of the most important sources of dramatic interest. Most religious and national ideologies, for instance, conceive of the universe as involving a dramatic conflict between the forces of good and evil played out on the stage of the world. In personal life also, the absence of conflict is identified with a dull, featureless existence. The institution of games and sports is evidence that, where a situation does not have enough conflict in it, conflict will be created artificially, either between individuals, as in chess, pairs as in bridge, or teams as in baseball, football, and so on. Prof. F. H. Knight is reported to have said that what people really want in the world is trouble, and if they do not have enough of it, they will create it artificially, the institution of sport being the proof.

On the other hand, there is a great deal of evidence that conflict in its nonsport aspect is usually felt as too much. Even though we may admit that some conflict is good, the word itself has a bias toward the bad. We think of the problem of conflict not usually in terms of how we get more of it but how we get less of it. We think of conflict in terms of family quarrels, separation, and divorce, or racial discrimination and race riots, or industrial disputes and strikes, or political conflict and revolution, or international conflict and war. These things we think of on the whole as bad, as tending to go too far and to get out of hand. Dialectitians like Hegel and Marx may defend conflict as a necessary instrument of change and progress, and sociologists like Simmel and Coser[1] may defend it as an instrument of social integration, but this still has to be a defense against the common prejudice. Conflict is discord, and the opposite of conflict is harmony; the words reveal the evaluational bias in the language and in the common experience. Discord may be necessary to make music interesting and to give it drama, but its significance lies in the ability of the composer to resolve discord into some meaningful harmony, however subtle. The essence of the drama of conflict is likewise its resolution; it is not the conflict as such that makes the drama but the resolution of the conflict as a meaningful process through time. A conflict that went on and on without end and without resolution would lose even dramatic interest; it would eventually become mere noise and confusion. It is the process of conflict toward some kind of resolution which gives it meaning and which makes it good. This is true even in sports and games; a game that went on interminably without any resolution would be intolerable.

We must, therefore, look at the ways in which conflicts are resolved if we are to assess their value and if we are to evaluate the institutions by which they are controlled. What we must look for here is ways in which a particular conflict process moves toward an end. This is not to say, of course, that conflict itself comes to an end, for conflicts are continually being recreated. Each particular conflict, however, can be thought of as having a life cycle: it is conceived and born, it flourishes for a while, and then certain processes that are probably inherent in its own dynamic system eventually bring it to an end. Resolution, as we shall see, is only one

[1] G. Simmel, *Conflict*, trans. Kurt H. Wolff, Glencoe, Ill., Free Press, 1953; and L. Coser, *The Functions of Social Conflict*, Glencoe, Ill., Free Press, 1956.

way of ending conflicts, and, out of the many ways of ending conflicts, it may not always be clear which deserve the reward of being called resolution. Resolved conflicts, however, are clearly a subset of ended conflicts, and we should study the latter first.

The first method of ending conflicts is probably the commonest, though by its very nature it is also the least noticeable. This is the method of *avoidance*. The parties to the conflict simply remove themselves one from another and increase the distance between them to the point where the conflict ceases from sheer lack of contact. A man who cannot get on with his boss quits or is fired. The man who cannot get along with his country emigrates. Teams between whom the conflict has become too bitter for sportsmanship stop playing with each other. Couples who cannot get along divorce. A customer who does not like one store finds another. Two friends who quarrel separate and do not see each other again. A quarrelsome faction within a church splits from it and forms another sect. Ideological or personal conflict within a party splits it, and two parties go off from the fission. Two atoms that cannot get along in a molecule split off and go their separate ways.

Avoidance is the classical method of resolving economic conflicts through pure competition; disputes about bargains are avoided simply because there is always another bargainer to go to. Political disputes are resolved by trading votes and logrolling and by a constant ballet of shifting political partners. Racial disputes are suppressed by segregation and by seeing to it that the races do not mix or only meet under rigid and stereotyped rules of behavior. Class conflict is avoided by cultural differentiation of the classes, with different speech and behavior patterns, so that the classes also do not meet except under formal and stereotyped conditions. International conflict may be mitigated by devices like arms control, which, in effect, move the nations farther apart. Avoidance always involves putting some kind of distance between the parties. The distance need not only be physical distance, though this is the most obvious and commonest form; it may take the form of social distance, as in segregation, or epistemological distance, as when two parties deliberately cultivate ignorance of each other and avoid overt communications. The Catholic-Protestant entente in the United States almost seems to follow this pattern.

The most extreme form of avoidance is *conquest*, the second form of ending conflict, by which one of the parties is, in effect, removed to infinity, or removed from the scene, leaving the victor in sole possession of the field. An interesting asymmetry in the avoidance pattern shows up clearly at this point. There are three forms of avoidance. One party may simply remove himself from the field; the avoiding party here does all the work. Both parties may remove themselves, though this is less likely, as once one party begins to remove himself, there is little incentive for the other to move. The third form is where one party forcibly removes the other. The parent carries the howling child out into the garden and returns to the house. The trade union or the church expels a dissident faction. One nation forces another by threats to withdraw from a field of conflict. This form of avoidance usually involves a good deal more work on the part of the active party than does simple self-removal, as the active party has to remove the other and then return to the field. Conquest is the extreme case of forcible removal, in which the removed party is removed completely. In a quarrel, one man kills another. In a war, one nation exterminates another. One race or group practices genocide on another. Fortunately, these cases are fairly rare, mainly because of the amount of work involved. Conquest, of course, can take place only where one party is conditionally viable with respect to the other. Two parties that are unconditionally viable with respect to each other obviously cannot practice conquest. Even if the parties are not unconditionally viable, the cost of conquest may preclude its attempt, and some other form of conflict conclusion must be practiced.

If the parties can neither conquer nor avoid each other, some form of *procedural* resolution of conflict is likely. In procedural resolution, the parties have to stay together and live with each other; conflict, in general, may not be resolved permanently in so far as the parties continue to exist in contact, but particular conflicts may be resolved simply in the sense that they come to an end as social systems and are replaced by other conflicts and other systems. We may distinguish three types of procedural conflict conclusion. The first is *reconciliation*, in which the value systems of the images of the parties so change that they now have common preferences in their joint field: they both want the same state of affairs or position in the joint field, and so conflict is eliminated. The second is *compromise*, in which the value systems are not identical and the parties have different optimum positions in the joint field; however, each party is willing to settle for something less than his ideal position rather than continue the conflict. In compromise, this settlement is reached mutually by bargaining between the parties themselves. The third type of conflict conclusion is the *award*, in which a settlement is reached because both parties have agreed to accept the verdict of an outside person or agency rather than continue the conflict. The compromise and the award are essentially similar in that they both represent less than the ideal situation for each party; they differ mainly in the method of arriving at the settlement.

To each of the three forms of procedural conflict conclusion, there corresponds an appropriate set of procedures. Thus, reconciliation is the result of conversation, argument, discussion, or debate that leads to convergent modifications of the images of the two parties. Compromise is the end result of a process of bargaining, in which mediation and conciliation may play an important part. An award is the end result of arbitration or legal trial. Neither the three forms of settlement nor the various procedures are completely separate in practice, though there is a tendency for one form to dominate in any particular case. Frequently, however, both reconciliation and compromise go on together; indeed, some reconciliation may be necessary before compromise is possible. Consequently, there are always likely to be elements of discussion and propaganda in bargaining situations. Similarly, in arbitration cases or in court proceedings, there are often elements both of reconciliation and of bargaining before the award is handed down, and the award will not be accepted unless it has been preceded by informal reconciliation and bargaining. One of the most difficult institutional problems in the handling of conflict is how to arrange for the right proportions and the right order of these various elements of the situation. Thus, legal procedings, such as suits, are often a poor way of handling conflicts in industrial relations, because of the difficulty of incorporating the necessary bargaining and reconciling processes in purely legal procedure. The same difficulty in marital conflict has sometimes led to the setting up of special marriage courts in which these more informal procedures can be employed.

Of all these processes, probably the process of reconciliation is the least understood, partly because very little research has been done on it and partly because of the complexity of the symbolic systems that are involved. We understand so little about the formation of value images that we can hardly be expected to understand the process by which these images are modified under the impact of mutual communication and discussion. The most we can do here is to make some suggestions and hope that social psychologists may be inspired to study this important and neglected field.

One obvious proposition is that a prerequisite to reconciliation is flexibility in the images, and especially in the value images, of the parties concerned. If the images of the two parties are completely rigid, it is clear that no process of convergence can take place. Rigidity in the image, however, may occur for a number of different reasons. The rigidity may be part of the value system of the image itself; that is, the person sets a high value on rigidity and the absence of change itself. Or the rigidity may be associated with insecurity in the valuation of the person himself; that is, he may be afraid to make any changes in the values that he puts on particular objects or goals because he sees such change as a threat to the valuation that he puts on himself. This is the problem of the identification of the image with the person, so that any change in the image is seen as a threat to the person. The person says in effect, "I am an X," where X may stand for Communist, Catholic, Pacifist, American, etc. Any attack on the X with which the individual identifies, then, is regarded as an attack on the integrity of the person; his value structure is not something that he has but something that he is. Thus we have, in effect, divided the value structure of a person's image into two parts: an inner core around which he integrates his personality and which holds him together and an outer shell which he holds or possesses but which does not constitute an essential part of the image of the person who does the holding or possessing. The core is rigid and not subject to small changes, though it may be subject to catastrophic reorganizations in conversion. The shell is not rigid and is amenable to the processes of modification under the stimulus of discussion and argument.

The success of the reconciliation process, then, clearly depends on how far the value structures of the parties in the field of conflict occupy the core or the shell of the value image. If the conflict is about a core value, reconciliation will be difficult or even impossible, short of very drastic experiences and conversions. If the conflict is about a shell value, change is possible, and so reconciliation is possible, though not all processes of communication lead to reconciliation. The problem is complicated by the fact that the boundary between the core and the shell is not fixed but is itself a result of the general value system and of the process of communication and argument to which the party has been subject in the past. Unskilled argumentation that seems to threaten the person of the other party may only serve to harden and widen his core of values and so make agreement all the more difficult. On the other hand, a dramatic act of renunciation symbolizing concern for the person of the rival may produce a drastic reorganization of his value structure with a shrinkage of the inflexible core and an extension of the malleable shell.

Reconciliation will presumably be easier if reconciliation itself is highly valued as a process by the contending parties. There may be an important difference in personality type between the *authoritarian* and the *reconciling* personality. The first has a very large core of particular values that he identifies with his person. Consequently, he is not interested in reconciliation but only in imposing his will and his values on others; the existence of differing values he regards as a threat to his person rather than as an opportunity for mutual learning. By contrast, the reconciling personality identifies his person not with any particular set of values or doctrines but with a learning process, a search for truth, and an interest in, and concern for, the welfare of others. Much work needs to be done on the nature of life experiences and perhaps even genetic selection, that lead to the predominance of one type or the other in a society. One may hazard a guess that the nature of the learning experience, especially in childhood, is of great importance in this connection. Where learning is associated strongly with pain and punishment, the personality resists the learning process; consequently, it tends to integrate itself as soon as possible around a large, hard core of values and doctrines, and it resists the learning process thereafter. This is the path to the authoritarian personality. Where learning is associated with rewards rather than with punishment, the personality integrates around the idea of continued learning rather than around a core of received truth, and the reconciling personality develops. This is certainly not the whole story. There is, however, great need for further work at this point to carry forward the pioneering studies of the authoritarian personality made by Adorno and others.[2]

The process of compromise through bargaining has probably received more attention than the other conflict-resolution processes. It is a process that can be more easily identified than the more subtle and less visible processes of reconciliation and, hence, is an easier object of study. It is also a process that is more subject to theoretical model building than the processes of value formation and change on which reconciliation is based. In this connection, the

[2] T. W. Adorno and others, *The Authoritarian Personality*, New York, Harper, 1950.

recent work of Schelling is of outstanding importance.[3] Bargaining is a positive-sum game, frequently nonsymmetrical between the parties, in which there is a curious mixture of cooperation and conflict—cooperation in that both parties with a certain range of possible solutions will be better off with a solution, that is, a bargain, than without one and conflict in that, within the range of possible solutions, the distribution of the total benefit between the two parties depends on the particular solution adopted. Thus, while both parties are interested in the adoption of some solution, they have divergent interests in regard to the particular solution that is adopted. This curiously mixed character of the bargaining game gives it an unusual character and raises problems that are quite different from those of zero-sum games, which are pure conflict, or games without any problem of division of gains, which are pure cooperation.

Schelling has called attention to the importance of *saliency* in the solution of bargaining problems. Bargains can frequently be struck when there is no communication between the bargainers, simply by the tacit observation on the part of both parties of some salient feature of the situation that makes both parties settle on the salient feature itself. A man and his wife who become separated in a large department store and who have made no previous arrangements for this contingency both gravitate to the lost-and-found department if they are of a humorous turn of mind, or perhaps to the main information booth if they are more sober-minded. People meet each other without prearrangement at the information booth at Grand Central Station, or at the crossroads on a map, or at noon if they are not given a time. Spoils are divided on a 50:50 basis, because this is the only division which is salient and which stands out from all the others. Even when there is communication between the bargainers, then the principle of saliency frequently governs the settlement. The reason is that, if any party stands out for a nonsalient settlement, the

[3] T. C. Schelling, *The Strategy of Conflict*, Cambridge, Harvard University Press, 1960.

danger of there being no settlement at all is very large; hence, as between a high probability of consummating an agreement at the salient point and a low probability of consummating what would be, if consummated, a more favorable settlement at some other point, each party chooses the salient point as having the maximum expected value discounted for probability.

Innumerable practical applications of the principle spring to mind. In economic bargaining, whether this is two individuals bargaining about the price of a car or a house or a trade union bargaining with an employer, there is a strong tendency to settle at round numbers and at convenient splits intermediate between the offers of the two parties. The 50:50 split is, of course, a highly typical pattern; the difficulties in the bargaining process arise through the psychological problem of establishing the final offers or the range to the split. Schelling has pointed out the great advantage that an irrevocable commitment gives a bargainer, provided that it does not preclude the possibility of any bargain at all. This leads to the paradox that the weakest bargainer is frequently in the strongest bargaining position, as his very weakness gives him a commitment that would be taken away by strength. The weak have nowhere to go, no place to which to retreat, and their very weakness makes their bargaining commitments irrevocable. Thus, the sick, the aged, children, and the insane have society by the throat; their very weakness gives them an unshakeable bargaining position. They say, in effect, "Support us, or we die, and our blood will be on your heads." Because of their weakness, this is no idle threat. Similarly, the fanatical, the devotees, and the religiously committed are in a strong bargaining position because of the irrevocable nature of their commitment. Jehovah's Witnesses are in a position of great bargaining strength vis-à-vis almost any society in which they live: they cannot be coerced, because they will die rather than give up their faith and practice, as, indeed, they died in thousands under Hitler. Before the fanatic, ordinary, reasonable men are helpless: they can be moved, and the fanatic cannot. If any bargain is struck, it must be on the fanatic's terms, for no other terms are possible. When a fanatic hits a different fanatic, of course, no bargain can be struck at all.

These considerations help us to understand the role of the conciliator and mediator in the bargaining process. This role is of particular importance in labor relations, where it has been worked out most completely. It is of growing importance, however, in domestic quarrels (the family counselor, for instance, plays much the same role in family conflict that the mediator does in industrial conflict), and it also is growing in importance in international relations. The mediator role may be quite informal, as when a mutual friend tries to mediate a quarrel, or it may be more formalized, as it is in industrial relations. In any case, the role is a complex one, with a whole spectrum of possible degrees of intervention into the conflict. At one end of the scale, we have simple conciliation, in which the conciliator simply tries to clear up misunderstandings. In conflict situations, there is always ample opportunity for unnecessary incompatibility of images. Messages between the parties have to pass through an intense emotional field in which they are likely to be distorted, so that the image that each party has of the other's position may be quite false. The conciliator has the advantage of being outside the emotional field that is created by the conflict. Consequently, he can both receive and give messages to either of the parties without the kind of distortion to which direct messages are subject. By acting as a go-between, therefore, the conciliator can transmit messages between the parties with greater accuracy than is possible with direct messages and so can achieve a certain reconciliation of images that would have been impossible without him. There are, however, limits to the function of conciliation. The elimination of misunderstanding will not necessarily eliminate the conflict or produce complete reconciliation of values and images of the two parties. Indeed, there may be occasions when conciliation can actually exacerbate a conflict; each party may think, quite wrongly, that the other party agrees with him, and the clearing up of this misunderstanding may make the parties realize that their conflict is deeper than they thought. This case, however, is rare, mainly because the emotional field through which direct messages from the parties have to pass is more likely to add hostility to a message than to take it away. Hence, the parties are likely to believe that each is more hostile than he really is, and conciliation, under these circumstances, is likely to reduce hostility.

Mediation, especially as the term is used in industrial relations, implies more outside pressure brought to bear on the parties than does mere conciliation. Conciliation simply in the sense of facilitating communication between the parties may not be enough: there may still be a residum of unreconciled images, and the situation requires compromise. The mediator may have an important role to play in the actual process of agreement on the bargain, especially where there is no obviously salient position in the field to which both parties can gravitate. A skilled mediator can create saliency by bringing the weight of his authority behind a solution that he thinks would be acceptable to both parties. Sometimes the solution introduced by the mediator may be a new position altogether that neither party has previously contemplated. This may involve a new principle, that of widening the agenda.

We can perhaps distinguish three functions of the third party here, in terms of the economic theory of exchange. The function of pure conciliation is simply to see that trading opportunities are not missed in the existing field of conflict through ignorance and a failure of communication; the conciliator, in this sense, is a broker, bringing the two parties together; that is, the conciliator brings the parties to the contract or conflict curve, in the language of Chap. 1, within the dimensions of the conflict as the parties perceive it. The second function is that of the widening of the agenda and the introduction of new variables in the field of bargaining. Two parties may have exhausted all their trading opportunities within a given set of variables, but when a new variable is introduced, new trading opportunities are opened up, and an impasse may be avoided. Even when all the trading opportunities and new variables have been exploited, however, the parties may find themselves on a conflict curve and unable to reach agreement. It is at this point that the third function of the mediator comes in, which is that of providing a salient suggestion around which a bargain may crystallize.

We have still not exhausted the functions of the mediator, however; if his suggestions do not create enough saliency in the field to permit the striking of a bargain, he may be able to introduce new elements into the field through outside pressure. He may, for instance, mobilize public opinion or threaten to mobilize public opinion on the side of one or the other of the parties, or perhaps even against both parties, and so force a sufficient reconciliation of position to permit a bargain. The impact of public opinion in the resolution of conflict by bargain is often important, but also its effects are often obscure. Each party will have reference groups, in the language of the social psychologists, whose opinion will be important to them. There will be, in fact, a series of concentric shells of reference groups ranging from the group with which the party identifies himself most strongly, which is likely to be small, to the group of the world at large, with which identification is likely to be weak. Thus, an employer is likely to be strongly influenced by the opinion of fellow employers in the same field, less strongly influenced by the opinion of employers in general, still less strongly affected by the opinion of the general public of his own country, and affected very little by opinion in other countries. A union representative will be strongly sensitive to the opinion of his fellow representatives in the same union, less sensitive to opinion in the labor movement at large, still less sensitive to opinion in the country as a whole, and so on. If a mediator can mobilize opinion in the closest and strongest reference group to the party concerned, he is most likely to have an effect; the larger and wider the· reference group invoked, the stronger will an adverse opinion have to be in order to produce an effect on the party concerned.

Where mediation is unsuccessful, so that, in spite of their own and of a third party's efforts, the parties cannot strike a bargain, the third form of procedural conflict tends to take over in the form of arbitration or court proceedings, resulting in arbitration awards or court judgments. In arbitration, a preliminary bargain has to be struck, in the sense that the parties have to agree to submit to arbitration. Sometimes this can be agreed on when the terms of the bargain itself cannot be struck. A further step toward agreement is necessary, for the parties must not only agree to arbitrate but must agree on an arbitrator. This second step is often more difficult than the first. However, a profession of arbitrators has developed, especially in the United States, to meet this need in both commercial and industrial arbitration. The successful arbitrator frequently operates as mediator and conciliator as well, for the closer his award comes to what the parties might have agreed upon in the absence of arbitration, the more satisfied the parties will be, and the better the reputation of the arbitrator. It is for this reason, perhaps, that, in the area of bargaining, both in commercial and in labor relations, arbitration is frequently preferable to more formal legal procedures, which are less open to preliminary conciliation and mediation.

An interesting conclusion that emerges from the empirical study of mediation procedures is that the negotiating process develops certain formal patterns that might almost be called rituals and that attempts to bypass or to cut short these rituals often destroys the negotiating process itself.[4] Thus, the parties begin the proceedings by somewhat bombastic initial statements that set the initial boundaries to the negotiations. There has to be a period of withdrawal after these initial statements to make it seem as if these are genuine commitments. The parties know, however, that these are not absolute commitments; otherwise, the negotiations would simply break down. There may follow a process of trading, by which mutual concessions are made. There may be attempts at commitment by, for instance, a strike vote of a union or a tactical movement of troops in a diplomatic negotiation. There probably has to be a

[4] See Ann Douglas, "The Peaceful Settlement of Industrial and Intergroup Disputes," *Journal of Conflict Resolution*, I, 69 (March, 1957).

latent period in which the incipient settlement is forming; sometimes the settlement crystallizes out of the negotiating procedure itself and sometimes as a result of outside intervention (nucleation).

The last procedural resort, of course, is law. In part, the law performs the function of arbitration, and the judge, or sometimes even the jury, hands down an award. The law, however, has more coercive power behind it than the arbitrator, for, behind the law, stands the system of police and punishment, the apparatus of jails, and, in some societies, even the threat of capital punishment. It would take another volume to examine the social system of the law and the manner in which it operates to resolve or to fail to resolve conflicts. It is a multifaceted institution. In some respects, as in the law of torts, it acts as a third party to the disputes of private citizens, instituting a procedure of conflict to which both parties consent because it is so deeply embedded in the structure of the society to which they belong. The importance of consent is easily forgotten in well-established societies where it can be taken for granted; where it is absent, however, as it may be in societies where the legal system is imposed by an alien power or where it is controlled by one group in the society, the most elaborate apparatus of legal procedure and institutions may not resolve the personal conflicts of the society. In constitutional law, the conflict of individual citizens or private organizations with the law itself may be resolved by procedures that test the law against a written, or even an unwritten, constitution.

In criminal law, the situation is much more complicated. Here, the law does not simply stand as an arbitrator of private quarrels but is itself one of the parties to the conflict. Much of the complexity of criminal procedure arises out of this dilemma, namely, that the law is both a party to the conflict and an agency for a settlement by award, that is, an arbitrator. In Anglo-American law, an attempt is made to resolve the dilemma by a sharp definition and differentiation of roles: the attorneys for the defense and for the prosecution symbolize the conflict; the judge and the jury symbolize the arbitration element. The conflict roles are highly stylized, as, indeed, is the whole procedure; this serves a function in resolving the dilemma imposed by the mixture of roles in the law, but it also has a cost, which may be quite high, in restricting the employment of informal mediatory and conciliatory procedure. The interaction of police, criminals, the courts, and the prisons as elements of a single social system is highly complex, and the realities often do not conform to the formal structure. Police and criminals not only have a symbiotic relationship with one another but often form part of a common subculture segregated from the rest of society. It may be, of course, that one of the most important functions of the police is to segregate the criminal subculture, even to the extent of becoming part of it, and, as long as this segregation is firm enough, the rest of the society can go about its own business. The persistence of the police-criminal complex, however, suggests that existing institutions have quite failed to solve the problem of eliminating crime. It may be, of course, that this is too ambitious an objective and that, if we limit crime to a segment of society, this is enough. On the other hand, the tendency for police and criminals to flourish together suggests that the problem of further limitation of this segment may require a rather different set of institutions from those we now possess.

Conflicts that cannot be resolved by appeal to existing law are frequently transferred to the law-making process in legislative assemblies. Here again, the proper description and analysis of the resolution of conflict in the legislative process would require another volume, if not many volumes. All political organizations have to develop a ritual of *settlement*, or decision. In an absolute dictatorship, the settlement is by the ukase of the dictator, though even the most absolute dictator presumably receives advice and hears arguments on different sides of a question. In a parliamentary democracy, the settlement is by majority vote of the legislature, perhaps with the further proviso of review by the executive or by the courts. Within the legislatures, as within the entourage of a dictator, various pressure groups will conflict. In the process of discussion and debate, positions may be modified, and a process of reconciliation goes on; in the final proposal, as it comes before the legislative body, compromise frequently plays an important part, and different groups bargain for support. The final decision, however, is of the nature of an award, except in those unusual cases where decisions are made by unanimous or virtually unanimous approval. We thus see all three of our conflict resolution procedures going forward in the legislative process.

An important distinction may be observed between *constitutional* and *legislative* settlements. A legislative conflict is settled for the moment by the passage of a law. This may not, of course, end the conflict but may merely transform it into a conflict about repeal of the first law or passage of an amending law. Legislative settlements, in this sense, tend to be temporary, though laws acquire a kind of constitutional status with the sheer passage of time and absence of successful challenge. Thus the prohibition amendment was passed and later repealed. The mere fact that it was embodied formally in a constitutional rather than a legislative change does not detract from the essentially legislative character of the enactment. The steel industry in Britain was nationalized by one government and denationalized by the next. Constitutional settlements are more fundamental and represent settlements of disputes regarding the rules of the legislative process. It may only be possible to detect the permanence of a settlement well after the event, of course. We can however, identify settlements like the American Constitution, the British settlement of 1688, and so on, as constitutional settlements. Where the legislative process is inadequate to resolve the political conflicts in a society, formal constitutional change, as in South American revolutions, sometimes takes its place, so that it is not always easy to distinguish one from the other except in the light of subsequent history.

When procedural conflict proves inadequate to deal with the intensity of the conflict in society or when there are no institutions for procedural conflict, violence is likely to result. The study of violence would again require a volume in itself; for all the importance of the phenomenon, there is surprisingly little theoretical or empirical study of it. It is not even easy to define. People can be killed or incapacitated with ulcers, and they can be injured by psychological violence just as effectively as they can with a gun. However, a distinction does not have to be clear to be important, and, at some point, there is a common-sense dividing line between procedural and violent conflict. Violence is most closely associated with conquest as a form of conflict settlement, though violence is descriptive of a conflict process rather than of a conflict settlement. It is quite possible, for instance, for conquest to be nonviolent, that is, for one party to be absorbed in another or for one organization to be dissolved by strictly procedural means. Departments are organized out of existence, countries are federated or united, organizations are laid down, and firms are bankrupted by purely procedural processes, without more than perhaps a trace of legal coercion lurking in the background.

Violence also does not necessarily lead to settlement. Indeed, it is perhaps the major evil of violence that it frequently inhibits settlement; for it often leaves no path to settlement open but conquest, and this may not be possible. Consequently, violence persists as a chronic disease of society; the procedures that might resolve the conflicts are too weak to prevent violence taking over, and violence in itself prevents the conflicts from being resolved and indeed perpetuates them. Violence, for instance, creates an atmosphere in which reconciliation is difficult and in which, indeed, each party is likely to move farther away from the position of the other. It likewise makes compromise difficult; one does not compromise with a man with a gun, and getting a gun oneself does not assist the process of compromise either. One does not negotiate from strength; one may dictate from strength, but one does not negotiate. The only place where violence may have a part to play in conflict settlement is where there is a sufficient monopoly or preponderance of violence in the hands of one party so that settlement can come about through conquest or award. Monopolies or preponderances of violence, however, seem to be unstable: where violence is not legitimated by procedures and constitutions, it tends to raise violence against it. Violence in itself, because it cannot perform the reconciling and compromising function, leads to the suppression rather than the resolution of conflict: it drives conflict underground but does little to eliminate it.

One of the great organizational problems of mankind, then, is the control of violence or, more generally, the control of conflict to the point where procedural institutions are adequate to handle it. The great course of political evolution, from the family to the tribe to the nation to the superpower, and, finally, one hopes, to the world government now in its birth pangs is testimony to the ability of human organization to extend conflict control to wider and wider areas. It is hardly too much to say that conflict control is government, and though government has broader functions than this, conflict control is perhaps its most important single task—the one thing which it must perform or cease to be government.

A purely political and legalistic attitude toward conflict control, however, catches only half of the problem. The ability to control anything depends on two factors: the magnitude of the thing to be controlled and the skill and appropriateness of the instruments of control. It is easier to control a dog than a lion and a stream than a hurricane. The political approach is through the instruments of control—courts, legislatures, assemblies, police, and procedures. This interest and emphasis is, of course, right and necessary. It may, however, lead to a neglect of the sources of conflict itself and of the possibility of controlling conflict at its sources. Thus we need to think about institutions for lessening conflict as well as for dealing with it. One example of this is the importance of economic development in lessening economic conflict. When there seem to be abundant opportunities for increasing the pie, the problem of sharing it falls into the background. Furthermore, in a rich society, the importance of economic conflict is lessened, simply because of the decline in the marginal significance of redistributed income. A conflict about bread is going to be more severe than one about caviar.

A field in great need of further exploration is that of the sources of psychological conflict and conflict-producing images, especially in the institutions of the family, the school, and the church, where these patterns are usually set. Reform here is slow, for conflict-producing personalities tend to reproduce themselves in their children, and it is hard to break into the process of culture transmission. Something can be done, however, at the ideological level and at the level of formal education. It is at this point that more knowledge is badly needed but also that there is hope for important changes.

The biggest problem in developing the institutions of conflict control is that of catching conflicts young. Conflict situations are frequently allowed to develop to almost unmanageable proportions before anything is done about them, by which time it is often too late to resolve them by peaceable and procedural means. To catch conflicts young, however, means that these dynamic social processes which lead to ultimate breakdown have to be publicly identifiable: we cannot deal with invisibles. It is fairly easy to look back with the wisdom of hindsight and see points in history at which conflicts that ultimately became unmanageable could easily have been dealt with. Thus, the First World War might well have been scotched in the six weeks before its outbreak if communications had been better and if there had been a quite simple apparatus of mediation: it was, at least at that moment, a war that nobody really wanted, and that happened because of a dynamic process that bred misunderstandings and misinterpretations of intention. The Second World War was of a different order; it must be diagnosed not as a result of the unwanted breakdown of an essentially unstable system, like the First World War, but as the result of an epidemic of political paranoia on the part of the German nation. The processes that led to it would have had to be dealt with earlier than, say, 1939. Just when the point of no return was passed is hard to say; it may have been at the point of

Hitler's reoccupation of the Rhineland, or it may have been later. To judge from the German trade statistics, February, 1937, marks the point at which the basic decision for ultimate war was taken by the German government; it was at this point that imports of certain strategic materials took a large jump.

It is easy to see that the institutions that might have prevented the two world wars were simply not present; it is more difficult to specify the institutions that will prevent a third, a possibly last, world war. Our knowledge of the dynamics of conflict processes is still primitive. Just as government efforts to prevent a business cycle may actually intensify it if poorly planned and badly timed, so efforts at conflict control may intensify the very conflicts that they are intended to control if they are based on too inaccurate knowledge of the social systems involved. Unfortunately, we cannot wait for perfect knowledge, and fortunately, we do not have to have perfect knowledge. There is some point in the growth of knowledge of social systems at which there is a net payoff for the institutions of control, and we have reason to hope that we are rapidly reaching this point in the case of conflict systems, if we have not already passed it; that is, even though, in the attempt to control conflicts, we shall make many mistakes, the successes will outweigh the failures.

The two greatest problems of control systems are first, signal detection, that is, how do we know when something needs to be done, and second, implementation, or how do we know what to do. I suspect that the signal-detection problem in conflict control is not so serious as it might seem. The problem is how to detect social situations that are in the early stages of a process that will lead eventually to destructive conflict if it is not checked. In any such detection or perception problem, there is always a chance of error. There are two types of error. We may give out a false alarm; that is, we may perceive the situation as requiring action when in fact it does not, and the problem will solve itself without action. We may give out a failed alarm; that is, we may say nothing needs to be done when in fact something should be done. It seems to be almost impossible to correct both these errors beyond a certain point; that is, if our detection system gives very few failed alarms, it will give a lot of false alarms, and we can avoid false alarms only at the cost of increasing the number of failed alarms. If both false alarms and failed alarms are costly this presents a very great dilemma. One suspects, however, that, in conflict control, false alarms are relatively cheap as compared with failed alarms; that is, the consequences of doing something that need not have been done are relatively slight, whereas the consequences of not doing something that should be done may be disastrous. There is no harm, then, in building a detection system that gives very few failed alarms, even if it gives a lot of false alarms: one can be tolerant of the false alarm. This is a very different situation from that posed by violent conflict, where false alarms and failed alarms may be equally fatal.

One would like to see an international organization for the detection of young conflict processes. The idea may seem impractical at the moment because people do not think in these terms; they think of conflicts as uncontrollable acts of God like hurricanes, and the idea of conflict control is a new one, even though the practice is as old as political organization. It was only a few years ago, however, that people thought of depressions and the business cycle in similar terms and talked about economic blizzards. Now the idea of depression control is accepted even in the most conservative circles. Similarly, one may hope that the idea of conflict control may receive equally rapid acceptance, in view of the immense crisis of conflict that we face.

The problem of implementation is, of course, much more difficult, and what to do once an incipient conflict process has been detected depends very much on the nature of the conflict itself. The problem is perhaps easiest in those areas where there are few specialized agencies for the conduct and encouragement of conflict, such as in race relations; here the counterconflict organization such as, for instance, the National Conference of Christians and Jews or the local interracial council can exercise a substantial influence. In labor relations also, conflict control is an important part of the practice of modern industrial relations, and the knowledge of industrial relations processes that has been accumulated in the course of a generation or more of study is now bearing valuable fruit. The problem is most difficult in the case of international relations, where there are specialized agencies for conflict (the armed forces) that have a vested interest in the preservation of conflict or at least of the threat of conflict, simply because conflict is the only reason for their existence as organizations. Even here, however, the sheer enormity of the cost of nuclear warfare is forcing the development of the institutions of conflict control. The current interest in arms control is a straw in the wind, and, in the case of international relations where the armed forces of the world form a social system with a dynamics of its own that is largely independent of the interests of the nations that support these forces, arms control may be nine-tenths of the problem. The problems of organization and of bargaining involved in setting up the institutions of arms control and, more generally, of international conflict control are difficult indeed; but it would be suicide for the human race to believe that they are insoluble. It has been the major theme of this work to show that conflict processes are neither arbitrary, random, nor, incomprehensible. In the understanding of these processes lies the opportunity for their control, and perhaps even for human survival. We cannot claim that our understanding is deep enough, and much work yet needs to be done, but it can and must be claimed that the understanding and, therefore ultimately, the control of these processes is possible. In that lies the present hope for mankind, for, without conflict control, all other hopes for human welfare and betterment are likely to be dashed to the ground.

16

EPILOGUE: THE PRESENT CRISIS

OF CONFLICT AND DEFENSE

The last chapter concluded the formal part of this volume. This is a work in abstract social theory. It purports simply to identify and build theoretical models of a set of social processes related to the phenomenon of conflict. Its theory is ethically neutral; in so far as it is useful to anybody, it may be equally useful to the nationalist as to the internationalist, to the militarist as to the pacifist, and to the communist as to the democrat. Even the previous chapter, which comes closest to the ethical judgment, treats this judgment as an abstract process, capable of producing many different ethical positions.

In this epilogue, I wish to go further and commit myself to what seem to me the implications of the theory I have developed, in the light of my own values. The reader is warned that his possibly different values may produce different conclusions. Nevertheless, this is not merely a matter of taste. Values must constantly be restructured by one's image of the world of fact and relationship. The theory of this volume represents a view of social reality that is different from what I must call, without intent of being insulting, the naïve view. The naïve view of the universe is egocentric and ethnocentric; for the naïve man, the sun goes round the earth, and society revolves around himself and his own group and culture. It is one of the first tasks of science, both natural and social, to destroy this naïveté and to exhibit man as part of a system the perception of which is liberated from perspective. The astronomer knows that the bright stars in our sky are merely near and that intrinsic brightness bears little relation to apparent brightness. Similarly, the student of social systems, by his very abstraction, develops a view of society that is, in theory, free from the perspective of his own person, culture, and nation. This Copernican revolution by which the illusion of perspective is perceived always represents the transition from the naïve to the scientific or even to the religious view of the universe.

This perspective revolution in the view of the universe, however, always produces a profound disturbance of the value system of the individual. This is true even in the physical sciences, and it is even more true in the social sciences. Values of rigidity, of combativeness, and even of loyalty that are quite consistent with the egocentric view of the universe are seen to be inconsistent with a scientific view. It will not be surprising, therefore, if the view of the social universe that is found in this volume will be associated with some transformation in basic values: it will be seen as a threat by those who hold egocentric values and as a reinforcement by those whose values have adapted themselves to the perspective revolution. The perspective revolution does not, of course, destroy either perspective itself or egocentric values. In the sight of God and in the light of social science, the child in a remote corner of Tibet is just as valuable as one of my own children. I must confess, however, that, even though I know the brilliance with which my own children shine in the sky of my attention is only an illusion of perspective, my personal concern and activity is heavily weighted in the direction of the near and dear. Brightness may be an illusion of perspective, but nearness is not; and it is quite compatible with the most universalistic of ethics to concentrate on the matters that are close at hand. Indeed, this is required; an ethical system that was so universalistic as to persuade a man to neglect his own children in the interest of spreading his attention over the whole wide world would be subject to severe criticism. The allocation of responsibility is an important task of any ethical system, and the allocation by nearness is the simplest and most workable, provided it does not lead us actually to believe the illusion of perspective.

We are still left, however, with a serious ethical dilemma that has become overwhelmingly acute in the modern world—that of reconciling the universal ethic that both science and high religion imply with the particularist loyalty to existing institutions and responsibilities. What we face in the modern world is a fundamental breakdown in the concept of defense as a social system, largely, as I have tried to show, as a result of the constant decline in the LSG affecting almost all institutions as a result both of physical and social invention. The concept of defense has always been somewhat naïve, as I defined it, in the sense that it has rested on an egocentric and ethnocentric view of the universe that takes the defended person or institution as given, known, and valued and the outside enemy as also given but unknown and negatively valued and regards the problem of virtue as that of the preservation of a little island of defended goodness in the middle of the howling chaos of the hostile world. There are times and places where this naïve view is not unrealistic, as when, for instance, Robinson Crusoe builds his stockade against unknown marauders. Unilateral defense against the vast unknown, however, soon passes over into a system of unilateral defense, in which two or more parties try unilaterally to defend themselves against each other. Once this happens, the naïve view no longer expresses the social reality; unilateral defense turns into a conflict system, the dynamics of which is not in the control of any one party but emerges as a result of the unconsciously coordinated decisions of all. Once this happens, the record of unilateral defense as a system is dismal. When individuals rely on it, we get a Hobbesian society, constantly re-enacted in gangsterdom, in which the life of a man is indeed nasty, brutish, and short and, to get away from it, men build political structures, enter into social contracts, and even submit to tyranny.

This is because, even with quite primitive means of violence, no two men are unconditionally viable with regard to each other. We must, therefore, as persons learn to live with conditional viability. This is why unilateral defense for persons has always proved to be unstable, even though new weapons and social situations may revive it from time to time, as in the cowboy era of the wild West.

Now, however, we face the same problem of the breakdown of unconditional viability in the relations of national states. Unilateral national defense has created an enormous amount of human misery through history, but, up to the present century, it has been a workable system, in the sense that it has provided occasional protected heartlands of peace in which civilization and the arts could flourish even though surrounded by a periphery of war. Now it is no longer workable; the decline in the LSG, coupled with the increasing range of the missile to more than half of the earth's circumference makes all heartlands hopelessly vulnerable. A beautiful example of this is provided by a Report on a Study of Non-Military Defense by the Rand Corporation.[1] The Rand Corporation is financed mainly by the United States Air Force, so that its studies must be accepted with the same kind of reserve that, shall we say, we might greet a study of the Reformation by Jesuits based on unpublished and secret documents in the Vatican; there is the same combination of honesty in the value system and bias in the commitment. By making what seem to me fantastically optimistic assumptions, this report concludes that, by taking adequate precautions, the United States might lose not more than from 5 to 85 million people, and the economy would recover almost to previous levels, assuming a gigantic effort, in 25 years. What the report does not say is that the purpose of all this misery and sacrifice is so that the next generation can go through it all again; that is, the purpose of national defense is to re-establish the system that gave rise to the catastrophe. Under these circumstances, unilateral national defense seems to me to be sheer lunacy; it can only persist as an ideology because of the

[1] Report R.322.RC, July 1, 1958.

smallness of men's imaginations and their refusal to let go of an outworn concept that has served them in good stead in the past. The abandonment of the ideology of unilateral national defense is particularly hard for Americans, who for 200 years have been served well by it, because of the accident of geography and history. Unless we abandon it, however, I believe we are doomed.

In this dreadful dilemma, where the ideas and values with which we have mostly been brought up have turned to poison in our hands, to what can we turn? The peace movement, one fears, is not adequate to meet this challenge. The history of the peace movement still remains to be written, and the movement is in great need of study and research. It can be traced back in Western history to mainly Christian origins. The early Christian church was pacifist in doctrine until it was taken over by Constantine. The monastic movement represents a pacifist withdrawal from the world, though not a direct criticism of it. From the time of the Reformation, each century has seen the rise of a peace church—the Mennonites in the sixteenth, the Quakers in the seventeenth, the Brethren in the eighteenth, and, more doubtfully perhaps, the Adventists in the nineteenth and Jehovah's Witnesses in the twentieth century. There were peace-movement elements in early socialism; the War Resisters International represents a very small secular pacifist movement. In the 1930s in Britain, the Peace Pledge Union showed signs of becoming an incipient mass movement. On the whole, however, the peace movement has been small in numbers and sectarian in outlook. It has kept alive the hope of peace, and it has provided a constant challenge to a blind acceptance of war as an institution. It has not, however, made much contribution to developing the institutions of peace, and it has not had much impact on the course of world events.

The invention of military conscription has forced the peace movement to channel its energies mainly into the defense of its individual adherents against the governments of their own countries. This is a very important conflict, but it does not have much to do with world peace. The struggle for the rights of conscientious objectors is part of the whole movement of defense of the individual against the power of large organizations. In so far as this struggle is successful, it is a tribute to the bargaining power of the inflexible; a man or a group that will die or go to prison rather than be coerced cannot be coerced. If society is convinced that a group cannot be coerced, they may be able to strike a successful bargain with society, simply because, in spite of their intransigence, they may be of more use to the society alive and free than dead or in prison. The inflexibly conscientious, therefore, are important defenders of the rights of all individuals against the pressures of society, and the bargains they strike frequently benefit those of less determination and are an important check on the power of organized society. Thus, while the lone pacifist is an important bargainer with society and helps to keep it from sinking into tyranny, he makes little contribution to the organization of society. He takes liberty, for liberty is something that people have to take: in a sense, it can neither be given to people nor organized by them; otherwise, it is not liberty. He does not, however, organize liberty; this is a political task for the compromisers and the bargainers, and, in a sense also, liberty has to be organized as well as taken.

Just as war is too important to leave to the generals, so peace is too important to leave to the pacifists. It is not enough to condemn violence, to abstain from it, or to withdraw from it. There must be organization against it; in other words, institutions of conflict control or, in still other words, government. The case for world government to police total disarmament as put forward for instance by Clark and Sohn seems to me absolutely unshakeable,[2] in spite of the fact that the march of technology has made some of their specific proposals obsolete. In general, we know the main lines of the kind of world organization that can eliminate the present dangers and give us permanent peace. What we do not know is how to get to it. The problem essentially is how do we bargain with each other,

[2] Grenville Clark and Louis B. Sohn, *World Peace Through World Law*, 2d ed., Cambridge, Harvard University Press, 1960.

THE PRESENT CRISIS OF CONFLICT AND DEFENSE 335

and especially how now do the nations of the world bargain with each other, to create a social contract and a machinery that will give the social contract stability. The world dilemma is illustrated admirably by the game matrix of Fig. 3.5, p. 50. We reproduce it below (Fig. 16.1) in terms of the social contract. If both parties keep the contract at N, all are better off; with the kind of payoff matrix shown, however, there is a payoff to either party in breaking

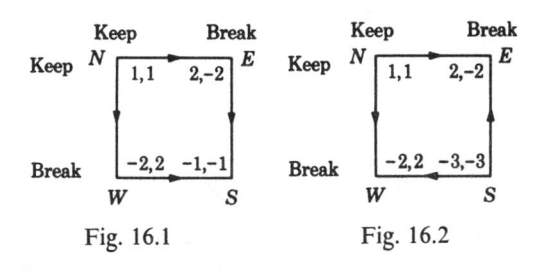

```
              Keep   Break                    Keep   Break
         N  ┌─────┬─────┐ E              N  ┌─────┬─────┐ E
    Keep    │ 1,1 │ 2,-2│          Keep    │ 1,1 │ 2,-2│
            ├─────┼─────┤                  ├─────┼─────┤
    Break   │-2,2 │-1,-1│          Break   │-2,2 │-3,-3│
            └─────┴─────┘                  └─────┴─────┘
              W      S                       W      S
            Fig. 16.1                      Fig. 16.2
```

the contract if the other party does not. If one party breaks it, however, the other must follow suit, and we end up in the Hobbesian state of unilateral defense and natural misery at S. The state we now seem to be in, however, is illustrated by Fig. 16.2. Here, the situation at S is worse than it is in Fig. 16.1, and if it becomes bad enough, it alters the whole character of the game, as we see from the arrows. Now, even if one party breaks the contract, it still does not pay the other to do so; the game as it stands will end up either at E or at W, depending on which party moves first. Figure 16.1 is the traditional position of unilateral defense; this has been the state of the world for many thousands of years. Now, the question arises, "Have we moved internationally into the condition of Fig. 16.2?" This might be called the pattern of unilateral virtue. It is a commoner pattern in human life than might be imagined. It is the pattern of long suffering. The peasant, the slave, the woman, and the underdog in innumerable societies have sat for generations at positions like E or W, unable to bargain to N and unwilling to fight to S. This, indeed, has been the characteristic feature of the internal relations of most human societies, just as Fig. 16.1 has characterized their external relations. For the heirs of the Enlightenment, however, this is not good enough. Responsible government is an attempt and, by and large, a fairly successful attempt to devise institutions that will keep us at the optimum at N in the internal relations of society. By devising orderly institutions for removing politicians from power and by devising constitutional checks through the courts, we make it more and more difficult for the powerful to break the social contract, and the Communist and democratic world alike share the ultimate ideal, as yet unrealized anywhere, of a society without aliens, without any excluded class or group, a society from which nobody shall be alienated. Now, the great problem before mankind is how to build responsible government at the world level. This is no longer a dream but a necessity, simply because the breakdown of the system of national defense makes it impossible any more to build defended islands of responsible government and peace in the midst of the Hobbesian wilderness of the warring world.

It is not too hard to see where we have to go; the difficulty is that no road leads there. Perhaps we should say more hopefully that the road to life, to government, and to organization always leads uphill. The easy roads, the intrinsic dynamics, always lead downhill to ultimate destruction. Both life and government are unstable castles of order in the midst of a universe of increasing entropy and chaos. They can be built, however, because of the learning process, because the gene can teach patterns to unorganized matter, and because the human organism can learn from its imagination, from its experience, and from others. Our hope for the future of mankind, therefore, lies first in the human imagination, which can create the forms of things unknown and so create the image of possible futures that have not been previously imagined. Secondly, hope lies in the learning process; man can take the images of possible futures and test them, partly in the imagination itself, partly in experience, and partly by trusting the word of the teachers who have tested the images.

Where, then, are the new ideas and the new images of the future that look like upward paths? One is clearly the idea of nonviolent resistance associated with the name of Gandhi. This is a powerful method of bargaining for a social contract. It is more sophisticated in its psychology than in military defense, and it fits well into the Schelling type of bargaining theory. It assumes that the enemy is not merely another, to be crushed or excluded from the society, but is part of the same social system as the defender. It is unfortunate that, in English, we have no word that expresses the positive aspect of *ahimsa*, or nonviolence. It is something, however, that we experience constantly in daily life, especially in the family: it is the characteristic activity of what I called in the previous chapter the reconciling personality. What was remarkable about Gandhi was that he was able to organize a large number of people into political movement of *Satyagraha* (truth seeking) aimed the establishment of a new social contract in the form of *swaraj*, or independence. This is perhaps the most important political idea of the twentieth century. We see it in operation at the moment, for instance, in the nonviolent campaign of Negroes in the United States for civil rights, full citizenship, and integration into American society.

There is great need for research into the dynamic processes of political movements of this kind and into the problem of the limiting conditions within which they are most likely to be successful.[3] The method is dismissed too easily by the militarists, who are committed to a less sophisticated and more primitive method of defense. It is perhaps welcomed too uncritically by the pacifists, who tend to assume its universal applicability. As with any powerful movement in human affairs, nonviolent resistance movements operate in the midst of a complex social system the course of which through time is the result of many interacting decisions and movements. Thus,

---

[3] The classic study by Richard B. Gregg, *The Power of Non-Violence*, Philadelphia, Lippincott, 1936, is still the best descriptive and analytic work in the field, in spite of, or perhaps because of, a certain amateur quality. The phenomenon has never been adequately studied by professional social scientists. *The Conquest of Violence*, by Joan V. Bondurant, Princeton, N.J., Princeton University Press, 1958, is a good recent work.

like military defense, nonviolent resistance may turn out to have unexpected and unwanted consequences. Even in India, for instance, the Gandhian movement led to the tragedy of partition and to one of the major human catastrophes of the twentieth century.

Another sign of hope is the interest in arms control that is now spreading even to the military. It may be that the institutions of peace will have to be worked out by conscientious military men, simply because they control the organizations that must be transformed if peace is to be organized. There is, I think, a largely subconscious feeling among military men who take their responsibility for national defense seriously that they are facing an unprecedented system breakdown. They may not think in quite the terms of this volume, and they will not have the prejudices of the author; but they are deeply worried about their inability, in the last analysis, to perform their traditional function of protecting the heartland from disruption and disorganization.

The interest in limited war is one straw in the wind. There is a nostalgia among the military and their academic friends for the good, old pretechnical days, when wars could be fought without the dangers of mass annihilation, and even for the good old eighteenth century, when war was still largely a professional business. Napoleon destroyed this idyll, and the democratization of war may well prove its ultimate undoing. The difficulty with limited war, however, is that there are no institutions for limiting it; its limitation depends on a tacit social contract between the opposing parties, and even though, as Schelling has shown, these tacit contracts may be of great importance and may be necessary to the formation of more explicit contracts, they do not seem adequate to carry the burden of the world's frightful danger. Furthermore, the simplest tacit contract and most obvious place to strike a bargain is at no war at all; the great weakness of limited war is that there is no salient configuration of the social system that limits it, whereas no war is a highly salient position around which a bargaining solution may cluster.

Arms control goes a little further than tacit contract. It may be defined as military cooperation with potential enemies in the interest of mutual security; its military object is presumably to restore unconditional viability and permit the re-establishment of the game of diplomacy without the constant threat of total disaster. Arms control unquestionably offers some real hope. It is the disunion of the military organizations of the world that threatens us with disaster, and the more organizational ligaments can be built between them, the better off we may be. A suggestive analogy is the elimination of religious war, though not by any means of religious conflict, by what now seems to us the very simple device of the separation of church and state. The idea that religion could be left to the personal preference of the individual and that, indeed, this would probably strengthen religious organizations rather than weaken them is something that would never have occurred to the man of the seventeenth century. This simple idea, however, has largely eliminated religion as a major source of violence, after centuries of devastation in its name. One wonders whether we may not now proceed to the separation of the armed forces from the state. The myth of the modern national state is that its armed forces are its servants, to protect it from having to submit to the will of other states or to enable it to impose its will upon others. What, in fact, seems to be the case is that the armed forces of the world form a social system of their own, almost independent of the states which support them and which they are supposed to defend. This paradoxical situation arises because what an armed force is organized for is to fight another armed force; hence, the existence of the national armed forces is completely self-justifying: each armed force justifies the existence of its potential enemy and has practically no other justification for its existence. In this, the military forces differ strongly from the police force, which is not organized against other police forces but against individual violaters of the law and which does not theoretically have a punitive but only an apprehending function. The business of the police, that is, is to bring the offender before the apparatus of the law to be tried, and if found guilty, punished; it is the courts, however, not the police, who are supposed to do the trial and punishment. This division of labor is not always strictly observed, but it represents the fundamental differences between a legal, responsible police force on the one hand and banditry, secret political police, and armed forces on the other.

One wonders, therefore, whether the path to national security does not lie through detaching and weakening the organizational and hierarchical bonds that bind the armed forces to the civilian state and through a corresponding strengthening of the bonds that connect the various armed forces of the world with one another. It may be more important to exchange generals with other countries, and especially with potential enemies, than to exchange professors and concert artists. The open-skies and open-spies proposals that have been in the air in-recent years are again straws in a very strange wind of change. Once we realize that the object of a disarmament conference is not necessarily to agree to disarm but to build an organization that unites the various national armed forces, the road to disarmament, which has seemed so hopeless, may be opened up. Once the armed forces of the world are united into a single organization, their functions obviously will cease, and, like the ideal Marxian state, they will wither away or, perhaps, one should say, fade.

Suppose now we get peace, real peace; what then? Our troubles are, of course, far from over. Mankind has very rarely had peace and is inexperienced in it. The few civilizations that have not had the institution of war, like that of Mohenjo-Daro and of the Mayans, are not wholly inspiring to contemplate; they seem to have been static, indeed stagnant societies endlessly repeating a ritualized and stylized form of life without change, adventure, discovery, or excitement beyond what ritual can offer. Both these examples probably came to an end through overpopulation, soil erosion, and a gradual worsening of conditions until a revolution of the proletarian cultivators destroyed the whole society. The warrior civilizations destroyed themselves too, of course, and the record of cruelty, destructiveness, and tyranny that these offer is no more pleasant to contemplate than the dullness of the unchallenged.

In my personal life, I see war only as a threat, with no virtues whatever. I lead a full and interesting life in peacetime, and I see nothing coming from war but misery and deprivation. I must recognize, however, that this is not true of all men and that, in the past at any rate, war has given color and excitement to otherwise drab lives, especially where it can be enjoyed by proxy. There is, therefore, an important problem facing mankind, failing its destruction, by the adjustment to permanent peace and the abolition of war as a social institution. We want peace, just as we want utopia, just as long as we are pretty sure of not getting it. When the choice is placed before us, however, as it seems to be in the modern world, between utopia or, at least, peace, which is something less, or annihilation, our embarrassment may become so acute that we choose annihilation. One sees this in the conventional cartoon image of peace as a wispy and rather bedraggled female in a bedsheet holding a wan olive branch as a corsage. She is not a girl that any red-blooded American or Russian would particularly want to go out with, much less make love to. Still, she haunts us. It is a specter even more frightening, perhaps, than that which Karl Marx invoked in 1848, because we have always thought in terms of war as a last resort. Now there may be no last resort, except doomsday, which is no resort at all. There is no defense, no isolation, no protection from the awful task of living together with monstrously strange bedfellows. As long as we had defense, we could simplify the task of living together by only loving the like and the lovable and by keeping away the unlike and the unlovable. Now we find ourselves all cooped up together on this little ball of a spaceship and forced to live together in peace for fear of wrecking it.

The problem is part of a still larger one, and we may have to think about the larger one before we can solve the smaller. The technical revolution in warfare that has made peace a necessity is part of a larger change in the knowledge, skills, and abilities of mankind through which we are now passing, which began to get noticeably under way in the seventeenth century and has been accelerating ever since. It is carrying mankind to a state of affairs so different from that of the civilized societies out of which it developed that it has been called postcivilization. We are still in the era of rapid transition and are not within sight of the final equilibrium state. An equilibrium state there must be, however, or at least a state that is not merely transition, for every transition must lead toward something. We only see very dimly what this high-level equilibrium might be like. It must clearly involve population control by means other than high infant mortality, which implies a revolution in family life and in sexual behavior that we have not even begun to accomplish as yet. If the expectation of life is going to be 70 years, then, in an equilibrium population, birth and death rates must be about 14, and the two-child family must be standard. It must likewise involve conflict control, so that the enormous powers that the new technology places in the hands of man are not used for his destruction. It will likewise involve boredom control, to prevent man from simply committing suicide from inanition in a utopian society. Of course it involves control of disease, ignorance, poverty, depressions, and tyranny, and it must involve some sense of high purpose for the human race, whether in the physical conquest of the universe, the conquest of man's own depravity, or in reaching out toward the divine. These are dreams, but they are dreams that we must dream, and dream well, if the vast dynamic process of change in which we are all caught up is not to take us to irretrievable disaster of one kind or another. There is no way back to Eden, to innocence or to ignorance; having eaten of the fruit of the tree of knowledge, it is Zion or nothing.

I was recently sitting in an airplane waiting to take off. It was spring, and a little bird was trying to build her nest in a little hole at the end of the wing. She flew busily in and out carrying bits of straw and twigs as the plane sat on the ground waiting for the signal to take off, and then the plane roared away and left her far behind. I could not help seeing in this a parable of our day. We are all going about our various tasks, each trying to build for himself a little shelter from the inclement world, a little defense against want or hardship or loneliness, and we are all building on the wing of a great sweeping process of change that may soon roar away with our little efforts, we know not where nor how. There were men in the cockpit, however, and we are men and not sparrows. We do have the gift of understanding, even of the systems that we create ourselves. It is not too much to hope, therefore, that man can learn to fly the great engine of change that he has made and that it may carry us not to destruction but to that great goal for which the world was made.

INDEX

Acceptability, 17, 86
Accretion, 103
Acculturation, 172
Adolescent revolt, 175
Adorno, T. W., 313
Age groups, conflict among, 199–203
Agriculture, 204–206
Airpower, effects of, 272
Alternation, 158, 249
Ambivalence, 90, 98
American Federation of Labor, 222
American Soldier, the, 173
Amish, 284
Analogy, 248
Anarchy, 187
Annihilation, threat of, 257
Apathy, 91–93, 179
Approacher, 89
Arbitration, 319
Argument, 292–295
Armaments, offensive and defensive, 258
Armed forces, 339
Arms control, 328, 338–339
Arms race, 34–35, 231
Audit, 183–184
Authoritarian personality, 313
Avoidance, 308
Avoider, 89–90

Balance of power, 28
Bargaining, 313–320

Bargaining area, 18
Bargaining power, 254
Bases, military, 262
Behavior, definition of, 7
 rational, 9, 151
Behavior Space, 3
Benedict, Ruth, 138
"Betweeness," problem of, 77
Births, 121, 131, 140
Blake, William, 97
Bondurant, Joan V., 337
Boulding, K. E., 20, 24, 95
Boundaries, critical, 265
 strain on, 264
Boundary conflict, 113
Boundary of equal strength, 231
Boundary of indifference, 61
Boundary of possibility, 6
Bribery, 49
Brown, J. S., 81
Budget, 183
Buffer state, 263
Buridan's ass, 81–82
Business cycle, 251

Character units, 141
Checkoff, 225
Christianity, 298–304
Circulation of elites, 110
Clark, Grenville, 334
Class conflict, 206
Coalitions, 55–56

Colonialism, 177
Communism, 286
Competition, 4
  spatial, 59–79
Compromise, 313–320
Conciliation, 316–317
Conflict, age group, 199–203
  boundary, 113
  class, 206
  definition of, 5
  dynamics of, 243–245
  ecological, 113
  economic, 189–207, 324–325
  ethical, 295
  field of, 153, 190
  group, 107
  heterogeneous, 166–167
  ideological, 277–304
  industrial, 208–266
  international, 227–277
  job, 181
  legislative, 322
  optimum, 305
  organizational, 145–165
  patterns of, 1
  personal distribution, 191
  protracted, 59
  range of, 14
  religious, 278
  resolution of, 307–328
Conflict absorber, 171
Conflict control, 324
Conflict curve, 13, 317
Conflict points, 12
Conflict set, 10
Conquest, 309, 323
  threat of, 257
Constitutional settlements, 323
Constitutionality, 186
Contagion, 125
Continuity, 158
Contract curve, 15–16
Conversion, 101, 122, 133–135
Cooperation, 52, 115
Core value, 312
Coser, L., 307
Costs of transport, 71, 262
Counterconflict organization, 327
Crimean War, 256

Critical boundary, 265
Cycles, business, 251
  diplomacy-war, 250
  fashion, 136–137
  submission, 52

Death, 121, 131, 140
Debate, 279, 293
Decision, 147, 150
Defense, 259, 267, 333
Deflation, 207
Devil, 30–31, 139
Difference equation, 22
Diplomacy-war cycle, 250
Directed graph, 42
Discussion, 294
Displacement, 93–94
Doctors, 128
Dominance, 116
Douglas, Ann, 319
Drama, 306
Duchess's Law, 190
Durkheim, Emile, 177
Dynamic system, 19
  perverse, 49–51
Dynamics of international conflict, 243–245
Dynamics of weapon development, 260

Ecological conflict, 113
Ecological equilibrium 114
Ecological succession, 120
Economic conflict, 189–207, 324–325
Economic groups, 112, 203
Edgeworth contract curve, 15–16
Elites, circulation of, 110
Emotional drive, 303
Empires, 269–271
Encroachment, 76–78
Enemy, 285
  as unifier, 162
Epidemiological model, 125–144
Epistemological processes, 288–298
Equilibrium, 20, 114
Ethical conflicts, 295
Evil, nature of, 301
Evocative power, 98
Exchange, 192
Expansion pressure, 154

INDEX

Factionalism, 160
False alarms, 327
Fashion cycles, 136–137
Field conflict, 190
Field of conflict, 153
First World War, 325
Freedom, amount of, 14
Freudian system, 170
Friendlies, 138
Frustration, 88–89, 169

Game of survival, 65–66
Game theory, 41–57, 192
Game, three party 53–56
Gandhi, M. 337
Gilbert, W. S., 297
God, 300
Gompers, Samuel, 209
Gregg, Richard B., 337
Group, 105, 171
  economic, 112, 203
  kinship, 111
  reference, 318
Group loyalties, 161
Growth-of-sickness curves, 130

Heisenberg principle, 291
Heredity, 157
Hierarchy, 147
Home strength, 230, 232
Hostiles, 138
Hostility, 152
Hotelling, Harold, 72, 75

Ideal society, nature of, 300
Identity types, 176
Ideological and ethical conflict, 277–304
Ideology, mutation of, 283
  power of, 280
Image, 96, 156–157, 292
Image of the future, 299
Image-lag, 164
Immunity, 134
Indifference curve, 298
Indifference set, 11
Industrial conflict, 208–226
Inferences, 289
Inflation, 207

Intensity and appeal, 281
Internal stability of organizations, 163
International conflict, 227–277
Interpretation of history, 299
Isolation, ideological, 284
I.W.W., 219

Jehovah's Witnesses, 315
Job conflict, 181
Job rationing, 215
Job role, 211
Jurisdictional disputes, 155, 223–224

Kaplan, Morton, 273
Kilkenny cats, 64
Kinship groups, 111
Knight, F. H., 306
Knights of Labor, 222

Labor law, 226
Labor Union, 219
Law, 320
  definition of, 4
Leadership, 109
Legislative conflict, 322
Lewin, K., 81
Limited war, 338
Location of firms, 73–78
Long-run effects, 197
Long suffering, pattern of, 335
Loss-of strength gradient (LSG), 79, 230, 245–247, 260–262, 268–269, 272
Lotka, A. J., 124
Love, 30, 33
LSG, see Loss-of-strength gradient
Luce, R. Duncan, 48

Malevolent hostility, 152
Man, nature of, 301
Market extinction lines, 69–71, 234
Market extinction point, 62
Marx, Karl, 286
Marxism, 298–304
Mathewson, Stanley B., 214
Maximin, 46, 91
Maximizing under constraint, 8
Mayo, Elton, 214
Mead, Margaret, 138

Mediation, 316–317
Miller, Neil E., 81–83
Minimax 41, 236, 238
Mixed marriages, 132
Mixed strategy, 47
Mobility, 198
Momentum, 21
Mother, rejection of, 134
Mutation, 124
  of ideologies, 283
Mutual viability, 235

National defense, collapse of, 333
  equilibrium of, 267
National interest, 275
Nationalism, 99, 298–304
Natural increase, 132
Nomadic empires, 271
Nonviolent resistance, 337

Offense, 259
Organization man, 178, 185
Organizational conflict, 145–165

Pacifism, 334
Partitions, 110
Party, 2, 106
  dominant, 58
  types of, 227–229
Payoff matrix, 41
Peace, 340–341
Peace movement, 333
Peer group, 172
Perception, 292
Perfect competition, 194
Personal distribution conflict, 191
Personnel management, 182
Perspective revolution, 330
Persuasion, 164
Perverse dynamics, 49–51
Piecework, 216
Police, 340
Police-criminal complex, 321
Postcivilization, 342
Predation, 115
Prediction, mechanical, 22–23
Price supports, 205
Price system, 195
Procedural resolution, 309

Projectile, 267
Proprioceptive function, 150
Protection, effects of, 196
Publican, 30–31
Punishment, 256

Quality, same as quantity, 3
Quandary, 83–84, 89

Raiffa, Howard, 48
Railroad, effects of, 271–272
Range of the projectile, 266
Rapoport, Anatol, 279
Rate of interest, 201
Rational behavior, 9, 151
Reaction coefficient, 26
Reconciliation, 310–313
Reconciling personality, 313
Reference groups, 318
Reformation, 102
Religious conflict, 278
Resistance, nonviolent, 337
Resolution of Conflict 307–328
Returns to scale, 233
Revolutions, 102, 174, 330
Richardson, Lewis F., 25, 34, 124, 141,
  142, 143, 144,
Richardson Processes, 25–40, 43, 61,
  64, 88, 100, 117, 169, 171, 231, 235,
  252
Right to quit, 185
Rigidity, 311
Ritual, 94
Ritual strikes, 218
River empires, 269
Role, 146, 156
Role-changing, 179
Roman Empire, 270
Russian Empire, 270

Sabotage, 179–180
Sacramental dogma, 302
Saint, 30, 139
Saliency, 314
Schelling, T. C., 254, 314, 315
Schizophrenic, 288
Science, tasks of, 249
Scientific process, 290
Second World War, 325

INDEX

Self-fulfilling images, 292
Self-image, 156–157
Semantics, 295
Settlement, 321–322
Shell values, 312
Shortsightedness, 37, 43, 50, 64–65
Shubik, M., 65
Sibling rivalry, 168
Signal-detection, 326
Simmel, G., 307
Small group loyalties, 161
Smith, Adam, 52, 193, 220, 221
Smithies, Arthur, 72
Social contract, 335
Social isolate, 174
Social organization, theory of, 304
Socialization, 167
Sohn, Louis B., 334
Solidarity, 162
Specialization, 193
Sphere of influence, 231
Stability of international conflict, 242
Staff, 148
Staying power, 65–66
Stouffer, S. A., 173
Strausz-Hupé, R., 59
Strength, 230, 232
    multi-dimensional, 268
Strike, 216–218
Submission, 32–33
    cycles, 52
Submissiveness, 116
Support, conflict about, 200
Survival area, 63
Symbolization, 281
Symbols, 96–100, 104
System boundary, 39

Taste as symbolic system, 103–104
Tertium quid, 283
Threat, 253–258
Three-group competition, 117–120
Tied values, 296

Touchiness, 26
Trading, 317
Trading set, 10, 12
Traitor, 180
Transport, costs of, 71, 262
Troeltsch, Ernst, 282
Trust, 184
Truth, 287
Tyranny, 187

Unilateral defense, 331
Union security, 224

Value, theory of, 303
Value ordering, 6
Values, 296
    core and shell, 312
    tied, 296
Vector line, 20, 27
Viability, 58–79, 235–242, 260, 332
    conditional, 273
    unconditional 232
Violence, 322–324

Wage bargain, 209–212
Wages, effects of unions on, 222–223
War, limited, 338
War as a cyclical system, 252
War moods, 141–143
War weariness, 143
Watershed dominance, 116
Watershed principle, 159
Welfare function, 8
World government, 334–336
World Wars, 325
Worldliness, 298–304
Worship, 302

Yes men, 149
Yogi, 30
Youth problem, 202

Zero-sum games, 44, 192